JOHN HUMPHRIES, a former   ...ue *Western Mail*, Cardiff, sheds new light on the Chartist Uprising of 1839 with this investigation into the lives of John Rees and Zephaniah Williams, two of the more mysterious leaders of a revolt that ended in the massacre of 22 demonstrators outside Newport's Westgate Hotel. A native of Newport, and educated at St Julians High School, the author has been a professional journalist all his life, firstly in Wales, then as a Foreign Correspondent, based in Brussels. As European Bureau Chief for thirteen Thomson daily newspapers, he travelled extensively, reporting on breaking news from all parts of Europe. After returning to Britain as London and City Editor for Thomson Regional Newspapers, he was appointed Editor of *The Western Mail,* the newspaper on which he began his career. John Humphries lives with his wife – and a very large garden – at Tredunnoc in the Usk Valley.

The Man from the Alamo

WHY THE WELSH CHARTIST UPRISING OF 1839 ENDED IN A MASSACRE

John Humphries

WALES BOOKS
GLYNDŴR PUBLISHING

Published in 2004 by Glyndŵr Publishing
Porth Glyndŵr, Higher End, St Athan,
Vale of Glamorgan, CF62 4LW.
www.walesbooks.com

ISBN 1-903529-14-X

*This publication was assisted by a grant
from the Welsh Books Council.*

Cover:
The facial composite of John Rees (left) was constructed
by Dr Charles Frowd at the University of Stirling (Psychology)
using PROfit Composite Software.

Also, the only known photograph of Zephaniah Williams (right),
taken in Tasmania not long before he died in 1874.
(Courtesy, National Trust of Australia, Tasmania, Latrobe Group)

Cover design: Welsh Books Council.

Printed and bound in Wales by
Dinefwr Press, Rawlings Road
Llandybie, Carmarthenshire, SA18 3YD

To Eliana
for her patience and assistance

Preface and Acknowledgements

With the passage of time, one of the most crucial episodes in British history, the Chartist Uprising in Newport, Monmouthshire, on November 4, 1839, slips out of our collective consciousness. A John Frost Square, an office block called Chartist Towers, and a set of murals on a concrete underpass somehow seem an inadequate memorial to what was suspected to be a plot to topple Queen Victoria and establish a republic. Even the bullet riddled pillars at the entrance to the town's Westgate Hotel where ten Chartists were killed and as many again fatally wounded by three murderous volleys from the 45th Regiment of Foot, the Sherwood Foresters, are no longer on public view. The mass grave in which ten demonstrators were buried at St Woolos Cathedral, not 600 yards from where they fell, has an anonymous marker, the identities of the victims of the massacre outside the Westgate still uncertain. Few artefacts from that day have survived, the display at Newport Museum commemorating the most momentous event in the city's history almost too trifling to be noticed.

Besides being the scene of the last armed rising on British soil, the Chartist insurrection at Newport is also remarkable for being one of the great riddles of British history. What impelled 2000 men, mostly colliers, some armed, to descend on Newport in the dead of night? Was it no more than a demonstration in support of electoral reform, or were there other forces at work? This book is not a dissertation on British Chartism, nor is it a biography of John Frost, its leader in Monmouthshire, although it is clearly impossible to avoid either. Events are driven by people, and in attempting to penetrate the fog that still surrounds the reasons for the Chartist Uprising I have reconstructed the lives of two of the main protagonists, Zephaniah Williams, transported for life for High Treason, and John Rees, alias 'Jack the Fifer', the man who got away. Rees was the 'Man from the Alamo' who fought to create the Republic of Texas; Williams established a Welsh mining colony on Ballahoo Creek in a remote part of Tasmania. In piecing together the lives of two extraordinary men I have been fortunate in obtaining access to hitherto unpublished sources, shedding new light on an intriguing moment in British history.

I would like to acknowledge my indebtedness for the assistance provided in Wales by the staff at Newport Library and Museum; the Gwent Record Office, in particular assistant archivist Colin Gibson and his colleague Dr Luned Davies; the Glamorgan Record Office; also Caroline Jacob at Merthyr Library; Emyr Evans, National Library of Wales, and my daughter-in-law Nerys Humphries for translating important Welsh-language documents. Without the help of John Molleston, Information Specialist at the Texas General Land Office, Austin, and Gus Morgan, a researcher in Mullin, Texas, I would never have picked up the trail of John Rees after he escaped from Wales. Lou Lionelli, Records Clerk at the Superior Court in Siskiyou County, California, narrowed down the search for the final resting place of the elusive Rees. In Tasmania, the staff at the State Archives Office in Hobart and Launceston Public Library provided invaluable help in piecing together what became of Zephaniah Williams and his coal mining ventures in Tasmania. They also led me to two fascinating documents: the list of almost 100 Welsh colliers and their families persuaded by Zephaniah to join him at Ballahoo Creek, and a map of his Tasmanian coal mines. Faye Gardam of Port Sorell filled in many of the blanks in Zephaniah Williams's Tasmanian odyssey. Then there was the Williams family Bible, carried 14,000 miles around the world when his wife Joan joined him in exile in 1854. For this I must thank Mike McClaren of Latrobe, Tasmania, who directed me towards Frogmore House, home of Mr and Mrs Kim Ransom, where the Bible has remained for 150 years! One day this priceless Chartist artefact must surely return to Wales, the centrepiece perhaps for a Chartist Museum and Research Centre where future historians can continue to unravel the mystery of the Uprising and the unique society from which it sprung, because there is much more to be discovered.

I am also grateful to my publisher and editor, Terry Breverton, of Glyndŵr Publishing. Without his support and encouragement, and Glyndŵr Publishing's commitment to telling the history of Wales, these latest revelations about the Chartist Uprising of 1839 might never have seen the light of day. Finally, I must mention Dr John Malcolm, a more recent settler in Tasmania whose home stands on the site of *"The Manor"*, the house Zephaniah Williams built for his family at Ballahoo Creek. Dr Malcolm told me where to find the Welsh daffodils that flower in spring!

JOHN HUMPHRIES
Plas Cwm Coed, Tredunnoc, Gwent.
May 27, 2004.

Contents

Abbreviations

GRO	Gwent Record Office
NPL	Newport Public Library
NLW	National Library of Wales, Aberystwyth
MM	*Monmouthshire Merlin*
CCL	Cardiff Central Library
GRO (CARDIFF)	Glamorgan Record Office (Cardiff)
GLO	General Land Office (Texas)
PRO	Public Record Office (Kew)
RA	Royal Archives (Windsor)
MB	*Monmouthshire Beacon*
TS	Treasury Solicitor Papers, Public Record Office
Bute XX	Bute Papers, CPL
NSW	New South Wales, Australia
HOC	House of Commons
HO	Home Office
LE	*Launceston Examiner*, Tasmania
CC	*Cornwall Chronicle*, Tasmania
GPO	Government Printing Office (Washington)

CHAPTER 1

Introduction

If John Rees alias 'Jack the Fifer' had not escaped to America then history's account of the Chartist Uprising in Monmouthshire in November 1839 might be very different, certainly less ambiguous. Then again, the affair which ended with twenty-two Chartists either dead or dying after the 45th Regiment of Foot threw open the shuttered windows of Newport's Westgate Hotel and discharged their muskets into the tightly-packed ranks of demonstrators, would make more sense if the alleged *'confession'* of Zephaniah Williams, one of three sentenced to death for High Treason, could be shown to be genuine beyond reasonable doubt. And why did John Frost leader of this supposed conspiracy to overthrow the monarchy, after a lifetime spent in close polemic conflict, never offer a word of public explanation for events that culminated in the last great show trial in British legal history? While much is known about Frost, 55-year-old draper, a former Mayor of Newport, magistrate, and figurehead for the Welsh Chartists, who were his mysterious partners Williams and Rees in an affair the Prime Minister, Lord Melbourne, admitted to the new Queen Victoria *"might have been very dangerous"*? Melbourne was a crucial influence on the young Queen, advising Victoria to ignore social matters, not even to read *Oliver Twist,* and to regard all public discontent as the work of an insignificant group of trouble-makers.[1]

Zephaniah Williams was a bankrupt coal owner running a beer shop from which he was expecting to be evicted.[2] Only months before the Chartist Uprising, he narrowly escaped a gaol sentence for hijacking, and then wrecking a colliery owned by the Mayor of Newport, Thomas Phillips, the man later knighted by Queen Victoria for organising the defence of the town against the Chartist mob. Is it credible that no sooner had he walked free from one

11

court, Zephaniah Williams, reputedly one of the most intelligent and astute men in the county, was of such a reckless disposition to embark knowingly upon an even more dangerous adventure destined to end either in civil war or before the courts, its ringleaders charged with the greatest of all felonies, High Treason?

The Tredegar stonemason, John Rees, was 24 years of age when all this occurred, about half Zephaniah's age. Both had lived and worked in Tredegar at the top end of Monmouthshire's Sirhowy Valley, but that would seem to be about all they had in common. If a person is judged by his track record alone, then Rees could be considered the only avowed republican revolutionary among the Chartist leadership, having not long returned from Texas where he fought in the "People's Army" during the successful struggle for independence from Mexico. Not only was he at the Alamo before it eventually fell to the Mexican General Santa Anna, Rees also survived the Goliad Massacre, still considered one of the most infamous war crimes perpetrated against American forces. The memory of these twin events, occurring as they did within three weeks of each other, has resonated across every battlefield on which Americans have since been engaged – *"Remember the Alamo"* as a powerful call to patriotism, *"Remember Goliad"* synonymous with the brutality of war. The experience could only have influenced Rees when he led the Chartists into battle outside the Westgate Hotel.[3]

Beyond poking a boyhood finger into the five 'bullet holes' in the scarred pillars at the entrance to the hotel, I had never thought much about the Chartist Uprising. That was until discovering the original pillars were of solid oak while those revered by visitors for a hundred years were fakes, made of plaster cast, evidently a bit of tourist kitsch decorated with holes by some wily former owner of the Westgate.[4] Despite this there never appeared to be any great mystery about the bloody struggle on the hotel's steps, except it seemed a huge sacrifice for what Professor David Williams in his acclaimed 1939 biography *John Frost: a study in Chartism* decided was nothing more than a large demonstration for electoral reform that went wrong.[5] His view has since been contradicted by two more recent studies of the Uprising: Ivor Wilks' radical assertion in 1984 that this was a republican workers attempt to overthrow the English Monarchy in the tradition of

Welsh self-determination, and David J. V. Jones' (1985) more plausible interpretation of events as a local rising originally conceived as part of a general insurrection.[6] The frustration for students of Chartism is that all three arrived at quite different conclusions, after raking through what was largely the same body of evidence and sources. This book sets out to make sense of these conflicting theories by investigating the lives and actions of two of the main protagonists, Zephaniah Williams and John Rees, before, during and after the events at Newport, in the process shedding new light on the affair from hitherto unpublished material.

At the start of the 19th century Britain's electoral system was unrepresentative, outdated and corrupt, a mere three per cent of the eight million population of England and Wales entitled to vote. The entire populations of great new industrial towns like Manchester, Leeds and Birmingham were totally disenfranchised without a single member of parliament, while villages with populations of fewer than forty, the so-called 'rotten boroughs,' were represented at Westminster, in some cases electing not one but two Members.[7] Pressure for reform peaked in 1819 when the radical Henry Hunt arrived at St Peter's Field, Manchester to address 80,000 people waving banners demanding "Vote By Ballot" and "Universal Suffrage." No sooner had Hunt started speaking, than the yeoman cavalry charged, slashing wildly at the crowd with their sabres. Eleven demonstrators were killed, many more injured, and some trampled in the panic to escape what became the Peterloo Massacre.[8] After this the government passed a series of repressive measures pushing parliamentary reform even further away. By 1832, however, reform had once again taken centre stage, the Whig administration of the 2nd Earl Grey extending the right to vote to townsmen occupying property with an annual value of £10. The Great Reform Act left many, of all classes, feeling a deep sense of betrayal because it meant six out of seven male adults remained disenfranchised.[9] Chartism sprang from this widespread disappointment. First published in May 1838 and agreed on August 6 as the new movement's manifesto, the Charter demanded:

1. All men over 21 to be given the right to vote.
2. Voting to be conducted by secret ballot.

3. The establishment of 300 constituencies of an equal number of voters.
4. Parliamentary elections to be held every year.
5. The ownership of property to be abolished as a qualification for a Member of Parliament.
6. Members of Parliament to be paid.

The work of William Lovett and the London Working Men's Association, the Charter, backed by a petition signed by 1,280,000, was presented as a draft Bill to the House of Commons by the Birmingham MP, Thomas Attwood in June, 1839.[10] After it was defeated, the movement split into two factions, the moral and physical force wings. Lovett, one of the founders, advocated peaceful persuasion, while Fergus O'Connor, publisher of the radical *Northern Star,* urged his Chartist supporters to *'go flesh every sword to the hilt.'*[11]

How Chartism galvanised the remote industrial valleys of Monmouthshire into action in less than a year, considering the geographic isolation of the mining communities, is one of the great riddles of British history. The slaughter outside the Westgate Hotel after 2000 rain-soaked colliers descended from the hills on a cold autumn night could only ever be justified by the Government's claim that the army had thwarted a rebellion, when what was intended might have been nothing more than a peaceful demonstration. It took barely ten minutes for the 30 soldiers of 45th Regiment of Foot, barricaded inside the hotel, to disperse the crowd with three musket volleys fired at almost point blank range, the Chartists scattering in all directions, leaving behind their dead and carrying away their dying. The only certainty about what happened was that rebellion had been expected to occur somewhere in Britain, ever since the storming of the Bastille by the Paris mob had deposed the established order in France fifty years earlier. The Chartists fitted the description as potential suspects, their demands for electoral reform seen as a cover for an uprising. At first, the Whig Home Secretary, Lord Normanby, sought to play down the situation at Newport, instructing the Mayor to select the worst offenders for trial. But the Magistrates would have none of this and within a few weeks of the event, 21 Chartists were awaiting trial for High Treason, while another 78 faced a variety of charges arising from the affair.[12]

The mainspring of legislation for dealing with treasonable activities is the Act of 1352, under which a person participating in a riot could be charged with High Treason, if deemed to have levied war against the realm. There was only one penalty for this, that imposed by Chief Justice Tindal on three of the Chartist leaders, John Frost, Zephaniah Williams, and William Jones, the Pontypool publican and part-time actor, at the Special Commission at Monmouth – "to be drawn on a hurdle to the place of execution . . . hanged by the neck until dead . . . the head severed from the body . . . the body divided into four quarters . . . and disposed of as Her Majesty shall think fit." While no corpse had been severed into quarters since the 18th century, the barbaric procedure had only been suspended, unlike disembowelment and the burning of the condemned man's entrails while he was still alive which had only been removed from the statue book twenty years earlier. Nevertheless, waiting in Monmouth Gaol for the sentence to be carried out, the three prisoners were tormented by their gaoler's graphic description of how it was intended to dispose of their bodies. Neither did punishment end with the horrible death of offenders; it extended to their families. Not only did those guilty of treason forfeit all their lands and property to the state, their immediate family and heirs were tainted through association by 'corruption of blood' and consequently banned from owning property. They were, in effect, ruined for life.[13]

Although the Whig Government considered the Uprising at Newport a threat to the monarchy, contaminating a large part of 19th century industrial South Wales, for some strange reason history rates it lower on the revolutionary Richter scale than just about every treasonable activity since the Gunpowder Plot in 1605. Even the Cato Street conspiracy in 1820, a bizarre scheme to murder King George IV and his entire Cabinet, seems at times more firmly lodged in the public consciousness than an uprising in Wales, which, as the years roll by, is buried ever deeper in the margins of history. Is this because rather than a real conspiracy, it was more the manifestation of a corrupt society; an explosive orgy of violence in part of the British Empire considered one step beyond civilisation – the so-called 'Black Domain' created by iron and coal, sustained by wage-slavery, and fed by ignorance? If this were so, how did such a degenerate society succeed in mobilising a revolutionary army under the very noses of the authorities? Some historians have suggested it was on account of the dominance of the Welsh language that the plan was kept secret until the last moment, even though it would appear that proceedings at Chartist meetings were held as often in English as Welsh, Zephaniah Williams on occasions acting as interpreter at the *Royal Oak* in Blaina.[14] Because the desperate social conditions prevailing in the Valleys would seem to offer the simplest and most principled motivation, the leaders of Welsh Chartism have been plucked from out of an incomprehensible fog as messiahs of modern socialism, their memory a socialist icon, the very stuff from which the cradle of the Labour Party was fashioned. Ivor Wilks in *"South Wales and the Rising of 1839"* is not alone in championing the attack on Newport as nothing less than an attempt to create *"an autonomous republic, a commonwealth, a commune of armed citizens."*[15] For Reg Groves in *"But we shall rise again: a narrative history of Chartism"* the Uprising was a genuinely revolutionary cry, and for Ness Edwards, socialist activist of the South Wales Miners Federation, 1839 saw the advent of the *"first independent political working class movement in South Wales . . . a result of insurrectionary fervour . . . being generated in the hearts and minds of the working class."*[16] But socialists are not the only ones to sift the ashes of Monmouthshire's failed Uprising in search of their roots. Republicans and monarchists alike, can find in the evidence presented at the Monmouth Treason Trials, the threads of a working class conspiracy to topple the monarchy and replace it with a Republic.

My interest in unravelling what remains a mystery to this day was revived during a visit to Port Arthur, the infamous penal settlement in Tasmania, formerly Van Diemen's Land, where Frost, Williams and Jones were eventually transported for life. Nestling in an idyllic bay, washed by the great Southern Ocean, and flanked by green hills, the eucalyptus forest now fully recovered from the depredations of convict labour, the settlement's penal history qualifies it as a World Heritage Site. The irony, well beyond the reach of the tens of thousands who suffered transportation from 1788-1868 (the youngest a child of eight from Preston sentenced to life for stealing a toy) is that this place is so incredibly beautiful that without its monstrous past Port Arthur would today almost certainly have become an expensive tourist retreat! On a hill overlooking the waterfront, not a stone's throw from the Triangle on which men were flogged to death, and within a few yards of the solitary confinement block, conveniently next to the madhouse for those unable to endure the silent, inky blackness chained to their beds, stands a small cottage with a wide colonial-style veranda. Now a museum commemorating some of the political prisoners who passed through Port Arthur, it was once the prison 'home' of William Smith O'Brien, leader of the Young Irelanders' failed attempt at winning Irish Independence in 1848. His death sentence was commuted to transportation by a government afraid of creating more Irish martyrs. O'Brien was fortunate in having as his brother Sir Lucius O'Brien, the 13th Baron Inchiquin, heir to Drumoland, who obtained an assurance that his aristocratic convict brother would be treated as a gentleman for the duration of his exile. Instead of a wooden bunk in a prison dormitory shared with fifty others, O'Brien was given this cottage on the hillside at Port Arthur, and the attention of a convict servant.[17] The cottage is also a shrine to one hundred "Canadian Patriots," mostly American citizens, in fact, dispatched to Van Diemen's Land after they crossed the border to join the Patriots' War in Lower Canada in 1837.[18] Almost out of sight, squeezed into a corner is a glass cabinet displaying a harp inscribed as having belonged to Zephaniah Williams "one of three *English* Chartists" incarcerated at Port Arthur.[19] Even though Monmouthshire was part of England in 1839, this confused epithet struck me as a pitifully inadequate commentary on an event, which some believe was the last great blow struck for republicanism in Britain.

Apart from Frost, whose battles with the local gentry were legendary, landing him in gaol in 1822 for libelling Thomas Prothero, the powerful, colliery-owning Town Clerk of Newport, precious little is known of the other leaders of the Uprising in Wales. Rarely off the front pages of the day, with a stream of vitriolic pamphlets, letters, and speeches, Frost's championing of the Charter was the inevitable progression in an adversarial life. Remarkably, however, while he had much to say about his incarceration at Port Arthur, he never once volunteered a detailed explanation for the events of November 4, although four years before he died at Stapleton, near Bristol in 1877, aged 93, he had agreed to contribute a series of articles about the affair to the *Newcastle Weekly Chronicle*. Nothing was ever submitted for publication, fuelling suspicions that somewhere there exists a half-finished account, possibly among the private papers he bequeathed to a mysterious Charles Groves.[20]

Unlike Frost, the only evidence of Zephaniah Williams' involvement with Chartism before the Uprising was the use of his beer shop, the *Royal Oak* at Nantyglo, as a meeting place, together with witness testimony linking him to the planning of the march during the preceding week. The total absence of any published contribution to the debate on electoral reform cannot be ascribed to ignorance. More than half the men who descended from the hills may have been illiterate, but not Zephaniah. A close reading of his letters and a pamphlet he published refuting the accusations of a local clergyman who accused him of being a deist, reveal an exceptionally well-educated individual for that period.[21]

In his convict record Williams is stated as being born in 1795, and a native of Merthyr Tydfil. When arrested after the attack on the Westgate he also described himself as a native of Merthyr.[22] Even though no baptismal record can be found to substantiate this, it is more likely to have been Merthyr, or its neighbourhood, than Argoed in Monmouthshire, assumed to be his birthplace largely on the basis of purely anecdotal evidence first published by Oliver Jones in *The Early Days of Sirhowy and Tredegar* (1969). The evidence Oliver Jones provides for this is his discovery that Thomas Williams, a man he believed to be Zephaniah's father, had owned a farm named Troedrhiwgyngy, near the village of Argoed, from which he concluded Zephaniah spent his early years either there or at a house also belonging to his father at Blackwood.[23] A Thomas Williams did own Troedrhiwgyngy Farm but it is clear from that individual's will he was definitely not Zephaniah's father.[24] Nor could Zephaniah have spent his early days in the house at Blackwood, which his father did build but not until 1822 by which time the Welsh Chartist leader was 27, married with a family and living at Penmaen where he owned his own colliery, supplying house coal to merchants in Newport and Bristol.[25] Williams was the son of a relatively prosperous yeoman farmer, originally from Penderyn in Breconshire who married Mary Thomas of Bedwellty in 1787. His father later moved to

Monmouthshire, first to Tredegar where he built two cottages, then later to Blackwood where he acquired coal-bearing land and built a house in 1822 on a site leased to his son Zephaniah by the entrepreneur and philanthropist John Hodder Moggridge. Zephaniah was eventually to inherit the properties at Tredegar and Blackwood.[26] Before his move to the Blackwood district Zephaniah lived for a time at Bovil House, Machen, on the estate of wealthy landowner, Llewellyn Llewellyn, whose daughter Joan he married in 1819.[27]

From his earliest days Zephaniah aspired to the entrepreneurial class he was eventually accused of seeking to depose. Minerals Agent for ten years to the Harford Bros., Quaker ironmasters at Sirhowy and Ebbw Vale, he was one of the most important and powerful middlemen on the coalfield, responsible for the hiring and supervision of collier gangs to supply the Harford furnaces with coal. Then, for no apparent reason, and only months before the Chartist Uprising in 1839, he quit the Harfords to run the *Royal Oak* beer shop at Blaina. As will be shown later, the suggestion he did so to campaign on behalf of the Chartists and electoral reform does not stand up to scrutiny.[28] The more satisfactory explanation is that either he had already lost his employment with the Harfords, or moved before that was likely to happen because by then he and others were facing the prospect of a lengthy prison sentence, even transportation for the break-in at Cwrt-y-Bella Colliery.[29] In an affair strewn with contradictions, one of the most ironic is that for all his involvement in Chartism, Zephaniah Williams had probably already qualified to vote in the first election following the 1832 Reform Act. Electoral registers for this period have not survived but he was a member of a Grand Jury of the Monmouthshire Quarter Sessions at Usk prior to 1839 for which he would have required the same minimum property qualifications entitling him to vote.[30]

Zephaniah Williams's descent from relative affluence into straitened circumstances is described in the *Monmouthshire Merlin's* account of his appearance before the Newport Magistrates, hours after he was arrested following the Newport Uprising:

> *"The room was at this moment crowded to excess when the prisoner Zephaniah Williams was brought in custody of*

two armed policemen and placed at the bar. We have seen this man in the days of his prosperity when he revelled no doubt in the anticipation of enjoyment of wealth and station; we have seen him take a leading part at Chartist meetings; and we were not prepared for the dismal, forlorn and hopeless expression which every look and gesture conveyed. His appearance is that of a man who having been totally disappointed in every hope, had abandoned himself to despair." [31]

By the time he was declared guilty of treason, Williams was a broken man. Asked by Lord Chief Justice Tindel what he had to say before sentence was passed, his face turned ghastly pale, his voice faltered as he disclaimed all knowledge of conspiracy to commit High Treason. He insisted he *"never entertained any notion of the kind imputed against me;"* that the greater part of the evidence against him was false; that he *"never entertained the least design of revolting against the Queen,"* adding, *"so help me God,"* his face quivering with intense agony as he pleaded his innocence. [32]

Four months later, bound for Van Diemen's Land and transportation for life, Williams made an astonishing confession to Dr Alex McKechnie, Surgeon Superintendent aboard the convict ship *Mandarin*. As the ship rounded the Cape of Good Hope, he signed a letter confirming everything the government and magistrates had suspected about the uprising. Among the questions this book will address is why Zephaniah confessed – the only one of the three prisoners to do so – when he was already destined for a fate most regarded as worse than death itself. The authenticity of the confession is crucial in explaining the Chartist Uprising in Monmouthshire because around it other authors, notably Ivor Wilks, Ness Edwards, Reg Groves, and David J. V. Jones to a lesser extent, have constructed their conspiracy hypotheses. [33]

John Rees, alias Jack the Fifer, was not the only Chartist still at large when Frost, Williams and Jones were dispatched to Van Diemen's Land but he was the most important, the magistrates offering a reward of £100 for his capture, the same as they had put on the head of Zephaniah Williams. If any man among the Chartist leadership could sustain a conspiracy to overthrow the monarch, then it was Rees who four years previously had enlisted in the People's Army of Texas under the command of General Sam Houston, the first elected President of the Republic of Texas, which was formed after a great swathe of territory had been seized from the Mexicans. Like most of the drifters and soldiers of fortune recruited from the saloons and coffee shops of Louisiana and Virginia to fight the war, on behalf of the wealthy Anglo-Texan plantation owners and slave traders, Rees had been persuaded by Houston's promise of land grants and citizenship in the new Republic. Most had arrived in Texas penniless, some with only the rags on their backs, but from this rabble was forged possibly the most politicised army ever to take the field in North America. Ill-disciplined and disorganised for the entire six months of the struggle, the army was from the outset a uniquely democratic force, the volunteers electing their officers by open ballot, and the rank-and-file participating in strategic planning before ever a shot was fired.[34] Distrusted by those whose interests they fought for, this army of social outcasts was, nevertheless, determined to have a voice in the new Republic and to share in the spoils of victory. Rees was one of 177 militiamen who, on the eve of the Texas Declaration of Independence, successfully petitioned the National Convention to admit their nominees to the committee drafting the Declaration, and to concede to every citizen soldier the right to a vote.[35]

Returning to Britain in February or March 1839 Rees would have scented another revolution on the horizon as the Whig government looked nervously over its shoulder for the first signs of trouble.[36] The earliest sign of the French revolutionary tendency crossing the Channel was at Pentrich in Derbyshire in 1817 when a few hundred men set out to capture Nottingham, only to flee in confusion at the sight of soldiers. Their leaders were executed for daring to challenge the status quo. After the Peterloo Massacre two years later, and the Merthyr Rising of 1831, many in authority believed the Chartist attack upon Newport was yet a further eruption of revolutionary agitation. As a reaction to the repugnant Truck Shop system and the dreaded debt collectors from the Court of Requests, the Merthyr Rising, in which 14 rioters perished, and Dic Penderyn (Richard Lewis) hanged, was more a crisis in working class identity than a manifestation of working class ideology, according to Gwyn A. Williams in *The Merthyr Rising* (1978). The raising of the Red Flag at Merthyr may have been in response to working class consciousness but this had been prodded into life by a string of local grievances rather than emerging from an inherent sense of ideological conviction or unity. Gwyn Williams seemed to feel the working class movement, as such, began taking shape eight years later with the Chartists.[37] If that were the case, then in Monmouthshire it was stillborn, a jittery government and paranoid aristocracy preferring instead to believe they confronted not the first signs of organised labour but revolution.

For much of the 1830s Britain seemed to totter on the brink of the revolutionary abyss, pushed there by the great social, economic and political upheavals following the French Wars. Anti-monarchist sentiment was running out of control across Europe like a bush fire. Charles X fled to England from France, £500,000 in gold hidden in his baggage; there was revolution in Belgium, revolts in the Germanic kingdoms of Hesse, Brunswick and Saxony; the Papal States were in turmoil; workers were in revolt in Lyons, and the Carlist Wars gripped Spain. Worse still, the 'French disease' was spreading ever nearer, infecting the Empire, for as this turbulent decade need its end, the young Queen Victoria faced rebellion in Upper and Lower Canada (1838-39). Now the firestorm threatened to engulf Britain.

The search for a convincing explanation of the aims of the Monmouthshire Chartists has been largely confined to the events rather than the main protagonists, John Rees being almost totally neglected, understandably perhaps because afterwards he seemed to disappear off the face of the planet. No statement, not a single reliable word has been found implicating Rees in Chartist activities preceding the Uprising, although there is hitherto unpublished witness testimony placing him in the front line on the fatal day. The reasons for the participation of Zephaniah Williams', a man clearly a cut above the rank and file, have leaned too often on anecdote and legend. All that has been really known until now is that he was the most secretive and cautious of the three convicted leaders, and became involved during the last days of planning. Rees remained an even more shadowy figure, rarely revealing a glimpse of his involvement. Was he the anonymous speaker at William Jones's public house at Pontypool who remarked,

"I am a young man but an old republican?" Or was he the veteran of the Texas War of Independence who instructed delegates at a meeting in Dukes Town, Tredegar, on the "organisation and arming of bodies?" Above all else, was Rees the man who fired the first shot outside the Westgate that triggered the murderous response from the soldiers hidden behind the hotel shutters? Or was it as some thought an army deserter killed in the melee, or as William Jones and John Frost believed an agent provocateur?[38]

Because he escaped to America, the case against Rees was never tested in court, the depositions of witnesses not heard. The Grand Jury, comprising the great and the good of Monmouthshire, was sufficiently convinced, however, that the evidence against him was strong enough to return a True Bill for High Treason. For 160 years the motives instrumental in persuading Williams and Rees to embark upon an adventure that could so easily have succeeded, had the marchers not been delayed by a night of torrential rain, have stared at us like blank pages in a half-finished book. Were they truly revolutionaries plotting to overthrow Queen Victoria as the Crown contended, or did they march recklessly into this affair, driven by a maelstrom of grievances, among which a fairer share of the indigenous wealth was paramount? If necessity is the mother of invention, then a conjunction of circumstances has the dynamic to propel people towards revolutionary turmoil regardless of political philosophy or settled plan. Once the tinder is in place, no flag needs to be raised, no banner waved, nor slogan shouted: all that is necessary is for someone to strike the match. By exposing for the first time the lives of John Rees and Zephaniah Williams to scrutiny, while exploring the conditions prevailing in the Black Domain from which they and 2000 others emerged to attack the town of Newport, this book hopes to shed new light on one of the most puzzling, at times incomprehensible, events in British history.

NOTES

1. 6 Nov 1839, entry in Queen Victoria's Journals (Royal Archives, Windsor Castle), *"At 12m to 4 Lord Melbourne came to me and stayed with me till 1/4p 4 . . . He read me 2 letters from Normanby; all quiet again. Frost, the ringleader, taken and shown himself an arrant coward; "If there had been a general rising," said Lord M, "it might have been very dangerous"*; L. G. Mitchell *Lord Melbourne, 1779-1848*, (Oxford University Press, 1997).

2. *Monmouthshire Merlin* property auction announcement, Gwent Record Office, 1 Nov 1833.

3. Discussed in detail in Chapter 4, 'Man from the Alamo'.

4. Gillian Holt, 'The Westgate Hotel, Newport,' *Gwent Local History*, No. 67.

5. David Williams, *John Frost: a study in Chartism* (Cardiff, 1939, University of Wales Press) p288.

6. Ivor Wilks, *South Wales and the Rising of 1839* (London, 1984, Croom Helm) pp246-251; David J. V. Jones, *The Last Rising: the Newport Chartist Insurrection of 1839* (Oxford, 1985), p209.

7. Public Record office, *The National Archives: Citizenship and Voting Rights before 1832.*

8. PRO, *The National Archives: the Peterloo Massacre 1819.*

9. PRO, *The National Archives: Citizenship and Voting Rights before 183.*

10. Williams, pp100-101; Lovett Collection, 122, 250, and 148, 56, 194.

11. *Northern Star*, 26 Jan 1839, and subsequent issues for evidence of O'Connor provocation.

12. PRO, HO 41/45, Home Office to Mayor of Newport, Nov 7, 1839.

13. William Blackstone, *Commentaries on the Laws of England*, Book 4, p94.

14. Close reading of Chartist Trials depositions, Newport Public Library.

15. Wilks, p 249.

16. Ness Edwards, *John Frost and the Chartist Movement in Wales* (Abertillery, 1924, Western Valley Labour Classics).

17. Richard Davis, *Revolutionary Imperialists: William Smith O'Brien, 1803-1864* (Dublin, 1998, Lilliput Press).

18. Allan Greer, *The Patriots and the People: The Rebellion of 1837 in Rural Lower Canada* (University of Toronto Press, 1993).

19. The harp might have originally belonged to Zephaniah's son Llewelyn who briefly joined his father in Tasmania, although it might have been expected to return with him to Wales. Faye Gardam, Secretary of the Devonport Maritime Museum and Historical Society, tells me the harp passed to Zephaniah's grandson, Llewelyn Atkinson, and was later given to Samuel Ready a musician at Latrobe whose son sold it Port Arthur Museum in the late 1980s.

20. In *Memoirs of a Social Atom*, (London, Hutcheson, 1903), pp200-202, W. E. Adams, Editor of *Newcastle Weekly Chronicle* reproduces a letter from John Frost dated Stapleton, 15 Dec 1873 in which Frost details his plans for a series of articles, adding, *"I have for years been thinking on*

the subject of my long and suffering life, and I feel anxious that the circumstances should be placed before the public in a way likely to be interesting to the rising generation." In this letter Frost says he was in his 89th year, confirming his birth as 1784, not 1786 as stated by several contemporary accounts during his trial; also see John Frost's will, Chartist Archives NPL for detail of bequest to Charles Groves. The only Charles Groves that can be positively linked to Frost is the one who founded the Young Chartists in Newport in partnership with Frost's son. Arrested after the Uprising he turned Queen's Evidence and was released without charge. So far, it has been impossible to discover what became of him.

21. Zephaniah Williams, *Letter to Benjamin Williams, A Dissenting Minister* (Newport, 1831), Chartist Archives, NPL.
22. Tasmanian State Archives, Hobart, Williams Convict Record, Prisoner 203, *Mandarin*.
23. Oliver Jones , *The Early Days of Sirhowy and Tredegar* (Tredegar Historical Society, 1969) p91.
24. National Library of Wales, LL1846/31, will, Thomas Williams, Troedrhiwgyngy, 2 June 1846.
25. Williams family bible discovered by author at *Frogmore House*, Ballahoo Creek, Latrobe, Tasmania.
26. NLW, LL/CC/1160, Thomas Williams, Letter of Administration, inventory.
27. Zephaniah and Joan Williams, wedding registration entry, St Tydfil's Church, Glamorgan Record Office, Merthyr Parish Records, p213, No. 637, 9 Aug 1819.
28. Oliver Jones, *The Early Days of Sirhowy and Tredegar* (Tredegar Historical Society,1969) p 92; Stockdale, MM, 23 Nov 1839.
29. *Monmouthshire Beacon,* Aug 1838.
30. Williams letter to wife 20 Sept 1843; *South Wales Daily News,* 28 April 1877, p 4.
31. MM, 7 Dec 1839.
32. MM, 18 Jan 1840.
33. NLW, 40/2, copy of 'confession' letter, Lord Tredegar Papers, 25 May 1840.
34. Gary Brown, *New Orleans Greys,* (Texas, 1999).
35. Convention Memorial, Archives, State Dept, Washington, Memorial No. 36, File Box No. 93, Letter No. V, Feb 1836.
36. For details of Rees' experiences in Texas and return to Wales see chapter, 'Land, Land, Land'.
37. Gwyn A. Williams , *The Merthyr Rising* (Croom Helm, 1978) pp224-230.
38. Newport Public Library, Chartist Trials, 7, Charles James Phillips.

CHAPTER 2

People of the Black Domain

'I have been down about three years; I don't know my age,
when I first went down I couldn't keep my eyes open. I
don't fall asleep now, I smoke my pipe, earns 8d a day.
Never been to school, can't say what tobacco is made of,
knows it comes from the shop, smokes half a quartern a
week. Thinks mother pays 8d for half a quartern.'

Seven-year-old William Richards, an intelligent and good-humoured
lad, his cap furnished with the usual collier-candlestick, his pipe
stuck firmly in his buttonhole, was one of 180 boys and girls
working in the mines and collieries at Sirhowy in1842 when R. H.
Franks delivered his report to the Commissioners investigating
child labour. It would seem from this that young Richards was
sent under ground as soon as he had the strength to lift a lump of
coal.

A slightly older lad, Jacob Morgan, aged 10, was employed
removing the cinders from the furnaces at Sirhowy.

'I have been at this work for only a couple of months. I was
before, for about two years, working with my father in the
colliery. I did not like working under ground; I would
rather work above. I believe they will give me about 3s a
week. The horse I drive comes out at six in the morning,
then it rests half an hour at nine o'clock, and again three
hours at dinner-time, then goes for journeys in the evening
until six o'clock.'

Evan Evans worked for the 'baller' in the forge alongside his
father. He did not know his age.

'I cannot say whether I am eight years old or not.'

Mary Ann Williams, 13, was paid 4s a week for a twelve-hour day.

> *'I keep a door in the colliery under ground. The place is very well, but would rather be at home . . .'* [1]

Of all the child workers, those employed in the iron works were the better educated. According to one account, seventy per cent at Sirhowy were able to read, an indication perhaps blast furnace work was superior to that in the coal and ironstone mines. Two thirds of the children employed under ground were illiterate, either because they were removed from school at an early age by their parents and sent down the pit, or because there were no day schools in the neighbourhood, leaving the non-Conformist or Dissenting Sunday Schools their only opportunity to learn anything, the clergy of the established Anglican church caring very little for the welfare of the labouring class. At least at Sunday School they were taught the rudiments of reading, writing and arithmetic, the teaching usually based around the scriptures and instruction by rote. Where day schools existed, the teachers were mostly unqualified, paid less than labourers, and frequently drawn from the ranks of crippled colliers, burned blast furnace men, and bankrupt shopkeepers. The average school age was estimated at eight, teachers often deliberately exaggerating this by recalling former pupils to swell the muster roll for visiting inspectors. Attendances were fragmented, two-thirds of all children receiving education that totalled less than a year. Many were removed from school for long periods by their parents whenever more gainful employment was available, as was often the case. When the Government Inspector, Seymour Tremenheere, a few months after the Uprising, compiled his report on elementary education in the parishes of Bedwellty, Aberystruth, Mynydd-islwyn, Trevethin, and Merthyr Tydfil, he concluded that half the children in an area with a population of 85,000, twice what it was twenty years earlier, never saw the inside of a day school. Parents were also suspicious of what many regarded as a tool of iron-masters and coal owners alike to keep workers poor and servile. For their part, the owners believed that once educated workers would become dissatisfied with their lot and fail to *"properly fulfil the duties of their station."* [2] Many of those claiming to read had only acquired the art of identifying some words and letters, like the initials of their own names. A large percentage of the prosecution witnesses at the Chartist Trials were illiterate, signing their depositions with their mark. Pitifully few read with ease and understanding. Zephaniah Williams, however, stood head and shoulders above his contemporaries in this regard, although exactly where he acquired his vastly superior education is unclear. His wife Joan, on the other hand, daughter of a prosperous farming family, was barely able to scribble her name in the parish register at Merthyr when they married in 1819.[3]

By 1839 work was plentiful and wages in Monmouthshire high, better than in any other part of Britain. The burden of the poor and destitute on the property-owning class was far more tolerable than elsewhere. If furnace men and mill men earning 25 shillings-60 shillings a week (£50 to £120 at today's values) were of a mind to, they could have accumulated sufficient savings to erect a cottage then costing about £60 to build (or £2,400).[4] While ironstone miners and colliers were less well rewarded, on 21 shillings-25 shillings a week, it was still more than twice what they might have expected as agricultural workers.[5] For children and women, weekly rates ranged from 3 shillings-12 shillings working under ground for coal owners who defied legislation outlawing the practice, one of the greatest offenders being the powerful Blaenavon ironmaster, Crawshay Bailey. Not surprisingly, a life of hard physical labour produced legendary feats of strength, one remarkable individual Will Rhyd Helig of Merthyr reputed to carry ten sacks of sand on a wheelbarrow, and another, a Penydarren carpenter, able to shoulder 700lbs of pipe. It was not uncommon for colliers to wheel barrow-loads of coal to Cardiff and Newport for sale.

From his very first day under ground a boy was worth a minimum of 6 pence a day, opening and shutting air doors, throwing small pieces of coal and ironstone into the trams, or handing tools to the men at the coalface. He learned early to become a good miner or collier but nothing else from the moment he went down the pit. One mother told Tremenheere how she had resisted her husband taking their seven-year-old son into the mines. Her other children, she said, had gone at eight, and afterwards *"they turned stupid and blind-like, and would not learn anything, and did not know what was right; and now they were like the rest, they went to the public-houses like men."* [6] Boys of ten and twelve would not hesitate to stop at the beer-shop for their noggin of rum at the end of a day's work. By the time they were sixteen, they took their wives from the coke-hearths or off the cinder beds at the ironworks, or from among those sorting and loading the coal trams at the collieries. In the Black Domain, because of the high wages, men could support a family at an early age and unlike many parts of the country where a large family was considered a heavy burden, here it was an investment, a means of generating more income. So great was the demand for labour, and so high were the wages during the seven years immediately prior to the Chartist Uprising, that a child's 6 pence a day was rarely necessary to sustain a family. But if money was relatively plentiful, eligible women were not. It was generally agreed that Merthyr was the surest place to find a husband!

Ironworkers and colliers worked hard, lived freely, drank heavily and died early, leaving no memento to their industry but a fading testimonial in some obscure chapel or churchyard. The average life expectancy in Britain in 1840 was 40.2 years, lower again in the South Wales Valleys where appalling social conditions existed, paradoxically, within a high wage society. Few men saved more than perhaps a weekly contribution to the local Friendly Society as insurance against illness and the cyclical volatility of the iron and coal trade which could put them out of work at a moment's notice. In the year ending November 1839, the month of the Uprising, only 20 colliers and miners had made a deposit in the Pontypool Savings Bank out of a population of 12,000. To cater for thirsty ironworkers and colliers sweating twelve hours a day at the blast furnace or cutting the rich, four-foot Mynyddislwyn seam, almost every corner had its public house, beer shop or Bid-All (unlicensed grog house). Although not as frequent as Glasgow where one in every ten houses was a dram house, the drink culture was overwhelming Welsh non-conformist moderation.[7] In response, temperance clubs like the Band of Hope flourished as chapels fought back with public declarations of "signing the pledge" against the demon drink. Excessive drinking was not peculiar to the South Wales iron and coal districts but even in a 19th century awash with beer and rum at every level of society, the Black

Domain distinguished itself in this regard. Much of the accompanying social disintegration can be attributed to the transformation caused by a population explosion of historic proportions, immigration into the minerals districts of Monmouthshire between 1820 and 1840 being greater than in any other county of Britain. By the end of this period, the populations of the five parishes, which previously recruited labour from rural Wales, were swollen by large numbers of in-comers from Cornwall, Somerset, Gloucester and Hereford, lured by the prospect of rich rewards from investing their labour in the great mineral adventure of the 19th century. Inevitably, immigration on this scale coincided with a decline in native Welsh-speakers to below 50 per cent in some parts of Monmouthshire by 1839. Nevertheless, the Welsh language continued to dominate the daily life of the county. Still linguistically remote from England, Monmouthshire was a frontier in every respect. Characteristically as Welsh as its neighbours to the west, it was unregulated and poorly policed, an Eldorado for fortune seekers and bolthole for the lawless, reckless and itinerant. There was good reason why a man sought by the authorities in the English border towns would be advised by family and friends to 'take to the hills.' The authors of the infamous Blue Books concluded from their investigation of education in the mineral districts of Monmouthshire that they contained a larger proportion of escaped criminals and dissolute people of both sexes than almost anywhere else in Britain. *"If the people have few virtues, they have great strength; if they have dark minds, they have strong passions and vigorous vices,"* they reported.[8] One such vice was 'The Bidding'. Most probably introduced to the valleys by migrant workers, the bidding was a popular social custom in West Wales where it was associated with marriages. Before a wedding, gifts were solicited from those who had previously enjoyed the generosity of the parents or relatives of the bride and bridegroom. The bidding was celebrated with a special ale, *cwrw bach*, distilled illegally and sold at inflated prices to recover the cost of the wedding, these occasions often ending in drunkenness. In the industrial valleys, the bidding degenerated into a weekend of binge drinking precipitated by some crisis or other, such as unemployment or debt. The individual concerned organised a drinking party as an excuse to forget his difficulties, to which he invited assorted males and females each of whom were expected to contribute towards the cost of a cask of beer and bottles of spirits. The participants soon became debauched, the orgies lasting all night and into the following day, often in the presence of children.[9]

No consideration of the evidence contained in the Blue Books of mid-19th century Monmouthshire can be undertaken without exercising some caution, the report of the Commissioners when published in 1847 widely criticised for being biased against the Welsh and the language for assuming that ignorance of English was synonymous with illiteracy. The three Commissioners were Anglicans with little understanding of education, Wales and the labouring classes. Most of the 300 witnesses interviewed were also Anglicans who believed in the paramountcy of the English language which, it was believed, led the Commissioners naturally on to their conclusion the Welsh language was *"a barrier to moral progress, pandering to prevarication and perjury, if not worse"* and that Welsh women were *"almost universally unchaste"* because of evenings spent at chapel meetings. For this the report earned itself the sobriquet of "The Treason of the Blue Books." This is not to say that because the report caused deep offence, this unique investigation by strangers into Monmouthshire's desperate social deprivation is invalidated. Very similar observations were made immediately following the Chartist Uprising by others closer to Wales and the labouring classes.[10]

One of the more benevolent ironmasters, G. S. Kenrick, of Varteg, set out to demonstrate how strong drink had become a necessity of life for the working classes to the extent it contributed directly to the attack on Newport. He did this by actually counting the drunkards in Trevethin, and found they totalled 1,962, or almost 12 per cent of the population, one tenth dying each year from alcohol-related illnesses, and accounting for half the annual death rate in the parish. The situation would not have been very different across the whole of the Minerals District of Monmouthshire and Glamorgan. Making a tally of the drunks proved not as difficult as Kenrick expected. One collier when asked about the number of drunks in his house, replied, *"Will you count them as I call their names? There's my son John, Jim, and William, Dick, Thomas. Ned and Joe, that make's seven; and then there's myself,"* and pointing to his wife, *"there's the old woman, you may put her down, for she gets drunk as well the rest of us."* That said, a steady collier spent less than five per cent of his monthly earnings on beer, which compares favourably with expenditure on alcohol 160 years later.[11]

Excessive drinking was most common at the end of the 'long pay'. Colliers were piece workers contracted to supply coal at fortnightly, four week or five week intervals. Only when the contract was completed, the coal delivered, was the master miner or Minerals Agent responsible for managing the gangs paid by the owners. Almost always payment was in gold or five pound notes, it being the custom to settle up in public houses or beer shops, as these were the only places working men could procure change. For providing his service, the publican received a discount of sixpence in the pound, which he returned to the colliers as beer. Inevitably, one drink led to another, the 'long pay' a major contributory factor in alcohol abuse, to the extent coal production declined dramatically at the start of the new contract as colliers recovered from over indulgence.

Frost, Williams and Jones all ran public houses, as did many of their Chartist lieutenants. Frost owned the *Royal Oak* at Newport, Williams took over the *Royal Oak* at Nantyglo. Before this he was landlord of public houses in Tredegar and Sirhowy, while Jones ran the *Bristol House* in Pontypool. Williams' life-long obsession may have been coal but he spent almost as much time in the licensing trade firstly in Wales, later Tasmania where he was even prosecuted for selling illegal grog. After hiring the colliers to dig the coal, how often did he take a further profit from the customary arrangements by obliging them to settle up at the public house or beer shop of his choice? Neither is it insignificant the Chartist Uprising coincided with the end of a 'long pay', the plans for the attack finalised at Blackwood on Friday 1 November, the marchers arriving in Newport at 9 a.m. on Monday 4 November, after their progress was delayed by a torrential downpour and frequent visits to public houses along the route.[11]

In a chronically over-crowded district described *as "teeming with grime, and all the slatternly accompaniments of animal power and moral disorder, with scarcely a ray of mental or spiritual intelligence,"* there would have been few places for

Top: Although child labour was prohibited by 1839, boys aged seven and eight were still sent underground to earn six pence a day. *Bottom:* Nantyglo in Monmouthshire, described in the infamous Blue Books as one of those towns *"teeming with grime, and all the slatternly accompaniments of animal power and moral disorder . . ."*

(Courtesy Newport City Museums and Heritage Service: Newport Museum and Art Gallery).

social discourse outside the public house and beer shop.[12] It was here that the new branches of the Workingmen's Association were formed as the Chartist movement spread like wildfire through the Monmouthshire and Glamorgan valleys during the winter of 1838, recruiting, according to Zephaniah Williams, an astonishing 50,000 members during the twelve months preceding the Uprising.[13]

That the movement advanced so rapidly is remarkable considering the remoteness of the Black Domain from mainstream political activity. Geographically and intellectually isolated from much of Britain, the six parallel valleys snaking their way towards the Bristol Channel, squeezed between mostly uninhabited moorland, were as distant from each other as England was from Wales. Roads were often little more than muddy tracks, the quickest way to Newport for those able to afford a ticket, the daily *Royal Mail* coach from Tredegar, or the twice-weekly *Waterloo*. A horse drawn vehicle, John Kingston's *Caravan*, ran along the Sirhowy Tram Road connecting Samuel Homfray's Tredgear Ironworks and the Harford Brothers Works at Sirhowy with Newport Docks. Apart from this, there was always the chance of hitching a hair-raising ride astride one of the iron or wooden trams careering down the steep gradients of the Sirhowy Valley Tram Road, everyone's life in the hands of the driver's mate whose job it was to slow the descent by ramming an iron bar between the wheels of the fifteen-tram convoy. Runaways were not uncommon, killing the horses, and sometimes passengers riding the forty-ton load of coal and pig iron.[14] By 1839 the steam engines replacing the horse drawn trams could haul twice as much, but still needed a full day for the round trip. By foot along the sixteen miles of tram road to Nine Mile Point, then on another nine miles to Sir Charles Morgan's Tredegar Park where his "Golden Mile" carried the coal to ships loading in the river, would have taken at least five hours. The Chartist marchers, most of whom came from north Monmouthshire, took twice as long to cover the distance, arriving at the Westgate not as planned under cover of darkness at 2 a.m., but well after dawn at 9 a.m.

Drovers' roads had existed for centuries across the bleak stretches of mountain upland, fanning out from the heads of the valleys towards the Brecon Beacons. Locally, smaller tram roads connected collieries, iron and limestone mines, but for the most part the lack of good, cheap communications contrived with geography to make these isolated communities, penetrated by little from the outside world. For the majority, the public house or beer shop was the only source of information about events beyond the Black Domain. Even though the Charter's famous six points were never published until the year before the Uprising and sales of newspapers were small, Chartism gained an extraordinary foothold in the Valleys in no time whatsoever. One bookseller, John Davies, of Tredegar, serving the parishes of Merthyr and Bedwellty with a combined population of 54,000, had so few customers he sold only 72 copies a month of three Welsh newspapers, and

62 copies of English newspapers each week.[15] Newspapers were passed from hand to hand, their contents read publicly to the illiterate gathered together for that purpose in public houses and beer shops. This was the most likely way Chartism was spread, by word of mouth, in the process electoral reform mutating until it became an antidote for everything.[16] At Zephaniah Williams' *Royal Oak*, his son Llewellyn, then aged 17, and later to become the acclaimed Welsh harpist 'Pencerdd y De', read customers extracts from the Chartist periodicals the *Northern Star* and *Western Vindicator*. Such readings, and the heated discussions that followed, sometimes fuelled by drink, were blamed by employers for the seditious and subversive torrent influencing their workmen.[17]

The Black Domain certainly lacked none of the ingredients to make a revolution. Wages might have been high but so was taxation. Income tax levied on high incomes during the Napoleonic Wars was abolished with the peace. But this only served to increase the burden on the poor from massive duties on imports to raise the revenue the Government needed to meet payments on the national debt, then consuming up to fifty per cent of the national budget. The burden of indirect taxation, combined with the Corn Laws designed to protect British farmers at the expense of British consumers, was crippling with tariffs imposed on 721 articles, ranging from 67 per cent on sugar, 96 per cent coffee, to a massive 843 per cent on tobacco and 140 per cent on rum. One disgruntled writer, commenting on this welter of taxes observed that *'the dying Englishman pours his medicine, which he has paid 7 per cent, into a spoon that has paid 15 per cent, flings himself back upon his chintz bed which has paid 22 per cent, and expires in the arms of an apothecary who has paid a license of a hundred pounds for the privilege of putting him to death.'*[18] When a sack of flour cost twice as much in Merthyr as it did in Bristol, such levels of punitive taxation were certain to loom large in the lives of all classes. While Frost considered the Charter's proposed electoral reforms essential to reduce crippling taxation, Tremenheere found on his visit to Monmouthshire following the Uprising that some of the women he interviewed actually believed the whole affair was about letting them have tea at two pence a pound.[19] Others swelling the Chartist ranks expected reform to deliver a system of national education and dismantle the abominated Workhouses. For those with a more garbled under-standing of the Charter, it stood for the redistribution of property, undoubtedly a popular idea in a district where a handful of power-ful employers owned almost everything. This was the so-called "seventh point" of the Charter. Never a publicly stated objective, it nevertheless gained such currency in Chartist mythology the leadership had great difficulty dislodging it as a "base and slan-derous calumny" spread by employers. But such was its appeal among rank-and-file, some testified at Chartist Trials they had joined the march to Newport because they believed the intention was to *"make the poor as rich as the rich."*[20]

This predisposition to believe anything they were told or was rumoured in the remoteness of the Monmouthshire valleys became very evident to Seymour Tremenherre, the Government education inspector, when he arrived at Pontypool Park, home of the Lord Lieutenant, Mr Hanbury Leigh, on Christmas Eve 1839 to begin his investigation into the moral and intellectual condition of a people that had contrived to keep secret from the magistrates and every other authority, a well-organised plan to seize Newport in the dead of night, a town twenty miles distant from the hill country. *"A silly cry was got up that I was sent down to take account of the number of the children, and that he Government intended to have one in ten put out of the way; and that I was to be shot, or treated as they proposed to treat the Lord Lieutenant, "* he recalled later in his autobiography.[21] The 'silly rumour' was reported by *The Times,* causing widespread alarm in the Black Domain. Some mothers were convinced the Government was planning to destroy all children less than three years of age. Others asked, *"Do you want to send them to Van Diemen's Land?"* while at Blaenavon it was feared the new Poor Law meant they would only each be allowed three children. At Pontypool, a woman remarked, *"Oh, I heard by the papers that you wanted to destroy all the children under four years of age, and I find now that it is true."*[22]

Kenrick had no doubt it was this *"grossest ignorance"* that incited the working class to distrust their rulers, culminating as it had in rebellion. As for those most culpable, Kenrick blamed the gullibility of the army of itinerant workmen that had moved into the minerals district. Awash as it was with immigrants, mostly single English men now that the labour supply from rural Wales was nearing exhaustion, the Black Domain was fertile ground for troublemakers. Having no intention of settling, and their sights set on making a large amount of money quickly, lodgers by 1839 represented a staggering one-fifth of the population. In Kenrick's view, they constituted an impressionable and dangerous entity *"at the mercy of the crafty and designing men who practise from time to time upon them."*

"They naturally think that whoever tells them that they are oppressed, wretched, miserable, must be their friend, and of course able to apply a remedy to all these evils and remove them," said Kenrick reporting the results of his investigation to the Pontypool Mechanics Institute. *"They are, therefore, predisposed to believe anything which the prophets may predict."* As for public houses, Kenrick saw them as places where robberies were planned *"where quarrels and assaults are promoted, from which discontent and rebellion spring, where the hard-earned wages of the artisan are squandered in riot and confusion, to the injury of his health and understanding, and to the ruin of his family. When wages are high, what becomes of the surplus earnings of the workmen? They go to the drunkard's savings bank, the public house."*[23] The Blaenavon iron baron, Crawshay Bailey, evidently agreed by forbidding his workmen from using the *Royal Oak*, just across the valley from his fortified mansion.

There is not a shadow of doubt this influx of immigrant workers from England, besides swamping the indigenous culture, created quite appalling over-crowding, one house in Pontypool having 21 persons of whom 13 were lodgers. Since the ironworks were never idle, beds in some cottages were rarely cold, as one man left for his shift, another moving in, sometimes sharing a room with as many as sixteen others. Cottages at Blaenavon were considered among the worst, one of these fitted with two tiers of bunk beds, like berths on a steam ship. It was not uncommon for a house to have five or six lodgers, some married, all sharing the same bedroom. But they offered an additional source of income that would have appealed to Zephaniah Williams as much as anyone. In the April immediately before the Chartist Uprising, Zephaniah faced eviction from the *Royal Oak* at Coalbrookvale, Blaina, after it was purchased by one of his sworn enemies,

Charles Brewer, a local ironmaster who regarded the presence of the Chartist leader as a particularly bad influence. No sooner had Zephaniah been sentenced to transportation than his wife Joan was evicted from the *Royal Oak*, which after passing between various owners was eventually converted into two terraced houses in what is today Queen's Street, Nantyglo.

Some years ago, the owner of one of the terraced houses that once had been the *Royal Oak* discovered, while making some renovations to it, a secret hatchway above a bedroom fireplace leading into the attic. Inside the attic was a room built of lath and plaster, totally sealed but for a narrow doorway giving access to a passageway that led from the attic to the ground floor. Was this a Chartist hiding place or annex for lodgers? All we do know is that something similar was constructed for lodgers at a house in Blaenavon, in this case an underground cellar-like room, with only a hole in the wall opening into a second similar room, this one reserved for female lodgers. When seen today, the two terraced houses converted from the *Royal Oak* seem hardly large enough to hold hundreds of Chartists preparing to wage a revolutionary war. But there was a lodge room – since filled with rubble – beneath the beer shop from which Zephaniah allegedly distributed weapons on the evening of the march to Newport.[24]

Alternately, the Black Domain, Disturbed District, or as Tremenheere preferred *"colonies in the desert,"* the five Monmouthshire parishes and neighbouring Merthyr, suffered unparalleled social deprivation. Whether wages were high or low seemed to make little difference to the prevailing conditions. Tremenheere found that absolutely nothing was done for the comfort and convenience of work-people; there were miles of unmade roads, deep in ruts and mire, besides rows of cottages. Schools were almost non-existent; there were no possibilities of amusement or comfort out of doors or in. Regulations were harsh and arbitrarily enforced, employers accepting no responsibility beyond paying wages. Social deprivation was endemic, ingrained in the very fabric of society to be inherited by succeeding generations, so much so that Tremenheere was surprised when the men and women of the Black Domain expressed astonishment the Government wanted to know about them, and that sympathy existed anywhere towards them.[25]

A district once described as *"revolting to civilisation,"* had good cause to conspire against ironmasters and mine owners, many of English origin, who had exploited its immense natural resources while offering nothing in return but wage slavery. These colonies in the desert were clustered in a tract of country about twenty miles east-west, ten miles north-south, forming an inverted triangle which had Merthyr Tydfil and Abergavenny as its base, and Risca its apex. Six parallel valleys ran north-south, the eighteen largest ironworks in South Wales located mainly at the heads of these Valleys where they opened on to cheerless moorland. Around each, the workers and their families congregated in rudimentary townships, some built at the highest elevations, exposed to the worst of the weather and separated from their neighbours by desolate mountain ridges inhabited only by sheep. The people were collected together in masses of four to ten thousand, their houses ranged along the steep escarpments and around the works in rows two to five deep. Almost everywhere the soil had been blackened by coal, or covered with mountains of waste from the mines and furnaces. The only roads between the rows of cottages were ankle-deep in black mud for most of the winter. Trams clattered day and night between the ironworks and collieries, almost brushing the sides of the nearest cottages. Rubbish and human waste were strewn about, creating a fecund breeding ground for disease. And illuminating this ante-room to hell was the glow from the furnace chimneys, from the bright masses of hot iron running through the rollers, and from acres of burning coal upon the coke hearths. Amidst the constant din from the forge hammers and the snorting of high-pressure steam engines, men bustled like tormented ants while great volumes of smoke were driven past and through their homes clinging to the mountain slopes. Such were the conditions in the Cinder Hole at Dowlais that one contemporary commentator, Mr G. T. Clark, of Talygarn, previously a Government employee in Bombay, observed, *"Bombay itself, reputed to be the filthiest under British sway, is scarcely worse."* Houses were built as barracks, not for comfort, sixteen men, women and children sleeping indiscriminately in a single room. Their water supply was the waste from the ironworks, or drawn from mountain springs and streams so charged with filth that outbreaks of typhoid and cholera were frequent.

While colliers thick with coal dust were predisposed to be clean, there were no baths or washhouses. The gunpowder they used for blasting they kept dry beneath their beds. Living and working in Merthyr was calculated to reduce an adult's life expectancy by almost 13 years, compared with that in Tregaron in Cardiganshire.[26]

In stark contrast, the owners lived like kings, ruling their own mini-fiefdoms as such. With very few exceptions, they saw their workmen only as the brute force needed to accumulate personal wealth. Isolated in their fortified mansions, they brandished their wealth like a weapon in the faces of those struggling to survive in communities debased by dirt, disorder and immigration, a shifting, restless mass they considered beyond the reach of moral influences. The status quo was underpinned by the iniquitous Truck Shop system through which the owners sought to enslave their workers for life even after it was banned in 1836. Drunkenness was not the only by-product of the 'long pay'. Far worse was the indebtedness it caused by forcing workers into the grip of credit at the company shop. In the early days of these valley settlements the company shop was the only reliable way of supplying the colonies in the desert. Because employment was erratic, many would have starved before the end of the 'long pay' without credit from the Truck Shop. But by the mid-19th century credit had become so entrenched, it proved impossible to eliminate the remuneration of labour by part payment in goods. All manner of devices were employed to circumvent the law. Commonest was the practice whereby a collier's wife was given cash by a clerk on entering the shop, which she immediately paid over the counter to settle the outstanding credit, her family never escaping the vicious cycle of credit and debt; her husband doomed to become a wage-slave forever. Paradoxically, company shops were regarded as insurance for wives against the recklessness or intemperance of their husbands, enabling them to draw credit slips against prospective earnings. Exchanged only in return for purchases at certain shops and public houses, these credit slips became a form of legal tender, everyone through whose hands they passed taking a discount. Very quickly, the Truck Shop had a monopoly, bankrupting the few independent shopkeepers daring to compete.[27]

The Truck Shop, one of the grievances leading to the Merthyr Rising, still fed revolutionary sentiment eight years later. Long after the Chartist Uprising the owners continued to regard credit as the only means of containing the lawlessness and insubordination of their workforce. One remarked to the authors of the Blue Books, *"If the masters had not some hold over such a set of men and were to make them entirely independent by giving them complete control over their high wages, they would work just when and how they liked, and the capital embarked in the works would be at their mercy. It is difficult enough to manage them as it is."*[28]

While criticising the Monmouthshire Welsh as slatternly, ignorant and self-indulgent motivated only by their worship of Mammon, the Blue Books did not shrink from placing responsibility for this degraded state upon the ironmasters and colliery owners, whom they said treated their cattle with more care and attention then their workmen. In return, the people mimicked the repulsive rudeness of those in authority over them, regarding their employers as the natural enemies of an exploited labour force. Neither believed the interests of capital and labour could be the same, both classes imagining themselves naturally antagonistic.[29] Given the backdrop to the Chartist Uprising it is not surprising the socialist trade union activist Ness Edwards should seize upon the conditions prevailing in November 1839 as the genesis for *"the first independent political working class movement in South Wales,"* and that Ivor Wilks saw it as an armed working class uprising. Even Gwyn A. Williams in *The Merthyr Rising* considered Chartism as a stage in the evolution of working class consciousness following the Merthyr Riots. Seen at a distance of almost 170 years, and with the benefit of socialist hindsight, no one can doubt the social conditions existed in Monmouthshire in 1839 for some form of confrontation between the classes. But was Chartism, a campaign for electoral reform, capable of cementing together social consciousness and political action, in the way necessary to build a working class rebellion? What it certainly failed to do, as we will see, is provide the political motivation and organisation necessary for such a feat, in a district where the pace of industrial revolution was far hotter than the pressure for social revolution.[30]

In rushing to invest in the great mineral adventure of 19th century Wales, the iron and coal employers were following a migratory trail that began in Tudor times when the first iron-workers arrived from England. Once the native woodlands of Sussex and Kent were exhausted, ironworkers moved to Wales for its superabundance of wood, water, ironstone, and later coal, which replaced charcoal for iron manufacture at Llancaiach-uchaf in 1553. Early coal mining was a level very much like a rabbit warren scratched into the side of a hill, at the point the seam broke the surface. Before 1849 explosions in collieries were rare, only becoming prevalent when levels with shallow openings gave way to deep shafts, the colliers, having no thought for ventilation, continuing to dust out the accumulation of 'fire damp' with their jackets before starting work at the coalface. But in the first half of the 19th century they were still literally only scratching the surface of a coal basin with the greatest vertical thickness in the world, 84ft of workable coal through 25 seams, enough to last 2,300 years at the rate worked in 1865. Tapping into this huge wealth led to a population explosion of historic proportions, Newport the first of the ports to capitalise on the rich hinterland, by 1833 exporting 441,000 tons of coal, three times as much as Cardiff. At the time of the Chartist Uprising, coal was being delivered on board at Newport at 10s a ton, a price not seen again for thirty years.

But Cardiff was soon to overtake Newport as the world's leading coal exporter, its predominance due initially to London's first Clean Air Act and the search by two London businessmen for cleaner coal, this ultimately leading to an elderly Welsh widow Mrs Lucy Thomas, owner of Waun Wyllt Colliery, near Merthyr. Although it had been noticed that some Welsh coal did not smoke as much as that from other parts of Britain, this failed to excite any interest until a coal merchant named Lockett joined forces with Sir James Duke, later Lord Mayor of London, to travel to Wales to investigate this peculiarity. It was 1830 and Cardiff the major outlet for iron and coal from Merthyr. On arrival, the pair took rooms at the Angel Hotel and as they settled down for their evening meal they were struck by the character of the fire in the room: the coal hardly smoked at all. Ringing for a maid, they instructed her to put more coal on the fire, which Lockett then stoked. Moments later, he turned to Duke and exclaimed, *"Our journey is ended, we need go no further."* The next morning they discovered from the merchant who supplied the Angel that the coal came from Mrs Thomas's Waun Wyllt Colliery. Finally arriving at the source, they agreed to buy her entire output at four shillings a ton, retailing this in London a few months later at eighteen shillings a ton. On their return journey to London, Lockett took with him a butter cask filled with lumps of Welsh coal so that he might make a fire and startle his friends with the blaze of the century![31]

This priceless discovery, with the potential to transform Wales in much the same way as the 1849 Gold Rush propelled California into statehood as the richest part of the Union, was almost wholly exploited by English capital, most of the profits repatriated to England. It was known as the *'Bristol Policy,'* on account of the fact some investors could make huge profits without ever entering the wilderness beyond the Severn Sea. This is not to say the indigenous Welsh had no part in this Eldorado, but usually only at the margins. As for the ironworks – almost all were owned either by English ironmasters or their immediate descendants. There was nothing very new in this. The exploitation of Wales's natural assets was placed beyond the reach of the indigenous Welsh four hundred years earlier, during the Reformation, when church lands and the rights to work the minerals beneath were redistributed by a Crown desperate for ready money to finance the war with France. The Tudor monarchs had sold seven-eighths of the confiscated monastery estates by the time of Henry VIII. Glamorgan and Monmouthshire had the highest concentration of church lands in Wales, most of these going to the Somersets, Earls of Worcester, the Herberts, the Morgans of Llantarnam, the Carnes of Ewenni, the Mansels of Margam, the Stradlings of St Donat's, and the Tubervilles of Pen-llin.[32] Well established at Court, these families were able to turn their contacts to good advantage and it was they and their descendants who leased to the 18th and 19th century English entrepreneurs rights to exploit vast reserves of ironstone and coal, and land for the construction of the ironworks. In return, a royalty was paid on every ton that was raised. One landowner was paid £40,000 in royalties from coal worked on just fifty acres. Such was the value of the famed four-foot Mynydd-islwyn Seam zigzagging across Monmouthshire.

This second wave of industrial conquerors was led by Richard Crawshay, of Merthyr, a farmer's son from Normanton, near Wakefield in Yorkshire. At their height in 1830, his Cyfarthfa and Ynysfach works had nine furnaces, on which 20,000 souls were dependent, Crawshay's annual pay roll totalling £300,000. His main competitor, the Guests at Dowlais, had 14 furnaces. Samuel Homfray, his family descended from Robert de Umfraville ("With the Beard") who had arrived with William the Conqueror in 1066, had six furnaces operating at Penydarren, his son, also Samuel, another five at Tredegar, in partnership with Thompson and Co. At the Plymouth Works, R and H. Hill had four. By this time, the Bristol Quakers, the Harford Brothers, had arrived in the adjoining Sirhowy Valley, acquiring first the Sirhowy Works (four furnaces) and then Ebbw Vale (3) where the first railway lines were manufactured. In the next valley again, Crawshay Bailey operated eight furnaces at Nantyglo after his brother Joseph inherited one quarter of Richard Crawshay's estate. Then there were the smaller ironmasters: Benjamin Hall whose fortune was also founded on an inheritance from the Crawshay estate; W. Jenkins, of Consett; Edward Williams, of Middlesborough; W. Evans, Windsor Richards, and later the Darbys, the Quaker family from Coalbrookdale who bought the Ebbw Vale and Sirhowy Works in 1842 when the Harfords went bankrupt. Smaller still was Brewer and Co., (2 furnaces), at Coalbrookvale, Blaina; Kenrick and Co., (5) at Varteg; C. H. Leigh and Co., at Pontypool (3); the British Iron Company (4), at Abersychan. Not only were they linked by industry, the ironmasters and landed gentry were joined in marriage. The first Samuel Homfray of Penydarren House married Jane, the widowed daughter of Sir Charles Gould Morgan, of the Tredegar Estate. It came as no surprise when the Morgans granted the Homfrays a 99-year lease to 1,200 acres of rich, minerals-bearing land at Tredegar on which Samuel Homfray junior and his partners Richard Fothergill and Matthew Monkhouse sited a new ironworks at a peppercorn rent. While the marriage was not a business arrangement, it formed a union, which paid dividends for both families. The Morgan family avoided bankruptcy in the second half of the 18th century and in return the new ironmasters were given an advantageous situation in the Monmouthshire Valleys. In effect, the landed aristocracy struck a profitable deal with the new captains of the Industrial Revolution. As the South Wales Coalfield filled up with iron and coal tycoons, so did the courts with litigation arising from intense rivalries between the owners. The period is littered with disputes over mineral deposits, rights, galeage, royalties, building-land, water supplies and transport routes. But for the most part, it involved the usual suspects: the same, tightly knit pack of ironmasters, mine-owners, and gentry. As for the indigenous Welsh, without capital they were marginalized and without the vote there was little they could do but watch the exploitation of the wealth beneath their feet. The few who did participate in this minerals bonanza, such as Thomas Prothero, Town clerk of Newport, and his business partner Sir Thomas Phillips, the Mayor who confronted the Chartists outside the Westgate, they considered themselves part of the established order, which Chartism was seen to threaten.

NOTES

1. Children's Employment Commission, First Report of the Commissioners – Mine, Part II (1842), (Appendix 2) pp619-620, pp624-629.
2. Seymour Tremenheere, Report of the State of Elementary Education in the Mining District of South Wales, 1840, pp175-191; Commissioners of Inquiry into the State of Education in Wales, Part II, Brecknock, Cardigan, Radnor and Monmouth, 1847, pp290-291.
3. GRO (Cardiff), Zephaniah and Joan Williams, marriage entry, St Tydfil's Church, Merthyr Parish Records, p213, No. 637, 9 August, 1819.
4. Bank of England calculates £1 in 1840 to be worth £40 at 2003 values.
5. Lecture, Pontypool Mechanics Institute, 1840, G. S. Kenrick, Varteg Ironworks. Chartist Archives, NPL.
6. Report of Mr Seymour Tremenheere on the State of Elementary Education in the Mining District of South Wales, 1840, pp182-183, Law Library, Cardiff University.
7. Kenrick, loc. cit. pp10-11, 14-15, 16-17.
8. Kenrick, loc. cit. p12; Commissioners of Inquiry into the State of Education in Wales, Part II, Brecknock, Cardigan, Radnor and Monmouth, 1847, p290, Law Library, Cardiff University.
9. Commissioners of Inquiry, loc. cit. p292.
10. Arthur Clark, 'The Treason of the Blue Books', *Presenting Monmouthshire*, 1964, pp29-32. All Parliamentary inquiries are known as 'Blue Books'.
11. Kenrick, loc. cit. pp18-19.

12. Commissioners of Inquiry into the State of Education in Wales, Part II, Brecknock, Cardigan, Radnor and Monmouth, 1847, p291, Law Library, Cardiff University.

13. NLW, Lord Tredegar Papers, 40/2, 25 May 1840, copy of Williams 'confession' letter.

14. W. W. Tasker, *The Sirhowy Tramroad and Railway in Monmouthshire* (Shrewsbury, 1960), Tredegar Public Library.

15. *Cofiaduron (Diaries) of John Davies (Brychan),* Cardiff Public Library.

16. NPL, Chartist Trials, Volume 15, William Howell.

17. Kenrick, p16.

18. Donald N. McCloskey, 'Magnanimous Albion: Free Trade and British National Income, 1841-1881', *Enterprise and Trade in Victorian Britain: Essays in Historical Economics,* No. 8.

19. Frost, *Western Vindicator,* 20 March 1839; Law Library, Cardiff University, Seymour Tremenheere, autobiography, *I Was There,* p38.

20. NPL, Chartist Trials, 15, William Howell.

21. Tremenheere, autobiography, *I Was There,* p37.

22. Kenrick, loc. cit. p9.

23. Kenrick, loc. cit. p16.

24. NPL, Chartist Trials, 15, Joseph Stockdale.

25. Tremenheere autobiography, *I was there,* pp37-38.

26. Charles Wilkins, *The History of the Iron, Steel, Tinplate and Other Trades of Wales* (1903), p303.

27. For general information about Truck Shops, see Arthur Gray-Jones, *History of Ebbw Vale* (1970), Oliver Jones, *Early Days of Sirhowy and Tredegar* (1969).

28. Commissioners of Inquiry into the State of Education in Wales, Part II, Brecknock, Cardigan, Radnor and Monmouth, 1847, pp290-291, Law Library, Cardiff University.

29. *Ibid,* loc. cit. p291.

30. Edwards, *John Frost and the Chartist Movement in Wales* (Abertillery, 1924, Western Valleys Labour Classes); Wilks, loc. cit, p249; Gwyn A. Williams, *The Merthyr Rising,* pp224-230.

31. C. Wilkins, *The South Wales Coal Trade and its Allied Industries* (1888).

32. Glanmor Williams, *Wales and the Reformation* (Cardiff, 1999), pp10-11.

33. Wilkins, loc. cit.

CHAPTER 3

Rise and Fall of Zephaniah Williams

The monopoly exercised over the iron and coal riches of the Black Domain by a small and powerful industrial clique was virtually unassailable by the mid 19th century when Zephaniah Williams confessed to a conspiracy, that, if only part true, was at the very least an attempt to smash the *status quo*. But long before this he had become personally frustrated with a system that excluded him from a share of the district's new wealth. In a century driven, not by social considerations, but by the scramble for the material advantage to be gained from industrial change, the vast majority in the South Wales Minerals District believed themselves unable to access the greater benefits of capitalism, because they had no electoral clout. For them, the ballot box provided legal access to assets, in this case, the wealth produced by the reserves of iron and coal beneath their feet. Without the vote, they were excluded from the legislative and legal processes, rendering them mere wage slaves in the Industrial Revolution, the greatest event in the history of capitalism. Locked out, as they saw it, by a largely 'foreign' elite, it was only a question of time before the South Wales workers sought alternative ways of accessing the profits of capitalism. This has led some like Gwyn A. Williams in *The Merthyr Rising* to conclude that the explosion of Chartist violence at Newport was the inevitable evolution of working class consciousness stimulated by that momentous week in the history of Merthyr Tydfil in 1831.[1] Twenty-four are believed to have died (although the real number will never be known), four transported for their part in it, and Dic Penderyn (Richard Lewis) hanged for the attempted murder of a soldier Donald Black outside the Castle Inn after thousands of rioters seized the town, destroyed the debtors court, redistributed property and raised the Red Flag. Nevertheless, the affair had all the signs of spontaneity and the culprits were prosecuted only for rioting, unlike the Chartist attack on Newport's Westgate Hotel eight years later, after which the charge was High Treason carrying a mandatory death penalty. Although the Government would find little evidence to prove so, it believed the Chartists plotted revolution because it was what it had expected.

What happened at Merthyr was the first shot in a turbulent decade for European Governments and Monarchies threatened by social and economic change. But it was another event, not the Merthyr Rising, which did more than anything to consolidate the feeling of alienation and deep resentment among the working classes leading directly, some believe, to what occurred at Newport. Six Dorsetshire labourers had been transported in 1834 for agitating together for higher wages and administering a secret oath, this despite the repeal of the Combination Acts in 1824 prohibiting trade unions. By the time the Tolpuddle Martyrs were transported the Grand National Consolidated Trade Union was claiming one million members although probably no more than 16,000 were paid-up members.

The idea that trade unions had existed in embryonic form, disguised as Friendly Societies during the period of their prohibition is unlikely to have been true of those formed in the Glamorgan and Monmouthshire Valleys.[2] While some expressly forbade political activity, even discussion, there was nothing in their rules to suggest they were anything other than societies for the mutual relief of their members in times of distress. When wages were volatile, the Friendly Society provided insurance against an uncertain future, the monthly contributions of workers their only form of savings, and the benefits they received when unemployed or ill their only social security. The alternative was to throw themselves and family on parish relief. The hardship and personal stigma of that became even worse after 1834 when the destitute were forced into Workhouses and families broken up.[3]

Usually meeting in public houses, Friendly Societies operated a strict code of conduct and discipline on club nights, including fining and expelling those who infringed this. Typical of a club rule for the preservation of good manners, the discouragement of vice, and the prevention of quarrels, contentions and disorders in the society was, *"It is hereby agreed – that if any member be detected of swearing, cursing, blasphemy, or of using provoking,*

*threatening or scurrilous language, or obscene discourse, or offer
to lay any wager in the club room, or shall make any reflections
on any member who have received any benefit from the Box, or
on any religion, or that will not keep his seat, or that will not be
peaceable and silent on being given notice, or if any member
presume to strike or challenge another member on the club night
or within one hundred yards of the club room . . . "* then that
member shall be fined (heavily) or expelled.[4] This would have
offered precious little scope whatsoever for covert political and
trade union activities. Moreover all Friendly Society rules required
approval by the Quarter Sessions, and club officials were bound
over to the Clerk of the Quarter Sessions to observe the rules and
maintain proper accounts.

Apart from details of Zephaniah Williams's early mining ventures, one of the first known authenticated records of his activities
in pre-Chartist Monmouthshire is a 1831 Quarter Sessions bond in
which he is named as a surety for a new Treasurer appointed by
the Bedwellty Union Society based at the Carpenter's Arms,
Blackwood. Zephaniah was bound over in the sum of £100 as
guarantor that the new treasurer complied with the Society rules
and fulfilled his responsibilities for the accounts. The bond document names the treasurer as William Jones Junior, and the second
surety as William Jones Senior. Whether the former was the same
William Jones who, eight years later, stood beside Zephaniah in
the dock at the Monmouth Special Assize is not known. What is
clear, however, is that by 1831 both he and William Jones Senior
were of sufficient substance to satisfy the court and, as members
of the Bedwellty Union Society, were obliged to obey its rules.[5]

Since the repeal of the Combination Acts in 1824 caused no
slackening in the rate at which the numbers of Friendly Societies
were being formed, this can be taken as further evidence they
were not a cover for trade union activity in South Wales. The ten
years up to the outbreak of Chartist violence witnessed a huge
increase in clubs, forty-two in the parish of Trevethin alone,
twenty in Aberystruth, and fifteen in Bedwellty. If this growth had
been concentrated in the last part of the decade it could have
been construed as directly linked to the rise of Chartism. But that
did not happen, for the rate of Friendly Society formation was
spread evenly through the decade.[6]

Whereas the Consolidated Trade Union failed largely due to the impact the victimisation of the Tolpuddle Martyrs had on workers generally, in South Wales the episode helped crystalise a class-consciousness that had previously not counted for much among a group for whom exploitation had become endemic, passed from one generation to the next; and a disease that continues to prevail even to this day. The Government's hostility towards trade unions and the widening gulf between rich and poor aggravated by crippling taxation, in particular the Bread Tax which by taxing imports of cheap corn penalised especially the labourer classes, was fertile ground for the new breed of Owenite socialists. One of these was Morgan Williams, eventual leader of the Merthyr Chartists, and another John Thomas, his co-editor of the bi-lingual newspaper *The Workman (Y Gweithiwr)*, launched the same year as the Tolpuddle Martyrs and considered Wales's first working class newspaper. The significance for the Chartist Uprising of the publication of *The Workman* is what clues it provides to the political relationship between Morgan Williams, John Thomas and Zephaniah Williams. Did the latter agree with the political senti- ments of the newspaper's co-editors? All three were middle-class radicals, as was John Frost. All were Welsh and spoke the lan- guage, although in the case of Frost this did not appear to extend to writing it with confidence since the one letter of his published by *Udgorn Cymru* (a later publication run by Morgan Williams) is clearly a translation from English.[7] No one doubts Frost, Morgan Williams and Thomas were politically active throughout the 1830s but the evidence for Zephaniah Williams being one of them can only be construed from his association with activists.

Morgan Williams was born at Penyrheolgerrig in 1808, the family moving there from Abernant-y-gwenith after its land was taken for tipping waste from the nearby ironworks. A weaver by trade, he was credited with designing the Chartist's green, white and blue banner and was secretary of the Merthyr Workingmen's Association, formed in October 1838 to fight for the Charter. But after the disastrous Merthyr riots of 1831, it was not surprising that he remained planted firmly on the 'moral force' wing of the Chartist movement.[8] His co-editor at *The Workman* responsible for the Welsh-language content, John Thomas, was a Carmarthen- born musician and teacher, better known by his bardic name

Ieuan Ddu. A pioneer of Welsh choral singing, and an accomplished harpist he ran a school in Merthyr for fifteen years, and was an enthusiastic eisteddfodwyr, composing a satire on the eisteddfod entitled *Cambria on Two Sticks,* in which he pays a tribute to Llewelyn Williams (Pencerdd y De), famous harpist son of Zephaniah Williams. Prominent among the Welsh speaking intelligentsia, he founded the Rhyddynofynwyr (Free Enquirers/Zetics) in Merthyr, and in May 1836 spoke at a meeting of the Sirhowy Cymreigyddion (Welsh Scholars) attended by the younger Williams who was introduced as the *"son of the cheerful and generous Welshman Zephaniah Williams."* According to *Seren Gomer,* everyone left this meeting at the Ancient Druid public house at Hollybush near Blackwood *"full of nationalist feelings about freedom and their native land."*[9]

Only one issue of *The Workman,* for May 1, 1834 has survived, and only four pages of that.[10] The curious ambiguity contained in its pages, if characteristic of other issues, reveals its co-editors Morgan Williams and John Thomas as campaigners in the Owenite socialist tradition sending out confused messages about trade unionism, self-reliance, co-operation, education and the environment. The one Welsh-language article, while critical of the sentences imposed on the Tolpuddle Martyrs for their 'foolishness,' reasserts the workers right to unionise, but cautions them about rushing their fences before the Union had proved itself, an astute observation in view of the imminent collapse of the Consolidated Trade Union. Critical of 'secret meetings,' the author, possibly John Thomas because he edited the Welsh section, chastises workers for not educating themselves to confront the employers, at the same time warning them to avoid improper action: *"to do nothing that is not right and good to do, by becoming like those who intend that which is not right."* In advocating the right to combine to secure *'reasonable advantage'* over immigrant workers, the author, nevertheless, urges his readers to *"make an effort to understand the situation of their masters."* Perhaps the most significant contribution the author makes to the debate over the reasons for the subsequent Chartist revolt is when he says every reasonable man knew what the workers had always wanted: *"to keep their hire when they are high from not going lower, to raise them when they are low."* Wage stability was a foremost consideration when the men from the hills descended on Newport in 1839.[11]

One of the English language articles, written perhaps by Morgan Williams, was far more strident, yet no more radical than the current sentiment among the labouring classes and their supporters. Bread prices in 1834 were low thanks to good harvests in the previous two years, this of critical importance for a country with a population of 25 million but only able to produce sufficient grain to feed 18 million, leaving the deficit to be covered by heavily taxed imports. Inevitably, poor harvests would require increased imports, the burden of taxation falling upon the main consumers of bread, the workers. The Bread Tax was blamed for starving the people, one of the consequences of it higher rents. Warning of a crisis ahead when the harvests failed, *The Workman* continued, *"That taxation in every shape is an evil we do not deny, but when wrung from the productive classes to support the idlers; when the poor man's bed is taken from under him for Tithe, to support a bloated clergy when assessed taxes are levied at the bayonet's point to pamper a stupid and imbecile aristocracy, when it makes all these, Taxation becomes an infernal evil and should be resisted . . . The wind is now asleep on the surface of the waters but how long we cannot say . . . How we shudder at a failure* (harvest) *for there is no revolution like that of the belly."*[12]

Talk of revolution was not uncommon at this time, especially where feelings had been inflamed by the punitive sentences imposed on the Tolpuddle Martyrs, seven years transportation, when *before* the repeal of the Combination Acts the maximum was only three months. References to the French Revolution, and reminders of the fate of Louis XVI and Charles X, littered denunciations of the idle aristocracy, employers, and the clergy. While it was fashionable for Owenites to be religious dissenters, even reject religion altogether, as it is suspected Zephaniah Williams did, they stopped short of political violence, believing instead the road to change was the environment and to change that was to change human nature, an idea more fully developed in the work of Karl Marx in the 1840s. Robert Owen, born in Newtown, was the founder of the Co-operative Movement and, true to his philosophy, *The Workman's* Welsh-language article emphasises this aspect of workers' action rather than what is today understood as political trade unionism.

How far Zephaniah Williams' association with Morgan Williams and John Thomas extended from social contact to political is hard to say. Thomas taught the harp and both Williams' were harpist families, Zephaniah's son Llewelyn – acclaimed as 'Pencerdd y De' (Chief Musician of the South) – likely to have been appointed Royal harpist if it had not been for his father's High Treason.[13] What is certain is that John Thomas was employed by Zephaniah as a clerk before returning to Merthyr in 1834 to launch *The Workman*, although that reveals more about Zephaniah as a man of substance and public stature than any political affiliation.[14] Evan Powell claimed, without producing a shred of attribution, in *History of Tredegar* (1902) that Zephaniah Williams was of one of the "influential gentlemen who patronised" the Tredegar branch of the National Union of Working Classes in 1830.[15] Even assuming this was correct, the anecdote has since been stretched to breaking point, Ivor Wilks in *"South Wales and the Rising of 1839"* promoting Powell's claim into his own assertion that Williams had long been active in radical causes, and was *"one of the founders"* of the Tredegar branch of the National Union.[16] There are similar problems of non-attribution with the consequent elevation of local anecdote into fact in passages dealing with Zephaniah's political past in Oliver Jones's *Early Days of Sirhowy and Tredegar*, 1969, and Arthur Gray-Jones's *A History of Ebbw Vale*, 1970.[17] In the absence of something more convincing, it is difficult to see the justification for Zephaniah's imagined reputation as a political activist of long standing. His robust and well-reasoned response to the slanderous attack made upon him by the dissenting minister, Rev. Benjamin Williams, might be referred to as evidence of Zephaniah's activism when in fact it could be little more than the intellectual, rational riposte of an agnostic, even atheist. *"I would advise all men,"* he writes in his reply to the Rev. Benjamin Williams, *"to take nothing upon trust, but all upon trial; whether in politics, religion. Ethics, or any thing else: to set down with a determined resolution; to examine closely; and to be directed by that which reason most approves."*[18] It is hardly surprising such a man reputedly had in his home a picture of the Crucifixion with the caption: 'This is the man who stole the ass.' For this, he earned the reputation of being a notorious deist.[19]

His reply, however, failed to silence the Rev. Williams who eight years later at a packed anti-Chartist meeting organised by the ironmasters at Coalbrookvale, Blaina, in the April before the Uprising, once again accused Zephaniah of denying the existence of God. The attack was pressed home from the platform by James Brown, owner of the Cwm Celyn and Blaina Ironworks. Clutching a copy of the Charter and pointing towards Zephaniah's public house, the *Royal Oak*, barely half a mile across the valley, he exclaimed, *"Who have we here at the Chartists' head to keep the tintinnabulum alive? Why a man who lives in the house above there, Zephaniah Williams, and what is he? Why, I will tell you. He is a man who will tell you there is no God, not Eternity – has no belief in either rewards or punishments, but that when we die we die as a dog, or as an old worn out horse. A few months ago, I was engaged on the borders of my native county Glamorgan in search of coal, near to the Rudry Iron Works, at which place this Zephaniah Williams was an underground agent and one day a fall came down in the mine work and mutilated a miner in a dreadful manner; and, in the poor fellow's agony, he shouted "O God save me-O Lord help me, etc, etc" in the hearing of this infidel, who coolly turned to the man and said, "you fool, to call upon God to help you, he cannot come if you call for a month, but if you were to say, 'O, Zephaniah, help me', I would do so directly."* Is it not notorious in our neighbourhood that this man holds infidel meetings at his house on the Sabbath day regularly? My friends, I will ask you what confidence you can have in a cause that holds such leaders as these at its head?"*[20]

When Chartists talked about wanting the franchise to make the *"poor as rich as the rich,"* what many of them probably meant was achieving the wage stability necessary to access the greater benefits they felt their labour warranted. They arrived at electoral reform because it would break the monopoly owners and the middle classes exercised over the legislative processes. By eliminating the wilful inertia of adherents to the status quo the excessive tax burden could be reduced, wages stabilised, and, in South Wales at last, the threat to employment caused by unrestrained immigration into the mining valleys contained. Whether it was

Owenite socialism or as David Jones maintains in *The Last Rising* something difficult to define precisely, it amounted to the same objective: a dramatic change in their living conditions.[21] As with all movements that countenance monumental changes in the social order, there was always the risk of attracting subversive elements. If republicanism was not on everyone's agenda as they descended from the hills, the notion was widely speculated upon, fuelled it must be said by employers blind to the sufferings of the working class. While wages in the Black Domain were certainly higher on occasions than anywhere else in the industrial world, they were accompanied by social deprivation in the filthy, over-crowded, disease-ridden shantytowns servicing the ironworks and collieries. Instead of alleviating these conditions, the owners perpetuated them through the repugnant Truck Shop system and the abomination of child and female labour, only to discover eventually that their perceived ownership of the land and its resources was not so secure as to sanction their oppressive conduct.

It is often claimed Chartism enjoyed mass support because members identified with leaders from the same disadvantaged social backgrounds. If this were generally the case, then Zephaniah Williams, son of a yeoman farmer, and mine owner in his own right, did not fit. According to probably the most reliable source, his convict record, he first saw the light of day in Merthyr Tydfil in 1795. At some point, his father Thomas Williams evidently acquired land in Bedwellty, near Argoed because at the time of his death in 1825 not only did he operate his own coal level producing more than 5,000 tons a year but was also in dispute over £400 in galeage, or royalties (amounting to £20,000 at today's values) due to his estate from 48,000 tons mined by the Argoed Coal Company.[22] His family's circumstances were sufficiently sound to allow the young Zephaniah to obtain a vastly superior education to that of his contemporaries, most of whom would never see the inside of a school. Exactly where this was obtained continues to confound researchers, the image of a young Zephaniah poring over his books after twelve hours underground not exactly what might be expected for the son of a relatively prosperous yeoman farmer. It is unlikely to have been delivered by the Welsh Circulating Schools, which frequented the Bedwellty, Mynydd-islwyn and Aberystruth Parishes from 1738 onwards. Usually based at a local farmhouse for a fortnight or so, the teachers provided only a nominal education, not much more than the Day Schools of 1840, adjudged as primitive by HM Inspectors. Excluding the remote possibility of an education obtained outside Wales, Zephaniah reveals in his reply to the dissenting minister and the letters (originally in Welsh) to his wife from exile in Tasmania a degree of scholarship available only at one of the free grammar schools existing at that time. If the family had moved to Bedwellty relatively early in his life, then Lewis School, Pengam, established circa 1770 would have been an obvious choice. King Henry the 8th School, Abergavenny (1543) was the next nearest, the others being the Haberdashers Company School at Monmouth (1614), another at Llantilio Crossenny (1654), and, finally, the Roger Edwards School at Usk (1621).[23] A further possibility was the school at Merthyr established by Taleisin Morgannwg (ap Iolo), son of the celebrated bard and historian Iolo Morganwg, founder of the modern National Eisteddfod of Wales in 1792. Morgan Williams, the Merthyr Chartist leader, and co-editor of *The Workman*, as well as other contemporaries of his were pupils, but Zephaniah might have been too old by the time it gained its prominence as a centre of learning.[24] There were six works schools in Monmouthshire, the earliest of these, Capel Waun y Pound, opened in 1784 midway between Beaufort and Sirhowy. Paid for from subscriptions deducted from the wages of ironworkers, the works schools offered only basic reading and writing.[25]

If Zephaniah Williams had links with the Merthyr radicals it was probably John Thomas rather than Morgan Williams. From a letter he wrote from the convict ship *Mandarin,* John Frost appears to have been more familiar with Morgan Williams. Writing to a man he clearly regarded as a close friend, Frost remarks, *"I little thought when you were at my home in October last, that so great a change was about to take place. Then, the father of a happy family in easy circumstances, possessed of extensive political influence, now a convict bound for New South Wales under sentence of transportation for life, ...but if the people of the hills of Glamorganshire, Monmouthshire, and Breconshire act wisely, firmly, we shall still see our native country."* Frost concluded with his sincerest regards to Morgan Williams and all *"our old and true friends,"* expressing the hope *"that the spirit which once animated the men of the hills"* was not dead.[26] Not once in any correspondence from Van Diemen's Land did Zephaniah Williams mention Morgan Williams but he did John Thomas, whom he regarded as a true friend, according to a letter he wrote to his wife from exile.[27]

It was sometime around 1830 that Thomas moved to Monmouthshire, not long after Zephaniah was appointed Minerals Agent for the Harfords. Also engaged in coal mining in his own right, he had need of a clerk, Thomas, nevertheless, appearing to divide his time between clerking for Zephaniah and the philanthropist and magistrate, John Hodder Moggridge. Moggridge's family were wealthy clothiers from Bradford-on-Avon who inherited an estate at Dymock in Gloucestershire where Moggridge lived the life of country gentlemen serving for a time as High Sheriff (1809). Exactly why he moved to South Wales is unclear but from his subsequent business interests, Moggridge was probably another of those attracted by the potential rewards from investing in the district's rich mineral resources. After purchasing the Plas Bedwellty Estate, he later moved to Llanrumney Hall near Cardiff while his new mansion was being built in a beautifully secluded part of the Sirhowy Valley, immediately across the river from a wooded area known locally as the Black Wood. This was to become South Wales' first garden village at Blackwood, Moggridge's Owenite-experiment in social engineering.[28] Although a stranger to the area, he was already a magistrate by 1812, and as a wealthy philanthropist wormed his way into the radical, reformist undercurrent that preceded Chartism, in the process striking up a friendship with two of the most active local radicals, John Frost and Samuel Etheridge. Having failed to win Barnstaple in the 1818 election, Moggridge challenged the mighty House of Beaufort for the Monmouth Boroughs two years later, Frost seconding his nomination. Not long afterwards, however, they had become bitter enemies, Frost and Etheridge accusing Moggridge of corruptly pocketing fines paid to him as a magistrate and exploiting the workers leasing the cottages in his Blackwood Garden Village. In an open letter, Frost launched a ferocious and libellous attack on Moggridge, denouncing him as a fraud who portrayed himself as a person burning with love for the human race while, in truth, he lacked the milk of human kindness. Moggridge never seems to have replied to these astonishing charges.[29] Perhaps he never needed to because shortly afterwards he must have been delighted to be one of the magistrates who gaoled Frost for six months for an equally savage libel on Thomas Prothero, Town Clerk of Newport!

Moggridge's idea for the garden village at Blackwood was inspired by the distress suffered by the poor he encountered on settling in Monmouthshire. Workers capable of earning the highest wages in the industrial world during the good times were laid off without a moment's thought or penny compensation if their employers got the slightest whiff of a downturn in the market. The ironmaster at Gadlys, Aberdare was especially notorious for this. The moment his chimneys stopped smoking was the signal the neighbourhood dreaded. This terrible uncertainty broke the spirit of ironworkers and colliers whose working lives swung wildly between misery and relative affluence, crime and drunkenness. Advised by the social reformer Robert Owen, Moggridge evolved a plan to select certain workers who had demonstrated they could maintain themselves and their families during the good times, and offer them help to continue doing so when economic conditions turned against them. Each was leased a small piece of ground to build a cottage, Moggridge advancing a loan, repayable with interest over an agreed period. The terms, including the ground rent, were supposed to be more favourable than what was normally charged, although John Frost thought otherwise, believing Moggridge's motives more self-interest than benevolent. There might have been some truth in this because like many of his contemporaries Moggridge's concern for the condition of the poor was partly motivated by a desire as a property owner to reduce the burden of poor relief on the rates.[30]

The success of his Blackwood Garden Village, or New Village as it was first known, hinged on the cultivation by the tenants of the gardens allotted to each cottage. Moggridge calculated the garden could produce sufficient vegetables to support a family during the down times in the ironworks and collieries. The first three leases were taken up in 1820, one of these by Zephaniah Williams for his father to build a cottage on plot No. 3.[31] By the spring the cottages were built, gardens dug and planted with potatoes, swedes, cabbages, all a novelty in a district where the cultivation of vegetables was widely regarded as hopeless on account of the Welsh weather. For the next two years everyone waited for the 'pioneer' families to fail but they faired much better than their sceptical neighbours. Soon, the demand for leases exceeded even Moggridge's expectations. Next he built a market house with public meeting room above, later used as a non-conformist chapel and schoolroom. Shops and a public house followed, and so did two similar experiments at Ynysddu, a few miles down the Sirhowy Valley and at Trelyn, near the Rhymney Ironworks. By 1829, Blackwood Garden Village had 1500 inhabitants, one of the very first of these Thomas Williams, Zephaniah's father.[32]

The relationship between the Williams family and Moggridge was sufficiently close for the wealthy philanthropist and magistrate to be appointed one of the administrators to the estate when Williams senior died in 1825, aged 73, at his cottage at Number 3, New Village, Blackwood. The inventory compiled by Zephaniah showed his father's personal effects including royalties, coal stocks, and leases on three cottages to be worth just over £1,000 (£40,000 at today's values), a substantial estate for that period.[33] The furnishings in the cottage reflected the father's standing as an affluent, retired yeoman farmer, of a certain status within the community. Among the cutlery were sets of silver teaspoons and tablespoons, silver sugar tongs, and silver ladle, and as might be expected from a family with more than a passing interest in the licensing trade, sets of wine and rum glasses. The most valuable item was a silver trinket box valued at £6 (£240). There was a large mahogany table for special occasions, and a deal one for daily use, together with several sets of chairs. Pictures and mirrors decorated the walls, and every window was curtained. Bedrooms were furnished with feather beds on brass bedsteads, and cupboards filled with supplies of bed linen, sufficient if needed for the comfort of visitors. This leasehold property was valued at £165-4-6. By comparison, the two cottages at Tredegar also owned by the father were, together, worth £97. The material evidence could not be more conclusive: in the 1820s at least, the Williams family enjoyed a degree of affluence, forming part of that small but increasingly influential middle class buffer between the gentry and the working masses. While most of his father's personal effects passed to his widow, Zephaniah inherited among other items, a mare and colt, thirty underground trams, twenty tons of tram plates, colliers tools, an anvil, bellows and vice, in short, the fixtures and fittings of a thriving business.[34]

Moggridge had by this time moved into his new home at Woodfield Lodge, directly across the River Sirhowy from the Williams household. He was also one of the most powerful figures in Freemasonry – Provincial Grand Master at Bristol.[35] Despite the apparent closeness between Williams and Moggridge, there is no evidence Zephaniah was himself a mason. This is not to say he was not. Few membership records survive from a period when freemasonry was almost as active in South Wales as Friendly Societies, and an influential friend like Moggridge would have been useful to Zephaniah's coal-owning aspirations. In return perhaps Zephaniah was able to provide a man who saw himself as a social reformer with access to the radical community.

Whatever brought the two together, evidently the mistrust that ended Moggridge's friendship with Frost and Etheridge did not extend to Williams or for that matter to the Merthyr radicals if the John Thomas (Ieuan Ddu) employed by Moggridge and described by the printer Etheridge as his "John-of-all-work" was, indeed, Ieuan Ddu from Merthyr. It is possible to make several connections indicating they were one and the same person. The first is that Zephaniah Williams employed Ieuan Ddu as a clerk at Blackwood; then came Etheridge's intriguing reference to the John Thomas employed by Moggridge *"robbing a Jew at Merthyr,"* and, two years after this, when a bankrupt Zephaniah Williams was forced to sell the cottage at New Village in 1833 the tenant is named in the auction notice as John Thomas.[36]

Nineteenth century pamphleteers were invariably pathologically scurrilous. In this instance, Ethridge's 40-page pamphlet published in 1830 savaged Moggridge's character and conduct as a Magistrate, the main thrust not only that he pocketed the fees and fines received in his magisterial duties, but that he sought to appoint his son Matthew as a magistrate so that he might also fleece the poor which would enable him to *"gallant with the girls a little more, or pay them better for it."* Neither was the Garden Village experiment excluded from this vicious tirade, Etheridge declaring, *"After you failed your electioneering project at Bridgewater and Monmouth, you soon found out that the people smelt a*

*rat, as we say: or in other words, that you was not exactly what
you ought to be, or wished the public to think you was; that you
was become more attached to the granting of leases, and seeing
the stones and mortar put together at Blackwood, than you was
to the interests or welfare of the public."* [37]

Whoever "John-of-all-work" was, if Etheridge is to be believed
then not only did he collect fines and fees on behalf of Moggridge, he was sufficiently literate to handle all the necessary paper
work, including the drafting of summonses. Etheridge claimed he
had evidence Thomas sometimes acted outside the law, and on
occasions had been forced to refund monies illegally levied on a
poor person's goods. The Newport printer roasted Thomas,
observing, *"There is one thing I have heard, and likewise been
informed of it by letter, namely, that John Thomas, your man-of-
all-work, is a sort of stipendiary, Constable of yours; to whom you
pay fifteen shillings per week, whether you find him many jobs or
few; and that you pocket all the rest of the fees yourself; and that
you and him charge for summonses, warrants, and serving levies
of distress, etc. I should like to know if this information is correct
or not: I know that John has never been presented, or his name
ever returned at a Court of Leet; and that therefore he is not a
regularly appointed Constable of the parish, nor ever acknowledged as such by any of the other magistrates: this I think is very
proper; but considering the many jobs John does, and many of
them dirty jobs too, I think that his salary is by far too little:
especially as he has on some occasions got into a scrape, and
have been obliged to refund; but more of John hereafter."* Despite
a promise to address the subject of John Thomas in a future
pamphlet, nothing materialised, leaving only Etheridge's curious
footnote hinting at some dastardly deed committed by Thomas
"against a Jew at Merthyr." [38] Admittedly, this does not sound like
John Thomas, musician, teacher and Owenite co-editor of *The
Workman,* the man employed by Zephaniah Williams as his clerk,
also at Blackwood. The description, and activities for which the
Thomas in the Etheridge letter is blamed, would be more applicable to Constable John Thomas, of Merthyr, who was attacked
and beaten by rioters during the rising of 1831. Known as the
'terror of Merthyr' (Shoni Crydd), he was accused of blackmailing
owners of beer shops and was one of the most feared and hated

men in the town. By 1834, however, he was dead, leaving his four children destitute.[39]

John Thomas, Blackwood clerk and co-editor of *The Workman* was certainly a contemporary of Zephaniah Williams. Born in the same year of 1795, he taught for a time at Machen where Zephaniah and his wife Joan had also lived. Joan's family had an estate at Bovil Farm and it was here that Zephaniah sunk Bovil Colliery, the eventual cause of his bankruptcy. On the balance of evidence, the two Thomas's would seem to be one and same person, although Etheridge's portrayal of Thomas as Moggridge's disagreeable lackey, exploiting the Monmouthshire poor for their own interests, is remarkably different from Thomas (Ieuan Ddu), the esteemed Welsh-speaking music teacher of Merthyr. Is this explained by a clash of cultures? Etheridge was a monoglot Newport printer, elder statesman of the local reformist pre-Chartist movement, and wedded more to the traditional radical values espoused by Tom Paine and William Cobbett than any specifically Welsh interests or sensibilities. Etheridge is most remembered for severing all connections with Chartism six months before the Uprising because of the predominance of 'physical force' men from the Valleys. Frost on the other hand could at least understand Welsh, and may well have spoken it although he wrote always in English. There is not a scrap of evidence he considered Chartism and the language incompatible although the relevance of the Charter declined the further it penetrated into the Welsh heartland. The subsequent allegation, that the Uprising was entirely the work of English speakers, was a charge vehemently denied by Welsh scholars.[40] By publishing articles in both languages, *The Workman* tried to bridge two cultures in an increasingly bi-lingual society. Yet no specifically Welsh issues are addressed in the newspaper's one surviving edition, England being the only context in which the mainstream issues are discussed. After analysing the content one is left to wonder, whether what was hailed as the first working class newspaper, was targeted at the workers or the 19th century equivalent of the chattering classes. No surprise perhaps that when the time came, those of a more radical disposition turned to the more militant Chartist mouthpieces the *Western Vindicator* and *Northern Echo*. Political protest in the Monmouthshire and Glamorgan Valleys had settled down following the Merthyr Rising, the workers getting on with their lives after the battering they suffered. It was also a boom time in the iron and coal industries and there were rich pickings!

Zephaniah Williams set out at an early age to carve a future for himself as a geologist and mining engineer. After his marriage at Merthyr in 1819 he had settled first at Machen, then at Cwm-corrwg in Bedwellty, close to Penyderi Farm, which formed part of his wife's (Llewellyn) family estate. A year later Joan gave birth to the first of their five children, only two of whom, Llewelyn and his younger sister Rhoda, were to survive. The births and deaths of all five are recorded on the first page of the Williams family Bible, which I discovered at Frogmore House on the banks of the River Mersey in north-west Tasmania, where the Williams family was eventually reunited. The house, a palatial red-brick property erected by George Atkinson, Zephaniah Williams' son-in-law, is located a short distance from Ballahoo Creek. It is here that Zephaniah established his first mining camp. Neither he nor his wife ever lived at Frogmore, the house not being built until after their deaths. Incredibly, although ownership of the house has passed through a dozen hands during the last one hundred years, the Williams family Bible and two oil paintings by Zephaniah's granddaughter Joan Boadle have never left it. One of the paintings is believed to be a self-portrait by the artist, the other of the house and its immediate surroundings. Apart for the cover, the English Bible is in pristine condition, and an impressive object, six inches thick, measuring perhaps eighteen inches by twelve inches, so heavy that it was difficult for my wife to hold for me to photograph this historic piece of Welsh memorabilia. One hundred and fifty years before the Bible re-surfaced at Frogmore House, Joan Williams had taken it to Tasmania when she joined her Chartist husband in exile. If it were true that Zephaniah was the notorious Deist, his scepticism had not shaken his wife's faith, the first page of the Bible inscribed, *"Joan Williams. Her book. August 22, 1834. Buried at St Paul's, C/E* (Church of England*) East Devonport."* From this one wonders whether she made the entries inside the cover or they were added later, possibly by the grand-daughter. Although names, birth dates and deaths of all five children are recorded, not a single baptism is mentioned. As remarkable as the Bible's survival is inexplicable, is that Joan had carried it

The author's wife holds the Williams family Bible.

fourteen thousand miles, sacrificing other family treasures to accommodate this weighty tome on a perilous voyage lasting three months. Arriving in Tasmania, she faced another hazardous journey by sailing cutter around the coast from Launceston, to the Mersey River and six miles up it to Ballahoo Creek.

Aware that she was never going to return to her native Wales, Joan Williams evidently refused to be separated from her solitary link to the three children she had left buried in Monmouthshire. The first of these was born at Cwmcorrwg, Bedwellty, in 1820. Named Rhoda, she died when she was seven. By the time Llewelyn was born in 1822, the family had moved to the neighbouring parish of Trevethin. He survived, but not his sister Joan and brother Thomas, whose births were recorded in the family Bible as Penmaen in Mynyddislwyn Parish. Llewelyn's youngest sister, another Rhoda, who eventually travelled with her mother to Tasmania, was the last-born, also at Penmaen.[41]

Top: Frogmore House on Ballahoo Creek, built by Zephaniah Williams' son-in-law, and where the Bible has lain for 150 years. *Bottom:* Births and deaths of the Williams' children recorded in the Bible, while the inscription on the left-hand page reads, *"Joan Williams, Her Book, August 22, 1834."*

Not long after Zephaniah moved to Cwmcorrwg, an early attempt to establish himself as a coal owner landed him before the High Court accused of illegally avoiding payment of galeage (transport charges) on coal raised from a mine in the Sirhowy Valley. With two coal merchant partners, William Pritchard of Bristol, and Thomas Webb of Pillgwenlly, Newport, Zephaniah had leased the rights to mine coal beneath land at Heol-y-Ceisaid on Penyrhiw Farm. At that time, landowners within eight miles of the Monmouthshire Canal had the exclusive right to build and operate tram roads connecting collieries and mines to the canal for the transport of coals, minerals and other goods. Benjamin Hall (whose son became the first Lord Llanover) was one of the principal beneficiaries and built what became known as the Benjamin Hall Tram Road. The lease to operate and maintain the tram road had passed to George Maule (later Treasury Solicitor responsible for prosecuting the Chartist leaders), John Llewellyn and Joseph Kaye. Among the land and mineral rights acquired by Hall where his tram road crossed other properties was Penyrhiw Farm on which the brothers, Lewis Lewis and Evan Lewis, operated a level and paid the tram road operators the usual and accustomed tonnage to move their coal. Without permission from Benjamin Hall, the Lewis's had leased part of the land to Zephaniah and his partners who promptly dug a second level without informing anyone, and proceeded to mine coal for several years before the tram road operators Maule, Llewellyn and Kaye suspected something fishy was happening beneath their feet. On investigation they discovered that not only was a second level operating, illegally, but the coal from it was being moved on a clandestine underground tram road built by Williams and company to avoid paying tonnage on Hall's Tram Road. Apparently, Williams and his partners had hatched a scheme some years previously to connect their level to the Monmouthshire Canal by a circuitous underground route, which included tunnelling beneath the parish road, thus avoiding a "considerable amount" in tonnage dues. Ignoring warnings to cease operations, Zephaniah continued to raise coal until served with a notice threatening an injunction if he proceeded with his "wrongful acts and schemes." For a while mining stopped and the clandestine tram road was decommissioned. But when he thought it safe, Zephaniah resumed operations, at which point a High Court injunction was issued on March 29, 1826, restraining him and his partners from raising coal from the level. Any breach of the injunction meant an immediate fine of £5000, a huge amount in those days. Not only were the three partners put immediately out of business, so were the Lewis brothers for cheating the Lord of the Manor of his royalties as owner of the mineral rights.[42]

Rivalry for the coalfield's riches was intense, those without the financial resources to negotiate legal access to ironstone and coal reserves often resorting to dubious practices. Unauthorised levels, and underground encroachment on seams already being worked by others were among the most common. Only a small amount of capital was needed to drive a level into the side of the hill where coal could be seen to outcrop, then using the 'pillar and stall' method to mine it. The colliers dug stalls off the underground roadway, leaving pillars of coal to support the roof as they advanced. When the seam was exhausted, they withdrew from the stall, removing the coal pillars as they did so, and allowing the roof to collapse. Few colliery owners employed more than 100 men in the 1830s. Deep shafts were not generally necessary, so much of the coal at that time on or near the surface. Ironmasters employed Minerals Agents like Zephaniah Williams to organise the contracts and labour to keep their furnaces regularly supplied, these agents or master miners exercising considerable power and influence on the coalfield. When in response to Government pressure to abolish the Truck Shops, Sir John Guest was persuaded in 1846 to pay workers directly, rather than through middle-men, there were forty agents responsible for the supply of ironstone and coal to the Dowlais furnaces.[43]

After losing the level at Penyrhiw, Zephaniah Williams in 1828 became Minerals Agent for the Harford Bros. at Sirhowy. Reputed to know every foot of underground workings in the area, he would have been familiar to colliers throughout the coalfield. Notwithstanding his new responsibilities, he embarked on an even more ambitious private venture, again in partnership with the Bristol and Newport coal merchants, Pritchard and Webb. On this occasion the enterprise was perfectly legal, the partners signing a lease permitting them to search for coal beneath 99 acres at Bovil Farm, Machen. The mineral rights were owned by a large consortium of mostly aristocratic speculators hoping to strike lucky by investing in what they hoped would prove to be coal-bearing land, the rights to which they then sold or leased to yield a quick profit without actually needing to sink a mine, a not uncommon occurrence in early 19th century coal rush days. The consortium imposed stiff conditions on the partners, including a ground rent of £93-15 a quarter for the 25-year duration of the lease, this to be paid whether or not coal was found. If the venture proved successful, there was an additional royalty of one shilling a ton. More seriously, under the terms of the lease Zephaniah and his partners were given only 18 months to start raising coal.[44]

The colliery was sunk at Bovil, but the enterprise was a disaster, bankrupting the three partners by November 1833. Presumably to pay off his debts, Zephaniah was forced to sell the family's three leasehold cottages, one at Blackwood occupied by John Thomas and two at Tredegar by auction at the King's Head Hotel, Newport.[45] Thomas it seems returned immediately to Merthyr to co-edit the very first issue of *The Workman,* which appeared three months after the sale of the house he had rented from Zephaniah.

Zephaniah must have been hugely disappointed by the failure of the Bovil Colliery since it was in an area he knew well, his father-in-law, Lewellyn Llewellyn, having built Bovil Mansion at Machen. But by the time the old man died in 1834, the Llewellyn Estate was in financial trouble, the family moving to another of their properties, Penyderi Farm in the Sirhowy Valley. Zephaniah's brother-on-law Thomas Llewellyn meanwhile continued to live at Machen where he was responsible for the administration of what remained of the family estate on behalf of his widowed mother, another brother Henry, and sister Joan, Zephaniah's wife.[46] And it was Thomas Llewellyn who was instrumental in orchestrating Zephaniah's most audacious undertaking on the eve of the Chartist Uprising five years later – the attempted hijacking of Cwrt-y-Bella Colliery running beneath Penyderi Farm and owned by two of the most powerful men in Monmouthshire, Thomas Phillips and Thomas Prothero. Both solicitors with extensive coal producing properties, they were the 'new rich,' rare examples of local men whose rise to pre-eminence and wealth without the advantage of privilege or patronage had elevated them to the ranks of the landed gentry. Besides being Town Clerk of New-port, Prothero was election agent for the Tories and in many ways stood for all that was wrong with the unreformed electoral system. Powerful and rich, he sat alongside the likes of Samuel Homfray, the Tredegar ironmaster, on the Monmouthshire Canal Board, and was appointed a director of the Newport Docks Company when it began the construction of the new dock at Pill in 1836. From his collieries in the Monmouthshire valleys Prothero exported coal from his own wharf on the River Usk, and built the *'Hercules'*, one of the first steam engines to operate on the Monmouthshire Tramway. For twenty years he had been Town Clerk during which time, according to John Frost, Prothero had lined his pockets at the expense of the townspeople. In what was a very litigious age, Frost paid for his libel of the Town Clerk with six months in gaol. Prothero was one of the giants among litigants, never hesitating a moment to use the courts, mostly successfully, to settle his disputes. His partner Phillips was not cast from exactly the same mould, but if it were true there was such a thing as a Chartist hit list, then these two were reputedly at the top of it. As it transpired, Phillips was knighted by Queen Victoria for his bravery as Mayor of Newport in organising the defence of the town against the Chartist invasion, and Prothero was involved in much of the questioning of Chartist suspects after the revolt collapsed. Zephaniah Williams could not have chosen two more formidable adversaries when in June 1838 with his nephew Edmund Llewellyn and a gang of colliers he broke into Cwrt-y-Bella Colliery running beneath his mother-in-law's farm and, literally, brought the roof down with the deliberate intention of sabotaging coal production and seizing the colliery.[47]

When Llewellyn Llewellyn died in 1834 the estate was placed in trust to be sold, until then its affairs managed by his eldest son, William Llewellyn. Penyderi Farm where Llewellyn Llewellyn's widow Jane lived with another son Edmund, sat on top of twelve acres of coal, the seam extending into an adjoining property, Cwrt-y-Bella, from where it was mined by Thomas Phillips and Thomas Prothero. For many years, and without any apparent objection from the older Llewellyn, Cwrt-y-Bella accessed its coal, and drained and ventilated the colliery by means of a level driven beneath Penyderi Farm. Not a penny tonnage had ever been paid or asked for this way leave until the family found it necessary to raise a £4,000 mortgage on the farm from a Worcestershire minerals speculator, Henry Goude. Even though the pair of Newport solicitors were never able to produce a legally binding agreement permitting them free access to the coal from Penyderi Farm, William Llewellyn had refrained from mounting a legal challenge on the family's behalf on account of Prothero's terrifying reputation as a litigant. Later he was to say he could not stop them using the level without bringing *"Mr Prothero about my ears,"* and that Prothero *"would not accede to any reasonable proposal if there was the least room for litigation."*[48] Instead, William approached Prothero and asked for a way leave agreement. When twelve months passed without any sign of an agreement, and no one locally was prepared to move against Prothero for fear of becoming involved in expensive litigation, Henry Goude, the mortgagee, with the support of the Llewellyn family, instructed a Dudley solicitor, James Maughan, to serve notice on Prothero and Phillips that henceforth they were required to pay one penny way leave on every ton raised from Cwrt-y-Bella through the level passing beneath the farm. Neither were they permitted to continue draining the colliery on to Penyderi Farm without permission from the Llewellyn's. If the Newport partners failed to comply, they were told steps would be taken to halt coal production at Cwrt-y-Bella Colliery.[49]

In a period when coal owners were vigorously elbowing each other aside, either legally and illegally, to reach the rich four foot Mynyddislwyn Seam zigzagging its way across Monmouthshire, such a threat would normally have prompted a litigious response from Prothero and Phillips. Instead, they ignored it, believing perhaps no one would dare interfere with a colliery employing 40 colliers and raising 35,000 tons of coal in the previous three years alone. But they reckoned without Zephaniah Williams and his brother-in-law Edmund Llewellyn. With the full support of Goude and his in-laws, Zephaniah and Edmund, assisted by a gang of five colliers began sinking a shaft on June 5, 1838 from a field on Penyderi Farm directly above the Cwrt-y-Bella level. Working day and night, the intention was to break through into the level and bring down the roof, blocking the only access to the coalface. Discovering what was afoot, Thomas James, the colliery manager, accompanied by Thomas Phillips' son, hurried to the level where they confronted the men underground and ordered them to leave the level immediately. The intruders refused to move and sent immediately to Penyderi Farm for help from Edmund Llewellyn. No sooner had he arrived and the situation turned distinctly ugly, teetering on the edge of violence in an underground level no wider than six feet, the roof too low for a man to stand upright and lit only by candlelight. Snatching up an axe, and flourishing it in their faces, Edmund Llewellyn ordered James and Phillips junior "off the premises," warning he would kill the first person that trespassed on his land again. Turning to the younger Phillips, he added menacingly, *"Perhaps that will be you."* And he gave him an ultimatum to deliver to his father and partner Prothero: they had used the level too long, said Edmund, and would use it no longer.[50]

For the moment, the manager and his companion retreated, to consider the consequences of what would happen when the shaft broke through into the level. Not only would the roadway be obstructed by debris from the pit, preventing the movement of coal, the lives of forty miners would be endangered by the lack of adequate ventilation at the coalface. Four days after the shaft was started, the entire labour force walked out and coal production ceased. At 10.30 p.m. Saturday, June 16, the colliery manager James was told Zephaniah and his crew of shaft sinkers were about to break through at a point where the level was supported by an arch. Hurrying underground, James found one intruder destroying the supporting arch and another completing the shaft so that it was large enough to admit a man into the level from the surface. The two men, John Thomas, aged 42, and Rowland Richards, aged 30, were both seized by James and his workmen, taken away and detained at his house. When James returned to the colliery two hours later at about 2 a.m. the Sunday morning, he spotted a light in the level, and on investigating found Edmund Llewellyn standing across the roadway near the bottom of the new shaft, and Zephaniah Williams at the top. Edmund had two pikes at his side, and as James advanced warned him that if he came further he would *"knock his brains out,"* a threat reinforced by Zephaniah who shouted down the shaft in Welsh, *"If there are any men in the level beat them to the Devil."* Fearing for his life, the colliery manager could only watch as two of Zephaniah's gang, Evan Jenkins and Robert Lewis spent the next two hours with sledgehammers and iron bars demolishing first the arch and then the timber supports, causing the collapse of fifty yards of roof, and completely blocking the colliery. Throughout the destruction of the level, Edmund stood guard with his pikes to prevent James and his workmen from interfering. So extensive was the damage, it would be many weeks before the level could be cleared of debris and the roof repaired for coal production to resume.[51]

Prothero and Phillips sought immediate restitution for the damage caused to Cwrt-y-Bella. The two colliers who had been seized by the colliery manager, Thomas and Richards, appeared before the Monmouth magistrate and ironmaster Samuel Homfray on June 21 charged with causing malicious damage to a colliery arch. Both were fined thirty shillings, ordered to compensate the owners for the damage with the alternative of 14 days in Usk Prison where they remained for the duration of their sentence, no one offering to pay their fines, costs or compensate Phillips and Prothero. On the advice of John Frost, William Llewellyn, who throughout the affair acted as an intermediary between the family and Goude, refused to pay the fines of the two convicted colliers, Thomas and Richards, although he did assure their families they would be provided for while they served their sentences. Almost simultaneously, an action was started in the Chancery Division of the High Court by Phillips and Prothero against Goude, the minerals speculator, Jane Llewellyn, the widow, and another brother Henry Llewellyn. By this time, William Llewellyn was close to panic, warning Goude's solicitor Maughan they were up to their eyes in lawyers and he doubted whether they would ever escape their clutches. *"I have received a note by messenger from Zephaniah Williams wanting very much this affair should be settled as soon as possible as he has drawn on himself the displeasure of his master, Mr S. Harford, and also Mr Phillips of Newport, who had been doing some business for him some time ago. He (Phillips), undoubtedly, will do all he can to him for having anything to do with sinking this shaft at Penyderry and that will be almost the means of his ruin,"* Llewellyn told Maughan. *"I very much wish we could put an end to the pro-*

ceedings pending against brother Edmund, Zephaniah Williams and the two men as I have finally ascertained that a warrant is in the hand of the police officer to apprehend them as soon as he can, to convict them for felony. . . . I expect every hour to hear that those parties are apprehended and shut up in some lock up house or another as no mercy will (be) *shown them whatever.*"[52] What is evident from this is that the year before his involvement in the Chartist Uprising, Zephaniah feared the sinking of the pirate shaft would cost him his job as Minerals Agent for the Harfords, and this, more than anything else, explains his sudden departure from Tredegar, a few months later, to take over the *Royal Oak* beer shop at Coalbrookvale, Blaina.[53]

Zephaniah's concern was well grounded. On 8 August, 1838, along with his nephew Edmund, and another two workmen involved in the break-in, Evan Jenkins and Robert Lewis, he appeared before Bedwellty Petty Sessions to answer summonses of "riotously and tumultuously assembling to injure a building or erection usual in conducting the business of a mine" at Cwrt-y-Bella Colliery. Sitting beside Samuel Homfray on the bench was none other than Zephaniah's employer, the Quaker ironmaster, Summers Harford, in addition to which the prosecution was conducted by Mr Thomas Phillips, junior, the man Edmund had threatened to kill! Their situation must have seemed hopeless.[54]

Never more so than in mid-19th century Britain was the sanctity of property held in greater esteem. A man could beat his wife close to death and pay only a few shillings fine, but the theft of a horse or a pheasant from the Lord of the Manor was good for seven years transportation. Zephaniah and his companions must have been conscious from sentences imposed at the most recent Monmouth Assizes of the range of offences meriting the severest punishment. At the April 1837 sitting, the judge dispatched two to Van Diemen's Land for life for horse stealing and another pair for the theft of just £8. A certain Thomas Adams, aged 27, got seven years for passing a base coin, counterfeiting. At the following Assize in March, 1838, twelve prisoners, three of them women, one only nineteen, were sentenced to various terms of transportation, nothing less than seven years. The raid on Cwrt-y-Bella Colliery had become, according to the *Monmouthshire Beacon* a "*Most Important Mining Case,*" on account of the perpetrators reckless disregard for property rights.[55] Not that it was a unique event. Something similar had happened the previous year in Glamorgan and while the legislation covering such an occurrence was ill defined, a conviction might easily have meant transportation for life. With gaols in England so over-crowded that prisoners shared three to a bed, transportation was a means of exporting the problem. Since criminality was widely regarded to be a genetic defect, transportation removed the defectives from the English gene pool.

Nor was this Zephaniah's first brush with the law. Some years earlier he had appeared before Monmouthshire Quarter Sessions at Usk Town Hall charged with ten others of unlawful and riotous assembly, and beating and wounding a police constable at Michaelston-y-fedw. The only detail to survive from this case is the result: Williams not guilty but another man sentenced to six weeks hard labour.[56] The alleged break-in at Cwrt-y-Bella Colliery and the demolition of the level, was in a much higher league, sufficiently grave for the Grand Jury to issue a True Bill for the indictment to be tried by Sir Thomas Erskine at the Monmouth Assizes on March 27, 1839. To everyone's astonishment, the case was thrown out on a technicality.[57] The prosecution made the mistake of charging Zephaniah and his companions under the wrong statute! Mr Justice Erskine admitted he was partially to blame for failing to read the depositions before he referred the case to the Grand Jury. If he had done so he would have seen there was no basis, under the statute specified by the prosecution, for the serious charges against the defendants. In his opinion, the prosecution should have realised the statute by which it was proceeding did not apply to this case, especially in view of a similar case in which he had adjudicated the previous year.

Zephaniah Williams walked free on March 30, escaping by the skin of his teeth almost certain transportation. What is more remarkable is that seven months later he is leading the Chartist attack upon Newport, supposedly the signal for a revolution to topple the monarchy. Neither had the litigation arising from the break in at Cwrt-y-Bella gone away. Phillips and Prothero were pursuing a civil action against Zephaniah's wife's family and the Worcestershire speculator Goude. No longer employed by the Harford's, Zephaniah had moved his family to the *Royal Oak* in early 1839 but even that was not secure. Only the tenant, the property had been sold to his powerful neighbour and enemy, Thomas Brewer. The Blaina ironmaster had bought the freehold in March for the express purpose of ridding the area of a man he rated a bad influence on his workmen. Despite all this, the day after being cleared by the court at Monmouth, Zephaniah makes his first reported public appearance at a Chartist meeting numbering more than one thousand outside the *Royal Oak* on which occasion he is described by William Edwards, the Newport reformist baker, as "one of the best Chartists he had met."[58]

What was it that induced a bankrupt who had already narrowly escaped possible transportation, whose recklessness at Cwrt-y-Bella Colliery left his wife's family close to ruin, whose inheritance disappeared in failed mining ventures, and who was waiting to be evicted from the *Royal Oak*, to follow, in close succession, one reckless adventure with another? It is impossible even to guess what part his personal situation and straitened circumstances influenced his involvement with the Chartists. His fortunes at their lowest point, desperate and bitter, even railing against the grievances and conditions prevailing in the Black Domain, Zephaniah Williams would seem the most unlikely person to seek intentionally to execute a revolution. Leading a demonstration for electoral reform as a means of addressing the injustices suffered by the workers was entirely different to plotting to overthrow the Monarchy. But this is exactly what he confessed to six months afterwards, although it is implicit in the argument of this book there needed a more determined finger on the trigger to transform a demonstration into High Treason.

NOTES

1. Gwyn A. Williams, *The Merthyr Rising* (1978), pp229-230.
2. Gwent Record Office, W. H. Baker, 'Friendly Societies in Monmouthshire to 1850', *Presenting Monmouthshire*, No. 13, Spring (1962), 33-39, GRO.
3. After the Poor Laws were revised in 1834 parishes could no longer distribute money and were grouped together in Poor Law Unions. Rate of assistance for the poor became generally less and discontent was widespread when this was followed by the construction of Workhouses.
4. 'Friendly Societies in Monmouthshire to 1850', loc. cit., 37.

5. GRO, FSB 6/42, Bedwellty Union Society bond, 1831.
6. 'Friendly Societies in Monmouthshire to 1850', loc. cit., 36.
7. NLW, *Udgorn Cymru* published translation of Frost 1840 letter from the convict ship *Mandarin* to his wife Mary in Bristol, provided for publication with covering note from Mrs Frost, dated 22 Sept 1840.
8. For detail of Morgan Williams, political activist, see *The Merthyr Rising*, pp58, 60, 74f., 84ff., 94, 110, 227; *Merthyr Express* article about Morgan Williams, 5 May 1956, Merthyr Public Library.
9. David Morgans, *Music and Musicians of Merthyr and District* (Merthyr 1922), pp28-33, p28, pp210-211; for John Thomas (Ieuan Ddu), Williams, *The Merthyr Rising*, pp85-87, 227.
10. NLW, *The Workman*, 1 May 1834; also see R. D. Rees, *Glamorgan Newspapers under the Stamp Acts*, (1959), Morganwg, iii, p76.
11. *The Workman*, p1, p14.
12. *ibid*, pp14-15.
13. NLW, Robert Griffith, *Llyfr cerdd dannau* (Manchester), p325; NLW, Eisteddfod Genedlaeothol 1887 (Caerludd), p143.
14. David Morgans, *Music and Musicians of Merthyr and District* (Merthyr 1922), pp28-33, p28, pp210-211.
15. Evan Powell, *History of Tredegar: subject of Competition at Tredegar chair eisteddfod held Feb 25, 1884* (Newport, 1902), p48.
16. Wilks, p95.
17. Oliver Jones, *Early Days of Sirhowy and Tredegar.* (1969) p92, 94; Arthur Gray-Jones, *A History of Ebbw Vale* (1970), p170.
18. NPL, Zephaniah Williams, *A Letter to Benjamin Williams, a Dissenting Minister* (Newport, 1831); GRO, *Monmouthshire Merlin,* auction notice, 1 Nov 1833, describes John Thomas as the tenant of the cottage at Blackwood Williams inherited from his parents.
19. Williams, *The Merthyr Rising*, p86.
20. NPL, pamphlet concerning Great Anti-Chartist Meeting, 29 April 1839.
21. Jones, *The Last Rising*, p206.
22. NLW, LL/CC/1160, Thomas Williams, Letter of Administration, inventory.
23. E. T. Davies, *Monmouthshire Schools and Education to 1870,* pp 93-94; A. Wright, *The History of Lewis School, Pengam* (Newtown, 1929, Welsh Outlook Press).
24. Morgan Williams, *Merthyr Express,* 5 May 5, 1956.
25. Oliver Jones, *Early Days of Sirhowy and Tredegar.*
26. NLW, Lord Tredegar Papers, letter from Frost to Morgan Williams, from *Mandarin,* 4 June 1840.
27. NPL, Williams letter to wife from New Norfolk, 21 April, 1844.
28. T. D. Fosbrooke, *Abstracts of records and manuscripts respecting the county of Gloucester* (Gloucester, 1807), vol. 2, pp238-9; GRO, *The Oriental Herald,* vol. XXI (1829), pp210-322.
29. NPL, for details of Moggridge's Owenite views see five pamphlets he wrote; NPL, PM160 342 MOG, pamphlet, Samuel Etheridge; NPL, *John Hodder Moggridge, Esq.,* open letter from John Frost published as pamphlet; for description of Blackwood Garden Village, see B. Ll. James, 'John Hodder Moggridge and the founding of Blackwood', *Presenting Monmouthshire,* No. 25, 1968, pp25-29.

30. B. Ll. James, *Presenting Monmouthshire,* loc. cit.
31. NLW, LL/CC/1160, Thomas Williams, Letter of Administration, inventory.
32. B. Ll. James, 'John Hodder Moggridge and the founding of Blackwood', *Presenting Monmouthshire,* No. 25, 1968, pp25-29.
33. Bank of England calculation at today's value for the pound sterling.
34. NLW, LL/CC/1160, Thomas Williams, Letter of Administration, inventory.
35. Library and Museum of Freemasonry, BE60 (BRI) POW, taken from *A History of Freemasonry in Bristol,* A. C. Owell and J. Littleton, 1910.
36. NPL, PM160 342 MOG, Samuel Etheridge, pamphlet.
37. *ibid.*
38. *ibid.*
39. Obituary, *Merthyr Guardian,* 14 June 1834.
40. Sian Rhiannon Williams, *Oes y Byd I'r Iaith Gymraeg* (Cardiff, 1992).
41. Williams Family Bible remains at Frogmore, now owned by Mr and Mrs Kim Ransom.
42. GRO, D43.4764, High Court Injunction, 29 March 1826.
43. Oliver Jones, *Early Days of Sirhowy and Tredegar.*
44. GRO, D43.1491, Bovil Colliery lease, 1828.
45. For evidence of bankruptcy, see Notice of Auction, Nov 1, 1833, *Monmouthshire Merlin.*
46. GRO, D124.00771-73, letters from William Llewellyn.
47. *ibid.*
48. *ibid.*
49. *ibid.*
50. GRO, Chartist Miscellaneous, Thomas James affadavit, Chancery Division.
51. *ibid.*
52. GRO, D124.0773, letter from William Llewellyn, 25 June 1838.
53. *ibid.*
54. *Monmouthshire Beacon,* 12 Aug 1838.
55. *ibid.*
56. Monmouthshire Quarter Sessions, April 1832.
57. *Merthyr Guardian,* 13 April 1839.
58. *Western Vindicator,* 31 March 1839.

CHAPTER 4

The Man from the Alamo

John Rees, alias 'Jack the Fifer,' is first heard of not in Wales but at Banks Arcade, New Orleans in October 1835, four years before the Chartist Uprising. He was barely 20 and not long arrived in the United States. At that time, New Orleans was the most cosmopolitan city in America, attracting adventurers from all parts of the world, some of the most adventurous meeting on the evening of October 13 in the coffee room of the three-storey red-bricked Banks Arcade on Magazine Street.

A few days earlier, the first skirmish in the Texas War of Independence had occurred at Gonzales at the confluence of the Guadalupe and San Marcos rivers when the mayor, Ezekiel Williams and seventeen others held off 200 Mexican cavalry, ostensibly a dispute over the return of a cannon loaned to the inhabitants as defence against marauding Indians. Its significance, however, was not lost on the Anglo-American settlers, of which there were only 40,000 in a territory the size of Britain, France, Germany and Spain combined but still an integral part of the sovereign Republic of Mexico, governed by President Antonio Lopez de Santa Anna from Mexico City. The battle at Gonzales was about the erosion of settler rights and liberties, although a sizeable body of Anglos supported the Mexican centralist government, partly due to concern about a possible slave rebellion.[1]

The relationship between Anglo-American settlers and the Mexican Government had from the time of the first colony been fragile, at best an uneasy truce held together by the offer to colonists of an inexhaustible supply of virtually free land. The inducement of a "league and a labor" (4,605 acres) for the head of each settler family at twelve and a half cents an acre was Mexico's best defence against Indians and an expansionist United States set on extending its territory from the Atlantic to the Pacific. The agents, or 'empresarios' commissioned by the Mexican Government to attract new settlers had an even better deal: 67,000 acres for every 200 families they introduced. One of those 'empresarios' was Stephen Fuller Austin, founder of Anglo-American Texas and its representative in the Coahuila state legislature, which administered Texas. By adopting a conciliatory policy towards the central government, Austin had procured for colonists special tax concessions and exemption from settling debts incurred outside Texas. The Government was also persuaded to turn a blind eye to slavery, which continued in Texas long after it was abolished by the Mexican legislature. But this fragile harmony between the Anglos and a government in Mexico City, frequently engulfed by political upheavals, began falling apart in 1830 with the passage of a law banning the further colonisation of Texas by settlers from the United States.[2] Nevertheless, they continued arriving, crossing the Sabine River from Louisiana, bringing their slaves with them. Infuriated by the crackdown, the Anglo-Americans at first demanded state government for Texas, sending Austin to Mexico City to negotiate with Santa Anna. Not only was it refused, but Austin did not return for 28 months, after his arrest on suspicion of inciting insurrection. When he eventually got back to Texas in 1835 he added his support to the campaign for independence at the Consultation Convention convened on November 1 at San Felipe, 'capital' of the Austin Colony.[3]

Before this, the majority of settlers believed Texas could develop as a free and prosperous Mexican state. But there had always been a faction wanting conflict with Mexico as a means of legitimising dubious land deals, under cover of either independence or annexation by the United States. Furthermore, a new 'slave state' as a member of the Union would tip the balance in the US Congress in favour of the South. There had already been several abortive attempts at breakaway, one of these the 1826 Fredonia Rebellion, which Austin had in fact helped the Mexicans subdue. A German, Adolphus Sterne was arrested for his part in this and sentenced to be shot for smuggling weapons in barrels of coffee to Haden Edwards, leader of the Fredonians. With the assistance of his Masonic friends, Sterne escaped the firing squad on condition he never took up arms against Mexico again. From his base in New Orleans, beyond the reach of the Mexicans, he continued, however, to agitate for an Independent Texas.[4]

The meeting at Bank's Arcade organised by Sterne recruited two companies of militia to form a new regiment, the New Orleans Greys, to be sent immediately to reinforce the small band of Texans commanded by Austin marching on San Antonio de Bexar, then held by a Mexican garrison. On the outskirts of San Antonio on the opposite bank of the river stood the Alamo, the fortified mission destined to become the site of the most cele-brated military engagement in Texas history and symbol of patriotic sacrifice.

Sterne offered the first fifty to enlist in the New Orleans Greys a free rifle. John Rees was one of these. In no time at all, 120 men, a third of them young, single, adventure-seeking foreigners with little previous military experience, had enlisted in the "Army of the People" for either three, six or twelve months.[5] Rees signed on for a year, almost certainly persuaded not by any acute political consciousness, but by the promise of his new Commander in Chief Sam Houston that every single man committing himself to the struggle for Texas independence would receive automatic citizenship in the new republic and with it a headright grant of almost 1,500 acres. New Orleans was plastered with placards proclaiming free land for homesteading, once Texas was freed from the corrupt regime of Santa Anna. Newspapers were filled with accounts of what awaited immigrants in the promised land, Houston's promise ratified two weeks later when the Provisional Government formed at San Felipe declared Texas would *"reward with donations in lands, all who volunteer their services in her present struggle and receive them as citizens."*[6] From the very first day he arrived in Texas, Rees would be a *de facto* Texan with the same rights as those born there or who migrated across the Sabine River from the United States.

A large proportion of the army during the Texas War of Inde-pendence was composed of foreigners, their imagination fired by the prospects of war and adventure. In contrast, many settlers were ambivalent towards the war with Mexico, preferring to let others fight while they remained at home on their plantations along the Brazos River. Those who did rally to Sam Houston's call to arms demonstrated all the characteristics of citizen-soldiers, discharging themselves during lulls in the fighting or at the end of the period they had contracted to serve. The struggle for independence almost collapsed in the spring of 1836, not because the army was defeated but because the settlers returned to their farms to plant their crops! From the very outset, the "Army of the People" was bedevilled by a lack of continuity in membership, leadership and organisation, due to the rank-and-file's insistence on electing their officers and being involved in strategic and tactical decisions. The military organisation grew from the bottom up, company representatives elected to form a council or board of war. Such excessive democracy caused fragmentation. The only coherent policy was the struggle for independence. The "glorious band" which fought the War of Independence were *not the wealth of the land (but) . . . in the main the poorest citizens,"* according to Mosely Baker, a Congressional candidate. The New Orleans Greys epitomised this, one observer describing the men enlisting at Bank's Arcade as social and economic outcasts collected *"from the very dregs of cities and towns . . . the most miserable wretches the world ever produced."*[7]

For uniform, the New Orleans Greys were issued with surplus grey 1825 US army fatigue jackets and trousers of the kind worn by slave stevedores on the New Orleans waterfront. Black sealskin forage caps with flaps at the back protected their heads against the fierce Texan sun. The muster roll for the Second Company, New Orleans Greys, when it arrived at San Antonio lists John Rees as one of its original 68 members.[8] Among his army buddies were Michael Cronican, William Durham and William Lockhart Hunter, three men who were later involved with Rees in a conspiracy to acquire thousands of acres of land in Texas. Cronican was a printer and newspaperman from Boston, Massachusetts, Hunter became a Chief Justice and member of the Republic of Texas House of Representatives, while Durham was an English immigrant from Norfolk.

The Second Company New Orleans Greys embarked from New Orleans on October 17 aboard the *Columbus* bound for Velasco, a cluster of ramshackle sheds, one filthy hotel and half a dozen grog shops on the bank of the Brazos River, where it emptied into the Gulf of Mexico. The climate on the coast was sub-tropical, the humidity oppressive, flies and mosquitoes a constant torment. A cholera epidemic had ravaged the population not long before the arrival of the Greys, the first volunteer unit to join the Texas revolution. The voyage across the Gulf through uncharted waters, hidden sandbars, avoiding hostile Indians and pirates, was generally considered dangerous but on this occasion uneventful, the *Columbus* arriving at Velasco on October 22. Despite its appearance, Valesco had become a major port of entry for immigrants to Texas, 25,000 having arrived in the previous four years. Away from the coast, the banks of the Brazos River were dotted with sugar and cotton plantations and the palatial homes of some of the wealthiest families in Texas. After confirming Robert C. Morris as its captain for three months and a Virginian William Cooke, second in command, the Greys boarded the *Laura* for the 25-mile trip upstream to the small town of Brazoria. With them they took two six-pounder cannons, which they were to drag overland on the final leg of their journey to San Antonio. At Brazoria, the Greys were welcomed as conquering heroes although they had still to confront the enemy. According to one account, *"speeches were made and sumptuous dinners prepared for us, and by the time we had emptied some dozen baskets of champagne, we had in our imagination conquered all Mexico."* The welcome was the same at Victoria a few days later but once the fighting started the Anglos fearing the worst from the advancing Mexican armies, fled eastwards.[9]

Much of the time on the 250-mile journey from Brazoria to San Antonio was spent scavenging for food and capturing wild mustangs, fiercely independent animals inclined to dump their riders on the ground before flying off across the prairie, saddles under their bellies, lariats dragging behind, equipment and supplies strewn in all directions.[10] Most of the Greys, however, were still on foot, rifles slung across their shoulders, knapsacks on their backs, carrying provisions, powder horns and equipment. At La Bahia de Goliad they crossed Coleto Creek where two months later most of them were to die in an action greater than the Alamo in terms of patriotic sacrifice. On the final leg of the journey to San Antonio the weather turned cold and wet, and by the time the Greys arrived on November 7 the "Army of the People" was on the point of collapse, plagued by desertions as settler volunteers quit to return home to prepare for the spring planting. One thousand Mexicans had resolutely defended the town and fortified mission for six weeks, while another thousand reinforcements were on their way. Discipline among the besieging Texans, meanwhile, had broken down and was no better among the Greys when they arrived. The once identifiable uniforms were now assorted rags. On their feet, shoes and moccasins rather than boots; only a few wore socks. For headgear, some wore Mexican sombreros, others coonskin caps, even tall 'beegum' hats. Not every man had the luxury of a rifle or shotgun. They seldom washed either themselves or their clothes, and little attention was given to the preparation of food. The smallest scratch quickly became infected, corn-liquor the only antidote for pain and disinfecting wounds. Bandages were re-used after boiling, and, when even these were not available, the men resorted to applying spiders-webs to heal open wounds.

There was no roll call, just a signal to rise and prepare breakfast after which, if there was nothing to fear from the enemy or marauding Indians, the raw recruits split into small groups, galloping off in all directions to scavenge for food. But for Sam Houston writing to a friend, A. Hutchinson in November 1835, *"No men are more patriotic or brave on God's earth, than what the boys of Texas are."* Rather like those who participated in the Chartist Uprising in Wales four years later, the personal motives of the rank-and-file varied considerably. Some sought refuge from the law, others wealth, while one volunteer, John S.Brooks described his motivation as *"defiance to tyrants – our watch word is 'Texas and Glory', our war cry is 'Liberty or Death,'* which was not dissimilar from the sentiments at least some of the Chartists were to express on their march to Newport. For Brooks, the Texas War of Independence was a struggle by the weak and oppressed.[11] By late November the Texan camp was looking deserted. Austin had resigned his command, and had been sent as special commissioner, to persuade the United States and other governments to recognise and support the new republic. Replaced by Edward Burleson, the first suggestion was to withdraw to Goliad for the winter. But before this could happen, the rank and file decided among themselves on a final assault, Benjamin Milam and Francis Johnson leading a dawn raid by 300 volunteers on December 5.[12]

By then, William Gordon Cooke, who had taken command of

the Greys Second Company, gathered together volunteers to storm the town, appealing to their patriotism with a famous call to arms that reputedly saved the Texas revolution: *'Who will join old Ben Milam in storming the Alamo.'* Milam was killed by a sniper's bullet on the second day as the fighting raged from house to house, the New Orleans Greys in the vanguard of the battle.

The Mexican General Martin Perfecto de Cos had split his forces between the Alamo Mission and the town of San Antonoio de Bexar. While the six-pounders the Greys had dragged across the prairie from Velasco bombarded the Alamo, Cooke and his volunteers clambered across the roofs of the adobe houses, pouring fire down upon the Mexicans hiding below. Still unable to dislodge the defenders, they hacked their way through the soft adobe walls of houses to engage the Mexicans hand-to-hand. But the Mexicans continued to hold out until Cooke and a group of Greys seized the priest's house on the main plaza, from where they directed fire into the Mexican positions, creating such a panic that the Mexicans retreated into the Alamo Mission. The following morning December 9, Cos discovering his cavalry had deserted during the night, surrendered. He was allowed to retreat south towards Mexico with what remained of his army, the Texans not having either the forces or supplies to hold such a large group of prisoners.[13]

The Mexicans lost 150 men; the Texans suffered 35 casualties, more than half of these New Orleans Greys. Rees was not among the wounded, displaying, not for the last time, a disposition for surviving the tightest corners. The fall of San Antonio and the capture of the Alamo was the first major campaign in the Texas War of Independence. For whatever reason he had enlisted, Rees could but not have been affected by the incongruity of a war fought, not on behalf of the poor and oppressed but to defend a land-rich, slave owning elite. Not that these Anglo-American settlers had no genuine grievances against the Mexican dictator Santa Anna. His imposition of Spanish language education, the pre-dominance of the Roman Catholic church, and an overly centralist regime were all issues with which the Anglos quarrelled, but were nothing compared to the material and aspirational constraints imposed by early 19th century vested interests in Wales. Against one of the largest armies in the world, the "Army

Top: The Alamo at San Antonio de Bexar, about fifteen to thirty years after the battle, when it was being used as a supply debot by the US Army *(courtesy Catholic Archives, Austin)*. Captured first by Rees and his New Orleans Greys in December 1835, it fell three months later to the Mexican Army led by General Santa Anna, all 187 of its defenders either killed during the battle, or executed afterwards. *Bottom:* The Mission church at Goliad where 400 Texans were held prisoner before being marched out into the desert and shot, only 28 surviving, one of those being John Rees.

of the People", not much more than an ill-equipped, untrained, ill-disciplined mob, ready to desert or take extended leave whenever of a mind to, had seized the initiative at San Antonio and the Alamo. When the war started, the politicians who plotted the uprising, at first sought only statehood for Texas within a federal Mexico. Not so the People's Army. From the moment the first shot was fired, the militia were united in their demand for a fully independent Republic of Texas, within which, as new citizens, they would share in its future prosperity through the exercise of their electoral and democratic rights. Sam Houston had promised them that! Taking the field as a loud-talking mob, fond of wild riding and shooting, fistfights and hard liquor, the army had no enthusiasm for Mexican federalism, only independence. After its first success at the siege of San Antonio and the Alamo, it developed a radical ideology that distrusted society outside the military domain, some elements threatening to help themselves to the wealth of the country without regard for the law. The majority of Anglos they regarded as *"Sunshine Patriots,"* shirkers who deserted for the smallest reason. [14] This, together with a chronic shortage of food, medicines and equipment festered until discontent manifested itself in the full-blown politicisation of the People's Army. Ten days after the victory at San Antonio, the Goliad garrison adopted a unilateral Declaration of Independence for a "free, sovereign and independent state."[15]

Immediately following the victory at San Antonio most of the *"Sunshine Patriots"* returned to their homes, leaving eighty per cent of those still defending the town and Alamo recruited from outside Texas. Split by political bickering, the army was on the point of collapse and had descended into what was then described as a *"labyrinth of anarchy"* more dangerous to itself than its adversaries. There was also a leadership hiatus after the Mexican capitulation. When Burleson left San Antonio to join Austin as a Texas emissary to the United States, Francis W. Johnson was appointed commander of the remaining troops. Johnson and his associate James Grant were essentially land speculators, members of a group of empresarios awarded six million acres in land grants by Coahuila province, only to have this frozen by Houston for fear of antagonising local Mexican sentiment. Determined to secure their land, Johnson and Grant persuaded two-thirds of the 300 men remaining at San Antonio, among them Rees and most of the New Orleans Greys, to join an expedition to seize the strategically important Mexican border town of Matamoros, on the western bank of the Rio Grande. Only 100 troops remained to defend San Antonio and the Alamo, and fearing a Mexican counter attack (which occurred three months later with the fall of the Alamo) Houston rode south to intercept the expeditionary force at Refugio. There, the Commanding Officer's impassioned appeal to their patriotic spirit persuaded the bulk of volunteers to abandon what became a military disaster, most of those who pressed on to Matamoros with Johnson and Grant either being killed or taken prisoner:[16]

"Comrades, we must seek to maintain such patriotic fire and not use it up where it will be of no benefit. Soon, friends, I believe, soon will the enemy under Santa Anna raid our peaceful savannahs, soon will their bugles urge their soldiers to our destruction; but that mighty word – freedom – will inspire us. . . . But to be victorious, citizens, it is necessary that we stand united . . . let us prove to them what a nation can do which is united. Though weak in numbers, it will rise up on masse and boldly speak out: 'We want to be free.' Let us show them that when nations rise up for the cause of justice, the Almighty will carry the banner. These, comrades, are the most dangerous, because he who is not with us is against us . . . no other help remains for us now than our own strength and the knowledge that we have seized our arms for a just cause" (cheers) ". . . let us then, comrades, sever that link that binds us to that rusty chain of the Mexican confederation . . ."[17]

One can only speculate about the extraordinary parallels John Rees might have drawn between these events in Texas, and the situation he confronted on returning to Wales a few months before the Chartist Uprising. The Chartists also had enemies in their midst, ironmasters, coal owners, and their collaborators, many of whom evacuated their families to the safety of Cheltenham and Bath for the period immediately preceding the arrival of another People's Army, the men from the hills. If land and freedom were synonymous in Texas, Rees may also have believed that in his native Wales the exercise of freedom was impossible, unless the grip of an immigrant, all-powerful aristocratic clique was broken. To what extent were the momentous events then unfolding in Texas shaping Rees's revolutionary spirit? Not only was his path crossed by some of the giants in the pantheon of the new fledgling nation, Stephen F. Austin, Samuel Houston, William Travis, James Bowie, Davy Crockett: the ragged army outside San Antonio was cast in the radical tradition of the Roundheads and French Revolutionaries, and as Paul Lack in his penetrating study of the Texas Revolution concludes, *"imbued with a strong sense of individual rights and freedom, and sympathy for the oppressed."* Throughout the struggle for Texas, there was a prevailing sense of guilt that the large majority of those who were to win its independence were recruited from among the poorest to fight for Anglo settlers concerned more with protecting their cotton and sugar plantations, than the struggle to create the new republic. Even when Houston proposed conscription as a means of diluting the influence of the volunteer army, conscripts would have still been permitted to pay substitutes to fulfil their military obligations, not dissimilar from compulsory militia service in Wales at that time. Like the Chartists, the Texan volunteers were concerned with the over riding right of suffrage because this was their only way to change the system. The People's Army considered itself the embodiment of the people's sovereignty, a force for revolutionary change that was soon posing a threat to civil order. It was described as a large debating society with decided opinions on all major issues of the day, often taking the most extreme positions. Because of weak political leadership, the leadership of Texas changing six times in twelve months, the army, despite all its indiscipline, exercised *de facto* dominance, the spectre of a mutiny, which eventually came but failed, hanging over the heads of those who ignored its representations.

The army's celebrated democracy was instrumental in producing two of the greatest disasters in American military history: the fall of the Alamo, and three weeks later the Goliad Massacre. Insisting on an input into strategic decision-making, a capricious rank and file bickered over who should command what remained of the garrison at San Antonio. Unable to agree, a compromise was reached with Travis and Bowie elected joint leaders, Travis to remain at the Alamo with fewer than one hundred men, while Bowie took his volunteers to a camp on the Medina River. Meanwhile, the expedition led by Grant and Johnson had split after Houston's intervention, those who continued on to Matamoros routed by the Mexicans. The remainder, including Rees and the New Orleans Greys waited at Goliad/Refugio for reinforcements and their new leader to arrive, Colonel James Fannin, slave owner, slave hunter and slave trader. At Refugio, their ranks much depleted by casualties and desertions, the Greys were re-formed as the San Antonio Greys, Samuel Pettus, who had enlisted with Rees as a private six months earlier, elected Captain of the 2nd Company.

It was the end of February 1836 and the political focus was on the new Constitutional Convention, convened for early March at Washington-on-Brazos. Fearing they might be denied representation on this historic occasion by Anglo settlers, the volunteers exercised their political muscle in a petition addressed to the Convention, signed by 177, one of these Rees, demanding that as citizens of their adopted country enjoying the same property rights as settlers they be permitted to send delegates to the Convention. The Convention agreed to admit two delegates from the People's Army to participate in the final drafting of the Texas Declaration of Independence, which was confirmed and published on March 2. Like the People's Charter drafted two years later by British Chartists, the petition from the Peoples Army of Texas to the Convention was grounded on an appeal for freedom through universal suffrage, *"We consider the elective franchise the dearest privilege of freedom and particularly in this important crisis in the affairs of Texas, we feel ourselves entitled and confidently expect to have a voice in forming a government which will claim our obedience, support and protection. A government which we anxiously hope will restore order out of confusion and chaos, and render Texas what her soil and climate entitles her to be, a prosperous and happy country."*[18]

The over-riding reason for the Declaration of Independence signed by the 54 delegates to the Convention at Washington-on-Brazos was stated to be the failure of the Mexican Government to fulfil its promise to provide Texas with a republican constitution similar to that of the United States; secondly, the subsuming of

Texan welfare into the wider interests of its larger Mexican neighbour, Coahuila province. Freedom of religion, the absence of a public education system and denial of trial by jury were among other grievances. The declaration severed all political connection with Mexico, constituting Texas as a free, sovereign and independent republic, fully invested with all the rights and attributes belonging to independent nations. What input the militia volunteers had in the final declaration, can only be guessed at, although Edward Curran, one of the two delegates from the Peoples Army at Refugio, was a member of the committee responsible for its drafting.[19]

Four days after the Declaration of Independence, the Alamo at San Antonio fell to the army of Santa Anna. Three weeks later the Mexican president ordered the massacre of Fannin's command, after it surrendered at the battle of Coleto Creek. About the only thing that could have saved Travis, Bowie and the 189 defenders besieged in the Alamo was if Fannin had hurried to the relief of the mission, several days march from Goliad where his army of 400 was garrisoned. His indecision delayed all hope of this. Fannin was subsequently blamed by many, not only for the fall of the Alamo, but for the massacre of most of those under his command at Goliad three weeks afterwards.

The importance of the Alamo was that it was one of two fortresses on the two roads leading to Texas from the Mexican interior, the other being at Goliad. By the time Travis replaced the seriously ill Colonel Jim Bowie as commander of the Alamo, it had been heavily fortified, the 68 who remained from the original garrison joined by Bowie's volunteers and Crockett's Tennessee riflemen. Soon, they would face 1800 of Mexico's most battle-hardened assault troops, their only real hope if Fannin mounted a rescue mission from Goliad, some ninety miles south-east.

Fannin dithered, neither destroying Goliad and retreating to the Guadalupe River as Houston had ordered, nor marching to relieve the Alamo, which the Commander-in-Chief knew was what the Goliad garrison most wanted. Efforts to persuade Fannin to leave for the Alamo almost succeeded, the army setting out but getting no further than the bank of the San Antonio River before being ordered to return. By March 6 it was too late, the Alamo falling on the thirteenth day of the siege. After the walls had been breached by Santa Anna's artillery his troops stormed the fortress. It was all over in ninety minutes. Travis was among the first to die. Jim Bowie, ravaged by illness, was shot in his sick bed. Crockett, among the seven who survived the initial onslaught, was executed. Only several non-combatant women, children and slaves were spared. In letters a few days previously, Travis complained that he had lost faith in Fannin and also with the revolution's political and military leadership: *"If my countrymen do not rally to my relief, I am determined to perish in the defence of this place, and my bones shall reproach my country for her neglect."* [20] Certainly the Greys held Fannin responsible for a disaster in which many of their comrades perished. What they did not know at that time was that very soon most of those that remained would be led to their deaths when Fannin finally gave the order to abandon Goliad. If *"Remember the Alamo"* was to become an exhortation to bravery for Americans on battlefields all over the world, *"Remember Goliad"* would resonate as one of the greatest war crimes of the 19th century.

On December 30, 1835, Santa Anna had obtained from the Mexican Congress a decree to the effect that all foreigners taking up arms against the government should be treated as pirates and shot. That was why Crockett and the handful survivors of the initial assault on the Alamo were executed. Texas was considered still part of Mexico. When the 400 volunteers commanded by Fannin abandoned Goliad on March 19, they knew what to expect if captured, although their main adversary General Jose de Urrea, now in hot pursuit, had no stomach for summary executions. The retreating garrison was soon in trouble, a cart breaking down as the column crossed the San Antonio River, the largest of its cannon falling into the water. This incident sufficiently delayed Fannin and his men, for Urrea's advancing cavalry to prevent the Texans from reaching cover amongst the timber along Coleto Creek. Caught in a shallow depression some six feet below the level prairie, and with no time to reach higher ground, Fannin called a council of war, which was still discussing what action to take when Urrea attacked. In their exposed position on the open, gently undulating prairie with no cover but the tall grass, the Texans formed a hollow square, three ranks deep, each man armed with three or four muskets, Rees and the San Antonio (formerly

New Orleans) Greys, on the front line. The Greys, the most experienced of Fannin's army, took the brunt of the Mexican fire but succeeded in repulsing three separate assaults by the Mexicans. One of the Greys, a young German, Herman Ehrenberg, later described the scene as *"dreadful to behold."* [21]

"Killed and maimed men and horses were strewn over the plain," he wrote. *"The wounded were rending the air with their distressing moans. . . . Herds of horses were running about without riders, while others were wallowing in blood and kicking about furiously . . . the countless bugles of the Mexicans from all directions sounded for the attack. The cavalry itself rapidly advanced from all sides at once, not in closed ranks but in broken formation and with yelling and constant firing. . . . We were soon enveloped in such dense smoke that we were occasionally obliged to cease firing and to advance slightly on the enemy in order to see our sights. The whole prairie as far as one could see was covered with powder smoke and thousands of lightning flashes quivered through the dark masses accompanied with the incessant thunder of the artillery and the clear crack of our rifles. . . . Many of our people were either severely wounded or killed. All our artillerymen with the exception of one Pole had fallen and formed a wall around the now silent cannon, which were no longer effective as the range was now too close."* [22]

When even this onslaught failed, Urrea sent sharpshooters into the tall grass to snipe at the Texans, inflicting further casualties among the defenders, until they were silenced by Texan sharpshooters firing at the flashes in the darkness. During the night, a shortage of water and the inability to light fires made it difficult to treat the wounded. The night then turned wet, a cold wind blowing in across the prairie. With ammunition low and little artillery support, the Texans knew they could not sustain another assault. The able bodied could have probably reached the Coleto timberline under cover of darkness but rather than abandon their wounded, they dug trenches and erected barricades of carts and dead animals in preparation for the next day's final battle. During the night, Urrea was reinforced by fresh troops and artillery, positioning these on the slopes overlooking the Texan position. At daybreak on March 20, the first artillery round fired by the Mexicans convinced Fannin their situation was hopeless. His troops then sent him out to negotiate what they believed was an honourable surrender, on condition they would be returned to the United States. But the surrender document, which Fannin signed without revealing its terms to his troops, had stated they would be *"subject to the disposition of the supreme government."*

Those prisoners able to walk were marched back to the fortress at Goliad. The wounded, among them Fannin, were left on the battlefield for two to three days before they were also imprisoned in *Fort Defiance,* as it was known to the Texans. Surrounded by a collection of miserable Mexican *adobes,* the fort stood above the San Antonio River, beneath it a brilliant white sandstone escarpment through which floodwater had cut deep furrows. Behind the fort's seven-foot thick walls were the ruins of an old church, and it was here the majority of the captured Texans were imprisoned, packed so tightly together many could only sleep standing up. After two nights in this dungeon without food and water, the Mexicans slaughtered some steers, the prisoners having to eat the meat raw. General Urrea sought clemency for the Texans, but with his mandate from the Mexican Congress, Santa Anna on March 23 ordered the execution of the *"perfidious foreigners."* Suspecting General Urrea might not comply with this, Santa Anna instructed the commanding officer at Goliad, Col Jose Nicolas de la Portilla, to execute the prisoners. After wrestling with his conscience overnight, Portilla formed the 360 able bodied Texans into three groups, marching them on to the prairie at dawn on Palm Sunday, March 27. The Texans had no idea what awaited them: some thought they were being repatriated, heading for the Gulf port of Copano and a passage home. So convinced were they, that the previous night the prisoners were heard singing *"Home Sweet Home"* in anticipation of their release. Others among the three columns heading off in different directions across the prairie, escorted on either side by Mexican foot soldiers, believed they were being taken to gather firewood. John Rees and what remained of the Greys formed part of the column heading along the road in the direction of the Texan-occupied town of Victoria. About three quarters of a mile from Goliad, however, each column was halted. The guards quickly formed themselves into a firing squad, raised their rifles, and firing from such close range most of the Texans were killed by the first volley.[23]

The German Herman Ehrenberg, at 18 the youngest member of the New Orleans Greys on that infamous morning, and one of the few to escape, published his first account of the massacre on his return to Germany in 1843:

"Probably a quarter of an hour had passed since we had left the fort, and not a word had passed over our lips nor over those of the enemy. Everyone seemed to have dropped into deep reflections. Suddenly the command of the Mexican sounded to march off to the left from the main road: and as we did not understand the officer led the way himself. My companions in misfortune still carelessly followed the leader. To our left a little five or six feet high mesquite hedge extended straight to the roaring San Antonio River about a thousand yards away, whose clear waves here at right angles pushed their way through bluffs between thirty to forty feet high, which rise practically perpendicularly from the water level on the side. Our feet were directed down the hedge and towards the river. Suddenly the thought seized everyone: 'Where with us in this direction?' This, and several mounted lancers to our right, to whom we had previously given no attention, confused us. And now we noticed that the line of the enemy between us and the hedge had remained behind and was now lining up on the other side so that they formed a double file there. Unable to comprehend this movement, we were still in a maze when a 'Halt!' was commanded in Spanish, which ran through us like a death sentence. At that moment we heard the muffled rolling of the musket volley in the distance. Involuntarily we thought of our companions, who had been separated from us and evidently led off in that direction.

"Astonished and confounded we looked at each other, and cast questioning glances at ourselves and then at the Mexican officers. Only a few of us understood Spanish and could not or would not obey the order. Meanwhile the Mexican soldiers, who were barely three steps away, levelled their muskets at our chests and we found ourselves in terrible surprise. Only one among us spoke Spanish fluently, whose words seemed incomprehensible to him. In doubt he stared at the commanding officer as if he wanted to read a contradiction on his features of what he had heard. The remainder of us fixed our eyes on him to thrust ourselves on the

threatening enemy at the first sound from his lips. But he seemed, as we were, possessed of the unfortunate hope that this order was a naked threat to force us into Mexican service. With threatening gestures and drawn sword the chief of the murderers for the second time commanded in a brusque tone: 'Kneel down!'

"A second volley thundered over to us from another direction, and a confused cry, probably from those who were not immediately killed, accompanied it. This startled our comrades out of their stark astonishment, which had lasted from five or six seconds. New life animated them, their eyes flashed and they cried out: 'Comrades! Listen to that crying, it means our brothers, hear their cry! It is their last one! Here is no more hope – the last hour of the Greys has come! Therefore – Comrades!'

"A terrible crackling interrupted him and then everything was quiet. A thick smoke slowly rolled toward the San Antonio. The blood of my lieutenant was on my clothing and around me quivered my friends. Beside me Mattern and Curtman were fighting death. I did not see more. I jumped up quickly and concealed by the black smoke of the powder, and rushed down the hedge to the river. I heard nothing more and saw nothing. Only the rushing of the water was my guide. Then suddenly a powerful sabre smashed me over the head. Before me the figure of a little Mexican lieutenant appeared out of the dense smoke, and a second blow from him fell on my left arm with which I parried it. I had nothing to risk but only to win. Either life or death! Behind were the bayonets of the murderers, and before me was the sword of a coward that crossed my way to the saving stream. Determinedly I rushed upon him. Forward I must go, and the coward took flight in characteristic Mexican gallantry. Now the path was open . . ."

Reaching the riverbank, Ehrenberg, according to his own account, shouted *"The Republic of Texas forever"* as he threw himself into the water.[24]

The Welshman John Rees was another of only 28 to survive the executions on the prairie. Most of those not instantly killed were pursued through the tall grass, shot or bayoneted. Fannin and forty of the wounded unable to join the death march, were later executed inside the fortress at Goliad, Fannin blindfolded and the last to die. Rees made it to the San Antonio River. A fascinating account of his escape was revealed for the first time in a pension application, made to the Texas War Department by another survivor of the massacre, William Mason. This hitherto undiscovered source confirms that the Rees who enlisted in the New Orleans Greys and was a member of Fannin's command at Goliad was a Welsh speaker known to his comrades as "Jack Rees".

Mason, who served in Duval's Company, describes how they were marched along that same narrow path as Ehrenberg towards the San Antonio River, halted and then were fired upon:

"All that was not shot down broke for the San Antonio River. Some were killed betwixt that and the river and some in the river and some after they had crossed. A man by the name of Rees and myself went through the bushes to the edge of the prairie and there laid down all day. When night came, Rees said he could strike the Guadalupe River below Victoria. We travelled all night and the next morning we found ourselves right in the division of the Mexican Army and they took us the second time. They took us in their camp but would not allow us to be questioned together. Rees told them that he was a Welshman and happened in Texas and they pressed him in the army. They asked me if I wasn't one of Col. Fannin's men that made their escape the day before. I told them I was not."[25]

Ehrenberg corroborates the story, recalling that when he too was re-captured by the Mexicans he was placed in the same company as Rees, and winked at the Welshman as a signal not to show any sign of recognition. The young German was being interrogated when *"without any warning, I was confronted with several Texan prisoners, all of whom with one exception, were unknown to me. That one was Jack Rees, who like me succeeded in escaping the massacre, but who, likewise, was forced to surrender again through lack of food. A wink from me alerted him, and we stared each other in the face like waxwork figures; but our inner joy, at knowing that a comrade had been saved, threatened to destroy the mask we had put on."*[26]

Besides Rees, there were only five other survivors from Pettus Company of New Orleans Greys: William L. Hunter, William

Brenan, Benjamin H. Holland, Milton Irish, and David J. Jones. The last named should not be mistaken for David Jones 'Dai the Tinker', one of the Chartist leaders who along with Rees was never caught. Not much is known about Jones, the Goliad survivor, except that two years to the day he escaped the massacre, March 27, 1838, he was hanged in Houston for murder. Exactly how Rees survived untouched by the first volley, is not clear, but the chances are that he was one of a handful of prisoners who, like Benjamin Holland, another of the six survivors from Pettus Greys Company, suspecting the worse, sprung at the Mexican soldiers moments before they fired, then dashed for the river in the confusion. Or as William Hunter did, Rees may have lay hidden among the bodies of his fallen comrades before crawling off into the tall prairie grass where he met up with Mason.[27]

William Lockhart Hunter had the most incredible escape of all. Born in Virginia in 1809, Hunter joined the Greys with Rees at New Orleans in October 1835. They fought together at San Antonio de Bexar and he was also a signatory of the Convention Memorial. Rees, Hunter, and for that matter, Holland were army comrades, united in battle and survival. Whereas Rees and Holland escaped unscathed from the first volley fired by the Mexicans, Hunter was hit, lying unconscious for some considerable time, his body covered by that of a dead comrade. On regaining consciousness not only had he been shot, clubbed and bayoneted, but stripped of his clothing, except for his undershirt and drawers. Crawling to the river, he hid in the water until nightfall before crossing. Now weak from the loss of blood, Hunter was found by some Mexicans and given food and clothing. Once his strength recovered he was taken to the home of a pioneer widow, Mrs Margaret Wright on the Guadalupe River, hiding there until Santa Anna was finally defeated by Sam Houston at the Battle of San Jacinto.[28] In later life, Hunter became a judge in both Goliad and Refugio counties, also serving in the Congress of the new Republic of Texas. Before that, however, he was involved with Rees, and other veterans from the New Orleans Greys in a series of deceptions to defraud the new republic out of several thousand acres of land.

The Mexicans never swallowed Rees's tall story about being a wandering Welshmen pressed into service by the wicked Texans.

Like many others, he was imprisoned until Houston routed Santa Anna at the decisive battle of San Jacinto three weeks later on April 21, then exchanged for Mexican POWs. By May 6, with the war won and the New Orleans Greys virtually eliminated, Rees enlisted for a second time, joining Captain William Graham's Company of Volunteers based at Navidad Camp on Galveston Island.[29] Two other former members of Fannin's command, William Durham, the Englishman, who missed the massacre being on leave at the time, and Augustus Sharp, from New York, another Goliad survivor, also re-enlisted with Captain Graham whose company had not long arrived from New Orleans where it was mustered into service on April 15. Before reporting for duty, Rees and Sharp took leave, sailing from Galveston to New Orleans arriving on June 22. During the voyage, Rees addressed a letter to the "Auditor of Public Accounts of the Republic of Texas" authorising him to pay William Sawyer, master of the *"Good Hope"*, the value of a draft for $20 to cover the cost of his passage, this, presumably, to be deducted from monies due to him for his army service.[30] The pair were still on leave when the roll was called on July 25. This stated Rees's age as 21, the only occasion throughout his service in Texas and subsequent involvement in the Chartist Uprising there is any mention of his age.

NOTES

1. *Bexar Archives, Barker Texas History Center, University of Texas at Austin. Miles S. Bennet, "The Battle of Gonzales: The 'Lexington' of the Texas Revolution,"* Quarterly of the Texas State Historical Association *2* (April 1899).
2. The first imperial colonisation law was that passed by the *Junta Instituyente,* Emperor Agustín de Iturbide's rump congress, on 3 January 1823. For more detail see: Eugene C. Barker, *Mexico and Texas, 1821-1835* (Dallas: Turner, 1928); Hans Peter Nielsen Gammel, comp., *Laws of Texas, 1822-1897* (Austin, 1898), 10 vols; Mary Virginia Henderson, 'Minor Empresario Contracts for the Colonization of Texas, 1825-1834', *South Western Historical Quarterly,* 31, 32 (April, July 1928).
3. Gammel Laws of Texas, loc cit.; 'Journal of the Permanent Council', *South Western Historical Quarterly,* No. 7, April 1904.
4. Adolphus Sterne Papers, Texas State Archives.
5. *ibid.*

6. Gammel Laws of Texas, loc. cit.
7. For details of recruitment to Revolutionary Army see, 'Texas Revolutionary Army', *Texas Historical Association,* No. 9, April 1906; Paul C. Lack *Texas Revolutionary Experience* (Texas A and M University Press, 1992).
8. Index to Military Rolls of the Republic of Texas, 1835-1845, H. David Maxey.
9. Gary Brown, *New Orleans Greys* (Republic of Texas Press, 1999), p37.
10. *ibid,* p38.
11. John E. Roller, 'Capt. John Sowers Brooks', *Quarterly of the Texas State Historical* Association, No. 9, January 1906.
12. The Austin Papers, ed. Eurgene C.Baker, Washington GPO, 1914-1928.
13. *New Orleans Greys,* loc. cit., Chapter 4.
14. Paul D. Lack, *Texas Revolutionary Experience.*
15. For the Goliad Declaration of Independence, drafted by Ira Ingram, see *A Texas Scrapbook,* comp. Dewitt Clinton Baker, 1875.
16. Brown, *New Orleans Greys,* pp154-159.
17. *ibid,* loc. cit. pp154-159.
18. Convention Memorial, Archives, State Dept., Washington, Memorial No. 36, File Box No. 93, Letter No. V, Feb. 1836.
19. Texas Declaration of Independence, *South Western Historical Review,* Nos. 30, 31, April, July 1927.
20. John H. Jenkins ed., *The Papers of the Texas Revolution,* 1835-36 (Austin Presidial Press, 1973).
21. During his lifetime Ehrenberg wrote several accounts of the Battle of Coleto Creek and the Goliad massacre. He named the first (1843) edition of his book, *Texas und seine Revolution.* The 1844 edition was entitled *Der Freiheitskampf in Texas im Jahre 1836,* and the book was published again in 1845 *as Fahrten und Schicksale eines Deutschen in Texas.* In 1925 Edgar William Bartholomae translated the 1845 edition into English as a master's thesis at the University of Texas. *Texas und Seine Revolution* is one of John H. Jenkins's Basic Texas Books.
22. Ehrenberg, *Texas und seine Revolution.*
23. John H. Jenkins ed., *The Papers of the Texas Revolution,* 1835-36 (Austin Presidial Press, 1973).
24. Ehrenberg, *Texas und seine Revolution.*
25. Mason Pension application: Texas State Library and Archives Commission, Republic Claims, micro-film reel 227, frames 424-449.
26. Ehrenberg, *Texas und seine Revolution.*
27. Goliad Survivors: Fannin and His Men (unfinished), Herbert Davenport, 1936.
28. Daughters of the Republic of Texas, 'Founders and Patriots of the Republic of Texas' (Austin, 1963); Austin Book Exchange, *Biographical Directory of the Texan Conventions and Congresses 1832-1845* (1941).
29. H. David Maxey, *Index to Military Rolls of the Republic of Texas, 1835-1845,* provides Captain William Graham's Company muster roll.
30. Texas State Archives, Micro-film Reel 87, frames 224-228 for copy of Rees's draft against army pay. Author's note: *Captain Graham handed*

over command of the company to Captain William Elliott in July 1836. Whether or not Rees returned to Galveston to take up his enlistment with Captain Elliott is unclear although he is on the company's muster roll of August 31, 1836 as enlisting for a year, having enrolled on October 22, 1836. This is obviously an error, Rees having first enrolled in New Orleans on October 13, 1835 and discharged on October 10, 1836. it was a mistake that almost cost Rees dearly when eventually he came to claim his land bounties for service during the Texas War of Independence; Captain William Sawyer's voucher for payment, Reel 126, frames 589, 590.

CHAPTER 5

Land, Land, Land!

Immediately following Houston's victory over Santa Anna at San Jacinto, the new Government of the Republic of Texas acted quickly to deal with a volunteer army, which having defeated a tyrant raised the spectre of military domination. But the war had lasted not seven months and the army's sudden military success helped curb the radical tide, by limiting its needs and therefore the potential for revolution.

Almost the first thing that Houston did was to encourage volunteers to take unlimited leave, in the hope most would never return. Next, the Senate meeting at the provisional capital, Columbia, in November 1836 codified army regulations, making offences of some of the prevailing abuses. Being absent without leave became a court martial offence. Taking booty was outlawed. After Santa Anna's defeat at San Jacinto, volunteers had abandoned their positions to plunder the Mexican general's Treasury. In future, even the indiscriminate firing of weapons, a favourite pastime of soldiers to relieve the boredom, and spontaneous beating of drums would be prohibited. As for anyone engaging in seditious activities, the penalty could be execution. Informers were duty bound to expose troublemakers, as every effort was made to tame the army's revolutionary tendencies.[1]

A tented settlement sprung up at Columbia to accommodate the veterans awaiting discharge, and a herd of steers driven in and slaughtered to feed them. The army that defeated the might of Mexico was not as large as might have been expected: only 3,685 had, at any time, served in the People's Army, 40 per cent of these foreigners. Enlisted men were paid twenty dollars a month and promised free land. Because the new Republic of Texas had only $55 and 68 cents in its Treasury, those lining up for discharge were paid not in cash but drafts, promissory notes, bits of paper guaranteeing payment for their services at some future date. The republic was, however, land rich, the very first Congress passing an Act fixing its western boundary along the line of the Rio Grande all the way to the river's source, and then further north again to the 42nd parallel. At a stroke, the Republic seized 350,000 square miles, including eastern New Mexico, and parts of Colorado, Oklahoma, Kansas to add to Texas, all of it once the sovereign territory of Mexico.

On October 15, 1836, five days after his discharge, Rees was at Columbia collecting a draft for $142 and six cents from the Auditor of the Texas Republic, Asa Brigham. This included $30 compensation for the rifle, given him by Sterne in New Orleans, and surrendered to the Mexicans after the Battle of Coleto Creek. The remainder would have been his pay for military service, roughly six months at $20 a month. Two old army colleagues, William Hunter, now recovered from the wounds suffered escaping the Goliad Massacre, and William Brenan, another of the 28 survivors, testified his claim for the rifle was genuine.[2] Not surprisingly, the discharge of volunteers was something of a veterans' reunion, for besides Hunter, Brenan and Sharp, all Goliad survivors, also present were James Welsh and R. Reed. Both members of Fannin's command, they were fortunate to be on leave at the time of the Goliad Massacre. While in Columbia, Welsh, 6ft 8 inches tall and a former blacksmith, deposited with a lawyer for safe keeping four pieces of land scrip, one of these the property of John Rees, on whose behalf he and Reed claimed to exercise power of attorney. Shortly afterwards this scrip became a negotiable security exchangeable for land at 50 cents an acre.[3]

Almost the first thing the Congress did was to begin the process of converting its huge public domain into hard cash, by issuing land scrip for sale in the United States and Europe to pay off the national debt. It also set about fulfilling its pledge to reward the volunteers of the People's Army with land grants. Besides scrip, which was used for many purposes, the Republic issued three other types of land grant: headright grants made to colonists as an inducement to either settle or remain in Texas during the war; Bounty Warrants as a reward for service for those enlisting in the War of Independence; and Donation Certificates. The last were also known as "battle donations," 640 acres of land promised to soldiers out of gratitude and appreciation for the services they had rendered. Those qualifying for the Donation Certificate included all who fought at the Siege of Bexar de San Antonio (the first Battle of the Alamo) from December 5-10, 1835. In addition to this, Rees was also able to claim a Bounty Warrant for serving in the Army of the Republic from October 1835 until his discharge after the defeat of Santa Anna.[4]

At the end of the Texas War of Independence in April 1836, Rees was entitled under an Act of the Convention passed on March 14 to a Bounty Warrant of 960 acres for the nine months he had served from October 22, 1835 to October 10, 1836. According to Ivor Wilks in his article for the *Welsh History Review* he queried this, claiming a later discharge date, October 29, which qualified him for the larger entitlement of 1280 acres for twelve months service.[5] Without waiting for this to be resolved, however, and within five days of his discharge from the army, Rees assigned his rights to the 960 acres to Griffin Bayne on October 15, 1836. Even though no warrant for this land was issued until January 5, 1838, Rees was permitted to sell or barter his rights to it in advance. In this case his assignment document lodged in the Texas General Land Office states, *"I transfer the within claim to Griffin Bayne for value received, Witness my hand and seal this 15th day of October 1836,"* signed *John Reese*. The Texas War Department's Chief Clerk, Charles Mason, testified the assignment was *"a true copy of the origin at transfer which is now on file in the War department."*[6]

As many as 50 per cent of Bounty warrants were treated as negotiable instruments to be sold, bartered, exchanged, or willed as soon as they were issued. But rights were rarely traded, as in this instance, *before* the issuance of a warrant, Ivor Wilks concluding from this that Rees was in a hurry to cash in his assets, leave Texas, and return to Wales, there to involve himself three years later as a leader of the Chartist Uprising.[7] This would be difficult to challenge if it were the only Texas land-deal in which Rees was involved. What I have discovered is a series of transactions involving a man named Rees (or Reese), together with sufficient circumstantial evidence, to place him in Texas in December 1838, less than a year before the Uprising in Monmouthshire. All this assumes that the John Rees of Texas 1835-1838 was the same Rees who led the Chartist attack on the Westgate Hotel. On balance, the evidence suggests it was. Not only did his experience of "wars in foreign parts" qualify him for leadership, but a hitherto undiscovered account of his escape to America after the Uprising in which he mentions his plans to return to Texas provides further confirmation that this was one and the same man.[8]

No record survives of how much Rees was paid for selling his Bounty Warrant entitlement to Griffin Bayne. Republic land was then changing hands for twenty-five cents an acre, so at the very most he would have received $240. If this was as Wilks suggests John Rees's fare home to Wales, then for the next two years he had an impostor in Texas conspiring with his former army comrades in a scheme to defraud the Republic of thousands of acres of land. After following the 'land trail', and investigating other soldiers of the same or similar names, also entitled to Bounty land, I remain convinced there was no impostor; that John Rees, alias 'Jack the Fifer' was implicated in the frauds.[9]

Fraud and land were synonymous in Texas. The favourite ploy was for a discharged soldier to claim his Bounty Warrant twice, in different Texas counties. The fraud was not difficult to perpetrate in a fledgling Republic whose first Congress in 1836 established 23 counties, all of which were sparsely populated and poorly administered. Rather than wait for the 960 acres he had been granted in Milam County, to be adjusted in line with his later discharge date, he assigned it immediately to Griffin Bayne, then submitted a new claim, this time in Refugio County, for another 1,280 acres for the same period of service.[10] By the time the warrant for this was issued in 1838, Rees had already assigned his rights to the land to James Welsh and J. N. Reed, both of whom had served with him in Fannin's command. No transfer document can be found in the Texas General Land Office for this transaction. All that can be said is that Rees disposed of this fraudulent claim to Welsh and Reed on or before November 26, 1838, the date the warrant was issued to Welsh and Reed. The two men would have needed to satisfy the Texas General Land Office the transfer from Rees had taken place.[11] Wilks, in his essay for the *Welsh History Review*, is mistaken in believing that this second application from Rees was nothing more than redress for the original mistake over his discharge date. There is not a scrap of evidence he asked his former commanding officer in the New Orleans Greys, William Cook, by then acting Secretary of War, or anyone else, to correct the error.[12] The second Bounty Warrant was not issued to Rees to correct an administrative error; it was issued as a direct result of a fraudulent claim.

There is no way of knowing what Rees received for the sale of his rights to 1,280 acres of land in Refugio County to which Welsh and Reed, as his assignees, became entitled when they bought his fraudulent warrant. It is not likely to have been more than $160 because a year later Reed assigned his share to his partner Welsh for $80. The chances of the fraud ever being detected were also remote after a fire in the Texas War Department and Texas Adjutant General's Office in 1855 destroyed the records of all Bounty Warrants, Donation Certificates, and military service records. Also lost were muster rolls and army papers, proving the entitlement of Texas Revolutionary Army veterans to public land. The fire was almost certainly started deliberately by those involved in fraudulent land transactions. But the Rees fraud was detected in 1860. Concerned about its dwindling public domain, the Republic established a Court of Claims to investigate illegal claims by checking land grants against the only surviving record – the surveys returned to the Texas General Land Office before the land was patented, or transferred from the public domain into private ownership.[13]

When Commissioner W. S. Hotchkiss examined the second Rees Bounty claim in 1860 he rejected it, writing across the warrant, "*a claim of 960 acres in the same name – for part of the same service – commencing at the same time – returned to the GLO* (General Land Office) *and patented.*"[14] The fraud was detected only because the 960 acres Rees had legitimately assigned to Griffin Bayne in October 1836, on his discharge from the Revolutionary Army, had by then been surveyed and final title (patent) to the land located in Erath County issued to Bayne. It might have been expected the affair was at an end when the Court of Claims declared the second warrant a fraud, both having been granted to the same John Rees. But thirteen years later, the warrant rejected by Commissioner Hotchkiss in 1860 re-appeared, in the possession of Benjamin C. Franklin. Appealing to the State Legislature against its earlier rejection, Franklin criticised Commissioner Hotchkiss for ignoring the possibility of the existence of two John Rees's, both with similar service records, and, accordingly, both genuinely entitled to Bounty Warrants. Even if they were one and the same person, declared Franklin, he was the *"innocent purchaser"* of the second warrant and should not be penalised. The State Legislature agreed with this, approving an "Act for the Relief of Benjamin C. Franklin" on June 4, 1873. Title to the disputed 1280 acres of land in Refugio County finally passed to Franklin and his heirs on January 14, 1876.[15]

Surveying and patenting were the final stages in transferring the ownership of Republic land to settlers and volunteers. The owner of the warrant selected his land from the vacant and unappropriated public domain. The warrant was then presented to a duly licensed surveyor to make the survey, and attach field notes describing the tract and showing its position on the county map in relation to older surveys. This was then forwarded to the General Land Office in Austin, and the patent was issued, formally transferring ownership of the land out of the sovereignty of Texas. While the patent always recorded the name of the grantee, whether soldier or settler to whom the warrant was originally issued, it was not necessary for that individual to settle the land. All that was required was for any transfer to be properly witnessed, usually by the chief justice of the county. Some of these transfers were scribbled on the back of warrants, others executed on separate forms.

The significance of Rees's next two land deals is that they place him (or his impostor) still in Texas in February and June 1838. In line with the promises made by General Sam Houston, headright grants were offered as an inducement to new settlers during the struggle for independence. The more settled and developed the area, the greater the value of the lands, and the more tax revenue for the new republic. Without population, Texas would remain a wilderness. All those who arrived before March 2, 1836 were entitled to claim a first-class headright certificate issued in the counties where the applicants resided. John Rees qualified having arrived in Texas with the New Orleans Greys in October 1835. The entitlement for a single man was one third of a league, 1461 acres. To claim this, Rees was required to appear *personally* before the County Board of Land Commissioners and swear the following oath:

"I, John Rees, do solemnly swear, that I was a resident citizen of Texas at the date of the declaration of independence, that I did not leave the country during the campaigns of the spring of 1836, to avoid a participation in the struggle, that I did not refuse to participate in the war, and that I did not aid or assist the enemy, that I have not previously received a title to any quantum of land, and that I conceive myself justly entitled, under the Constitution and the Laws to the quantity of land for which I now apply." [16]

In addition, Rees needed to produce two credible witnesses to prove he was in Texas at the time stated. Once approved by the board, he paid $5 for the certificate, the fee shared between the clerk and board members. There were four categories of headright certificate, the most important first-class, the significant difference between this and the others that the grantee did not need to homestead the land: in short, as with Bounty Warrants, it was a negotiable security.

Rees (again spelt Reese) appeared before the Board of Land Commissioners in Brazoria County to apply on February 1, 1838 for his first-class headright certificate. The clerk recorded that D. Gallaher and William T. Austin testified to Rees's presence in Texas prior to March 2, 1836. A few months before Rees's application was heard, William Austin was the Brazoria County Clerk, and is named as a witness by several applicants before the Land Commissioners that day. He clearly had a vested interest in proceedings, a number of applicants having already assigned their headright claims to him. As for Rees's second witness, D. Gallaher, it was almost certainly an assumed name because Dominic Gallagher was one of Fannin's command massacred at Goliad. Two months before John Rees appeared before the Land Commissioners in Brazoria he had sold his rights to Andrew Robinson for $500, agreeing to be bound over by Robinson for a further $1000 to deliver title to the land. That transfer was also witnessed by Gallaher and Austin. [17]

Rees's application for his headright entitlement of 1461 acres was approved by the Commissioners and the deal with Robinson settled. On the schedule of approved certificates, May 2, 1835 is given as the date of Rees's emigration to Texas although John

Rees of the New Orleans Greys did not arrive until the October. But the same date is given for every settler appearing before the Brazoria Board that day, probably agreed upon arbitrarily by the Land Commissioners who were often dealing with their friends and neighbours and found it hard to reject what they suspected were fraudulent applications. The first Texas Government Land Commissioner, John P. Borden, who served during this period, 1837-1840, was told by one County Commissioner when he began his investigations into fraud, *"Now, Sir, please imagine to yourself a board crowded with near 200 applicants on the first day of the opening of the Land Office and on subsequent days from 50 to 100 . . ."* Fraud was so widespread that Borden reported in 1839 that anyone holding fewer than ten headright grant certificates was *"considered a small operator in this line."*[18] That there was widespread indifference to this plundering of the new Republic's public domain, and that whatever fraud was detected was only by accident, is hardly surprising. Not only was this a new nation with all the administrative imperfections that inevitably entailed, but Texas was still in the dawn of Anglo-European colonisation. The whole of Brazoria County, an area three times the size of Monmouthshire, had a population of fewer than 1600 whites with perhaps twice as many black slaves. A typical Southern slave-based society, the banks along the rivers and creeks were lined with prosperous sugar and cotton plantations, soon to make the county the wealthiest in Texas. One hundred years later it became even richer, producing 30 million barrels of oil a year.[19] None of this would have been in any way apparent to the veterans of the Texas War of Independence, scrambling to submit their fake claims to the Land Commissioners at Brazoria. What they saw was a humid, sub-tropical prairie of prime farmland spread along the Gulf Coast, too much of it monopolised, they probably thought, by wealthy plantation owners who never lifted a finger during the War of Independence. Very soon, however, the Texas Congress was compelled to act to prevent the public domain from being depleted by fraud, and in 1840 approved "An Act to Detect Fraudulent Warrants."[20]

Rees and his pals were again waiting in the queue when a Land Office opened in Harrisburg County (now Harris) on June 6, 1838, to process applications. Michael Cronican and William Durham, both of whom also served with Rees in the New Orleans Greys, witnessed the filing of his claim for another first-class headright certificate for 1476 acres, on this occasion testifying correctly that Rees arrived in Texas in October 1835 and that afterwards had participated in the battle for San Antonio de Bexar. Before enlisting in the People's Army, Cronican was a newspaperman from Boston, Massachusetts. Afterwards he founded two Texan newspapers before dying in a cholera epidemic. Durham was an Englishman from Norfolk whose family migrated to the United States. Settling in New York, Durham joined the Greys at the same time as Rees, and was promoted sergeant at San Antonio. Awarded 1280 acres for his military service, he died from yellow fever in Houston two months after witnessing Rees's latest fraudulent claim. Cronican, Durham and Rees served together for the duration of the war, alongside William Lockhart Hunter, the man to whom Rees immediately assigned this latest land acquisition. Not only was Hunter one of the most celebrated of the Goliad survivors, he was chief justice of neighbouring Goliad County, good enough reason why the Harrisburg Commissioners never probed too deeply this bogus claim. The land surveyed on Hunter's behalf two months later (August 30, 1838) was on the San Antonio River, six miles below the town of Goliad. Significantly, Hunter is referred to in the survey notes as being the "assignee of John Rees." For once his name is spelled correctly, perhaps a sign Hunter was more familiar with the successful applicant than the Land Commissioners who on the certificate they issued spelled it "Reese." Although the claim was validated in 1842 by a Board of Commissioners set up to detect bogus applicants and forged certificates, Hunter who served on four of the Republic of Texas Congresses, never patented the land. By June 1858 it was too late, the Court of Claims declaring the certificate void after discovering Rees had claimed twice.[21] Today three quarters of what is now Harris County is covered by the sprawling metropolis of Houston and thirty satellite towns.

The land scam involving Rees and his comrades would seem to be too protracted for the central figure, John Rees (or Reese), to have been an impostor. Further research might show those associated with the Welshman made similar bogus claims, these in turn supported by other army veterans. Apart from this clear evidence of his implication in what appears to have been a widely accepted racket, to which for some time at least the authorities turned a blind eye, the dates of his various applications, both legitimate and false, locate Rees, the Chartist leader, in Texas in the middle of 1838. There is even further evidence placing him in Texas as late as December 1838, less than a year before the Chartist Uprising of November 1839. If this were the case, as my investigations show, how did he manage to assume such prominence in the Chartist movement? After Frost, Williams and Jones were rounded up, John Rees became the "most wanted" man in Britain, believed by some to be the real leader of the Welsh rebellion. The Monmouthshire magistrates certainly rated his apprehension a top priority, and were to despatch police constables far and wide in their search for him.

If it is accepted on the balance of evidence that the John Rees in Texas was the man who later was to lead the attack on the Westgate, then the dates of his various land grant applications are hugely significant. Applicants for headright grants were required to appear before the Land Commissioners in person, and the Harrisburg County Clerk recorded in June 1838 that "John Reese personally appears." The significance of this dissolves, however, if there was a bogus Rees at large in Texas, invented by former comrades to plunder the Republic of its public lands, confident their deception would not be detected because Rees had returned to Wales. They would have justified what was generally regarded as daylight robbery, by the sense of alienation felt by the still largely penniless veterans of the People's Army. Privately, the provisional President, David Burnett, regarded the volunteers as *"an unprofitable tribe of adventurers"* and with his conservative supporters wanted to renege on the land grants in order to keep the public domain intact for entrepreneurial exploitation.[22] At the end of the war, the palatial mansions of the plantation owners still lined the banks of the Brazos River, untouched by the revolution, their owners and their fortunes still in place.

But Rees had one more reward to collect for his military service. This is the last piece in the jigsaw, the final piece of evidence placing him still in Texas in December 1838. The Congress of the Republic on December 21, 1837 approved an Act rewarding every soldier engaged in the siege of San Antonio de Bexar, the first battle for the Alamo, with a Donation Certificate for 640 acres of land.[23] Also included was a similar provision for all those men in the action under Fannin at Coleto Creek, which culminated in the Goliad Massacre. A soldier who participated in both engagements was allowed, however, to claim only once. To receive his grant a soldier needed to produce for the Secretary of War a certificate signed by the commandant of the company to which he belonged and countersigned by at least one field officer, accompanied by an affidavit from the claimant to the effect his claim was just, true and original, and that he had never presented such a claim before.[24] The procedure was far more fraud-proof than previously, and although the supporting evidence for Rees's claim was probably lost in the fire at the Texas Adjutant General's Office, it must have existed otherwise his certificate would never have been issued. Significantly, unlike the Bounty Warrants for length of military service, and headright grants for settlers, both of which were transferable, recipients of Donation Certificates were not permitted to sell or mortgage their land *"during the lifetime of the recipient."*[25]

Ivor Wilks asserts that Rees returned to Wales immediately following the end of the Texas War of Independence in 1836 and, consequently, would not have known of his entitlement for *"having fought bravely at Bexar"* because the award of Donation land was not approved until the Act of Congress in December 1837. In the circumstances, he, therefore, concludes Rees could not have applied for his award until he returned to America *after* the Chartist Uprising.[26] My research has shown that Rees (or, possibly, an impostor) was in Texas "personally" filing claims for headright grants in February and June of 1838, by which time he would have certainly known, if only from his association with his old army comrades, that the Congress had agreed in December 1837 to make donation awards to Bexar veterans.

The Donation Certificate issued in the name of Rees was dated December 20, 1838, according to Thomas Lloyd Miller in *"Bounty and Donation Land Grants of Texas 1835-1888."* Miller is considered the leading authority on Texas Republic land claims. While the date on the original certificate in the archives of the General Land Office in Austin is illegible, Miller has confirmed it from other sources in the National Archives in Washington. This places Rees still in Texas at the end of 1838, two years after Ivor

Wilks says he returned to Wales, and only ten months before the Chartist attack on the Westgate Hotel.

The 640 acres to which Rees became entitled were located in Travis County on Hampton Creek where it runs into the Pecan Bayou, about seven miles above the confluence with the Colorado River. The patent, the document formally transferring the land, was completed on March 14, 1853. But the recipient was not Rees. It was more likely to have been a *"Mr Brown,"* to whom the General Land Office delivered the file on March 15, the day after it issued the patent for the transfer of this allotment of public land into private ownership. By this time Rees had no involvement whatsoever in the land on Hampton Creek, and certainly did not homestead it, as some have suggested. The confusion has arisen because land awarded by Donation Certificates was patented in the name of original grantee, irrespective of whether the grantee, in this case Rees, was ever on the land, alive, even in Texas at the time. Many grantees conveyed their land by deed before a patent was ever issued and those conveyances were never filed with the General Land Office. Certificates changed hands often, especially after March 2, 1848 when the prohibition on the sale or transfer of Donation Certificates was lifted.[27] As will be seen from Chapter 10, the Rees Donation Certificate was widely travelled!

Before 1848, a Donation Certificate, unlike other rewards for military service and settler land grants, was not negotiable, the grantee prevented from selling it, even giving it away. All Rees could have done in 1838 was select land somewhere in Texas, have it surveyed, then patented to himself for homesteading. Evidently the Welshman had no intention of farming in Texas. His final reward for services, the non-negotiable Donation Certificate, was consequently a worthless piece of paper to be folded up and tucked away in a back pocket, which is exactly what he did. Perhaps, on occasions, he showed it to friends in Wales as evidence of his Texan adventure and proof of his military experience, potentially an invaluable asset as the Monmouthshire Chartists prepared for the Uprising. But above all else, this tattered certificate with its missing pieces, not only placed Rees, crucially, in the United States as late as the beginning of 1839, it also provides a vital clue to what became of him when he fled Wales in the aftermath of the failed attack on the Westgate Hotel in Newport.[28]

NOTES

1. Hans Peter Nielsen Gammel, comp., *Laws of Texas, 1822-1897* (Austin, 1898), 10 vols; John H. Jenkins, ed., *The Papers of the Texas Revolution, 1835-1836* (Austin, 1973, Presidial Press); Joseph Milton Nance, *After San Jacinto: The Texas-Mexican Frontier, 1836-1841* (Austin, 1963, University of Texas Press).

2. Texas State Archives, John Rees, draft 670, Micro-film Reel 87, frames 224-228.

3. Texas State Archives, James Welsh, Claim Reel 112, Frame 274.

4. Gammel, *The Laws of Texas*, I, p925, p951, p953.

5. Wilks, 'Insurrection in Texas and Wales: the careers of John Rees', *Welsh History Review*, 11,1 (1982), p78.

6. Bounty Grant 1612, Milam County, issued 5 January 1838, Texas General Land Office.

7. Wilks, loc. cit, p 75-78, p 87-88.

8. NLW, Rees letters from United States, *Cambrian*, 28 February 1844.

9. A John Reese served in the Revolutionary Army from 6 March 1836, the day the Alamo fell, until 7 June 1836, for which he received Bounty Warrant 2390 for 320 acres, dated 15 February 1838. On 1 March 1859, 213.33 Acres of this award was patented to him in Montague County, Patent 295, Vol. 7, Abstract 629, GLO File 745. This Reese was also issued with duplicate Bounty Warrant 607, GLO file 1057, for 320 acres in Jones County on 31 January 1850 for the same period of service but the warrant was not patented, after it was rejected by the Commissioner of the Court of Claims, because the original warrant had been used. This was further evidence fraudulent claims were widespread.

10. Bounty Grant 4456, Refugio County, issued 26 November 1838, Texas General Land Office.

11. John Molleston, Information Specialist, Archives and Records, Texas General Land Office.

12. Wilks, loc. cit. p78.

13. Thomas Lloyd Miller, *Bounty and Donation Land Grants of Texas 1835-1888*, Chapter 5, pp47-53; also warrant 4456, loc. cit.

14. Bounty Grant 4456, Refugio County, issued 26 November 1838, Texas General Land Office.

15. Benjamin C.Franklin, Petition to Texas State Legislature, concerning Warrant 4456, Texas State Archives.

16. Thomas Lloyd Miller *The Public Lands of Texas 1519-1970*, p32.

17. Headright Grant 250, Brazoria, issued 1 February 1838, Texas General Land Office.

18. Miller, *The Public lands of Texas,* loc. cit p33.

19. *History of Brazoria County* (1940); *Brazospot Facts,* June, 1964.

20. Thomas Lloyd Miller, *Bounty and Donation Land Grants of Texas, 1835-1888,* pp32-33.

21. Headright Grant 552, Harrisburg, issued 6 June, 1838, Texas General Land Office.

22. Paul C. Lack, *Texas Revolutionary Experience*.
23. Gammel, *The Laws of Texas*, I, 1450-1451.
24. *ibid*, pp1450-1451.
25. *ibid*.
26. Donation Certificate 266, issued 20 December 1838; Wilks, loc. cit. p88.
27. Wilks, loc. cit. p88; John Molleston, Information Specialist, Archives and Records, Texas General Land Office; Miller, *Military Land Grant Legislation*, Chapter 2, p32.
28. Miller, *Bounty and Donation Land Grants of Texas, 1835-1888*, pp42-43; Rees Donation Certificate 266.

CHAPTER 6

Men from the Hills

Not one of the 236 depositions taken by the magistrates in the aftermath of the attack on the Westgate Hotel, or any of the 36 witnesses called at the trials, mentions John Rees as being involved in the preparations for the Uprising. Besides Oliver Jones's claim that Rees worked at the Tredegar Ironworks after *"wars in foreign parts,"* the only evidence of his return from America by the spring of 1839 is a single entry in Welsh, in the diary kept by the Tredegar newsagent and scholar John Davies (Brychan), who counted among his friends 'Jack the Fifer,' and John Thomas, former clerk to Zephaniah Williams and Merthyr co-editor of *The Workman.*[1] Davies was closely associated with the Merthyr intellectuals and the Welsh scholars who met regularly at the Ancient Druid public house at Hollybush in the Sirhowy Valley. His diary entry for April 24, 1839 notes he had *"bailed out John Rees from Tytywyll at Rhymney."* Tytywyll was the 'Dark House', the lock-up attached to the Rhymney Iron-works, which like other works employed its own constables. If this was the Chartist John Rees then was his incarceration connected in any way with an intriguing diary entry Davies had for the previous day, April 23, when he notes visiting Nantyglo to hear the English Chartist leader Henry Vincent speak?[2] This had been one of Vincent's last speeches before he and the fiery New-port baker William Edwards, with two others, William Townsend, the wine merchant's son, and John Dickensen were arrested and gaoled for between six and twelve months for attending illegal meetings.[3] The gaoling in August of four men who were regarded, certainly in Monmouthshire, as standard bearers for electoral re-form was critical in propelling the Monmouthshire Chartists towards revolt.

Despite the disappointment of the 1832 Electoral Reform Act, the demand for universal suffrage had not gone away, just stalled, and it would be only a matter of time before public discontent focussed on some other vehicle for procuring a more broadly based and just democracy. The working classes had given massive support to the middle-class campaign for the 1832 Reform Act, but it had failed to enfranchise them. Since then, the 1833 Factory Act had regulated child labour but not adult hours, an amendment to the Poor Law treated poverty as a crime, committing entire families to the workhouses, the 'poor law bastilles,' while the failure of the trades unions, after the trail of the Tolpuddle Martyrs, resulted in an increasing number of workers being forced into signing contracts prohibiting them from combining to improve pay and conditions. And the inevitable, predicted by Morgan Williams and John Thomas in *The Workman* five years earlier, had happened: the harvests were disastrous, a recession in trade followed, and so did widespread public unrest. The Chartist Movement burst upon this scene in May 1838 with the People's Charter and its famous six points. From that winter, the movement spread like wildfire through the Glamorgan and Monmouthshire valleys, Zephaniah Williams claiming that by the time of the Uprising there were fifty branches with 50,000 members.[4] Even after allowing for the exaggeration political movements are prone to make, it was an unbelievable organisational feat, especially in view of the short time the Chartists had to organise Valley communities, isolated from mainstream political activity, and whose communications were primitive. The workers did, however, have their Chartist newspapers, Henry Vincent's *Western Vindicator* launched in February 1839 and published in Bristol, and Fergus O'Connor's *Northern Star,* both of which were widely read in public houses and beer shops across the district. Not surprisingly, the Chartists functioned largely as independent cells, the difficulty in co-ordinating activities accounting for a great deal of the confusion and factionalism that ended with the massacre at Newport and was eventually to lead to the movement's collapse. Unlike English Chartist branches recruiting mostly from the ranks of the craft unions, those in South Wales were more representative of the labouring classes.

The first Welsh branches were probably Newport, Merthyr, and Newtown. At Newport, the radical printer Samuel Etheridge was the first treasurer. By Christmas 1838 the Merthyr Workingmen's Association, formed that October with Morgan Williams as its secretary, was strong enough to organise several thousand members for a march from Merthyr to Penyrheol in support of the Charter. This was quickly followed by the election of John Frost as the South Wales delegate to the inaugural meeting of the National Convention in London on 4 February.[5] The Convention was the Chartist 'parliament' and executive, some members even placing MC (Member of the Convention) after their names, a silly idea not imitated by Frost who was content to describe himself as *"a reformer for twenty years."*[6]

Zephaniah Williams is first mentioned as speaking to a thousand Chartists of the Blaina Branch of the Workingmen's Association on the hillside behind the *Royal Oak,* on March 31, 1839, only the day after he walked free from Monmouth Assizes following the Cwrt-y-Bella Colliery break-in and sabotage.[7] At this meeting he is described by the Newport baker William Edwards as *"one of the best Chartists"* he had met.[8] While the *Royal Oak* at Coalbrookvale, Blaina, undoubtedly became a Chartist headquarters, nothing is known of any activity there before March. The significance of this is that not only does it reduce further the time the Chartist leadership had for conspiring together, it also reflects upon the extent of Zephaniah's involvement and the validity of his later 'confession' to participating in a revolution to overthrow the monarchy and establish a Republic of England (never any mention of Wales). Whatever he may have been accused of doing and saying, as far as can be seen much of it must have been behind the scenes, because there is only one recorded instance of Zephaniah having entered the public debate raging over Chartism, when he wrote to the *Silurian,* in response to attacks made upon him at an anti-chartist meeting at Coalbrookvale organised by Crawshay Bailey on April 29. Among his critics on that occasion was the Rev. Benjamin Williams, the same dissenting minister with whom he had a public spat eight years earlier, and his target was much the same: Zephaniah's deism. To this Williams retorted that his difficulty in accepting the Revelation did not invalidate his argument for universal suffrage, accusing the employers of deliberately provoking violence.[9] Not even in jittery mid-19th century Monmouthshire could this be read as incitement to riot.

The same could not be said about either the young firebrand Vincent or the veteran political fighter John Frost whose inflammatory speeches and articles in the *Western Vindicator* pushed the Monmouthshire Chartists in the direction, if not of violent revolt, at the very least some kind of attempt to shake the status quo. A charismatic speaker, Vincent, the son of a London goldsmith, was twenty-five years of age, his youth and good looks soon establishing him as the 'darling' of the Monmouthshire Chartists, especially among female supporters who flocked in their hundreds to welcome him, whenever he returned to Newport to drum up support for the Charter in the mining communities.[10] Close on his heels were Government spies gathering the evidence the Whig Government needed to bring charges against him for incitement. The principal 'recruiting officer' for Chartism in Wales and the West Country, Vincent published a diary of his travels in the *Western Vindicator,* in which he calculated that during thirteen months campaigning on behalf of Chartism he had spoken two hours a day and travelled 6,071 miles.

Arriving in Newport on March 25, the streets were blocked by four thousand people as Vincent addressed the crowd from the back of a wagon. *"God speed the plough,"* one woman shouted from the crowd, as the Chartist 'missionary' spoke figuratively of a plough turning over the bad soil of the aristocracy. At the end of the meeting Vincent was asked by his adoring female listeners to sing *"The Patriot,"* a revolutionary Chartist song. Afterwards he reported, *"Bless their kind little hearts! Of course, I accommodated them. We then adjourned; the ladies falling in procession four abreast and an immense procession of men following in the rear. . . . The Newport ladies are progressing with great spirit to the terror of the aristocrats of the town and neighbourhood."*[12]

The following day, taking a chaise over the hills to the next meeting at Pontllanfraith, Vincent was impressed with *"the defensible nature of the country in the case of a foreign invasion."*

"A few thousands of armed men on the hills could successfully defend them," he noted in his diary, adding, *"Wales could make an excellent Republic,"* a statement subsequently used by some to give substance to the allegation of a plot to replace the monarchy with a South Wales republic, when in fact Vincent, a man capti-

vated by the valleys, was probably only indulging in harmless reverie.[13] What was more significant from his observations at that time was his obvious awareness of the main grievance of those engaged in the iron and coal trades: *"They are said to have good wages, but I found this far from being the case. Work is very irregular, so that what is gained in wages is lost from the uncertain state of the labour market."* Expressing his regret at being unable to speak Welsh, Vincent clearly regarded it as impressive language, to which the people were passionately attached: *"How better they would be if possessed of law-making power."*

Arriving at Blackwood that evening, he was led into town by one hundred small girls singing a radical song. *"It was a pleasing sight,"* he wrote, *"to see such children assembled to pray for the success of a cause upon which their future happiness and freedom depended."*[14]

Vincent's 'missionary' work on behalf of the movement in Monmouthshire was interrupted by an event in April that did for Chartism what the prosecution of the Tolpuddle Martyrs had done for trade unionism in 1834: helped to de-rail the movement. The Whig Government's policy was to contain the Chartists by forbidding their meetings but where this failed, send in troops. Vincent had arrived in Devizes from Newport for a huge meeting on Easter Monday April 1, which the magistrates had forbidden but still took place. Very soon Chartist marchers clashed with the local Yeomanry and a detachment of 14th Lancers, during which Vincent was struck on the head by a stone.[15] A few months later there was a similar outbreak of violence, this time on July 4 in Birmingham, where the National Convention was meeting. Again, a meeting of marchers was prohibited, and there was a bloody struggle when a detachment of metropolitan police tried to disperse the crowd, the riot only ending with the arrival of the dragoons.[16] These, and similar confrontations began to wear down Chartist resistance, especially in England where the rivalry between the 'moral' and 'physical' force factions threatened to tear the movement apart.

Vincent had been seriously hurt in Devizes so did not return to Newport until April 21, when, joined again by the baker Edwards, he took a gig into surrounding hills. It was early spring, and Vincent was enchanted by *"primroses and pretty wild flowers peeping from under the hedge-rows . . . hills and valleys clad in beautiful virgin green . . . birds singing merrily."* At the *Halfway House*, Gellygroes, the pair feasted off Welsh mutton and greens washed down with coffee before mounting a platform to address 1,500 persons *"amongst whom were some well-dressed ladies."* After he had spoken about the Charter for two hours, and other speakers had addressed the meeting in Welsh, Vincent and Edwards led a procession of marchers lining up five abreast into Blackwood where they were met by two hundred children waving flags and carrying flowers and singing *"Here's a health to Radical Boys."* At Blackwood, three thousand Chartists listened to his speech which *"infused new fire and energy into all present."* The missionary's progress through the Sirhowy Valley continued on to Pontllan-fraith and a crowd of 4,000 gathered to hear him speak outside the *Greyhound*, where he spent the night, after a sing-song retiring to bed exhausted at 2 a.m.[17]

The next day it was over the mountains and Vincent's first meeting with Zephaniah Williams at the *Royal Oak* in Blaina, a man he described in his diary as *"one of the most intelligent men it has ever been my good fortune to meet with."* As Vincent, the baker Edwards, and Zephaniah were walking towards the *Royal Oak* for tea prior to the mountainside meeting, they had a remarkable encounter with the notorious Monmouthshire ironmaster, Crawshay Bailey. Vincent's account of the exchanges that took place with this *"rank Tory"* provides an interesting insight into the mounting tension between masters and workers:

"Bailey: 'Which is Vincent?' – To which I answered, 'My name is Vincent, Sir.'

Bailey: 'If I had known you about to address the people this morning, I would have had you put in the pond.' – 'Why, Sir,' said I, 'I thought you were a Conservative gentleman, and of course a moral-force man.'

Bailey: 'Damn your moral force; what business have you here amongst my men; I employ a great number of men and I give you notice that if you speak to the people on the hill tonight, I will upset you and have you put in the pond.' I smiled at this and said, 'Where will you get the men to do it?' He then pointed over to the blazing furnaces where his men were working, and said,

'There!' I replied, 'My life on the issue, Sir, they will not oppose me; I will beat you on your own ground.'

A running conversation then took place between Edwards and Bailey, in which Edwards charged him with a few awkward things. I then said, 'Well, Mr Bailey, I wish you a good day; I hope you will not forget your threat; depend upon it you will be beaten.' He bowed and we separated."

That evening six thousand men gathered on the hill behind the *Royal Oak* to listen to Vincent speak. But before he could begin, Crawshay Bailey's son arrived accompanied by a dozen clerks and managers and started barracking the speakers. Vincent *"lashed them unmercifully"* until the younger Bailey losing his patience, exclaimed, *"Human nature can't stand it"* and cocking up his head asked, *"What is the meaning of the word Tory, Mr Vincent?"*

" 'THIEF!' was my reply. I told him to look into the dictionaries – I told him the name first originated in Ireland, where the brigands were termed Tories.' He then asked me, 'If I were for a Republic.' I answered, 'I am for giving the people the power of electing their own rulers, and whatever government they may chose to form, is the only legitimate government.' (loud cheers). He then said, 'Are you for a revolution?' I answered, 'Yes; because revolution means change – and we need a change – and intend to have one.' He then said something of our insulting nature, when the people drove him and the clerks off the ground and would have killed them if I had not begged of the people not to hurt them. Thus ended the threat of 'putting me in the pond!' Success to the brave Welshmen – they are noble fellows!"[18]

Next morning, Vincent continued on to Pontypool, increasingly fascinated by the countryside through which they travelled, describing it as, *"the most delightfully-romantic tracts of country it has ever been my good fortune to see. Such beauty of scenery! Lofty hills – valleys luxuriant with foliage – fruit trees blossoming in the gardens – and all around wearing the appearance of gladness and gaiety."* But by then he had entered the pristine farmland of the Usk Valley, across the mountain from the squalid, congested iron and coal communities in the county's eastern valleys. The Black Domain ended at Pontypool, the coal seams not re-surfacing again until the Forest of Dean. Abergavenny was a different world, as it is today, untouched by the devastation of mining. Pontypool on the edge of the coalfield produced Vincent's largest audience, an estimated 12,000 travelling from all directions to hear him speak from the bedroom window of a house.[19]

Vincent's confrontation with the powerful Bailey family at Coalbrookvale in the very heart of its fiefdom, confirmed him as the champion of workers still governed by the Master and Servants Act, and liable to serve thirty days hard labour for leaving their master's service without permission, and twelve months for stealing wood from his hedgerows. His later imprisonment for holding illegal meetings only stiffened the resolve of the men from the hills. Even from Monmouth Gaol Vincent continued to incite revolt, on October 5, only one month before the Uprising, smuggling out a statement for the *Western Vindicator*, which promised them, *"Your day will come – from this gaol I tell you it will come; all the power of oppression is as nought; we will blunt the bayonet and break the chain. Great events are in the womb of time, and their birth will be a thunderclap of joy to the universe."* Then a week later: *"We are on the brink of revolution! People, be sturdy – be firm – but above all be prudent. Your cause will triumph."*[20] In the next two issues, however, his mood changes and for the first time Vincent urges *"patience and perseverance,"* offering to explain how best to change the existing system in a future edition of the *Western Vindicator*.[21] We can only speculate whether this transformation was linked to the treatment he suffered in prison, or whether Vincent decided he was pushing too hard on the door that led to the uprising. Those he spent months whipping into a frenzy of anticipation with promises of the Charter, must have found it difficult to understand his increasing ambivalence, leading eventually to Vincent renouncing violence. But the legacy of his incitement to republican revolution was that at least some of those who joined the march to Newport believed that was what their demonstration was all about. Into this unstable political environment stepped John Rees. Recently returned from the Texas War of Independence, his head filled with thoughts of freedom and revolutionary fervour, Rees could have been expected to see the Chartist objective in the same terms, certainly more clearly than Zephaniah Williams, and even John Frost who was as guilty as Vincent in retreating from the expectations he had raised.

By the beginning of March, Frost was already alerting the working classes of Monmouthshire to prepare themselves for revolt, writing in the *Western Vindicator, "It is a duty incumbent on you to rouse yourselves from that apathy which has too long held you in slavish submission to men greatly your inferiors in honesty and natural talents. . . . England expects every man to perform his duty, and Wales will, I hope, respond to the call. Your families, as well as your country, demand exertions on your part – Obey the call."* Sometimes camouflaged by ambiguity, the inflammatory declarations buried among more moderate language, the message at the centre of Frost's exhortations was clear: *"Justice is on your side; patience, firmness and perseverance are alone required to ensure success. . . . With the people of England it is now a question of principle . . . the cry which is now heard from the extremity of Scotland to the extremity of Wales is the people's Charter. . . . Is there any power that can withstand the will of the people? . . . Is there any divine authority that one man shall command and that another shall obey? Obedience, aye!! Yes, there must be obedience. We are for order. Order is Heaven's first law. It is the law of the Chartists: but we must know whom we are to obey. . . . Once more, countrymen, consider, consider seriously, the advantages that the industrious classes would derive from just lawgivers. We should once more hear our country called Merry England. Yes, and I hope the day is not distant when that name will be properly applied to our beloved country."*[22] Such rhetoric seems almost designed to spread confusion among a rank-and-file that could only have concluded it came directly from the National Convention, delivered to them by their delegate John Frost. Add to this the Newport draper's acidic attacks on an idle, aristocratic clique manipulating a corrupt system to live in luxury at the expense of the producers of wealth, the working classes, and Frost is as much to blame as Vincent for stoking resentment, if not for planning and presiding over the attack on the Westgate.

From the speeches of the two in the months immediately pre-ceding the Uprising, they appeared to compete for the most extra-vagant language to excite their supporters. Nevertheless, both stopped short of specifically advocating republican revolution although Vincent came closest on several occasions, his heavy hints like a verbal wink and a nod! That could not have been more obvious when addressing a meeting in April at the *King's Head* public house at Pontypool he described how Chartist lodges throughout England, Scotland and Wales were waiting for one word *"Now!" "And when the word 'Now' is given, then will our hands east, west, north and south be simultaneously stretched out and we will lay hold upon the pillars of the constitution and we will rock it and toss it to and fro until it shall totter from its foundation and base, up to the very highest point of it – there shall the pretty little bauble which is placed on the top of this pillar of the constitution be unable to keep its seat – it shall totter and reel to and fro – and at last even it shall fall."*[23]

Chartist violence was moving closer, the next outbreak occurring at Llanidloes at the end of April. When the local magistrates discovered the Chartists were arming themselves and drilling secretly, and asked the Home Office for help they had to content themselves with three London policemen. Sure enough, when the Chartists heard of their arrival they called a meeting, after which three of their members were arrested and held in the Trewythen Arms Hotel. The hotel was stormed, the prisoners released, the riot lasting until midday. One of the London policemen was found hiding in a cellar, the other two in a hayloft.

As the summer wore on, the Chartists became increasingly con-cerned by the Government's success in arresting leaders, thereby discouraging the rank and file. When the petition with its 1,280,824 names, demanding the Charter, was treated with disdain by the House of Commons, only 46 of its members voting for it, the only action the Convention could agree upon was its 'ulterior motives,' central to which was the 'Sacred Month,' a month-long general strike during which strikers would abstain from all intoxicating liquor. Also included in this action was a series of measures designed to destabilise the Government: (1) withdrawal of all bank savings (2) conversion of paper money into gold (3) dealing exclusively with trades people favoured by Chartists (4) adopting

Chartist candidates for the next election and, as freemen, (5) exercising their rights to arm themselves for self-defence.

That the Chartists who attacked Newport's Westgate Hotel were armed only for purposes of self-defence became a cornerstone of the defence Frost, Williams and Jones presented at their trial. Zephaniah Williams, in particular, before setting out from the mountainside at Nantyglo, insisted on this from all those marchers under his command. But once again, the instruction had been confused, if not pre-empted, by statements Vincent continued issuing from his prison cell right up until the last month before the rising, much to the annoyance of the authorities.[24]

Standing on his prison bed, and dictating his dispatches to the *Western Vindicator* to a visitor, the advice of the 'little captain' as he was affectionately known, was clear: *"Be ready at a moment's notice to take up arms to repel the unjust attacks of all foreign and domestic tyrants."* Then on September 11, he urged his followers, *"To your tents o' Israel! Every man to his post. As the storm thickens, redouble your energies; attend to your organisation – spread political knowledge and never relax your exertions until the land of your fathers be the birthplace of freedom."*[25]

All efforts by the Convention to obtain remission of Vincent's twelve-month sentence failed. So did plans for the 'Sacred Month' of protest, provisionally fixed for August, while on September 14 the Convention dissolved itself. Frost was not surprised at this, blaming its failure on a general lack of ability among the delegates.

Frost now began pulling back, suggesting that perhaps the best way to press their case was for 20,000 Monmouthshire Chartists to march ten abreast in support of his candidature for the Monmouth Boroughs constituency. By the autumn, Chartist agitation seemed to be declining. Frost actually mentioned this in a letter to the Lord Lieutenant as justification for the mitigation of Vincent's prison regime.[26] If Frost truly believed this, and there is no reason to suspect otherwise, how was it, as Ivor Wilks asserts, that plans were in place for a workers' revolution, arms distributed, and contacts made with Chartists in England to co-ordinate a national rebellion? Mobilisation on this scale may well have been talked of, but the evidence indicates precious little preparation until a series of meetings in the week immediately preceding the Uprising, hardly a springboard for what Wilks describes as *"a fervid expression of the emerging proletarian consciousness of South Wales."* [27] The grievances certainly existed. Vincent, for one, may have endeavoured to politicise them; but there is no sign the main body of marchers were motivated by anything other than their enfranchisement which, after the disappointment of the 1832 Reform Act, was regarded as the all important antidote. Their democratic consciousness had long since emerged, as demonstrated by the reform battles that proceeded Chartism. To exercise it is what they hungered after, because without the vote labour would never access the legislative processes essential for change. A more plausible, less complicated explanation is that the Chartist bandwagon, at least in Monmouthshire, had been driven so hard by Vincent and Frost, in particular, it was impossible to turn: that there was a determination because of the cancellation of the 'Sacred Month,' the failure of the petition, and collapse of the Convention for some sort of local protest, comparable with the notion of a purely local rising preferred by David Jones in *The Last Rising*.[28] That is not to say there were not others, like the known revolutionary John Rees, marching down to Newport with quite different intentions in mind.

If Zephaniah Williams was correct when he estimated there were fifty lodges, or branches of the Workingmen's Association (Chartists), in Monmouthshire and Glamorgan with between 100 and 1,300 members each, then almost every adult male was a member.[29] When Tremenheere conducted his investigation in 1840 into the state of education in the disturbed mining area – defined as the parishes of Bedwellty, Mynyddislwyn, Trevethin, Aberystruth and Merthyr – the population totalled 85,000, of whom one fifth were children, forty per cent of the remainder women.[30] Most of the Chartist branches in Wales were congregated in the five parishes, so if Zephaniah was right and the average membership of branches was 700, taking the median of his range for calculation, then there were at least 35,000 Chartists in the two counties, either a gross exaggeration for someone's benefit, or a remarkable rate of growth for a movement that had existed in Wales for less than twelve months! Not a single document has survived from this Herculean organisational feat, giving rise to the inevitable speculation that all branch records must have been destroyed rather than allowed to fall into the hands of the authorities. In 1936-1938 it was reported the licensee at the *Rolling Mill Inn,* Blaina, had discovered an iron chest stuffed with the virtually indecipherable records of the old Blaina Chartist Lodge, which he burned![31] The Blaina Lodge was based at Zephaniah's beer shop, the *Royal Oak* in 1839 but his son Llewellyn was once publican at the *Rolling Mill.* If the Chartists did destroy their records, as would have been sensible in the aftermath of the Uprising, then what happened to the Chartist treasury? The membership subscription seems to have varied according to means, although sixpence was the most common amount collected by 'captains' from members of their work gangs and also from public houses and beer shops.[32] If Zephaniah's membership estimates were correct then the collection of 30,000 to 50,000 sixpences meant a substantial 'war chest;' yet there is not a single mention of the use made of Chartist funds in any of the surviving records from that period. In fact, the movement seemed so short of cash after the three leaders were transported, that public appeals were necessary to raise funds to help their families, described by Morgan Williams, the Merthyr Chartist leader, as being in straitened circumstances.[33]

Might the Chartist 'war chest' have been used to buy arms? A meeting in Newport in April between a Liverpool iron merchant, Joseph Johnson, and William Townsend, who was later gaoled with Vincent for organising illegal gatherings, suggests this was happening if Johnson's version is to be believed. At this meeting, Townsend offered to buy 200-300 muskets and 500-600 cutlasses for cash but, surprisingly perhaps, Johnson rejected the order because he was "disgusted."[34] The Government's policy of authorising the arming of the middle classes undoubtedly encouraged the Chartists to do the same although only for self defence, Vincent insisting as early as March 1839, *"It is true some of the Chartists talk of arms and the right of the people to arm . . . but so did the Whigs.*[35] All the Chartist record shows is that pikes were distributed, some from a room under Zephaniah's beer shop, and the occasional pistol was procured in the days running up to the march.[36] Many of the marchers could have had their own weapons as it was common practice to keep a shotgun on the wall above the fireplace. Zephaniah Williams, however, was very specific in his instructions as to how the men under his command should behave on the march, explaining they were going to Newport to show *"they would have the Charter as the law of the land"*; that there would be no shedding of blood for the cause, and that all the marchers were to take care not to break the law nor touch anyone's property.[37] If they were arming covertly, which would have been necessary for what the authorities believed they had in mind, it is quite impossible to estimate what weapons they may have had, unlike the middle classes who were actively encouraged by the Home Office to prepare themselves for the anticipated outbreak of public disorder. Associations were formed in Monmouthshire for the "Protection of life and Property", the Home Secretary authorising the Lord Lieutenant Leigh to issue to their members in Pontypool and Monmouth with 50 brace of pistols and 50 cutlasses, and another 200 brace of pistols and cutlasses for special constables if the situation should deteriorate.[38] With tension rising, the yeomanry from twenty parishes met at the *Royal Oak*, Christchurch on the Newport-Chepstow Road to swear loyalty to the Queen and to uphold the constitution. Those attending, among them John Frost's son-in-law Harry Fry, were urged to *"keep their powder dry, and make their horses stand fire"*[39] Judging from the 150 assorted arms, mostly shot and ball, and makeshift pikes, recovered from outside the Westgate after the Uprising by constable Moses Scard, the two thousand men who descended on Newport were hardly armed to the teeth.[40]

By October every public house in Monmouthshire seemed to have a Chartist lodge or was affiliated to one. Five of these, the *Coach and Horses*, Blackwood, *Royal Oak*, Blaina, *Bristol House*, Pontypool, *Star Inn*, Dukestown, and *King Crispin*, Bryrnmawr, were to figure most prominently in the preparations for whatever was eventually planned for Monday, November 4.

The *Star Inn* at Dukestown was the first Chartist Lodge to be formed at Sirhowy, followed soon afterwards by others at the *Miners Arms* and *Red Lion*, all in an area where there were five public houses and 28 beer shops amongst only 151 dwellings. Zephaniah Williams counted John Morgan, landlord at the *Star,* a close friend.[41] He would also have been familiar to local workmen many of whom he employed when living at Sirhowy for ten years as Minerals Agent for the Quaker ironmasters, the Harford

Bros. Attached to the public house was the Star Field, the scene of some of the largest Chartist meetings held in the valleys, one of the most important of these on August 12 after the 'Sacred Month' had been cancelled, partly out of concern that a strike during the onset of an economic recession when wages were already being cut would have persuaded the ironmasters to close their works permanently. By now the Dukestown Lodge at the *Star Inn* had a reputation as a stronghold for the 'physical force' faction of the Chartist movement, John Rees and his friend David Jones (Dai the Tinker) both active in the area as 'captains.'[42] But on this occasion the meeting ended peacefully enough in the singing of hymns and Chartist songs, and instructions to John Frost to appeal again to the Home Secretary Normanby for the release of Vincent when he next attended the Convention as a delegate.

All was to no avail. The Convention was dissolved in September and Frost hurried back to South Wales to confront an angry crowd on October 3 at the rear of Zephaniah Williams' *Royal Oak* at Blaina demanding immediate action. While Frost managed to prevail upon them to be patient by explaining that the rest of the country was not ready and that to act precipitously would be disastrous, the Newport Chartist was sounding less than fully committed, suggesting the Chartists re-direct their efforts into supporting his nomination to contest the next General Election. With the more militant wanting nothing of this, he promised the meeting that if they did not get the Charter soon he would *"head the ranks of anything that will take place."* That was still not good enough, and at a secret delegate meeting that same evening at the *King Crispin* beer shop, at Brynmawr, lasting until the early hours of the morning, any idea Frost still had of extricating himself evaporated, when he was forced to consent to drawing up lists of those in authority to be executed in the event of a rising, according to an account by the eccentric Pontypridd surgeon and Chartist leader, Dr William Price. Frost opened the meeting, explaining, *'I have called you together to ask will you rise at my bidding, for it must be done?'* At which point, one of the delegates, an old solider named David Davies, of Abersychan, who had served 25 years in the army and fought at the battle of Waterloo, got up and said, *'I will tell you Mr Frost, the condition upon which my lodge will rise, and there is no other condition, so far as I am concerned. The Abersychan Lodge is 1,600 strong; 1,200 of them are old soldiers; the remaining 400 have never handled arms, but we can turn them into fighting men in no time. I have been sent here to tell you that we shall not rise until you give us a list of those we are to remove – to kill. I know what the English Army is, and I know how to fight them, and the only way to success is to attack and remove those who command them – the officers and those who administer the law. We must be led as the children of Israel were led from Egypt through the Red Sea.'* Dr Price claimed that after every delegate had spoken in the same manner Frost promised he would not call on them to rise, until he had given them the execution lists. The commitments wrung from Frost were understandable. Some members, among them Price, had scented that for all his inflammatory speeches and rousing articles in the *Western Vindicator,* Frost did not have the stomach for a fight.[43]

Dr Price's account of this meeting, and a private one with Frost that followed on Saturday evening 26 October, is included in his memoirs written forty years later. The Pontypridd doctor was to become famous as pioneer of legalised cremation when he cremated the body of his son. Price believed Frost's nerve had failed and that he wanted a less ambitious form of protest. Of his meeting with the Chartist leader in the week before the Uprising, he wrote afterwards: *"I refused to agree to anything except what had been decided at the Twyn-y-star meeting to which Frost replied, 'What! Do you want us to kill the soldiers – kill a thousand of them in one night? Dear me, dear me, I cannot do it, I cannot do it' and he cried like a child and talked of heaven and hell."* It must be said the doctor's account of events needs to be read with caution. Price did not like Frost and while he was engaged with the Chartists in the early months, he appears not to have been involved in concocting the final plan, disappearing to France until it was all over. But he did attend the meeting on October 3 at Zephaniah Williams's *Royal Oak* at Coalbrookvale, Blaina, the last public meeting the Chartists held in the hills before the march and at which the rank and file were evidently determined to release Vincent. When Price wrote forty years later that he had been bound by the decisions taken at the *Twyn-y-star,* he probably meant the secret meeting at the *King Crispin.*[44]

What meetings were held afterwards were for delegates only, the most important of these occurring in the week immediately preceding the Uprising, the first at the *Star Inn*, Dukestown, on Monday, 28 October, and attended by delegates from most of the coalfield communities. Zephaniah Williams and the Bristol watchmaker's son, William Jones, landlord of the *Bristol House* public house in Pontypool, were present although John Frost may not have been. With nothing resolved, it was decided they should all meet again soon to finalise plans. Delegates had split into moral and physical force factions, the latter wanting to challenge the authorities immediately. In the meantime, it was resolved to hold nightly lodge meetings at which members would be encouraged to arm in self-defence.[45]

The following night, Tuesday 29 October, William Howell, a worker at the Blaina Gas Works, went to Zephaniah Williams' *Royal Oak,* having decided that in view of the trouble that was brewing, he and his wife would be safer if they joined the Chartist Lodge. The beer house was full, Zephaniah addressing a crowded room. *"Now my lads this is a good cause, you have five articles to attend to,"* he said, explaining one was to destroy the Poor Houses, another to have Free Trade, another to *"have the poor as rich as the rich,"* and to vote for Members of Parliament. According to Zephaniah, all of these were easily obtained and without shedding of blood, if the poor stuck together. Howells also claimed the Chartist leader assured them their wives and children would be cared for while they were away and that there were a *"great many gentlemen giving their money to support the cause."*[46]

Not satisfied by this, Howell's wife Rachel later returned to the beer house for further assurances from Zephaniah that her family would be supported when the men were away. That Saturday was the end of the long pay at the Blaina Gas Works and, not unlike other workers, their debt would be rolled over into the next month. Rachel Howells reminded Zephaniah of this by asking him for the name of a shop to provide her family with credit while her husband was away. *"He did not say where the men were going to,"* Rachel Howell said in evidence to the examining magistrates, *"nor what they were going to do."* Of all the Chartist leaders, Zephaniah Williams was the most secretive, many of his followers certain of only one thing when they set off for Newport: their weapons were supposed to be for self-defence only.[47]

On Wednesday 30 October, Zephaniah was at the *Navigation Inn,* Crumlin, promising the marchers there would be no bloodshed although they should carry arms of some sort. When he arrived back at the *Royal Oak* the same evening, he revealed for the first time there would be large meeting of Chartists on the mountain that Sunday. They would get the Charter, he assured his listeners, if they remained united and refused to work. Before the night was over, he was off again to Blackwood, stabling his horse there for the next three nights.[48]

On Thursday 31 October and Friday 1 November, the Chartist leaders Frost, Williams and Jones based themselves at the *Coach and Horses,* Blackwood where Richard Pugh was landlord. There had been a lodge there for about nine months, started by the shoemaker Owen Davies, the purpose at first to collect a few pennies to buy newspapers. At the beginning it was not described as a Chartist Lodge, but when colliers began joining in April and May, discussions focussed on the Charter, especially after a visit from Henry Vincent. Pugh, the landlord, collected subscriptions from new members and the secretary William Barwell issued membership cards. Zephaniah Williams and William Jones both slept at the *Coach and Horses* on the Wednesday night after a meeting. For the first part of this crucial week, Frost appears to have kept his own counsel, leaving Williams and Jones to alert the lodges that something was imminent, although no decision on its form was taken until Friday, November 1, when about thirty delegates gathered at the *Coach and Horses* around midday.[49]

Understanding exactly what happened at this vital meeting has proved especially intractable beyond the fact it lasted for four hours, after which the delegates dispersed to rally their troops for a march on Newport. As for the purpose of that march, according to William Davies, son of a Blackwood shopkeeper, it was to *"seize all authorities, wherever they could be found, and stop the mails, so that the people of the north would know they had succeeded."* Davies attended the meeting but what he claimed occurred was tainted by the fact that after his capture the 19-year-old turned Queen's Evidence. If he had not absconded, first to England, then a second time to France, he would have been a key prosecution witness against Frost, Williams, Jones and many others. The next most damaging account of what transpired at the crucial Blackwood meeting came from Job Tovey, a Blackwood collier.

Tovey was not a delegate to the Friday meeting, but spent a large part of that day drinking at the *Coach and Horses*. More significantly, he claimed to have received a first hand account of the final plan from Frost himself, when the Chartist leader spent the Friday and Saturday nights at Tovey's Blackwood home. A Chartist since the Blackwood lodge was formed at the beginning of the year, Tovey counted fifty men entering the delegate meeting. When it ended, Frost asked him for a room for the night. The following morning, Saturday November 2, the Chartist leader is supposed to have explained over breakfast how he was planning to take the men down to Newport on the Sunday evening. Those unable to arm themselves, would be able to seize weapons from the Workhouse at the top of Stow Hill where they would *"give three cheers which would so frighten the mayor that he would die in his bed and it would produce such an effect on the soldiers that they would throw down their arms."* They would then take possession of the town and stop the mail for Birmingham where Chartists would be waiting to see if it arrived late, because that was intended to be the signal for them to rise up and make the Charter law of the land. Frost told Tovey *"they had been fighting long enough for others and it was time they should now fight for themselves."*

During Saturday afternoon young William Davies arrived at Tovey's accompanied by a stranger he introduced to Frost as a delegate from the North, with two letters for the Chartist leader who, after reading them quietly, tossed both on the fire. The stranger was urged to leave immediately to alert the northern Chartists to the Monmouthshire men's plans. Frost remained at Tovey's throughout Sunday, receiving a great many callers, one of whom said that Zephaniah Williams was gathering his men at 6 p.m. They needed to be at the Cefn (outside Newport) by 10 p.m. and Newport by 3 a.m., said Frost, who spoke of sending a company to seize the powder magazine and arms at Tredegar House which they would convert into a barracks. He also confirmed they planned to release Vincent from Monmouth Gaol. As the evening wore on, Frost told Tovey's wife that by the time he next returned to Blackwood, *"many of tyrants and oppressors heads would be off."* Asked by her what they would do for food, he said there were storehouses with plenty of flour at Newport and deer in the park for the Chartists to butcher. Then, joining William Davies and the large number of men gathered outside the *Coach and Horses*, he gave the order to march, the column moving off towards Newport accompanied by a *"great wailing and crying"* among the large number of women and children lining the road out of Blackwood. Whatever suspicions some may have had of Frost's commitment, he now assumed the role of Chartist general. At Cefn and the *Welch Oak* public house, on the outskirts of Newport, he was to be joined by Zephaniah Williams and 2,000 men from Nantyglo and Blaina, all that he believed he needed to seize the town. William Jones was also on his way from Pontypool with a similar size force, or so it was believed. In fairness, once the die was cast on the Friday night, Frost did not abandon his 'soldiers' until minutes before the massacre on the steps of the Westgate.

If Tovey was to be believed then the Chartists' intentions could not be clearer. If Zephaniah Williams 'confession' made months later aboard the convict ship *Mandarin* was true, an earlier plan for simultaneous attacks on Brecon and Abergavenny had now been abandoned, and Newport was the only destination that Sunday night. Even though Tovey escaped after the attack on the Westgate, he was arrested on December 23, which meant his testimony was available to the Crown a week before the Special Commission sat in Monmouth. In the absence of William Davies still on the run, Tovey's evidence was the most damaging in that it confirmed everything the Crown suspected. So why was he never called to testify? The suspicion remains he was a Government spy and was sure to be uncovered by the defence when it investigated the witness list. As it happened, the list of witnesses was never delivered to the defence by the Crown in sufficient time for proper investigations to take place!

Zephaniah Williams was also marshalling his troops but with a great deal more circumspection as to their objective. Lists had been compiled organising Chartists into companies of ten, each led by a captain. Ostensibly, to facilitate the collection of weekly membership subscriptions, the process took on a more sinister construction when it was discovered the 'captains' at the Argoed Lodge had been secretly briefed on what was planned for the Sunday. Members there became even more alarmed when George Reed arrived in Argoed on the Sunday afternoon with a message from Frost, instructing them to arm themselves for the march on Newport, stop all traffic, the post, the coach, and remain to guard the town. On hearing this, one man objected, saying, *"I thought it was proposed to carry the meetings peaceably through the country but instead of that we are going to carry arms against the law."* To this, Reed replied, *"If we do not break the old law we will never get a new one."* Another asked where Frost was, someone else adding for good measure, *"If Frost don't lead us down to Newport we wont go one step."* That captains were appointed is not in doubt. John Rees and David Jones were widely regarded as Chartist captains in the Dukestown and Sirhowy areas while Richard Davies, a collier accused of looting during the Uprising, named his captain as Thomas Giles.[50] What is not clear is the extent to which their roles were militaristic. The exchanges between members of the Argoed Lodge are significant as evidence of the confusion among the marchers before they set out.

By the Saturday, Zephaniah was back in the Lodge Room at the *Royal Oak* in Nantyglo. He spoke about the Charter and how £5 and £2 notes would be abolished once it became the law of the land. Members were told that the time and place of a great meting would be revealed the next day. By 3 p.m. on Sunday afternoon the beer shop was packed. Zephaniah stood on a chair or table instructing everyone to return home, change their clothes, collect some bread and cheese, and meet on the mountain between Nantyglo and Ebbw Vale about a mile away. For defence, they should arm themselves with guns, pikes, even sticks. Turncoats were warned that Chartist spies were in place at Llanelley, Brynmawr, Nantyglo and Blaina. They would not accept any 'old women's' excuses. For those who remained at home the consequences would be serious. They might even *"die like dogs,"* said Zephaniah. For the very first time he hinted at what the march was all about. It was to be a united demonstration of strength, he explained.[51]

The night had turned wet and cold. After changing into warmer clothes in preparation for the march, Zephaniah was next seen by

135

Richard Hawkins in a small side room. Hawkins had gone to the *Royal Oak* to settle a bill with Zephaniah for drinks charged to his slate. He found the Chartist leader standing at a table rolling twenty or thirty cartridges in paper and tying them at both ends. A former corporal in the Marines, Hawkins swore they were cartridges although later he conceded they might have been plugs of tobacco for sale to customers at the *Royal Oak*.[52]

By Sunday evening, the beer shop was filled with Chartists, over-flowing into the road outside as William Howell and his wife Rachel set out for chapel. Near the *Royal Oak,* four of the crowd seized Rachel's husband and dragged him away. *"I took hold of my husband's arm to go safe,"* she re-called. *"I was near out of my senses. They pushed me from him; I was near falling. One man in particular pushed me against the wall and I was hurt. I did not see my husband again until the Tuesday evening."* As William Howell was taken off to the meeting on the mountain, he saw several men enter a door to the cellar beneath the lodge room, re-appearing minutes later with pikes.[53]

George Lloyd was paid each month at the *Royal Oak* at the end of the 'long pay.' That Sunday when he arrived someone pointed a dagger at his throat, thrust a mop handle into his hand, and marched him off to the meeting on the mountain where Zephaniah was standing in the rain on a 'tump' addressing a crowd of between 4,000 and 5,000. *"My dear Chartists,"* he was saying, *"you need not be afraid for we are bound to be at Newport at 2 o'clock. The soldiers will not touch you."* Hearing this the crowd whooped, and shouted, *"We do not care for them."* Then with a great cheer they headed off into the stormy night, breaking windows, drumming on doors, and forcing occupants from their beds. Lloyd was pushed along with a stick in his back, and at Abercarn thrown in the canal when he tried to escape. Not everyone knew where they were headed or for what purpose. Zephaniah would only say they were *"taking a turn as far as Newport."* The unfortunate William Howell was convinced they were marching to London! From the direction they were taking, it must have soon become clear that Monmouth and the release of Vincent from gaol was not the immediate objective. Zephaniah was pressed on this by a farmer Thomas Saunders as he sheltered with others in a barn at Tynycwm. No further than Newport, was all he would say.[54]

Walking beside Williams for some of the way after leaving the mountain, Edward Richards, a collier from Blaina, heard him repeatedly tell marchers there was no danger so long as they did not break the law. A mile from the blast furnaces at the Harfords Ebbw Vale Iron Works, it struck Richards the blast had been blown off the furnaces. If the molten iron were allowed to cool inside the furnaces, the works would be out of production for weeks and workers laid off. Pointing this out to Zephaniah, the Chartist leader retorted, *"Let them put it out, to the devil,"* at which point he left the marchers briefly, possibly to secure the blast furnaces from sabotage. Near the ironworks he met a man who said he would get himself killed at Newport to which Zephaniah replied, *"No. I hope we shall come back safe. Nobody will be killed there."* [55]

In Monmouthshire's eastern valley, William Jones spent most of Sunday on the hills rallying his men. They were to leave the Racecourse at Pontypool for Newport at about 10 p.m. The Pontypool contingent had the shortest distance to travel but in the event was the last to arrive, and then, only when the action was over. The tactics were the same as at Nantyglo and Blackwood: those resisting were press-ganged into joining the march. One of these was a labourer, James Emery. That morning he had heard Jones speak at Pontypool about a proclamation, which would be posted at Newport on the Monday. Headed, "That we, the Executive Government of England . . .," it was signed, "John Frost, President." As always, Jones was supremely confident about the outcome of the night's activities. *"I'll bet any money,"* he boasted, *"that before Wednesday night we shall either have the Charter or all will be pardoned or the Government will be in our hands."* Whatever action was planned, the Pontypool men were the least prepared for it, according to a report from the lodge a few weeks earlier. Merthyr, on the other hand, had 2,000 well armed and organised Chartists although only a handful ever took part.[56]

The descent of the men from the hills was accompanied by a continuous downpour. Public houses, beer shops, homes and farms along the route were raided, weapons, food and drink seized as the marchers sought shelter from the appalling weather. Henry Vincent's exhortations to the Chartists to abstain from strong liquor, to *"keep their hands clean,"* would have sounded pretty hollow that night. Several times Jones and Williams evicted marchers from public houses, Williams at one point despairing they would ever reach Newport. The 3 a.m. deadline for the rendezvous with Frost and Williams at the *Welch Oak* came and went with the Nantyglo company still several hours from its destination. Shortly after midnight, Henry Smith, a Dorsetshire stable lad at the *Coach and Horses* public house in Llaniddal was woken by his employer James Samuels and told to hitch the horse to a tram. Entering the taproom he found it crowded with marchers, Zephaniah sitting in a corner drying his clothes near the fire. The

The route taken by the three companies of Chartists led by Frost, Williams and Jones, the latter getting no further than Malpas on the outskirts of Newport before turning back, after he was told of what had happened outside the Westgate.

tram road passed in front of the *Coach and Horses* and Smith was to take Zephaniah with four others down to the rendezvous with Frost and Jones at the *Welch Oak.* As the tram descended the last few miles to Newport, marchers crowded alongside it waving spears and pistols. At the *Welch Oak,* more time was lost rounding up the men for the next stage of the journey into Tredegar Park, which they reached as dawn broke. Mary Charles, the landlord's daughter, said there were about 300 men outside the public house and they spoke only of going to Newport to *"take the poor house."* Four she noticed, in particular, huddled together as if they were leaders. One of these, a man of about 30, seemed to have come from the town where he reported there were only 60 soldiers. It seemed generally agreed *"Newport would not be worth anything in a day or two."* [57]

The case against Frost, Williams, Jones and others for High Treason was to a large extent based on an alleged conversation Frost had with James Hodge at Pye Corner, about midway between the *Welch Oak* and Tredegar Park on the town's outskirts, where the marchers were to gather for the final leg of the journey into Newport. Like so many others who sought to save their own skins after the Uprising by claiming they were compelled to take part, Hodge's statement was always suspect. What he alleged was that at Pye Corner Frost ordered all armed men to the front of the column, at which point Hodge exclaimed, *"In the name of God what are you going to do; are you going to attack any person or place?"* Frost replied they would attack and take Newport, blow up the bridge, stop the Welsh mail proceeding to Birmingham, and that would be the signal for a national uprising. Hodge told Frost he was like a butcher leading a flock of lambs to the slaughterhouse. Before it was too late he should order the men to return to the hills. Only the previous week Hodge had started work for Thomas Prothero and his partner, the Mayor of Newport, Thomas Phillips. At the trial it emerged that Prothero was also the examining magistrate responsible for extracting Hodge's account of the alleged conversation to which no one else was privy. But during the march Frost was reported to have had a similar conversation with John Harford, another of those pressed into joining, Harford alleging the aim was to seize the Workhouse and the soldiers stationed there. This would seem to explain why the

Chartists planned to arrive at Newport in the dead of night, perhaps indicative of a deeper conspiracy than a mere show of force. But the 24-mile journey from the mountain at Nantyglo to Newport took almost ten hours, much longer than it should have taken. Instead of arriving under cover of darkness, the Chartists never reached the Westgate until it was fully light.[58]

Where were John Rees and David Jones as the marchers converged on Newport? Jones had a conversation with Mary Thomas after he and others armed with guns and mandrills had burst into her father's public house at Newbridge at about 1 am. Apparently, Dai the Tinker's wife was very ill, and Mary who had known Jones for ten years inquired about her health. *"Worse than she has been before,"* he replied before leaving and after paying her for a jug of beer and some bread and cheese. Jones was next spotted by an Argoed collier, John Jones, in Tredegar Park, holding a large knife in one hand, a spear in the other.[59] There was some suggestion that it was the late arrival of the Sirhowy contingent led by Jones, that delayed Zephaniah's departure from the mountain. According to one account, Rees and Jones held a long conversation on Sunday afternoon at the *Globe Inn,* Tredegar before Jones started marshalling his men at the Star Field in Dukestown, where he had waited in vain for the Merthyr contingent to arrive. Some must have turned up because a Merthyr Chartist died outside the Westgate. More valuable time was then lost searching for deserters, before the Sirhowy Chartists headed up the mountain to join Zephaniah Williams for the march down to Newport.[60]

John Rees mustered his Tredegar Chartists at the back of the *Red Lion.* Once again time was lost searching for turncoats, the departure further delayed by a mob of women resisting the abduction of their men folk. At last, the Tredegar column was off, heading towards Blackwood to join Frost. As the column passed Bedwellty House, home of the Tredegar ironmaster Samuel Homfray, Jack the Fifer urged his men to cheer lustily.[61] Rees is next heard of firstly at the *Waterloo* public house and then at the Courtybella Weighing Machine on the boundary of Sir Charles Morgan's Tredegar Park. This was where the Morgan family made its millions from charging for every tram load of pig iron and coal carried across the Park's 'Golden Mile' to the wharves on the River

Usk at Newport. The rain was easing by the time Frost and Rees with their Chartists from Blackwood and Tredegar began arriving in the Park, at between seven and eight in the morning. Hundreds of men milled around waiting for instructions. Some were armed with pistols and muskets, others with mandrills, pikes and sticks. What they most wanted to know was the disposition of the 45th Regiment of Foot.

The next sighting of the Chartist column was about a mile further on outside the *Waterloo* public house near the bank of the River Usk. Samuel Smith and Thomas Pritchard, crew of the Harford Brothers' steam engine *Superb,* had the previous evening made a delivery to the company's wharf on the River Usk. With steam up early on the Monday, the locomotive set off on the return journey to Sirhowy, getting no further than the *Waterloo* when a group of hauliers coming down the tram road with their horses warned there was little point continuing because of the mob of men following behind. Pressing on, the engine had reached only as far as Gaer Pool before the crush of marchers on the tram road forced it to reverse back to the *Waterloo* until the crowd had passed.

If ever John Rees had been brought to trial, the crew of the locomotive *Superb* would have been key prosecution witnesses. As it happened, neither gave evidence although they did provide depositions for the examining magistrates. According to the fireman Pritchard, the man leading the column as it approached the *Waterloo* was Jack the Fifer. He wore a square cut coat called a pilot coat, and carried a pike in one hand and in the other a stick which he held in the air and shouted, *"Halt!"* As the column waited for orders, Jack the Fifer spoke briefly to a man (either Jones or Frost) wearing a blanket smock, after which he ordered the Chartists carrying guns to step forward. John Rees spent the next 45 minutes assembling the column six abreast with a gun carrier at the end of each rank as far as the weapons would reach. When this was done, he issued the order for the column to march towards the centre of Newport. Samuel Smith, the engine driver, confirmed most of what his fireman stated, except for the description of what Jack the Fifer was wearing. Smith said it was more like a dress blue coat than a pilot coat. Rees was definitely leading the column, with David Jones, a gun in one hand and horse pistol in the other, marching beside him.[62] On arriving at the *Waterloo* both entered the public house and were spoken to by Samuel Probyn, one of the Newport hauliers waiting for the marchers to clear away from the tram road. Probyn saw one of the leaders (possibly David Jones) replace his pike with a gun hanging over the fireplace, remarking as he did so, *"Exchange is no robbery."* But Probyn reminded him he could get transportation for that, the man replying *"Oh, I'm a Chartist."* Then turning to John Rees, Probyn asked him who his leader was. Rees turned and pointed to Frost in the road outside, adding, *"That's my leader."*[63]

The marchers spent about three-quarters of an hour at the *Waterloo* before continuing into Newport, via the Courtybella Weighing Machine where they halted. By this time, John Rees appeared to have assumed command, although the assertion by Ivor Wilks that at the meeting of delegates at Blackwood the Friday before he had been selected to lead the attack on Newport, cannot be substantiated. Frost was certainly still at his side, at the front of the column near the weighing machine, when they interrogated, two boys, John Rees, son of a police constable, and his friend James Coles, about the whereabouts of the soldiers. According to young Rees, at least a dozen had been moved from their barracks at the Workhouse at the top of Stow Hill to defend the Westgate Hotel. On hearing this, it was Jack the Fifer, not Frost who told the boys to deliver a message to the soldiers at the Westgate that *"they meant to have the Westgate by and by for themselves."* With a pistol in one hand and a pike in the other, the Fifer, not Frost, lined the Chartists into a military formation, and with those with weapons leading the way, gave the order to march up the Friars Lane, past the Workhouse where some of the 45th Regiment of Foot were garrisoned and out on to the top of Stow Hill, opposite St Woolos Cathedral. The two boys insisted another group headed off along Commercial Street towards the Westgate.[64] Following some distance in the rear, because there is no mention of him ever being anywhere near the front of the marching column, was Zephaniah Williams, rounding up stragglers as he went. As for William Jones, the Pontypool contingent had failed to rendezvous at the *Welch Oak*. Before the column moved off from Courtybella Weighing Machine, the operator,

Thomas Evans, estimated there were 5,000 marchers, 300 of these with muskets. Spotting a man with a wooden leg amongst them, Evans asked what he was up to. The man said he did not know, smiling as though it were of little consequence, at which point Evans remarked the man must not be satisfied with one wooden leg because he had come to Newport to get two! He was not the only one who on entering Newport still did not know what it was all about.[65]

By now the Mayor of Newport, Thomas Phillips and thirty soldiers of the 45th Regiment of Foot, together with approximately the same number of special constables were waiting at the Westgate. During the troubles 1,500 special constables were sworn in throughout the county in anticipation of an outbreak of violence. A rising had been expected for several months and Phillips and Prothero were both the targets for anonymous letter writers. In July, Prothero was told by one that every stone in Swindlers Hall, which was what the Chartists called his mansion, would be pulled to the ground; and that there were thirty thousand armed men at Blackwood, Mynyddislwyn and Pontypool. Another letter in identical handwriting advised Phillips to leave Frost, *"the most popular man in England,"* alone. As early as May, Capel Hanbury Leigh, Lord Lieutenant of Monmouthshire, one of the moderates among the gentry, was asked by Mayor Phillips to provide a cache of weapons for the Christchurch Association. Spies were ordered to report all suspicious activities to their masters, Phillips, Prothero, and the Tredegar ironmaster Samuel Homfray. By the Thursday before the Uprising, Phillips was alerted to expect trouble the following Tuesday. On the Sunday morning, Homfray told the mayor the rising would be immediate, the aim of the Chartists, he believed, to free Vincent from Monmouth Gaol. As tension mounted, several of the local gentry hurriedly fled the county, the Harford Brothers at Sirhowy moving their families to the safety of Cheltenham until it was safe to return. The coal owner Thomas Powell, of Bryn Colliery and Ironworks was warned by John Llewellyn, of Abercarn of a rising Sunday night and march on Newport.[66]

Probably the best-informed and most feared police officer in the county was Superintendent William Homan, of Tredegar. The one who arrested Vincent in London in May, Homan was a marked man among the Chartists. Based at Tredegar, a hotbed of Chartist activity, he would know sooner than most what was being planned. Homan had undertaken to keep the Marquis of Bute informed by supplying Captain Howells, commander of the Royal Glamorgan Militia, with regular intelligence reports. On October 29, the day following the crucial delegate meeting at the *Star Inn,* Dukestown, Homan wrote to Howells advising him the Chartists were *"still bent on mischief,"* adding, *"It is reported to me they are to have a simultaneous rise throughout the kingdom this week and arms have been issued and pikes. The magistrates are undecided as to what steps they should take at present. I much fear things will not end as quietly as imagined. You shall hear from me as events occur."*[67]

By the Sunday evening, the Mayor of Newport knew the Chartists were on their way when two special constables, Thomas Walker and Richard Webb, returned to the Westgate from a scouting expedition in the hills. Walker had been stabbed in the thigh and groin after they stumbled upon a group of marchers. Clinging to back of his horse, he barely made it back with his life. The second scout Webb had galloped out of range when someone took a shot at him. As the situation deteriorated, a number of Newport Chartists were rounded up and detained at the Westgate.[68]

By the time the Chartists reached the top of Friars Lane on Stow Hill, opposite St Woolos Cathedral, it was fully light, the rain had stopped and it promised to be a fine day. Drenched to the skin, marching six or eight abreast, a man with a gun positioned at the end of every other rank, the column set off noisily down the hill towards the Westgate at the bottom. One eyewitness said it was half a mile long, stretching from the *Six Bells* public house at the top of Stow Hill to the front door of the Westgate. His estimate of the number of men, four to five thousand, was probably an exaggeration since the last of the marchers were directly opposite the *Six Bells,* only a third of a mile from the entrance to the Westgate. If they were marching eight abreast, and avoiding the man immediately in front, a more accurate estimate would be nearer 2000, which was the figure the Crown Prosecutor chose to include in the treason charges preferred against Frost, Williams, Jones, and others. A column of 5,000 men, eight abreast would have stretched for over a mile, all the way back to the Courtybella

Weighing Machine. As it happened, Zephaniah Williams was at the very end of the column opposite the *Six Bells* rounding up the last of the stragglers when the first Chartists rushed the entrance to the Westgate. Wildly different estimates of the number that participated in the march were given at the time, during the trial, and since, one Crown eye-witness insisting three to four thousand men wheeled around the corner at the bottom of Stow Hill to face the Westgate, when the capacity of the square in front of the hotel was more likely to have been four to five hundred only.[69]

Whatever their number, most were not prepared for what followed next. Frost had boasted of establishing a headquarters at Tredegar House but they had passed through the park without touching this edifice of aristocratic power. Frost had allegedly told James Hodge they would stop the Welsh Mail to Birmingham as a signal for a national uprising in the North of England and elsewhere. But there was no direct Welsh mail service from Newport to Birmingham. All letters were sorted at Chepstow, and those destined for the north taken to Gloucester where they were transferred to the Bristol-Birmingham mail coach, which arrived in Birmingham at between two and three o'clock in the morning. If the non-arrival of mail from South Wales as part of this delivery was intended as a signal for a national Uprising, the Chartists had chosen a convoluted and inefficient method of communicating their intentions. Frost had also spoken of seizing the Workhouse at the top of Stow Hill where the remainder of the 45th Regiment of Foot were garrisoned. In the event, the marchers paid it not the slightest attention. Had the Chartists so modified their plans at Friday's Blackwood meeting at the *Coach and Horses* that they were heading for the Westgate, not with revolution in mind, but for a united and impressive public display of support for the Charter and for Vincent? The only certainty is that there was widespread confusion as to their intentions, when the Chartist column wheeled around the corner at the foot of Stow Hill led by a man waving a sword, identified as *"Rees the Fifer"* by the eye witness, Daniel Evans, the Newport tailor who at that moment was stood at the front door of his shop directly opposite the Westgate. Several witnesses spoke of a man detaching himself from the mob and advancing on the hotel. Special constable David Neck, clerk to a Newport solicitor David Williams, was on the steps at the entrance to the Westgate when a marcher with a gun in his hand approached the front door of the hotel. Henry Evans, a saddler whose shop was also across the road from the Westgate, claimed the first shot was fired by a solitary insurgent.[70]

Whether the Chartists were led by Rees was probed closely by James Kelly, for the defence, in cross-examining Daniel Evans, the tailor:

Kelly: Was there no one who appeared to you to be the leader? – *"Only this Rees the Fifer had a sword in his hand and he seemed to wave the sword."*

Kelly: Is he the one you would call the leader? – *"I do not call him the leader more than the others, because they all appeared to be voluntarily coming up."*

Kelly: Then do you think there were no leaders? – *"No, I will not say that; certainly there must have been a leader in bringing them to the place."*

Kelly: Was there anyone who appeared to be the leader? – *"I did not observe anyone alone but that one, and the man I heard give the command."*[71]

The command Evans heard above the din was *"In my men!"* or *"In my boys!"* as a group of marchers stormed up the steps at the entrance forcing their way into the hotel passageway. Others jumped through the windows after beating them in with make-shift spears, stout sticks tipped with iron. It was then the first shot was fired, although where exactly and by whom is disputed. Special constable Thomas Bevan Oliver, guarding the entrance to the Westgate, said it was in the passageway after the man who gave the order to invade the hotel demanded of him, *"Surrender yourselves our prisoners."* When one of the other constables shouted back, *"No, never,"* the insurgent levelled a gun at him and Oliver slammed the hotel door, striking the gun, which ex-ploded close to his head. It was then that firing started outside.[72]

Behind the shuttered windows of the hotel's long room, the mayor, Sir Thomas Phillips, waited, a copy of the Riot Act, which he never did read, in his pocket. Captain Basil Gray and his 30 soldiers had their muskets at the ready but not charged. Before the Chartists arrived the mayor and Gray agreed the hotel was the target and that the troops should take a defensive position, out of sight behind the shuttered windows of the long room. According to Gray, the hotel was struck by small arms fire almost immediately. As slugs and ball tore at the windows, the Chartists simultaneously rushed the front door, forcing their way into the passage. Ordering his men to load with ball cartridge, Captain Gray and the mayor threw open the shutters giving the soldiers a clear shot at the Chartists pressing against the hotel. But they also exposed themselves to gun fire, the mayor hit in the arm and hip, and one of the soldiers, Sgt James Daily struck by six slugs in the head and three in the hand. Although not disclosed at the time, Daily and the Mayor were not the only casualties inside the hotel: a second soldier, Sergeant Armstrong, was also wounded.

Ordered to return fire, the soldiers directed their first volley into the packed ranks of the mob in the road outside, then a second into the passageway where a number of Chartists had forced an entrance. In all, the soldiers fired three rounds each, about one hundred shots, all at point blank range. According to Daily, they knocked down the Chartists *"as fast as they appeared."* On seeing the first demonstrator fall in the roadway, the insurgents fled in every direction, leaving a handful to continue the battle in the smoke-filled hotel passageway, unable to make headway across the corpses of their fallen comrades. Ten minutes after the first shot, Captain Gray ordered a ceasefire.

Gray was convinced that the mob had knowingly fired on the military, the moment the shutters were removed from the long room windows. Neither did he doubt who fired first. Before the shutters were removed so that the soldiers could return fire, shots had entered the room from outside, striking the ceiling above the shutters. This was challenged, however, by the Crown's own witness Daniel Evans, the tailor, who said the soldiers fired before the shutters were opened: *"I think they fired up; they could not fire upon the mob; they could not see them."* Since the Mayor and Sgt Dailey were wounded simultaneously as the shutters were removed, and there were no further casualties when the soldiers were exposed to the crowd outside, the defence argued that this was because the insurgents stopped firing the moment they saw soldiers at the window. The Crown had only to produce Armstrong, the second of the regiment's casualties, to scuttle this argument,

Top: The Chartist marchers streaming down Stow Hill concentrated their attack on the bay window (far left of picture) where the troops were stationed. *Bottom:* Others stormed the entrance.

(Courtesy Newport City Museums and Heritage Service: Newport Museum and Art Gallery).

148

but his existence was never revealed, either in the immediate aftermath of the Uprising or during the trial. Sgt Dailey was not at all sure how many shots were fired from the crowd; five or six he thought before the regiment returned fire. The Mayor, Sir Thomas Phillips, had been watching the approach of the Chartists from a side window on to Stow Hill, and as the column wheeled around to face the hotel he hurried across the passageway into the long room where the soldiers were waiting. It was he, not Captain Gray, he insisted, who gave the order to load immediately he heard the first shot in the hotel passageway.[73]

Where were the ringleaders Frost, Williams and Jones when all this was happening? Zephaniah Williams was still at the top of Stow Hill, one third of a mile away. All he knew of what had happened was the sound of gunfire and smoke rising into what was by then a clear blue sky. Then suddenly he felt the rush of marchers hurrying from the scene. Momentarily, he tried to turn the tide, calling them cowards until one man retorted as he swept passed, *"The devil shall have me before Zephaniah Williams has me with him again. The soldiers are shooting us down."*[74] William Jones had not even reached Newport with his Pontypool contingent. The only sighting of Frost was by two customers in the Westgate Hotel who saw him walking along the pavement a few minutes before the firing started. But as the marchers reached the front of the hotel and the shout went up, *"Mr Frost, appearance to the front,"* he never showed himself and was not seen again until spotted near the turnpike road at Tredegar Park by the park keeper William Adams. Frost was walking quickly, a handkerchief held to his face as if he was crying, according to Adams. When asked by Adams what was wrong, he mumbled something incoherently before hurrying on in the direction of Cardiff along with several hundred others who were following.[75]

After the crowd had been dispersed, police constable Moses Scard found five dead in the hotel, four in the street and another in Friars Field. Many were wounded, dragging themselves back to the hills, only to die later, buried secretly by friends and families to avoid detection. Edward Dowling, proprietor of the *Monmouthshire Merlin*, and scourge of the Chartists, wrote of the scene outside the hotel, *"Many who suffered in the fight crawled away; some exhibiting frightful wounds, and glaring eyes, wildly crying for mercy, and seeking a shelter from the charitable; others, desperately maimed, were carried in the arms of the humane for medical aid; and a few of the miserable objects that were helplessly and mortally wounded, continued to writhe in tortures, crying for water."*[76]

Officially, the death toll was put as "upwards of twenty." Searching the street outside the Westgate, Scard recovered 150 assorted weapons, ammunition, powder and ball, some in the pockets of the dead. An eyewitness said that as the men fled their faces were black with gunpowder where they had bitten off the end of the cartridges they were ramming into their pistols. From one of those he arrested, Constable Scard recovered a Monmouthshire Workingmen's Association membership card with the slogan, *"Peace, law and order!"*[77]

Some of the Chartists in their rush to escape the soldiers' muskets fled down Commercial Street. Samuel Smith, engineer of the Harford's *'Superb'* rail engine whose return journey to Sirhowy had been delayed by the crush of Chartists on the tram road, was heading back to his engine along Commercial Street after visiting his lodgings. The engine's fireman Thomas Pritchard had already set out for Sirhowy, Smith intending to catch up with the locomotive further along the line, not unreasonable since the engine barely managed four miles an hour. Passing the *King William* public house, Smith was overtaken by John Rees followed by the man in the blanket smock, most probably David Jones, both hurrying away from the direction of the Westgate. Asked what had happened, Rees replied they had taken *"one pop at them"* with *"no loss to us."* A moment later, Dai the Tinker (David Jones) rushed up from the same direction, gun in his hand, and beckoning to Rees to hurry, the two quickly disappearing in the direction of Cardiff Road towards the *Waterloo*.[78]

When the engine crew stopped at Bassaleg to take on water, they were overwhelmed by Chartists escaping from the massacre at the Westgate, the men clambering aboard the empty trams, so many hanging on that when the fireman Pritchard looked back all he could see were the wheels of the trams protruding beneath the mountain of bodies. *"We ordered them to get off but it was no good,"* he said. *"At the Welch Oak a man with a spear told us to stop the engine which we did, and he said 'what the devil are*

*these you have got here on the trams?' Speaking to them in Welsh,
he said, 'Damn you, come down'. Some did but the crowd was
too many for him to conquer. Finding it was no good trying to get
them off he went towards Newport on the tram road.* "[79]

The Chartists were now in full flight. That they had fired knowingly at the Queen's troops, the cornerstone of the prosecution
for treason, was confirmed by a reported conversation John Rees
had later that morning. Henry Bailey met Rees not long after the
battle, and asked why *"they had run away when the battle was
won"* to which Rees replied, *'We made a retreat, then went back
and gave them another volley.'* [80]

The magistrates immediately dispatched their clerk Thomas
Jones Phillips with a warrant to search Frost's house, only a
stone's throw from the Westgate. Not only did Frost's wife and
daughters raise no objection to the search, they even helped by
directing the magistrates' clerk to the shelves containing Frost's
private papers. Later, much would be made of the fact that no
personal papers of Frost were produced at the trial, because they
contained nothing incriminating. Neither it seemed had the
Chartist leader made any attempt to hide anything, his papers set
out on his desk as if he had momentarily left the room. Doubling
back from Tredegar Park to Newport, Frost accompanied by
Charles Walters, a ship's carpenter from Chepstow who was seen
outside the Westgate with a gun, found temporary sanctuary with
the printer John Partridge. That evening, the clerk accompanied
by Constable Edward Hopkins arrived at Partridge's house armed
with a search warrant and on entering found the two fugitives.
Both were armed, Frost with three new pistols, loaded and
capped, a powder flask and some bullets. It was not long before
the Pontypool leader William Jones, who never got as far as
Newport, was captured in a field near the Navigation Colliery at
Crumlin. He had challenged his pursuers with a pistol but was
soon overpowered. The Pontnewydd radical John Llewellyn was
picked up trying to leave Swansea on the Carmarthenshire coach,
while Dr Price, who withdrew the Taff Valley contingent at the
last moment, was reputed to be heading for Egypt. He did get as
far as Paris where he remained for a few years.[81]

Rewards of £100 each were posted throughout South Wales and
the West Country for the arrest of Zephaniah Williams, John Rees,

and David Jones. For two days Williams lay low, hiding out with his in-laws at Penyderi Farm, near Argoed, while planning his escape from the country. Then on the Wednesday afternoon following the Uprising, James Brown, owner of the Blaina Iron-works, spotted the Chartist leader riding a pony in the vicinity of the works. A man detailed by Brown to follow Williams tracked him to Caerphilly and the home of his brother-in-law, Dr David Llewellyn. The local constable was immediately alerted to the presence of the wanted man in his neighbourhood but without the warrant, which was still in the hands of the police at Bed-wellty, failed to make the arrest. This allowed Zephaniah time to devise an escape plan with the assistance of his brother-in-law, Dr Llewellyn, who had married the sister of Richard Todd, the Cardiff-based Portuguese Consul. An influential businessman, Todd was a member of the Cardiff Council and a spirits merchant. As Portuguese Consul, he handled affairs on behalf of Portuguese ship owners trading in and out of Cardiff. More significantly for Zephaniah, another of Todd's sisters was married to Captain Head, the master of the *Comet*, then loading at Cardiff. With a letter of introduction from Todd to Head in his pocket, Zephaniah made his way by a circuitous route via Bridgend to Cardiff, arriving there on November 21, only to discover Captain Head had refused him passage and sailed. That afternoon, Zephaniah met Todd secretly to devise an alternative escape. Another vessel, the *Vintage*, was sailing on that night's tide for Oporto and the master, a Captain Williams, was persuaded to take the fugitive. After seeing Zephaniah safely aboard, Todd went ashore, and the *Vintage* set sail – only to run aground on a mud bank where it would be stuck fast until the next morning's high tide. In the mean-time, the Cardiff Constable, Jeremiah Stockdale, was informed by a local publican both Williams and John Rees were attempting their escape through Cardiff that night. In total darkness and accompanied by four officers, he rowed out to where the *Vintage* was grounded on a mud bank.

Captain Williams swore there was no one aboard apart from the crew, until Stockdale entered his cabin and found a fully clothed man asleep in a cot, his boots off, waistband unbuttoned. The man trembled violently when the constable woke him and at first all he would say was that he was a native of Merthyr and his name was Jones. The previous fortnight he admitted spending with Jane Llewellyn at Penyderi Farm, and twelve months earlier said he was employed by the Harford's at Sirhowy but left them because he *"did not like to stay."* In his pockets, "Jones" had a silver watch, a silver pencil case, a box of percussion pistol caps, 102 sovereigns, one half sovereign, two silver sixpences, eleven Spanish dollars, and a letter written by Todd to Captain Head of the *Comet*. Eventually, the mystery passenger admitted he was the fugitive Zephaniah Williams, was arrested and returned to Newport to appear before the magistrates. As for his luggage, the ship sailed for Oporto before it could be recovered.[82]

NOTES

1. Oliver Jones, *Early Days of Sirhowy and Tredegar,* p93; Sian Rhiannon Williams, *Oes y byd I'r iaith Gymraeg* (The Duration of the World for the Welsh Language), Welsh in the Industrial Area of Monmouthshire in the 19th Century (1992).
2. Cardiff Central Library,*Cofiaduron (Diaries) of Brychan (John Davies)*.
3. John Macdonell, *Reports of State Trials,* vol. iii, 1831/40 (London, 1891), pp1038-86.
4. NLW, 40/2, Lord Tredegar Papaers, copy of Zephaniah Williams's 'confession'.
5. Fred Pedler, *Merthyr Express,* 'Morgan Williams, the Chartist', 5 May 1956.
6. *Merthyr Guardian,* 9 February 1839; *The Charter,* 10 February 1839; *Monmouthshire Merlin,* 16 February 1839.
7. *Western Vindicator,* 6 April 1839.
8. *ibid.*
9. Williams letter, *Silurian,* 15 June 1839.
10. *Western Vindicator,* 31 March 1839.
11. *ibid.*
12. *ibid.*
13. *The Times,* 6 November 1839: report from Bristol dated 4 November 1839.
14. *Western Vindicator,* 31 March 1839.
15. *Western Vindicator,* 6 April 1839, *Cambrian,* 13 April 1939.
16. *Charter,* 28 July 1839.
17. *Western Vindicator,* 4 May 1839.
18. *ibid.*
19. *ibid.*
20. *Western Vindicator,* 5 October 1839.
21. *ibid,* 19, 26 Oct 1839.

22. *ibid*, 2 March 1839.
23. *Western Vindicator,* 20 April 1839.
24. PRO, HO 40/45, Thomas Phillips to Home Office, 12 August 1839.
25. *Western Vindicator,* 11 Sept 1839.
26. PRO, HO 40/46, letter from the Marquis of Bute to Home Office, 6 September 1839; Gurney, *Trial of John Frost,* pp515-516; NPL, letters dated 28 September 1839.
27. Wilks, *South Wales and the Rising of 1839,* p146; for wider picture of Chartist contacts prior to Monmouthshire Uprising, see Wilks, pp162-179.
28. David Jones, *The Last Rising,* p207.
29. NLW, 40/2, Tredegar House Papers, Williams 'confession', copy of letter, 25 May 1840.
30. Report of Mr Seymour Tremenheere on the State of Elementary Education in the Mining District of South Wales, 1840,pp 177-178, Law Library, Cardiff University.
31. *South Wales Argus,* 19 September 1936, 11 November 1938.
32. NPL, Chartist Trial depositions for numerous witness references to this.
33. PRO, HO 45/102, informer's account of Chartist meeting on Clerkenwell Green, 15 May 1841.
34. *Cambrian,* 29 June 1839 publishes an article by Johnson; PRO, HO 40/45, deposition of Joseph Johnson, 29 April 1839.
35. *Western Vindicator,* 23 March 1839.
36. NPL, Chartist Trials, 15, William Howell.
37. NPL, Chartist Trials, 15, Edward Richards.
38. British Parliamentary Papers, Accounts and Papers XXXV111, C.559, 1839: *Return of all Associations formed and armed for the Protection of Life and Property;* PRO, HO 41/14, Russell to Leigh, two letters, 13 May 1839, and Russell to Leigh 20 May 1839; Needham to Leigh, 10 May 1839; PRO, HO 41/13, Home Office to Officer Commanding, Militia, Monmouth, 8 May 1839; PRO, HO 41/14, Phillips to Mayor of Monmouth, 12 May 1839.
39. *Monmouthshire Merlin,* 6 April 1839; *Cambrian,* 19 April 1839; *Western Vindicator,* 26 April, Aug 3, 1839.
40. NPL, Chartist Trials, 12, Moses Scard.
41. Oliver Jones, *Early Days of Sirhowy and Tredegar.*
42. Oliver Jones, loc. cit. p93.
43. MB, 26 October 1839; David Williams, *John Frost, A Study in Chartism,* pp188-191.
44. *ibid.*
45. CCL, Bute Papers, xx. 72; *Silurian,* 16 November 1839; NPL, Chartist Trials, 11, James Emery.
46. William Howell, Chartist Trials, Vol. 15.
47. NPL, Chartist Trials, Rachel Howell, Monmouthshire Magistrates, Committal Proceedings.
48. NPL, Chartist Trials, 5, William Davies.
49. This and the subsequent paragraphs about the final preparations at

Blackwood are from the following sources: NPL, Chartist Trials, 5, Job Tovey, Esther Pugh, Richard Pugh, William Davies; *Merthyr Guardian,* 1 February 1840.

50. PRO, TS 11/502.1630; PRO, TS 11/502.1630; Matthew Williams, MM 17 January 1840.

51. *ibid.*

52. NPL, Chartist Trials, 15, Richard Hawkins.

53. MM, William Howell and Rachel Howell, 10 January1840.

54. MM, Thomas Bowen, George Lloyd, 17 January 1840; James James, Gurney, *The Trial of John Frost*; NPL, Chartist Trials, 15, Thomas Saunders.

55. MM, Edward Richards, 17 January 1840.

56. NPL, Chartist Trials, 15, 7, James Emery.

57. NPL, Chartist Trials, 5, Mary Charles.

58. MM, Henry Smith, 10 January 1840; Gurney, *The Trial Of John Frost,* James Hodge, pp304, 308-309; *The Times,* John Harford, 12 January 1840.

59. NPL, Chartist Trials, 5, 14, 15 Mary Thomas, Mary Williams, John Jones.

60. Oliver Jones, *Early Days of Sirhowy and Tredegar,* pp99-101.

61. *ibid.*

62. NPL, Chartist Trials, 14, Thomas Pritchard, Samuel Smith for description of Chartist approach to Newport from Tredegar Park.

63. PRO, TS 11/502.1630.

64. Rees, Coles evidence, Gurney.

65. NPL, Chartist Trials, 9, Thomas Evans.

66. PRO, TS 11/502.1630.

67. CCL, Bute Papers, XX.30, Letter from Homan to Capt Howells, 31 October 1839.

68. NPL, Chartist Trials, 4, Walker, Webb; NPL, Chartist Trials, 7, Homan.

69. For most reliable eye-witness evidence see, Henry Evans, Gurney pp223-226; Daniel Evans, Gurney pp226-230.

70. *ibid;* NPL, Chartist Trials, 15, David Neck.

71. Daniel Evans, Gurney pp226-230.

72. Thomas Oliver, Gurney, pp213-223, also Oliver, NPL, Chartist Trial, 9.

73. Basil Gray, Gurney, pp247-254; Sir Thomas Phillips, Gurney, pp233-239.

74. NPL, Chartist Trials, 15, George Lloyd.

75. William Adams, Gurney, pp230-233.

76. Dowling, *Rise and Fall,* p43; MM, 7 November 1839, p4.

77. NPL, Chartist Trials, 12, Moses Scard.

78. NPL, Chartist Trials, 14, Thomas Pritchard, Samuel Smith.

79. *ibid.*

80. NPL, Chartist Trials, 6, Henry Bailey.

81. Thomas Jones Phillips, Gurney, pp417-423.

82. Stockdale, MM 23 November 1839; CPL, Bute Papers, XX.79, D.Reece, 22 November 1839, 11 December 1839.

CHAPTER 7

Trial and Transportation

The Chartist Treason Trial broke new ground when the Special Commission began sitting at Monmouth on December 10. For all concerned, judge, jury, counsel and accused it was a unique and historic legal event. No treason trial had been held in Britain since the Cato Street conspirators twenty years earlier and much time would be spent pouring over legal precedents and opinions. According to the Lord Chief Justice, Sir Nicholas Tindal, who presided, the trial of Frost, Williams and Jones, the first of the alleged conspirators to appear, centred on three words: object, design and intention. To prove High Treason, arguably still the most serious of all capital crimes, the Crown was required to produce the testimony of two witnesses to an overt act, which in the eyes of the court constituted the levying of war against the realm.

When the first Treason Act was passed in 1353 war was usually levied against the monarch by a rival for the throne. Since then, the definition had been refined to refer to any insurrection obliging the monarch to alter the law or to remove his/her advisors. Neither did the overt act need be accompanied by the pomp and circumstance of armies facing each other across the battlefield. The Crown was required, however, to demonstrate that the insurrectionists were organised in great numbers and in a warlike manner. Even then, treason was not necessarily proven if it could be shown that the aim was to correct some local or private injustice such as, the Chartists might have claimed, the amelioration of the prison conditions suffered by Henry Vincent. What distinguished the Chartist Uprising from the Merthyr Rising a decade earlier, when the rioters were prosecuted for lesser offences, was that the Chartists were deemed to have a more general purpose affecting the state by seeking to alter the established law. Addressing the Grand Jury at Monmouth before it retired to deliberate on whether to return True Bills for the trial of those committed by the magistrates for treason, Lord Chief Justice Tindal took great care in explaining that the law was precisely defined to punish the guilty while not entangling innocent persons by reason of its uncertainty. For an overt act to constitute High Treason, said Lord Chief Justice Tindal, the prosecution would need to show the aim of the insurgents was to put down the authority of the law, shake and subvert the foundations of all government, loosen and dissolve the bands and cement by which society was held together, and the general confusion of property, by involving the whole people in bloodshed and mutual destruction: nothing short of civil war.

Having laid down precise guidelines for the Grand Jury, Tindal concluded with an extraordinarily prejudicial statement, which almost certainly today would have provided grounds for an appeal. Before sending the jury away to consider against whom indictments should be returned, Tindal observed: *"I would add, also, my most earnest hope, that it may be found in the result, that the great majority of those, who may have been involved in the guilt of these transactions, have been misled by the arts of wicked and designing men, and have thus sinned through ignorance and blindness rather than from premeditated guilt."* He went even further by suggesting a remedy for a *"state of mind and feeling so unhealthy and diseased,"* recommending a programme of religious instruction to teach Wales' younger generation to fear the Almighty and accept the laws of the country as being ordained by God.[1]

With this ringing in their ears, the Grand Jury, a veritable *Who's Who* of Monmouthshire, including the ironmasters Sir Benjamin Hall, Samuel Homfray, Joseph Bailey (Crawshay Bailey's brother), and Octavius Morgan of the Tredegar Park dynasty, took less than a day to return True Bills for High Treason against fourteen persons, two of these John Rees and David Jones, still at large. The Monmouthshire gentry had been delighted by the Home Secretary's decision to establish a Special Commission to try the Chartists. Now it would be satisfied with nothing less than convictions for an offence the law regarded as of the deepest dye, requiring the severest punishment. Only this would restore the Black Domain to its former state of slavish compliance. Whatever their object, design, and intention, the Chartists had challenged the ascendancy of the ruling class. In response, the establishment set about assembling the most powerful case to sustain charges of High Treason only satisfied by the execution of the ringleaders.

The roundup of activists and witnesses started immediately. Not that this was easy. The search for information was met by a wall of silence, in some instances with intimidation and violence threatened against collaborators. The Blaina ironmaster James Brown, one of the leading Chartist-hunters, complained to Thomas Jones Phillips, clerk to Newport Magistrates responsible for co-ordinating the collection of evidence, that witnesses against Zephaniah Williams had been intimidated. Two of these, James James and his brother-in-law had been violently assaulted. According to Brown, the Chartists were using Scotch Cattle terror tactics to discourage witnesses.

Scotch Cattle were a form of 19th century working class mafia that had existed in the industrial valleys of Monmouthshire long before the rise of Chartism. Because the population of the Black Domain lived in constant fear of losing job, home and security, the Scotch Cattle organisation, if there was such a thing, intervened after attempts at peaceful arbitration failed to deal with grievances, the most common of which was the social distress caused by the arbitrary reduction in wages by mine owners and ironmasters. The violence associated with Scotch Cattle was often directed at strike-breakers and blacklegs, and was usually preceded by secret meetings held in the mountains, accompanied by the firing of guns, blowing of horns and beating of drums. Those who continued to ignore warnings were likely to receive a midnight visit from a gang of ten or so miners, the leaders disguised by masks, handkerchiefs, cattle skins, and others with blackened faces. Some were even dressed as women, like the Rebecca Rioters of West Wales whose target was the burden of the toll-gates, although the cause of those disturbances was far more deep-seated than that. The first thing that an intended victim knew of the arrival of the Cattle outside their home in the dead of night was the rattle of chains and blowing of a horn. Windows were smashed, furniture and furnishings destroyed. Minerals Agents or master miners who profited from the colliers through their links with public houses and company shops, were also often the target for the midnight visit. In difficult times, the Cattle terrorised most of the mining valleys, and were active again in the aftermath of the Newport Uprising with threats to kidnap key witnesses.[2]

Whether these were real or imagined, key witnesses were moved from the valleys to secure addresses in Newport. Despite these obstacles, and with the help of spies and informers, and deals struck in return for promises of immunity against prosecution, the magistrates accumulated an impressive list of witnesses for submission to the Treasury Solicitor George Maule. By the time of the Special Commission, statements had been taken from 236 Crown witnesses, only one sixth of these, however, material witnesses with first hand accounts of what happened. Most of the preliminary examinations took place at the Westgate, presided over by the Rev. James Coles, of Michaelstone-y-fedw. He was especially hostile in his interrogation of Welsh-speaking prisoners towards whom he was autocratic and condescending, on one occasion threatening to arrest a witness, John Hughes, for 'smiling.' Coles was enthusiastically assisted in his cross-examination by John Frost's life-long enemy Thomas Prothero, the investigation moving rapidly to a conclusion on December 6 by which time 125 prisoners had been interrogated. A dozen of these were given gaol sentences or bailed, and twenty-nine committed to Monmouth Gaol, twenty-one accused of High Treason. After further committals to the Brecon Assizes, some sixty prisoners were awaiting prosecution.

Zephaniah Williams was sent for trial on November 25 after the magistrates heard eighteen hours of evidence against him. By the end of this he was a shadow of the man described on his wanted poster as 5ft 8 inches, of strong, square build, a bold talker with a blunt manner, and a swaggering walk. Even the usually aggressive Coles took pity, remarking as he committed Williams for trial, *"God forbid that I should add one pang to the suffering you appear to undergo."* Williams' physical and mental deterioration was partly attributable to sleep starvation, because each night he was chained to a gaoler. While Coles directed that Williams be treated more humanely, the handcuffing might have been explained by suspicions that Zephaniah was suicidal. John Frost insinuated as much when he revealed one of the three gaoled Chartist leaders had contemplated suicide.[3]

The hearty good health Zephaniah had always enjoyed was replaced by a black foreboding in Monmouth Gaol. For the several dozen Chartists awaiting trail on a variety of charges, he became a 'weather vein', the latest piece of bad news etched into his countenance.[4] Besides his overwhelming sense of hopelessness and sleep deprivation, there was also the debilitating diet of gruel, bread and potatoes, barely sufficient to keep a prisoner alive. After two months of this, most prisoners suffered digestive disorders, progressing into serious illnesses. Following four months in Monmouth Gaol, Henry Vincent was delirious, and suffering from liver failure. These conditions could have been alleviated had Chartist supporters been permitted by the magistrates to deliver food to the inmates.[5] Frost was soon in need of medical attention for digestive and biliary disorders, and Jones for a recurrence of a blood complaint. The prison chaplain, Rev. E. J. Gosling reported several Chartists confined to the infirmary, others in solitary confinement.[6] Meanwhile, Vincent and his three companions from the earlier sedition trial were moved into the female cells to avoid contact with the new arrivals, all of whom were held incommunicado and refused access to newspapers, pen and paper. The chaplain ministered to Frost regularly, but Zephaniah's agnosticism appears not to have been shaken by his experiences, the Rev. Gosling noting in his journal he had preached to him just the once, although he did "lecture" all three on January 14, two days before they were sentenced to death. Gosling was mostly interested in showing that the spread of Chartism was linked to the decline in religious observance, noting the lapse by two prisoners, Lovell and Walters from the Anglican faith, coincided with their increasing support for the Charter! The other evil, he identified, was the popularity among the 'lower orders' of publications pandering to 'depraved tastes.' Overseeing the prison regime was Governor Ford, a man whose inhumanity caused Frost to describe his incarceration at Monmouth as "*the greatest misery I have endured.*"[7]

In the public mind, Frost, Williams and Jones had already been tried and convicted. Any hope of a fair trial before a Monmouthshire jury was quickly swept aside by a hostile press and bigoted establishment baying for blood. William Foster Geach, Frost's stepson representing all three, unsuccessfully applied for the trial to be moved out of Monmouthshire. It was generally accepted that if Frost was convicted of High Treason, the others would follow, since much of the evidence was common to all three accused. For a conviction, however, the Crown needed to prove design, object and intent. The common design was allegedly the Chartist delegate meeting at the *Coach and Horses*, Blackwood, on Friday November 1 immediately before the Uprising when plans for the march were finalised. If the object was to seize Newport then that was the overt act of levying of war against the Queen. For the defence, Fitzroy Kelly ascribed a more moderate objective to the march on Newport: a demonstration only, in support of the Charter and for the amelioration of conditions suffered by Vincent and his companions in Monmouth Gaol. According to the Crown, the seizure of Newport by armed men was intended to convey a signal for a national uprising. While there was evidence that some marchers were armed, very few exhibits were produced from among the hundred or so assorted weapons and ammunition picked up from outside the Westgate where they were abandoned by fleeing marchers. Nor was there conclusive evidence of the widespread production of weapons in preparation for the march, only a few pikes distributed from a room beneath Zephaniah Williams' *Royal Oak* beer shop, and his encouragement to marchers to arm themselves for purposes of self-defence. Even more inconclusive was the claim that the signal for a national rising would be the non-arrival of the Welsh mail in Birmingham, after the defence demonstrated there was no such coach.

So unclear were the Chartist intentions, that the defence pressed on the jury Lord Mansfield's definition of High Treason, which required the prosecution to prove the crowd and the individuals so arraigned both guilty of a treasonable objective.[8] It soon became evident that while united in spirit, the Chartists had no common aim. For some it was the end of the 'long pay,' they had been drinking heavily during the march down to Newport, and really did not care.[9] Public declamations by Frost certainly pointed to treasonable intent in his accompanying, aiding and encouraging the Chartists. Yet this could not be seen as automatically implicating the marchers.

Of the 236 witnesses prepared by the magistrates, only a handful were material to the prosecution. Even these were of dubious quality, their credibility certain to be challenged if the defence had the opportunity to investigate the witness list. Contrary to statute, the list was not delivered until December 17, the defence suspecting the magistrates clerk, Thomas Llewellyn Phillips, wanted to allow it as little time as possible to investigate witnesses before the trial opened on December 31. Sir Frederick Pollock, leading for the defence, lodged an objection, but rather than delay proceedings, the Lord Chief Justice referred the matter to the Court of the Exchequer. Although this court was eventually to rule 9-6 in favour of the objection, the judges decided the late delivery of the witness list had no material effect on the outcome of the Monmouth trial.[10]

Two key witnesses were missing from the Crown's list. Nineteen-year-old William Davies, son of a Blackwood shopkeeper, and the only prosecution witness able to say exactly what went on at the crucial delegate meeting on the Friday at the *Coach and Horses,* had absconded for a second time. On the first occasion, immediately following the failed Uprising, he was arrested in Canterbury on his way to Dover and France. Escorted back to Wales, young Davies, probably under pressure from his father, turned Queen's Evidence, providing the Crown with statements incriminating Frost. But before proceedings started, he absconded again, hiding out with relatives at Llanelli before eventually placing himself beyond the reach of the Crown for the duration of the trial by escaping abroad.[11] After Davies, by far the strongest evidence against Frost as to what actually happened at the *Coach and Horses*, came from Job Tovey, with whom the Chartist leader spent the night and day immediately following the delegate meeting. Tovey was never called.[12] That left the Crown's case resting on the evidence of five men, Matthew Williams, William Harris, John Harford, James Hodge, and Richard Pugh.

Matthew Williams from Argoed swore to seeing Frost at the *Welch Oak*, afterwards in the company of a body of men in Tredegar Park, and, lastly, on the pavement by the Roman Catholic Church at the bottom of Stow Hill before the shooting started.[13] The most damning evidence looked as if it might be that of William Harris[14] who claimed he heard William Davies say to Frost before the marchers set off from the *Coach and Horses* on the Sunday night, *"There is enough to eat Newport."* But his evidence was discredited by the defence and withdrawn, leaving the prosecution case hanging on Hodge, Harford, and Pugh.

If Hodge's account of a conversation with Frost is correct, then the Newport draper had planned to attack and capture Newport, blow up the bridge, and stop the Welsh mail as a signal for national rebellion. Cross-examined, he was forced to admit, however, that no one else was privy to this conversation, and the credibility of his evidence thrown further into doubt when it was revealed that within a few days of providing his statement to Thomas Prothero, the examining magistrate, Prothero gave him work at one of his collieries.[15] John Harford's testimony of what Frost told the marchers about their intentions at Newport, was equally suspect. For thirteen days before his examination by magistrates at the Westgate for "carrying a sword in the mob," Harford had been detained in the Union Workhouse. On mentioning to the workhouse master there were certain things he could say against Frost, Harford was taken to the Westgate to repeat these to the magistrates in return for which it was alleged all charges against him were dropped.[16] The landlord of the *Coach and Horses*, Richard Pugh, was called to prove the Friday meeting, but apart from testifying to Frost's presence there, either knew nothing of what transpired, or was too cautious to admit to knowing.[17]

So that was it: a great deal of uncorroborated evidence, a great deal of hearsay. The only evidence that might be described as documentary proof of a conspiracy was a solitary piece of paper, seized from the home of the printer and former Chartist Samuel Etheridge, containing instructions for organising men into groups of ten commanded by captains. Etheridge was never charged with any offence and insisted the document referred to preparations for the 1790 rebellion in Ireland, and not the Chartists.[18] Either the Chartists destroyed all their papers – or never had any.

The weakness of the prosecution's case was clear from the summing up of the Lord Chief Justice. To the astonishment and dismay of the Attorney-General, Sir John Campbell, Tindal had from the beginning of the trial laboured for an acquittal although in Campbell's view *"no human being doubted the guilt of the prisoners."* For the sake of public order, the Attorney General believed the country needed a guilty verdict. But after listening to Tindal, he expected the worse and had retired to his lodgings to

From left to right: The trial at Monmouth with Frost, Williams and Jones in the dock on the right of the picture; Zephaniah Williams had difficulty focussing when sentence was passed, the Lord Chief Justice pausing a moment for him to recover; and Sir Thomas Phillips, Mayor of Newport, with his wounded arm in a sling.

(Courtesy Newport City Museums and Heritage Service: Newport Museum and Art Gallery).

consult with his legal team. In the event of an acquittal against Frost, they decided not to proceed against the others.[19] But the Attorney General had reckoned without the inherent prejudice of the Monmouthshire jury, which had probably convicted the Chartists before a word of evidence was delivered. It took the jury only thirty minutes to declare Frost guilty, adding a recommendation for mercy. The remaining Chartists were soon dealt with, the trial of Zephaniah Williams lasting longest from January 9-13, followed by Jones on January 15. The same day, Walters, Lovell, Benfield, Rees (another John Rees), and Jenkin Morgan changed their pleas to guilty of High Treason in return for a promise of a reduced sentence. All eight were sentenced to death, in the case of the last five this eventually commuted to seven years imprisonment.

Wearing the traditional black cap, Lord Chief Justice Tindal delivered the death sentence on the three Chartists leaders on January 16, warning them the jury's recommendation of mercy was unlikely to be successful. Zephaniah Williams listened, his eyes closed. When he opened them again, according to the *Monmouthshire Merlin* reporter in the court, he seemed to have difficulty focussing, leaning his head in his hand as if about to faint, causing the Lord Chief Justice to pause a moment for him to recover. At their own request, the three were placed in the same condemned cell at Monmouth Gaol to await execution, unaware of the massive campaign launched to save their lives. The Monmouthshire gentry responded with a rival campaign to reinforce the government's resolve to execute the conspirators. Petitioning the Home Secretary, the Grand Jury spoke of the feelings of outrage and insecurity in the county.

Isolated from what was happening, and denied access to newspapers, pen and paper, the three Chartists awaited their fate in Monmouth Gaol. Only when aboard the convict ship, *Mandarin,* bound for Van Diemen's Land weeks later, was Frost able to write to his wife Mary giving her a graphic account of the events that followed their sentencing.[20] Remarking that he for one would have preferred death to transportation, he wrote, *"Death is unavoidable and it is not of relative importance whether we meet it now or within a few years. The value of life depends on the use we can be to others; if we cannot use it for the good of family or society it is hardly worth defending."*

Preparations for the execution were well advanced, the hangman and headsman waiting in Monmouth, when forty-eight hours before it was scheduled on Saturday February 1 the Home Secretary, Lord Normanby, announced a postponement until February 6. Governor Ford was instructed to advise the prisoners not to raise their hopes because the lawful sentence would be assuredly carried into effect. Delivering the news to the three Chartists in the condemned cell, Ford tormented them with questions about how they required their remains to be dealt with following the execution. Frost later recalled how the Governor had talked of cutting off their heads with *"the same lack of feeling as if he was talking about geese."*

"We could tell from this unfeeling man's expression whether the news was favourable or not," the Chartist wrote to his wife. *"Sometimes he came through the cell looking like a wolf, which we took to be a good sign. We met him, however, without showing signs of fear, and instructed him to speak to our families concerning arrangements about our bodies."* [21] Some years afterwards, Frost put a more sinister construction on this grisly conversation, deducing it was all part of a Government plot to push the three Chartists into a suicide pact, thereby discrediting Chartism while avoiding the opprobrium of a public execution, and the widespread unrest this might cause at a time the nation was preparing celebrations to mark Queen Victoria's marriage.[22] The scale of support for the gaoled Chartists was exceptional, mass meetings held in almost every large town in Britain. One radical newspaper commented, *"If Frost is unfairly dealt with, no Crown in Europe will be worth one year's purchase."* In Monmouthshire, there was a wave of arson attacks, threatening letters and assaults levelled at those connected with the prosecution.[23] Unaware of what was happening beyond the prison gates, Frost, Williams and Jones were convinced their situation was so hopeless they talked together about a suicide pact. One of the three, most probably Williams in view of what was known of his mental and physical state, was the strongest advocate of this as a means of defeating the Government's objective.

"He thought it would be a most disgraceful death if we were to allow ourselves to be hung and afterwards to have our heads cut off and our bodies quartered, though the latter part of the

sentence probably would not have been carried into effect," Frost recalled later. The other two opposed suicide, Frost insisting it was exactly what the Government wanted. Listening to these nightly conversations just six feet away on the other side of the locked cell door was the turnkey, a man Frost was convinced had reported their suicidal tendencies to the Governor. This, he thought, even explained the seven-day postponement of the execution: the Home Secretary hoped that in the intervening period they might be persuaded into taking their own lives. Incredible as this might seem, Frost insisted his suspicions were confirmed fifteen years later while visiting America after receiving his conditional pardon. There he met another Chartist imprisoned at Monmouth at the same time. This man confirmed the turnkey was reporting their talk of suicide to the Governor. According to Frost, *"They knew what our conversations were, they knew that the subject of suicide had been discussed in the condemned cell and they thought that by holding out no hope they would induce us to do that which they themselves were afraid to do."*[24]

But on February 1, the day originally set for the execution, the Home Secretary announced their reprieve, commuting the death sentences to transportation for life. Just why the sudden change of mind, when most expected the Whig Government's resolve not to weaken, has never been clear.[25] While some believe there was Royal intervention, it is more likely their lives were spared after representations from Chief Justice Tindal to Normanby on the grounds of the legal objections raised at the trial.[26] That same night at about 10 p.m., the three prisoners were woken by the clatter of the gaol's iron gates. Moments later, Governor Ford came to their cell with the news they were to be moved immediately on the instructions of the Home Office. He did not say where. Chained together in heavy leg irons and loaded into a prison wagon driven at great speed through the night to Chepstow, escorted by five London policemen and a mounted guard of Lancers, the prisoners were put aboard the steam ship, *Usk,* which sailed immediately but not until Frost remonstrated with Governor Ford about the heavy chains they were forced to wear. *"I asked him whether it was for punishment or for security that they were being kept on us,"* he wrote his wife. *"Was it likely that we would escape from the steam ship? Then he took them away, grumbling and roaring like a bear.*" After anchoring briefly at Pill, near Newport, the ship proceeded to Portsmouth, the Home Secretary clearly anxious to remove their malign influence as rapidly as possible. Aboard the *Usk* the three were locked in a cabin, guarded day and night by two police officers, and a soldier armed with a bayonet. Even when allowed on deck there was a police escort, not that there was much opportunity for this on account of heavy seas, the voyage taking 15 days when usually it took four. The Chartist prisoners were destined for the prison hulk the *York* moored in Portsmouth Harbour, one of several decommissioned naval vessels located around the coast to accommodate the overflow from Britain's crowded gaols and as holding pens for those sentenced to transportation. After ten dreadful days aboard the hulk, Frost, Williams and Jones were transferred on February 24 to the *Mandarin,* berthed at Spithead. Dressed now in regulation prison clothes, speckled cotton shirt, round jacket, cotton trousers and cheap hat, the three were bundled aboard a barge and huddling from the cold beneath a piece of sail cloth, were delivered to the convict transport and a 14,000 miles voyage to the other side of world, lasting four months.[27]

Frost was admitted to the ship's hospital as soon as they arrived on board. That evening, having fallen into an uneasy sleep, he was woken by someone saying, "This, sir, is John Frost." Opening his eyes Frost saw the ship's infirmary was filled with military officers, the older of them identifying himself as Governor of Portsmouth. Approaching the Chartist leader's bunk, the Governor said, *"I have not come here Mr Frost for the purpose of reproaching you; I have come here to give you a little advice. If there should be the slightest commotion in this ship during the time she is on her voyage hence to Van Diemen's Land, the officer in command of the troops has the strictest orders to act with the greatest promptitude."* By now Frost was obsessed with the idea that the Government, having being deflected from carrying out the execution because of the fear of public unrest, still wanted them dead. Replying to the Governor's admonishment, he said, *"Would it not have been better that our lives should have been taken according to law, than that they should be taken on our passage to Van Diemen's? And do you mean that that promptitude will be evinced if I or any of us have nothing to do with any commotion?"* At this point the Governor left the ship, leaving Frost to contemplate what attempt might be made on their lives during the long voyage.[28]

In eighty years, 165,000 men, women and children, some hardened criminals, others machine breakers, pirates, patriots, deserters, political prisoners, trade unionists, slaves, or just land rights activists were transported to Australia, half of these to Van Diemen's Land, later Tasmania. Transportation was introduced in the 17th century, the majority of prisoners then deported to the American Colonies, until the War of Independence in 1776 brought this to an end. An alternative had to be found. British gaols were dangerously over-crowded, prisoners sharing three to a bed, a prison sentence as good as a death sentence in these disease-ridden pits. By the beginning of the 19th century Britain was assailed by a crime wave, every part of London the scene of executions, criminals strung from chains on every common and wayside. So vicious had crime become that in 1796 the Government offered 'blood money,' £40 for every capital conviction informers were able to deliver. The wide-open spaces of recently discovered Australia seemed the perfect answer. Transportation was justified as a deterrent, reforming the criminal class into useful members of society. But the availability of cheap convict labour was the real excuse and all changes and refinements to the system were dictated by this colonial requirement. By 1840 transportation was universally considered an abomination that corrupted, rather than reformed, those who suffered it. Sir William Molesworth, chairman of the House of Commons Committee that unsuccessfully recommended its abolition in 1838, described the Australian communities that sprung from penal transportation as being in a state of depravity not equalled in any part of the civilised world; more hideously vicious than any recorded in sacred or profane history. By the time Frost, Williams and Jones arrived aboard the *Mandarin* the penal colonies had become the British pest houses that stunk in the nostrils of mankind.[29]

It was not without justification that Sir Francis Forbes, Chief Justice of Australia, said he preferred death in any of its forms to transportation to Norfolk Island. Two thousand convicts were held on Norfolk Island, a thousand miles off the Australian coast, and at Port Arthur on the Tasman Peninsula. In both, the penal regime was of such savagery that the only respite for some was a murder pact, one convict killing the other in return for the certainty of being hanged at Sydney or Hobart Town. At Point Puer, the infamous children's penal colony in the bay at Port Arthur, children flung themselves roped together from the cliffs into the sea. Twenty-five miles across the Peninsula at Slopen Main were the Coal Mines, a punishment station rivalling any as a sink of depravity. Located on the edge of Norfolk Bay, there was only one realistic escape, across twelve miles of open sea. The alternative was the narrow isthmus of Eaglehawk Neck, a hundred metres wide, guarded day and night by eleven ferocious dogs with names like *Ugly Mug, Tear'em, Caesar and Pompey,* some placed on stages out in the water to detect absconders attempting to swim to the mainland. The most hardened criminals were detained at the Coal Mines, spending their days half naked, on their hands and knees dragging wicker baskets of coal from the coalface to the pit bottom. This inky blackness was ruled by the most degenerate, one hundred flogged on one morning alone for diverse crimes from buggery to assault. Not surprisingly, disease was rampant. Those for whom punishment ceased to be a deterrent were locked away at night like caged animals in cells one hundred feet beneath the surface, some never to escape this earthly hell.[30]

As political prisoners, Frost, Williams and Jones were confident they would escape the hell of Port Arthur. After all, it was for repeat offenders, which they were not. Customarily they could expect to be sent to one of the Probation Stations along the Tasmanian coast, there to serve two-to-four-years on public works projects before being granted a ticket of leave and released into the community to work for wages. This had replaced the practice of assigning convicts to free settlers or to Government officers. In either case, it amounted to slave labour, any convict who dared transgress or offend his master returned to a penal settlement for further punishment. Of the 211 convicts aboard the *Mandarin,* the three Chartists were to be the only ones destined immediately for the punishment settlement at Port Arthur, Frost to work as a clerk in the office of the Commandant, Captain Charles O'Hara Booth, Jones to supervise the boys at Point Puer, and Williams as a supervisor in the dreaded Coal Mines.[31]

With all this in prospect, it is not hard to imagine the cause of Chartism receding in their consciousness, to be replaced by profound apprehension, as the *Mandarin* headed down the English Channel in the teeth of a raging gale. The convict ship had not sailed far before its maintop and mizzen masts were brought down, forcing it into Falmouth for repairs. While these took place, Barclay Fox, a gentleman who had heard that the infamous Frost was aboard, persuaded Dr Alex McKechnie, the Surgeon Superintendent, to permit him to satisfy his curiosity by visiting the Chartist 'lion' in his cage. Assuming the disguise of a missionary distributing religious texts, and introduced as a friend by Dr McKechnie, Fox asked Frost whether there were any religious books or tracts in which he might be interested for the long voyage. Describing the encounter in his diary later, Fox wrote, *"Frost came forward and answered with the most consummate contempt for all children and old women's books. He 'would be obliged for a Pilgrim's Progress or some solid reading however'. He had made religion his study for 13 years. In answer to my question whether he did not consider the government had acted as leniently with him as it could, he answered with great emphasis, 'Not a bit of it. They have commuted my sentence to a much harder one. I should vastly prefer hanging to this slow lingering torture to which they have condemned me.'"* Both Jones and Williams who were in the same cell agreed with this sentiment, confirming to Barclay Fox the benefits of transportation. Frost's face was not easily forgotten, he said, wan and haggard and indented with deep furrows, small piercing grey eyes and a beetling brow surmounted by a shock of grey hair, displaying much character but little talent. *"All the bold badness without any of the sublimity of a Revolutionist,"* said Fox. As for Jones and Williams, he considered them to be *"inferior animals,"* Jones affecting a light carelessness and unconcern, Williams appearing to be nothing more than *"the brute man."* In return for his private peepshow, Barclay Fox sent Frost a copy of *Pilgrims Progress*.[32] The night before the *Mandarin* sailed from Falmouth on February 29 the Chartist prisoners had another visitor, on this occasion a Captain Shaw who had been invited by the ship's master Captain John Good to dine aboard. Shaw found the Chartists to be penitent, describing Frost as *"a decent, nice-looking old man"* who preferred execution to transportation.[33]

The *Mandarin* sailed south across the Bay of Biscay and down the west coast of Africa, towards Simon's Bay on the Cape of Good Hope. Once aboard the convict transport the men were mustered on deck, and issued with their regulation dress of jackets and waistcoats of coarse blue cloth, duck trousers, check or coarse linen shirts, yard stockings and woollen caps. This was a winter voyage, in which case they were also given flannel underclothes and raven duck overalls. The prisoners' quarters lay between-decks, two rows of sleeping berths, one above the other, each six foot square and made to hold four convicts, each man allotted 18 inches of space to sleep in. The three Chartists were locked away in a separate cell at the end of the prisoners' quarters reserved for the most dangerous prisoners. Food was considered adequate by the authorities, although not by the convicts. Six months earlier, when 136 rebels, mostly American citizens, convicted for their part in the rebellions in Upper and Lower Canada in 1838, were transported aboard the *Buffalo*, one of the prisoners, William Gates described the standard daily ration as one-half pound of bread, one-pound of meat, pork or beef alternatively, a pint of skilly (thin soup) in the morning, pint of cocoa or tea at night, a pint of water, and a small quantity of duff (flour pudding). Every convict received an ounce of limejuice and the same amount of sugar every day as protection from the scourge of sea voyages, scurvy. Disease usually brought aboard from the hulks was a major enemy, the overall death rate for men, one in every sixty-eight.[34]

Conditions aboard the transports had, however, improved by 1840. Most significantly, the practice of transporting male and female convicts together had been scaled back, although when this did happen the women still regarded transportation under such conditions as a sentence to prostitution, some preferring a public execution to the ignominy of a floating brothel. Such practices continued to be justified on the grounds that no conspiracy could be concealed while the women were paramours and spies. At one time, the first pick of concubines had gone to the captain and officers, each soldier and sailor afterwards permitted to attach himself to a female convict for the duration of the voyage. Between decks, the male convicts starved of sexual favours would occasionally invade the female quarters only to find themselves repulsed by a chorus of the foulest abuse.[35]

The *Mandarin* carried only four women, the wives of soldiers, one of these pregnant and destined to die aboard in the most distressing circumstances. It was the first voyage for Dr McKechnie, the Surgeon Superintendent, and while he blamed the woman's death on a lack of midwifery equipment, his inexperience may have been a contributory factor. The ship was off the West African coast when the woman suffered agonising pains. On examination, the doctor found the baby's head jammed and the pelvis deformed. Without the proper instruments he decided nothing could be done apart from alleviating her pain and *"trusting to nature."* By the following day she was dead, the head of a large female child so firmly fixed in the neck of her womb, it was impossible for McKechnie to remove it. Noting in his journal the need for convict ships to carry midwifery instruments, he said he might have saved the mother but not the child.[36]

McKechnie's responsibilities as Surgeon Superintendent extended far beyond the health of the convicts. For these he was paid according to the number arriving safely in Van Diemen's Land, in addition to which there were his special privileges, such as the freedom to import duty free goods into the colonies, usually liquor and tobacco. While the master and crew sailed the ship, McKechnie dealt with most other matters, among these security and the supervision of floggings. Ship board Magistrate, chaplain, mentor and physician, McKechnie was the most powerful man aboard the *Mandarin,* and the most vigilant, constantly endeavouring to distinguish stupidity from perverseness, genuine sickness from malingery. Not only did their lives depend upon him during a challenging and at times tempestuous voyage, the convicts knew a bad word from the doctor on their arrival could determine their fate. The Surgeon Superintendent appeared to befriend the Chartists promising to do what he could to make the voyage as comfortable as possible. All three felt indebted although Frost was suspicious of the surgeon's motives, hinting in a letter to his wife that McKechnie was short-tempered, read all mail before it left the ship and, consequently, might not be as trustworthy as he made himself appear. The Newport Chartist leader was sufficiently concerned to send one letter by a personal courier, a mysterious Mr George Rogers who seems to have disembarked from the *Mandarin* at Simon's Bay to return to Britain.[37]

Shortly before the *Mandarin* reached the Cape, Frost's suspicions, coupled with his foreboding that an attempt would be made on their lives during the long voyage, were probably the reasons he cautioned Zephaniah Williams not to involve himself in a rumoured plot to seize the ship. The potential for mutiny aboard a convict transport was always high, among a group of men society had consigned to the pest house of the world. Faced with an existence worse than most could imagine, no convict ship ever crossed the Equator without some plot rumoured or real, although of the 1,040 ships that transported convicts to Australia very few were successfully seized. On the slightest alarm, the convicts were loaded with chains, and fastened to ring bolts attached to the ship's side. Attempts at mutiny were brutally and quickly put down, the ringleaders flogged, thrown overboard or dispatched to Norfolk Island, the hell of hells.[38] An Irish rebel, Christopher Grogan, involved in a mutiny aboard the *Ann* in 1801 was given 250 lashes, and another, Marcus Sheehy, a United Irishman from Limerick, was executed on board by firing squad. More recent to this, a conversation between the Canadian rebels on the *Buffalo* about how easy it would be to seize the vessel and sail it to one of the United States ports was overheard and reported to the master by one of the conspirators, who expected to be freed in return for his betrayal. The prisoners were ordered below deck, the hatches locked while the crew searched for weapons and other evidence of a mutiny. Finding nothing, it was the informer who was punished in this case.[39] On most voyages, convicts commonly distrustful of each other shrank from the confidence required to plan and execute a mutiny.

If there were a plot, the Surgeon Superintendent would usually be the first to hear of it. Knowing this, Frost was uncertain what action to take when a few days before the ship reached the Cape of Good Hope he was handed a letter by another convict inviting him and his companions to lead an attempt to seize the *Mandarin*. If Frost failed to inform McKechnie, and the plot was later discovered, he, Williams and Jones would be accused of participating in a treasonable act and at the very least sent to Norfolk Island. Shown the letter, Zephaniah Williams was inclined to join the plotters until Frost reminded him that having *"made one mistake"* they should not risk another.

"Suppose we make the attempt and fail," said Frost, *"our death will not be a very honourable one for if we should not be killed at once, but taken prisoners, we are sure to be hung. There is no one to save us here; no agitation to keep the matter alive and frighten the government out of their intention."* If a mutiny were to succeed, he warned Williams it would not be they who were masters of the ship but the other convicts who after seizing the liquor supplies would most probably throw the Chartists overboard. *"For my part I shall have nothing to do with it,"* at which point Frost put the letter into the fire. Reflecting on the incident many years later, the Newport Chartist concluded it was another piece in his conspiracy theory. Because there was no proof the mutiny letter was written by a prisoner, Frost saw the government's hand in it, at the very least, its representative on board, McKechnie. No prisoner, he surmised, could obtain writing paper without the doctor knowing, or find the opportunity to write such a letter without being observed. It was a calculated attempt to trap them, and if it had succeeded the Government would have had its excuse to execute them. Arriving at Hobart Town, Frost believed McKechnie confirmed his suspicions when, as he left the ship, the doctor turned to the Chartist leader, and remarked, *"Frost, I am happy to bear testimony to your good conduct since you have been under my authority."* Then fixing him with his eyes, and tapping his nose knowingly, added, *"And let me tell you, you have said nothing, you have done nothing since you have been on this ship with which I have not been made acquainted."* For Frost this was confirmation the doctor knew of the bogus mutiny letter, might even have planted it. This, and the warning delivered by the Governor at Portsmouth, and his suspicions they were encouraged to commit suicide in Monmouth Gaol, was sufficient to convince Frost of a Government conspiracy to have them killed.[40]

Whether true wholly or in part, his suspicions about McKechnie reflect upon the authenticity of the Zephaniah Williams 'confession' letter, a copy of which was discovered by Frost's biographer Professor David Williams in 1939 among the papers in Lord Tredegar's Library at Newport. The letter, clearly marked 'Copy' at the top of the first page, is now in the National Library of Wales. [41] The alleged confession was made by Williams a few weeks after the rumour of the mutiny had spread around the ship. While it came to nothing, the weather turned foul, the *Mandarin* lashed by hurricane force winds of such ferocity the ship was close to capsizing. Even though all hatches were battened down, the sea still flooded the prisoners' quarters and hospital, pouring through the small mizzen hatch left open to prevent the convicts shackled below from suffocating. Despite the ferocity of the storm, Frost who had feared a sailor's grave suffered not a single attack of seasickness, writing, triumphantly, to his wife, *"So little do I now dread a sea voyage that I should like, in a good ship, and in pleasant company, a voyage to any part of the world."*[42]

The Williams 'confession' letter confirmed everything the government, magistrates, and Crown Prosecutors had suspected about the Uprising: that it was a revolution, the plan being to overthrow the Government of England and establish a republic. Newport was not intended to be the only target. Brecon would be seized by 5,000 armed men from Merthyr, followed by Abergavenny and Cardiff, gunpowder warehouses and provision stores taken, blast furnaces converted to manufacture cannon and arms of all descriptions, and magistrates and selected members of the aristocracy imprisoned or executed. The River Usk would be blocked to shipping and any troops sent by land resisted in every possible way. The successful capture of Newport would be the signal for a general Uprising by Chartists throughout Britain, this to be communicated by the non-arrival of the Welsh Mail in Birmingham.[43]

After the earnest denials at his trial, Zephaniah Williams appeared to capitulate aboard the *Mandarin,* admitting to the surgeon McKechnie everything the Crown had alleged when the Attorney General, Sir John Campbell, in outlining the case to the jury at the Monmouth Special Assize, said of the Chartist marchers:

"Arriving at Newport they were to attack the troops that were there; they were to get possession of the town, to break down the bridge which is there erected across the river Usk . . . they were to stop the mail; the mail bag from Newport not arriving at Birmingham in an hour and a half, it would be known to those who were in concert with them . . . that this scheme had succeeded. There was to be a great general rising; I hear nothing of any private revenge; I hear nothing of any private grievance; this was not a meeting for discussion; it was not a meeting for petitioning

*the Queen or either House of Parliament; it was not a meeting
arising out of any dispute between masters and servants . . . it
was not any sudden outbreak from want of employment, or from
want of food . . . the witnesses whom I (shall) call before you
speak the truth – that there was this public object, by armed force
to change the law and constitution of the country."*[44]

The importance of the confession cannot be ignored, because if
true, it offers evidence of a plot to depose the government and
monarch in what would rank as one of the largest conspiracies in
British history. Both Wilks in *South Wales and the Rising of 1839*
and David J. V. Jones in *The Last Rising: the Newport Chartist
Uprising of 1839* lean heavily upon it for their conclusions. Without the confession, Wilks would have found it extremely difficult
to conclude from the available evidence that the attack on the
Westgate was an attempt to establish *'an autonomous republic, a
commonwealth, a commune of armed citizens.'*[45] Similarly, the
merit of Jones' assertion that it was a *'local rising originally conceived as part of a general insurrection'* also needs the *'confession'*
to sustain it.[46] Because of it, both authors arrived at very similar
conclusions separated only by degree. Both were also critical of
Professor Williams for his judgment in ignoring the confession.
Wilks attributed this to Professor Williams' reluctance to give
authority to a document that undermined his premise that the
Uprising was nothing more than a monster demonstration that
went wrong.[47]

Professor Williams' decision to treat the statement as immaterial
was not because he doubted Zephaniah Williams was the author,
even though to this day the original has not been found, either
locally or within the archives at the Public Record Office, if it ever
existed. It was Zephaniah's reason for making the statement that
quite rightly concerned him. Neither can the circumstances be
ignored: Zephaniah confessing *after* the trial and sentencing were
long over, and he was half way round the world, bound for a life
of exile and years of imprisonment in a penal settlement widely
regarded as an abomination, a pest hole, an offence to civilisation. Professor Williams thought the reason was to curry favour
with the authorities, possibly in the hope of being rewarded with
some remission of sentence.[48] Zephaniah's only explanation was

that he had been persuaded to *"make this manifesto statement of our design"* solely on account of McKechnie's kindness towards him during the voyage.[49] There is little doubt McKechnie won the confidence of the three Chartist prisoners, even Frost who despite his suspicions wrote from the *Mandarin* to his friend Morgan Williams, leader of the Merthyr Chartists, suggesting the 'men from the hills' repaid the surgeon's kindness by making him a presentation of a ring.[50]

At the time of the Chartist Trials a number of alleged activists turned Queen's Evidence to save their own necks, including the youngster from Blackwood William Davies, who had the most damning evidence about what transpired at the vital meeting at the *Coach and Horses* on Friday November 1. This was never heard, however, because he absconded for the duration of the trial.[51] On the other hand, Frost, Williams, and Jones resolutely denied all allegations of an insurrection. Even aboard the *Mandarin* at the very time Williams was confessing to the surgeon, Jones was continuing to plead his innocence. In a letter from the convict ship dated May 1, 1840, to Dr J. Sloper, of Pontypool, he claimed Government spies incited the confrontation outside the Westgate. *"Our intentions were not treasonable,"* he wrote, *". . . the attack on the Westgate was never contemplated and was only put in practice by the emissaries of the magistrates, some of whom unfortunately fell, a sacrifice to their perfidy. . . . I ought never to have been banished . . . there was nothing to justify the government doing (it)."* It might be argued that Jones could quite honestly say this because he was nowhere near the Westgate when the conflict occurred. But he would have been as familiar with any plan for a national rising as Zephaniah Williams, the two spending a large part of the week immediately preceding the march in each other's company, and both at the critical November 1 meeting in Blackwood.

Whether or not Zephaniah's was a true account of what the Chartists intended, or a opportunistic concoction of everything they had discussed in lodges and beer houses during the weeks and months preceding the Uprising, one explanation for his collaboration could be that he had been broken by events and, consequently, ready to volunteer anything for the chance of gaining the slightest personal advantage. A statement that sounded as if it had been given freely was taken aboard a convict ship, in oppressive circumstances that today would most certainly have made it inadmissible as evidence. By his own admission to Frost, McKechnie boasted of knowing of everything that had occurred aboard the *Mandarin* during the four-month voyage.[52] If this were the case he would certainly have learned that Zephaniah was sufficiently desperate to consider joining those plotting to mutiny. It is not beyond the bounds of credibility that McKechnie, part of whose job was to 'police' the convicts with the assistance of a detachment of soldiers, exploited this desperation to extract the confession amidst the miserable conditions aboard the ship. Yet the statement was all too perfect, too precise, and too convenient for the government, confirming, as it did, a pattern of revolutionary events the establishment in London and Monmouthshire were expecting. But it was also incompatible with Zephaniah's behaviour before and during the march: his exhortations to marchers gathering on the mountaintop at Blaina to arm themselves but only for defence, his assurances there would be no bloodshed, and his genuine concern that no damage should be caused to property. When he heard that blast furnaces were being damped down, Zephaniah left the march, briefly, to investigate the situation, aware that if this were allowed to happen the consequences for the ironworks would be disastrous. This was hardly the kind of concern expected from someone about to wreck revolutionary havoc.[53] As for the national rising for which the attack at Newport was supposed to be the prelude, Zephaniah admits to knowing only what Frost had told him, and this seems inconclusive after the mysterious messenger from the North on the day before the march advised caution.[54] Significantly, Zephaniah's *Mandarin* statement makes it clear most of what was planned or simply spoken of at some time during the preparations, including the simultaneous attack on Brecon and Abergavenny, was not adopted, nor was the proposed assault on Newport's Union Workhouse where the soldiers were stationed. The reason for this truncated Uprising, if that was what was still intended, was, according to Zephaniah, that Frost had said, *"Let me have two thousand armed men with Zephaniah Williams with them, we will accomplish our objective with little trouble and as far as Brecon and Abergavenny, we will afterwards soon secure them.*"[55] It is hard to see how such a settled plan could have emerged from so much confusion, but if Zephaniah's confession accurately reflected the intentions of Frost, Williams and Jones, then the mass of ill-informed marchers who followed them to Newport for no clear reason were either cruelly and deliberately deceived, or the victims of subversives. This book inclines towards the latter because of the prominent role assumed by at least one known revolutionary, John Rees. He would not have been alone; all it required was a handful of activists to transform a peaceful although potentially volatile protest into revolution. G. D. H. Cole in his 1941 study of Chartism concluded it was not Frost who organised the Uprising but *"some successor of Dic Penderyn whose name history does not record, or some group of leaders who were themselves the victims of the desperate oppression of the Guests and the Crawshays . . ."*[56] What resulted from the subversive actions of a minority cannot, however, then be rationalised as the inevitable consequence of desperate oppression, because far from being motivated by some embryonic political philosophy, the vast majority of the marchers had no coherent objective beyond a demonstration in favour of electoral reform, which they hoped would address their countless grievances. In that regard, Zephaniah Williams was no different to the rank and file, and like Frost and Jones had no stomach for the revolution Rees and others tried to engineer.

It is somewhat surprising, that the one to confess among the three Chartist prisoners was not the older Frost who never expected to survive the voyage to Van Diemen's Land, nor the more vulnerable Jones, but the man who was commended for his remarkable courage and fortitude in captivity. This said, it stretches credibility to imagine Zephaniah had no other purpose for betraying his comrades than his gratitude to the doctor for some small kindnesses during an exhausting voyage. The most convincing explanation I believe is that Zephaniah was indeed the author, and that he volunteered, possibly under duress, an account of the Uprising he knew the authorities wanted to believe, hoping it might provide some respite when he entered the penal regime; but that when the statement was examined at the Home Office it was seen for what it was, an opportunistic fabrication of events that would not stand up to public scrutiny. What makes this the more plausible is that when the statement eventually returned to Britain at the beginning of 1841, the authorities chose to make no use of it whatsoever. This could not have been due to the confidence pact Zephaniah struck with McKechnie because this was broken when a 'copy' was made and sent to Octavious Morgan, magistrate son of Sir Charles Morgan of Tredegar House, and self-appointed Chartist hunter-in-chief. At a time when Chartist leaders were still at large, including Rees with a £100 reward on his head, Morgan and the Crown might have been expected to use the 'confession' to justify their prosecution of the insurgents and allay the considerable public disquiet about the savage sentences imposed on Frost, Williams and Jones. According to Ivor Wilks, the Home Secretary Normanby had always been anxious not to exaggerate what had occurred at Newport, only proceeding with the Treason Trials under pressure from the Tory opposition.[57] This might have been true a year earlier but by September 1841 the Tories were back in office and in the business of suppressing Chartism, free speech, and any further electoral reform.

None of this is to be taken as proof that the confession was a forgery, although in the continued absence of corroborating evidence it must remain unsubstantiated. No mention is made of it anywhere in McKechnie's log of the voyage, and the original has still to be found. Nevertheless, the copy produced for Octavious Morgan was in the same hand that also copied two letters sent by Frost from the *Mandarin* to Morgan Williams in Merthyr, and Fergus O'Connor, editor of the *Northern Star*.[58] It is not as incredulous as Ivor Wilks imagined, that Professor Williams should believe Zephaniah Williams was seeking some remission of his sentence in Van Diemen's Land by collaborating.[59] That he subsequently received no respite, and was despatched immediately with Frost and Jones to the Port Arthur Penal Settlement, in no way devalues this assertion. Zephaniah always suspected the fate of the Welsh political prisoners and their treatment had been predetermined by the Home Government, complaining to his wife they were more severely treated than the Canadian Patriots and O'Brien's Free Irelanders, all suffering transportation for High Treason.[60]

If there was little support for the Monmouthshire Chartists over what happened at Newport, there was widespread sympathy for them afterwards. A "Committee for the Restoration of the Exiles" was formed, the Merthyr Chartist leader Morgan Williams especially active, attending a meeting on Clerkenwell Common, London on May 15, 1841, in support of Frost, Williams and Jones. According to an account of the meeting provided by a police spy, Morgan Williams described the sentences as *"cruel tyranny"* and said their families were in extreme need. Williams also demonstrated once again the extraordinary contradictions that inhibited Chartism, on this occasion denouncing *'Negro emancipation'* and Animal Rights activists as humbugs, part of what he described was the then current *"cant of humanity."*[61] In May 1841 a huge petition calling for the return of the three Chartists was only narrowly defeated in the House of Commons. Even then, the Whigs whose Government was soon to fall, made no attempt to assure parliamentary victory by revealing the existence of the Williams 'confession.'

All appeals for a free pardon were opposed vigorously by the leading figures in the South Wales political establishment. The campaigns in 1841, 1844, 1846, 1847-1848 at the very least helped keep Chartism alive by infusing a new vitality into a movement ravaged by factionalism. At one stage, Fergus O'Connor, editor of the *Northern Star,* and strong advocate of liberty through martyrdom, was encouraged to lead a second Uprising. This came to nothing, even Henry Vincent renouncing physical resistance before his release from Monmouth Gaol. Writing to Morgan Williams from the *Mandarin,* Frost still hoped the *"spirit which once animated the men of the hills is not dead"* and would expedite their return to their native land.[62]

It would be sixteen years before his hopes were realised, and then only for himself, and never for Williams and Jones. Remarkably, he considered his experiences aboard the convict ship and his sufferings at Port Arthur *"may turn out for the best."* Before the voyage, Frost was filled with great foreboding because of his dread of seasickness. After the gales in the English Channel, the weather was remarkably fine, the Chartist leader suffering no ill effects all the way to the Cape where the *Mandarin* docked to take on supplies of fresh meat, fruit, vegetables, and water. After two months of salt beef and pork, scurvy had made its dreaded appearance and fresh provisions were the only way to prevent its spread. Illnesses festering in the crowded, stagnant atmosphere of the prisoners' quarters, spread rapidly once the ship entered the tropics, the convicts decimated by heat and weakened by sickness and a crude diet. Leaving Simon's Bay, the *Mandarin* was becalmed briefly, before encountering treacherous seas for the remainder of the voyage to Van Diemen's Land. Writing to a friend about this fifteen years later, Frost who had by then obtained a conditional pardon but not the amnesty necessary to return to Britain, said, *"If anyone had told me that . . . at the age of three score and ten to be in pretty good health, I should scarcely have believed him. When I was on board the Mandarin convict ship, a fortnight was the utmost I expected to live; and when aboard the hulk I lived for ten days on bread and water. By degrees I gained strength, and with an increase of resolution to bear my sufferings with patience and firmness.*

"One day when the ship was tossing about, I had before me a pretty tough piece of convict beef; and I had hold of the partition with one hand, and was attempting to cut the beef with the other, when I heard a chuckling above me. I looked up and saw the old boatswain laughing at me. 'Ah, Mr Frost,' said he, 'this voyage will be worth a thousand a year to you; it will teach you something of life.'

"I have seen life in almost every form; it is something to see in a convict ship – something to see in a penal colony. However, at last, which is something hard to believe, it may turn out for the best." [63]

NOTES

1. Joseph and Thomas Gurney, *The Trial of John Frost* (London, 1840), p4.
2. For Scotch Cattle, see David Jones, *Before Rebecca* (London, 1973), pp98-111; PRO, TS 11/502, Letter from James Brown to Thomas Jones Phillips.
3. MM, 30 November 1839.
4. NSW, Mitchell Library, Doc., No. 67366, Frost letter to wife from Port Arthur, 21 July 1840.
5. GRO, QSPR 17/4/6, Prosser.
6. GRO, MG.0017, Chaplain's Journal.
7. NSW, Mitchell Library, Doc., No. 67366, Frost letter to wife from Port Arthur, 21 July 1840.
8. Lord Mansfield, Lord Chief Justice, 1756-88.
9. NPL, Chartist Trials, 9, Thomas Evans.
10. Gurney, pp296-301.

11. NPL, Chartist Trials, 5, William Davies.
12. NPL, Chartist Trials, 4, Job Tovey.
13. NPL, Chartist Trials, 15, Matthew Williams.
14. NPL, Chartist Trials, 5, William Harris.
15. James Hodge, Gurney pp308-9, pp303-4; *The Times*, 13 January 1840.
16. John Harford, *The Times*, 13 January 1840.
17. Richard Pugh, *The Times*, 13 January 1840; NPL, Chartist Trials,5, Pugh.
18. NPL, Chartist Trials, 8, Samuel Etheridge.
19. Hon. Mrs Hardcastle, *Life of Lord Campbell* (London, 1881).
20. NLW, *Udgorn Cymru* , letter from Frost to wife, September 1840.
21. *ibid.*
22. NPL, Chartist Archives, Lecture, John Frost, Oddfellows Hall, Padiham, 31 August 1856.
23. *Northern Star*, 28 December 1839.
24. NPL, Chartist Archives, Lecture, John Frost, Oddfellows Hall, Padiham, 31 August 1856.
25. MCA, V, 70-3
26. Jones, *The Last Rising*, p197.
27. NPL, Chartist Archives, Lecture, John Frost, Oddfellows Hall, Padiham, 31 August 1856.
28. *ibid.*
29. HMSO, HOC session 1837-38, Volume No. XXII, Paper No. 669.
30. Tasmanian State Archives, Hobart, account of Van Diemen's Land prisoner, Marsh, and T. J. Lempriere, *The Penal Settlements of Van Diemen's Land*. Lempriere was Commissariat Officer, 1833-48; Frost, lecture 31 August 1856, Oddfellows Hall, Padiham.
31. M. N. Sprod, *The Convict Probation System: Van Diemen's Land 1839-* (Hobart, 1990, Blubber Head Press); George Rude, *Protest and Punishment* (Oxford, 1978). Sir Francis Forbes, chief justice of Australia, stated, in a letter to the Maconochie Committee on Transportation: *"The experience furnished by these penal settlements has proved that transportation is capable of being carried to an extent of suffering such as to render death desirable, and to induce many prisoners to seek it under its most appalling aspects."*
32. NPL, Chartist Archives, Barclay Fox's Journal.
33. J. G. Smith, 'Customs History of the Port of Newport', *Gwent Local History*, No. 46, Spring 1979.
34. Rude, *Protest and Punishment*, pp159-163.
35. John West, *History of Tasmania* (Hobart, 1852).
36. PRO, ADM.101/46/7, Journal of Dr Alex McKechnie.
37. New South Wales, Mitchell Library, Doc., No. 67366, Frost letter to wife from Port Arthur, 21 July 1840.
38. West, *History of Tasmania*: Rude, *Protest and Punishment*.
39. Samuel Snow, *The Exiles Return* (Cleveland, 1846).
40. NPL, Chartist Archives, Lecture, John Frost, Oddfellows Hall, Padiham, 31 August 1856.
41. NLW, 40/2, Tredegar House Papers, copy of Williams 'confession', 25 May 1840.

42. NSW, Mitchell Library, Doc. No. 67366, Frost letter to wife from Port Arthur, 21 July 1840.
43. Williams 'confession', copy of letter, May 25, 1840, Tredegar Papers, 40/2, NLW.
44. Joseph and Thomas Gurney, *The Trial of John Frost for High Treason* (London, 1840), pp58-72.
45. Wilks, p249.
46. Jones, p209.
47. Wilks, p248.
48. Williams, *John Frost: a study in Chartism*, p288.
49. NLW, 40/2, Tredegar House Papers, Williams 'confession'.
50. NLW, 40/1, Tredegar House Papers, letters from Frost to Morgan Williams and Fergus O'Connor, 4 May 1840, p380.
51. NPL, Chartist Trials, magistrates depositions, evidence of William Davies; *Merthyr Guardian,* 1 February 1840.
52. NPL, Chartist Archives, Lecture, John Frost, Oddfellows Hall, Padiham, 31 August 1856.
53. NPL, Chartist Trials, 5, James James, and others.
54. NPL, Chartist Trials, 5, Job Tovey, Susanna Tovey.
55. NLW, 40/2, Tredegar House Papers, Williams 'confession.'
56. Cole, *Chartist Patriots*, p146.
57. Wilks, pp216-217.
58. NLW, 40/1, Tredegar House Papers, letters from Frost to Morgan Williams and Fergus O'Connor, 4 May 1840.
59. Wilks, p248; Williams, p286.
60. Williams letters to wife, op. cit.
61. PRO, HO 45/102.
62. Frost letters to Morgan Williams, Fergus O'Connor, from *Mandarin,* op. cit.
63. *Cornwall Chronicle,* Frost letter to friend in London from New York, 21 November 1855.

CHAPTER 8

The Escape of 'Jack the Fifer'

The decision to commute the death sentences on Frost, Williams and Jones to transportation for life denied the aristocracy the vigorous exercise of the law it had expected. So infuriated were the local gentry that Octavius Morgan, son of Sir Charles Morgan of the Tredegar Estate, wrote to the Marquis of Normanby, the Home Secretary, the week following his decision, complaining that the magistrates felt the leniency shown the Chartists gave them no incentive to continue the search for those still at large.[1] The prevailing impression in the Black Domain, he said, was that the troublemakers could *"scoff at the law and magistrates."* Most prominent among these Chartist fugitives was John Rees ("Jack the Fifer") and his friend, David Jones ("Dai the Tinker"), both believed to be in hiding with as many as 13 others in the rugged, remote hill country in the neighbourhood of Hirwaun. But the magistrates were not inclined to invest further in a hunt for fugitives, whose eventual punishment would do nothing to discourage the still simmering rebellion. Two months after the Uprising, the district remained a tinderbox, hardly a week passing without rumours of the Chartists descending again from the hills. The tension was stoked by Henry Vincent's appeal to the Welsh from Monmouth Gaol not to surrender. *"Let there be no unmanly shrinking; nothing would grieve me more,"* wrote Vincent in the *Western Vindicator,* although not long afterwards he was to renounce the use of physical force in support of the Charter.[2] For his part, the other Chartist luminary, Fergus O'Connor, sought to present the prosecution of Frost as an attack on the common interest. *"The cause of Frost is the cause of the whole nation; in saving him the people do but save themselves,"* he wrote in the *Northern Star.*[3]

Up and down the country petitions were launched pressing the Home Secretary to pardon the three convicted Chartists. At the same time, there was talk of a further rising, a correspondent in the *Western Vindicator* writing of *"deluging the earth with blood."* Of the various attempts to explain the reasons for the Uprising, one of the most bizarre was the parallel another contributor to the *Western Vindicator* drew between Wales and Ethiopia. Describing the Welsh as the most unsophisticated people in Britain, comparable to those in darkest Africa since they relied entirely upon barter, the writer admitted they had one less known characteristic – patriotism. *"There are three things which a Cymro (Welshman) should love before all other – the nation of the Cymry; the manners, customs of the Cymry; and the language of the Cymry."* This sense of individual worth, concluded the writer, had found expression in the Charter's main points.[4]

On the day of the attack on the Westgate, 300 soldiers were stationed at Brecon, about 70 at Newport with smaller numbers of the 12th Lancers at Abergavenny and Monmouth. Within a week of the Uprising eight companies of the 45th Regiment of foot were on their way to Newport, 700 arriving at Bristol on the following Saturday evening after a forced march from Winchester in atrocious winter conditions. By the end of the week, Colonel Considine, the officer commanding the forces at Newport, had almost 1,000 men under his command. Scores of Special Constables were also sworn in to patrol the flashpoints, the ratepayers eventually having to foot the bill for 1,500 of these, and one thousand new police staffs and badges. Inevitably, there were many false alarms, especially while Rees, Jones and their gang remained at large. The aftermath of the Chartist Uprising – the search for and arrest of suspects, interrogation of witnesses, and increased policing – was to cost the county's ratepayers dearly. The total bill came to £1744-13s-9d, from November 4 through to the following April, the equivalent of £70,000 at today's values, £23,000 of this for additional constables at 3s for a night duty and 2s 6d for day patrols. By comparison, the cost of repairing the damage to the Westgate Hotel was remarkably little, £90-19s-9d, less than the £105-7s-0d bill (£4,200) from the hotel for providing food and drink to troops and the specials on duty. Much to the disgust of local ratepayers, all these expenses fell on their shoulders, neither the Home Office nor the Treasury being prepared to make a contribution.[5]

Their anger was relayed to the Home Secretary by Octavius Morgan in a letter to Normanby on February 9, the week following the commuting of the sentences. The government's failure to execute the sentences of the court was considered a defeat for law and order. *"A very considerable change has, within the last week, taken place in the feelings of the population of the mining districts of this county,"* wrote Morgan, *"and we understand the prevailing impression among them now is that the Chartists are stronger than the Government since the Government did not dare to carry the sentence of the law into execution, but were obliged to carry away the prisoners privately in the night and therefore that the Charter shall yet be the law of the land. This we have heard from very credible authority and we give it to your lordship as we have heard it."*[6]

Ostensibly, the purpose of the letter was to seek Home Office instructions on whether or not to pursue Rees and Jones. Their hideout was known, but feeling betrayed, the magistrates were refusing to spend more time and money, without an assurance the fugitives would be dealt with forcibly.

"I, at the same time, feel bound to state that such is the effect produced on men's minds by the proceedings at the Monmouth Special Commission that it is very much to be feared that individuals will not come forward with the zeal and alacrity they have hitherto done, or give evidence against them, should any recurrence of such circumstances take place, when they find that their exertions in support of the law and the furtherance of justice have been rendered pointless, and that the only result of such exertions has been to expose themselves personally to the vindictive feelings of those against whom they have ventured to appear as evidence," wrote Octavius Morgan. In support of this, Morgan reported to the Home Secretary instances of colliers whose lives had been so threatened after giving evidence to the Special Commission, it was no longer deemed safe for them to work alongside Chartists underground for fear of suffering serious harm.[7]

Stung by the criticism, Normanby instructed the Newport Magistrates to continue the hunt for Rees and Jones, rebuking Morgan for his criticism and analysis of the situation. *"Lord Normanby regrets some of the topics which you have introduced into your letter,"* his secretary replied, *"and would be sorry to infer from them any remission of that zeal which the Magistrates have hitherto shown: and requests the Magistrates to be assured of his continued support to them in the discharge of their duty. The information which you say you have received as to the increased confidence of the ill-disposed in consequence of the removal of the prisoners from Monmouth Gaol in the night time, appears to Lord Normanby to afford no just cause for apprehension."* [8]

On receiving this rather curt reply, Octavius Morgan decided to seek advice and who better for this than his cousin, the Tredegar ironmaster Samuel Homfray, one of the most enthusiastic Chartist hunters in the country. The magistrates' claim to know the whereabouts of Rees and Jones was really no stronger than a suspicion. So two days after receiving Normanby's letter, Octavius concluded that he had better confirm the supposed location of the Chartist hideout with another source and despatched special constable Thomas Watts to Tredegar with a personal letter for his cousin at Bedwellty House. The letter contained no mention of the Chartist hiding place. Watts was instructed to deliver that information verbally to Samuel Homfray, in anticipation he could confirm it, and then advise on how the gang might best be approached in their hideout, which was reputedly in an inaccessible part of the hill country. The plan was not to seize the entire gang, only those against whom the magistrates could build the strongest case. Watts was to return posthaste with Samuel Homfray's advice, Octavius adding for good measure, *"You will see I did not mince the matter in my letter to Lord N for I was determined he should have the truth which information it seems was not very palatable."* [9]

Returning by coach from Tredegar the next day, Watts evidently knew as much about the whereabouts of the fugitives, and the difficulties that could be expected in apprehending them as Samuel Homfray, who was reluctant to embark on another expensive manhunt after the leniency already shown to Frost and company. *"In the event of a failure the money would be out of my own pocket,"* he complained to his cousin although he did confirm those in hiding had formerly been employed at his Tredegar Ironworks, including Rees as a stonemason.

After arranging to meet Octavius the following Thursday at Newport to discuss matters further, Homfray advised that only Rees and Jones should be taken, and that to do this agents would need to infiltrate those protecting the Chartist hideout. *"By acting in this way and not molesting but rather making friends with the others you may take them,"* he added. But in a footnote to his letter, Homfray warned his cousin, *"It appears to me that if Rees and Jones are at the place named and are to be taken that it will require one or two determined men . . . they will do more in that place than a dozen others – it is a remote out of the way spot at least a stage beyond civilisation."* To emphasise to his cousin the remoteness of the hideout, Homfray underlined *'a stage beyond civilisation.'*[10]

A little chastened, perhaps on account of Normanby's brusqueness, Octavius and the chairman of the Newport bench, Rev. James Coles, replied to the Home Secretary on February 22 reaffirming their determination to apprehend Rees and Jones, against whom True Bills for High Treason were outstanding.[11] Constable Watts and Sergeant Fairbrass, the latter a member of a team of officers seconded from London to assist the local police, were chosen as the *'two determined men'* despatched into the wilds of north Monmouthshire and Glamorgan on the trail of the fugitives. After two days and a night combing the area where the suspects were believed to be hiding, they returned empty-handed. Either their information was wrong or the fugitives had long since disappeared from Wales. According to one report, the pair had fled the neighbourhood of Hirwaun as early as November 7 the previous year. This reported sighting at Hirwaun certainly has merit, in the light of a letter Rees wrote from the United States in 1841 in which he gave details of his escape. Nevertheless, Watts and Fairbrass charged the county £3-2s for their efforts and hire of horses. Merthyr Tydfil Constables Millward and Williams also thought they were closing in on Rees when towards the end of November they were tipped off that he was hiding in a house at Hirwaun, only to discover that if he had been he had fled before they arrived. But they did pick up the trail of Pontypool beer shop keeper, John Llewellyn, another of the Chartist leaders for whose apprehension a £100 reward was offered. Followed to Swansea from Hirwaun, Llewellyn was seized boarding the coach for Carmarthenshire.[12]

If any person were likely to apprehend Rees and Jones, it would most probably have been William Homan, the police superintendent at Tredegar. This man knew more than anyone about what the Chartists were planning, and had already been paid the equivalent of £3,600 for hunting for Zephaniah Williams without success. The £100 reward for Williams' capture was eventually paid to his Cardiff colleague Superintendent Jeremiah Stockdale, who arrested the fugitive just before he escaped to Portugal.[13] But it was Homan who had arrested Vincent in London on May 7 the previous year and who had also alerted Captain Howells of the Royal Glamorgan Militia to the Uprising five days before it occurred. In the aftermath of November 4, the superintendent set off with two constables to distribute wanted posters for Williams, Rees, Jones and Llewellyn throughout Monmouthshire and Glamorgan. The £100 reward on the head of Rees and Jones was offered by the ironmasters Crawshay Bailey, of Nantyglo, and William Brown, of Blaina.[14] Post boys spent seventeen days distributing the posters as far away as Aberystwyth and Cardiganshire, Hereford and the borders, even across the Severn to Bristol where local police complained the description of the fugitives was not sufficiently detailed.

Because of this, a new poster was produced describing John Rees as: *"About 5ft 8 inches in height – rather thin in the face – rather light hair – dark sandy whiskers – full eyes – long neck – pale dark complexion – rather blunt manner – and when drunk very talkative – walks upright – has a military air when walking. Had a blue pilot cloth coat on the day of the riots and black hat."* No mention is made of his age.

According to anecdotal evidence, Rees and Jones escaped together. For several months, there were reports of the pair being sighted performing in public houses in the West Country, before they disappeared completely, Rees to America while Jones returned later to Wales to live the rest of his life dressed as a woman.[15] Newport police superintendent Edward Hopkins claimed Rees had been seen playing his fife, accompanied by Jones, in a public house near Bristol. But he gave up the search after visiting eight public houses, afterwards travelling to Shrewsbury to investigate another reported sighting of the pair in the *Rover* beer house.[16] From new evidence it appears none of these reports were correct; that Rees was long since gone.

Until now the only proof Rees reached America came in a short report published by *The Times* in February 1844, which refers to a letter Rees had written to a friend from Virginia. Similar reports appeared in the *Monmouthshire Merlin* and *Monmouthshire Beacon* a few days later. But the original source of these reports has now been discovered. *The Times* account was taken from the Swansea-based *Cambrian* newspaper, the *Merlin* and *Beacon* repeating the truncated account published by *The Times*, unaware that a fuller version of not one but two letters from Rees had been published by the *Cambrian*. *The Times'* Wales correspondent, named Foster, was then based in Swansea. Unfortunately, his abbreviated account of the Rees letters created the enduring impression they were written in 1844 although it is clear from the original, much longer extracts published in the *Cambrian* that the first letter was written on St David's Day 1841.[17]

These extracts were sent anonymously to the Editor of the *Cambrian,* after the identities of those who assisted in Rees's escape were deleted, either by the recipient or some person who had had sight of them. Jack the Fifer's first letter dated Virginia, March 1, 1841, and not as has been supposed from *The Times* report "March 1844," indicates he fled Wales long before the magistrates discovered his hideout which he confirms was, indeed, at Hirwaun. Leaving there, he *"travelled day and night"* to Chester, a distance of about 150 miles in the middle of winter, probably following the old drovers roads from Brecon to Builth Wells, Llandrindod Wells, Newtown, and Welshpool, before reaching the border town. From his letters, it appears Chartists and their sympathisers assisted almost every stage of his escape; and that he knew from the moment he left Wales precisely where he was headed in the United States. While several Chartist leaders outside Wales condemned the Newport Uprising as reckless, the assistance given Rees implies widespread grassroots sympathy across Britain.[18] Sanctuary would certainly have been available at Newtown, a hotbed of Chartism, and where a riot had occurred the previous year that ended in the transportation of the ringleaders.

His escape, however, was not entirely undetected by the authorities, two unidentified police constables pursuing him all the way to Chester. According to Rees, these he evaded by striking up a conversation with a *"sergeant of the artillery"* which seems to have persuaded his pursuers he was not their man. This, the first of two references in his letters to an association with the army, might be taken as inferring Rees was familiar with the military. Does this explain how he acquired his alias "Jack the Fifer"? His military bearing, together with anecdotal evidence that he had seen service in "foreign lands," is probably explained by the time he served in the People's Army during the Texas War of Independence. But what about the origins of that alias? Might Rees have served earlier in the British army, even local militia? The popularity of the fife as a domestic instrument in the 19th century arose largely from its use by the military, the Fife and Drum being the customary way of issuing orders and signals to troops before the advent of the bugle. Army muster rolls prior to 1840 only list pensioners and deserters and Rees was neither, which is not to say he did not serve in the army. As for the local militia, all males over the age of fourteen were conscripted for three years unless able to pay another person to serve as their substitute. Unfortunately very few militia enrolment lists survive. However he got his alias, it stuck although it seems specific to Wales as there is no evidence it was ever used during his service in Texas. That Rees was called "Jack" by Herman Ehrenberg in his account of their escape from the Goliad massacre, has probably no great significance since Jack for John was then commonplace! The likelihood he saw military service before Texas is improbable. John Rees was only 20 when he first went to Texas in 1835, so the most likely explanation for his alias is that he acquired it from performing in public houses.

From Chester, Rees travelled by coach to Liverpool where he found himself again pursued by *"a police from our own country."* Liverpool was the main port of departure for emigrants to America. But with someone on his tail, he appears to have left almost immediately by train, first for Manchester, then on to York and Leeds. Evidently, Rees had sufficient funds to pay for what was then a relatively new and expensive form of transport. Whether it was by coincidence or in anticipation of having to make a quick getaway, several of the arrested Chartists were found to be carrying substantial sums of cash. At Leeds, Rees, by this time desperate to reach a port from which he could escape Britain, took a coach to Sunderland. Arriving at Boroughbridge, an important coaching centre on the Great North Road from London to Edinburgh, he was arrested on suspicion. But luck was on his side, *"Through being steady and sober, I made my escape, and shortly after reached the residence of . . . where I got a very good situation and met good reception at . . ."* he writes. After a short time in Sunderland, Rees pushed on to Newcastle only to be recognised by a man named Vaughan *"who tried his best to betray me, and to deliver me up, but fortunately for me, the master of . . . worked at Newcastle."* Alerted to the danger, Rees was taken to a safe house in the country while Chartist friends found him passage on a ship to America. The master of the vessel, the name of which is deleted from the published extract, was another Chartist.[19]

Once aboard the ship for America, Rees expresses his relief. *"Having so far succeeded and escaped all the danger I was exposed to, I now considered myself a little more secure being on board but not yet safe,"* he writes. The unidentified master of the vessel provided him with all *"the comforts and necessaries to make myself comfortable. He treated me extraordinarily well – if I had been his own brother he could not have shown more kindness to me."*

The ship was bound for Quebec, the Atlantic crossing exceedingly rough, taking ten weeks on account of severe headwinds. Storms brought the mast down, forcing the vessel into St John's in Newfoundland for repairs. During this time Rees obtained work on some kind of Government project at St John's, but panicked and fled, leaving behind all he possessed, when he encountered *"two soldiers which I had enlisted,"* although they had failed to recognise him. This reference once again hints at previous military service since Newfoundland would have been garrisoned by the British Army. Knowing he risked capture, the longer he remained in a British colony, Rees sailed for Boston.

"My only and chief object was to get to the United States, which I have at last accomplished where in spite of all their tyrannical power I considered myself safe," he wrote of his arrival in Boston. From there he took a ship to New York and was befriended by Chartists who had also fled Britain. By now, his not inconsiderable funds, sufficient to pay his way across Britain, the Atlantic and through Canada to the United States, were almost exhausted and he needed to work. This he found as a stonemason helping build a church on Brooklyn Island, opposite New York City.

The mystery surrounding John Rees takes another twist in the final paragraph of his first letter. This ends with the clearest indication he knew exactly where he was headed. Moreover, the missing words are perhaps more intriguing than what he actually says: *"My employer was very kind to me, and I might have remained with him; but feeling a great desire to come here to see . . . and family, I exerted myself to the utmost to save money, sufficient to bring me here which I succeeded in a short time. I took a schooner from New York to . . ., a distance of 4 to 500 miles; arrived here in a few days, where I met with . . . and family, all in good health, and comfortable circumstances, and now remain with them."*

Whose family? Was it his? Was this a reference to relatives who had previously settled in the United States? Virginia was full of Welsh colliers and their families. It would explain how Rees at the age of 20 wound up enlisting in the New Orleans Greys. A five hundred miles voyage from New York would have taken him to Virginia, perhaps Alexandria, Portsmouth, Richmond or Norfolk, all ports of entry for settlers heading for the Appalachian Coal Basin, stretching from Kentucky to Pennsylvania. Not only did west Virginia produce 300,000 tons of coal in 1840, it was also a major centre for iron making. The Appalachians had become a magnet for thousands of Welsh colliers and ironworkers in search of a new life. By the middle of 19th century large numbers of Jones', Williams', Davies' and Rees's had sailed for the New World from Newport, Cardiff, Swansea, Aberaeron, Aberystwyth, Caernarfon, even from smaller Welsh ports. Whatever family offered John Rees sanctuary in Virginia it was one with whom he was well acquainted.

His second letter, also published by the *Cambrian*, was undated and the extract much shorter, expressing, firstly, his great sadness at having to leave his native land *"at my advanced years."* If the Texas and Chartist Rees were one and the same person, Jack the Fifer would have been 26 on arrival in Virginia, not an advanced age by today's standards. But it must be remembered that in 1840 average life expectancy in Britain was 40.2 years, due largely to the appalling levels of infant mortality. The equivalent age today would be 48 when a man might make the same observation on being banished from his native land. The remarkable escape of the Chartist Rees from his remote hideout in the Welsh hill country, dodging pursuers as he criss-crossed Britain, the perilous Atlantic voyage, which could so easily have ended in ship-wreck, then the journey from Canada to freedom in the United States and south to Virginia in search of friends, was at one and the same time hazardous and arduous, more likely to be accomplished by a younger, rather than older man, accustomed to surviving difficult conditions. Rees, veteran of the Texas War of Independence, survivor of the Goliad Massacre, was a man of stamina and spirit.

Arriving in Virginia he at last felt safe although homesick. He wrote, *"The feelings which occupied my mind when on my passage often made me sad; but when taken in consideration, I rejoiced it was not for theft nor murder,"* he wrote. *"In my next letter I shall be better provided to give you a description of this country; but so far I like it well, more so to think that I am in a country where no tyrannical power is displayed."*

Clearly unrepentant, Rees was more anxious to discover what had happened to certain unnamed *"rascals"* whom he accused of stealing his chest, and also for news of Frost, Williams and Jones, having heard of a petition for their release. *"I saw an account some weeks back of a petition being offered to liberate them. I trust it will be granted,"* he commented. Finally, he asked to be remembered to his friend, David Jones, the Tinker, and asked for news of his whereabouts.

The clue to what happened next to Rees centres on a statement in his second letter to the effect he had *"been offered a commission as an officer in the army to go to Texas; whether I shall accept it or not I cannot at present describe."* [20] His former experience in the Army of the Republic of Texas would have marked him out as an excellent candidate for a commission. By 1841, the Republic of Texas was in its fifth year. But although the Texans had won their independence, Mexico still refused to recognise the new republic and the border along the Rio Grande needed defending against Mexicans and Indians. For this, the cash-strapped government of the republic once again offered a bounty of 240 acres of land, to be located anywhere in Texas, to men serving in a frontier regiment. Land! The very mention of it could not have failed to excite Rees's interest, given his previous enthusiasm for acquiring bits of Texas by hook or by crook. Despite the destruction of records in the Adjutant General's Office by arsonists a decade later, a record has survived of a John Rees re-enlisting in the Army, but not until 1846, by which time Texas had been annexed by the United States. There is now incontrovertible evidence this was Jack the Fifer, because tucked away in this man's pocket was the Donation Certificate awarded to John Rees: the Welshman's reward of 640 acres for his part in the Siege of San Antonio de Bexar. Even though the republic had ceased to exist, the certificates were still valid, on condition they were not sold or mortgaged during the lifetime of the beneficiary. The rights to this block of Texas wilderness, which Rees probably never saw, will prove to be the umbilical cord linking the various episodes in the life of Jack the Fifer.

NOTES

1. NLW, 40/2, Tredegar House Papers, Octavius Morgan letter to Normanby, 9 February 1840.
2. Vincent, *Western Vindicator*, 16 November 1839, 7 December 1839.
3. O'Connor, *Northern Star,* 30 November, 7, 14, 21 December 1839.
4. Rokup, A. B. Gomer, 30 November 1839, *Western Vindicator.*
5. GRO, Q/Misc.P.T. Acc. 0003/16, 26, 27, 28, 30, 4 November-22 June 1840.
6. NLW, 40/31, Tredegar House Papers, Morgan letter to Normanby, 9 February 1840.
7. *ibid.*
8. NLW, 40/32, Tredegar House Papers, Normanby reply to Morgan, 15 February 1840.
9. NLW, 40/33, Tredegar House Papers, Morgan letter to Samuel Homfray, 16 February 1849.
10. NLW, 40/34, Tredegar House Papers, Homfray letter to Morgan, 17 February 1840.
11. NLW, 40/35, Tredegar House Papers, Morgan, Coles letter to Normanby, 22 February 1840.
12. GRO, Q/T ACCB 5-6 (1831-1847).
13. PRO, TS 11/502.1630, Stockdale; PRO, TS 11/ 503.1631, Homfray to Thomas Jones Phillips, 7 November 1839; PRO, HO 40/45, TS 11/50.
14. PRO, TS 11/502.1630, Crawshay Bailey, Thomas Brown reward, 7 November 1839.

15. Jones, *Early Days of Sirhowy and Tredegar.*
16. PRO, TS 11/503.1631, Edward Hopkins, letter to magistrates clerk at Newport, 15-16 November 1839.
17. NLW, Rees letters from United States, *Cambrian,* 28 February 1844.
18. Publicola, *Western Vindicator,* 30 November 1839.
19. NLW, Rees letters from United States, *Cambrian,* 28 February 1844.
20. *ibid.*

CHAPTER 9

Prisoner of the First 'Gulag'

'The moral filth of Great Britain was accumulated in vast and fermenting masses in the penal colonies, whence moral typhus, plague, pestilence, and all manner of hideous disease; and these British pest-houses stank in the nostrils of mankind.'

Sir William Molesworth,
House of Commons report, 1838

The last word on transportation to the American colonies, which ended abruptly with the Declaration of Independence, came from one of its signatories, Benjamin Franklin, who drew an analogy with *"pouring cargoes of rattlesnakes on the shores of England."* Banishment was recognised as a form of punishment during the reign of Queen Elizabeth I when a criminal was branded for life by an 'R' burnt into the shoulder, the mark as wide as an English shilling. Loss of country was deemed to be a penalty more severe than any domestic form of punishment short of the scaffold, but the system was not formalised until 1717, when Parliament decided the nation's colonies would benefit from cheap convict labour. The responsibility for transportation was at first privatised, ships' masters free to sell their charges for £20 a head on arrival in the American colonies. At a price usually provided by family and friends, wealthier convicts were freed to spend the rest of their lives as exiles although it remained a capital offence to return to Britain. By 1779 the government was casting around for a new repository for the sweepings of its gaols and Poor Houses. Dockyards, salt mines, even exchanges for Christian slaves held by the Islamic countries were all considered as a means of disposing of a burgeoning criminal class. The answer was found finally in Britain's newest colonies, New South Wales and Van

Diemen's Land, far enough away for a Europe filled with wars and revolution to pay any attention to this experiment to drain the homeland of its tainted blood. To this day, the British Government has never accepted this experiment in social engineering precipitated a human tragedy rarely equalled in its ferocity and depravity. Only the realisation eighty years later it was impossible to hold tens of thousands of people in perpetual bondage ended transportation, but not before it had built a monster, an antipodean Sodom and Gomorrah from the material of British prisons.

The arrival of the *Mandarin* in the Derwent River opposite Hobart Town on June 30, 1840, coincided with an investigation into the convict system by Alexander Maconochie, private secretary to Sir John Franklin, Governor of Van Diemen's Land.[1] Maconochie was scandalised by what he found. By its sixtieth year, transportation had a settled appearance: savagery had become institutionalised. The convict was a slave, a stranger to morality whose only interest was the vague hope of liberty. Without wages, he robbed; miserable, he was drunk; the artful escaped; the careless were punished. Self-respect was utterly destroyed and if not habitual criminals, those born to better things were blindly sacrificed to satisfy the same political objectives. An offender by accident not habit suffered the same bondage, any principles surviving from education or upbringing, drowning in the recklessness and depravity of those around him on the chain gang. Plunged into utter despair, the convict's state was worse than that of the Afro-American slave, the only respite hard liquor, Van Diemen's Land becoming the most drunken speck on the ocean of human existence, tens of thousands dying from alcohol abuse.[2] But did some of this seem vaguely familiar to Frost, Williams and Jones? In Monmouthshire's Black Domain, ironmasters and mine owners treated their cattle with more consideration than their workers.[3] In Van Diemen's Land, a free settler was given a cow by the Government for every convict assigned to his land! Prisoners cultivating a plot of land staked its entire produce for credit in rum. Tattered promissory notes fluttered around the colony like confetti, the largest fortunes accumulated by many settlers derived entirely from the rum trade. It was not uncommon to see men squatting around a bucket of spirits and drinking from it with quart pots, until either it was emptied or they were incapable, not once ever moving from the spot. For liquor, and its twin vice, gambling, they traded everything, even the clothes off their backs. Crime rampaged through the colony, peaking in 1845 when it was higher in Van Diemen's Land than in any place in the civilised world, and for several years traders in Hobart were compelled to sleep on their shop counters. Many ticket-of-leave convicts permitted to move freely around the colony either never found or sought work, preferring instead to prey on others.[4]

With robbery likely to occur at any house, at any hour of the day, it is hardly surprising the number of free settlers dwindled to only one in 1844. Public executions were so frequent – fourteen in the course of three days – they came to be regarded as rather dull public spectacles. Hanging was generally reserved for murder, armed robbery and for stabbing a police constable but had also been imposed for political crimes.[5] The most dreaded sentence was to be committed to one of the penal settlements at Port Arthur, Norfolk Island and Sarah Island in Macquarie Harbour, usually reserved for repeat offenders. Underpinning this regime was flogging, and on a scale unparalleled in British penal history.

By the time Frost, Williams and Jones arrived in Van Diemen's Land the atrocities committed in the name of judicial punishment had made Britain a pariah state. The abolition of transportation was still rejected by Lord Russell, Secretary of State for the Colonies, although he did agree to modify the regime in 1840, the year the Chartists arrived, by introducing a new Probation System. Up until then, convicts were assigned as servants to free settlers from whom they received food and clothes instead of wages. Besides the convict's labour, the settler received one hundred acres of free land for each assignee, and one cow. The system with which this was replaced meant that after spending a preliminary period on public works at one of the probation stations located around the coast, a convict was issued with his ticket-of-leave allowing him or her to work for wages, either for settlers or government departments. The next step towards freedom was a conditional pardon permitting the convict to leave the colony but never return to Britain. A free pardon was rarely granted, and then usually only to political prisoners.[6] The Tolpuddle Martyrs of 1834 and the three Welsh Chartists were among the few to receive it, and when it eventually came for Frost, Williams and Jones in

1857, it was really more part of a general amnesty announced by Queen Victoria to mark the end of the Crimea War, because by then the Chartists were all but forgotten. The first political prisoners to benefit from the new probation system were the Canadian rebels arriving in Hobart five months before the Chartist leaders. The Canadians were in fact mostly American patriots caught up in the Canadian border skirmishes of 1838, and rather like those held by the United States in Guantanamo Bay in Cuba after the Second Iraq War, their detention was generally regarded as contrary to international law. On arrival in Van Diemen's Land they were sent immediately to the Saltwater River Probation Station on the Tasman Peninsular, spending most of their sentence in relative comfort and causing little trouble.

Frost, Williams and Jones expected similar treatment to the Canadian Patriots but no sooner had they arrived in Hobart on June 30 than they were transferred to the colonial schooner *Eliza* for transport down the coast to Port Arthur, a penal settlement whose infamy terrified the most incorrigible criminals. Before the *Eliza* sailed, the Governor, Sir John Franklin boarded the vessel to explain personally the detailed regulations under which they would be placed and advise on their conduct. His vacuous assurance they were not being sent to Port Arthur for punishment, or treated differently from other political prisoners opened a wound which, certainly for Zephaniah Williams, never healed even when Franklin, the Artic explorer disappeared with his entire crew when searching for the North West Passage. In Zephaniah's opinion, Franklin remained *"the lying brute* (who) *delighted in the misery and punishment of his fellow creatures."*[7] However, his promises must have seemed genuine enough when the following morning the *Eliza* entered the sheltered waters of the stunning bay in which the penal station sat. Flanked by soaring cliffs, sandy beaches and dense forests, from a distance it would have borne little resemblance to a prison location, but more like an English country village, its most prominent feature a solid stone-built church complete with belfry and spire, and surrounded by neat gardens. The clue to its real purpose would have been the men in yellow uniforms quietly weeding the vegetables and flowerbeds. To the left of this momentary glimpse into Arcadia, the prison barracks, four-storeys high, screened from the sea by trees and set into the foot of a hill, almost invisible against the brown coastal scrub lapping at the water's edge. At that time it housed 1,200 prisoners, the largest number ever accommodated at Port Arthur. Next to it were the punishment cells, tiny capsules, barely large enough to hold a pig let alone a man, whose inky, silent, blackness drove inmates insane. The solitary confinement block was huge, divided into ten passageways lined with fourteen cells, a round hole in each cell door, the only ventilation in the ceiling. Treated as animals, the inmates groped like dogs in the dark for the scraps of food, thrown to them by gaolers padding around the complex in stockinged feet to magnify the silence. After surviving this ordeal for sixteen weeks, Zephaniah Williams was hooded, before being released into the blinding glare of daylight. As for those driven crazy by this early form of psychological torture, they were simply moved next door into the asylum. Above this place of savagery, perched like a terrifying symbol on the hill, sat the iron Triangle against which offending convicts were strapped and flogged, the floggers selected from amongst the strongest and most brutal of the inmates.

Directly across the bay were the shipyards where the convicts built schooners from the timber cut from the forests and hauled to the settlement on the shoulders of gangs of thirty, forty convicts chained together, winding their way through the bush like giant centipedes, the largest logs furnishing masts and spars. Before this, another gang would have stripped the bark from the felled timber into ten foot sheets, rolling it into bundles carried on their heads to Port Arthur for lining the roofs and walls of convict huts. The only beasts of burden permitted at Port Arthur were convicts, driven on constantly by ruthless overseers chosen for their cruelty from among the convict ranks.[8] Other gangs cut and hauled stone from the quarries and at the dockyard men worked for hours up to their waists in water. Behind Port Arthur and linking it to Norfolk Bay on the opposite side of the Tasman Peninsular, was a ten-mile wooden railroad built by slave labour and along which wagons loaded with supplies, sometimes passengers, were hauled by convict gangs. The track ended just short of Eaglehawk Neck, the narrow land bridge joining the peninsular with the mainland, guarded night and day by dogs and a detachment of soldiers, this the only escape route from Port Arthur other than by sea.

Top: The prison settlement on Port Arthur, where once 1,200 convicts were held, is now a World Heritage site. *Bottom:* left, the cell in which Zephaniah Williams was held in solitary confinement for four months, and right, his harp, on display in the Patriots Museum at Port Arthur.

On arriving at Port Arthur, the three Chartists were paraded before the Commandant, Captain Charles O'Hara Booth, who according to Williams presided over proceedings *"in the plenitude of his vanity waiting to receive his victims."*[9] Stripped of their clothes and issued with yellow prison uniforms, they listened for two hours as the commandant's clerk read out the regulations enforced at the penal settlement, designed to subdue the inmates and discourage escape. Above all else, Booth regarded escape as a personal failure and was unsparing in his efforts to apprehend absconders, hunting them down with his dogs until they could be returned to Port Arthur, hungry, ragged and paraded in chains as an example to the other inmates. The extent to which Booth resorted to flogging is disputed. As might be expected, the verdict of those on the receiving end was very different to the official view. According to Thomas Lempriere, for ten years Commissary at Port Arthur, the commandant only used the lash as a last resort: *"We know he detests the use of it and it is with regret, when he is compelled by the necessity of maintaining strict discipline, that he causes corporal punishment to be inflicted."*[10] The Commandant was certainly a firm believer in the administration of psychological terror as an instrument of discipline and if it had been at all possible would have held every prisoner in solitary confinement. A French naval officer, Captain C. P. T. Laplace, shown around the penal settlement when he came ashore after his ship had anchored in the bay, was surprised how tranquil it appeared, almost as though the prisoners had been sedated. Asked how he had achieved such perfect discipline, Booth attributed this to, *"Severe punishments; by impartial justice, as impassive as that of fate; by untiring vigilance; by demanding absolute silence from the prisoners."* Claiming he rarely used corporal punishment because it degraded the culprits still further, the Commandant said he obtained the best results from solitary confinement, which was more dreaded by the convicts: *"It subdues them by forcing them through boredom to make salutary reflections on the past and future. That is why they generally come out better than when they went in; but, unfortunately, this improvement does not last long."*[11] Although Booth's superiors in Hobart and theirs in turn in London preferred to close their eyes to the atrocities perpetrated by Booth's gaolers, accounts of the brutal treatment suffered by prisoners did occasionally escape into the world beyond the Tasman Peninsula. The *True Colonist* published a sensational account accusing Booth of flogging a gentleman convict, a former army officer, to the point he was driven to commit suicide while the *"barbarous treatment"* suffered by another convict in solitary confinement caused him to starve himself to death.[12] And from the eyewitness evidence of Williams and Frost there must have been very many occasions of *'last resort'* because flogging was constant, the ground beneath the Triangle frequently soaked in blood. The Chartist prisoners soon found it was scarcely possible to move without violating a rule or regulation invoking some form of punishment. Even the expression on a convict's face was deserving of retribution, the failure to salute the Commandant's office on passing another good reason for a flogging. Williams documented much of this in a series of remarkable letters to his wife from which it is possible to piece together the horrors of Port Arthur, a system, he concluded, designed to corrupt and demoralise mankind.

Writing to his wife, he explained that, *"Having a piece of coin, a knife, thread and needle, tobacco or tobacco pipe in our possession, not saluting our officers properly, or even the office itself when passing, and no one inside, and a thousand of other trifling things too numerous here to mention, all visited with some kind of punishment, either so many weeks or months in chains, solitary confinement on bread and water, or the lash."*

As magistrate as well as Commandant, Booth was judge and jury. But the implementation of this wretched system was delegated to the overseers he selected from amongst the convicts, it being too disagreeable an occupation for gentlemen. If a convict overseer suspected a man had money, anything of value, he was tormented, driven *"almost to death"* until he surrendered it, then taken before the Commandant, accused of some trifling offence on the evidence of the overseer and flogged *"every stripe taking away some flesh 'till the blood runs down his heels."*[13]

Although Williams considered the Commandant's litany of regulations *"infernal rubbish"* penned by the *"Christian Devil himself,"* he immediately formulated for himself a rule of conduct as a means of surviving the regime. He promised his wife he would be humble, obedient, and submissive.[14] Incredulously, Frost was pleasantly surprised by his first impressions of Port Arthur, unless this was no more than a brave face given the circumstances. While Williams was sent as an overseer to the Coal Mines, and Jones as a supervisor at Point Puer, the juvenile settlement, Frost was assigned to the relatively comfortable position of clerk in the Commandant's office from where he wrote cheerfully about Port Arthur in his first letter to his wife Mary who by then had moved with their family to Stapleton, near Bristol:

"I understand that a strong feeling was produced in the colony by our being sent down to Port Arthur and I have no doubt that great indignation will be felt in England, Scotland and Wales when it is known. It will be said that we are on the chain gangs and that we are treated as the vilest of the vile; I wish that truth should prevail and for that reason I have stated the facts; God knows that the very best situation in Port Arthur is bad enough privation and suffering; but our situation is one of comfort, compared with that of many prisoners." [15]

A year later Frost discovered how vicious the regime at Port Arthur could be. That was how long it took for his first letter to reach England, be read by someone in the Colonial Office and for instructions to be sent replacing his comfortable office job with two years in a chain gang. All mail was censored by the Commandant who, unfortunately for Frost, neglected to remove from this first letter a reference to Lord Russell, which, when read by officials in London was seen as implying some impropriety on behalf of the Colonial Secretary, by suggesting he might be tempted to pry into the letter's contents. Frost had forgotten all about the letter when he was called into the Commandant's office and told, without a word of explanation, instructions had been received to send him to the chain gangs. Nothing could be worse for a man of Frost's age (by then 57), temperament, and intellect to be chained alongside those he considered coarse, depraved criminals. Now he would work and sleep with them, thirty-to-forty to a dormitory, only eighteen inches of bed space for each. When he infringed a second time by failing to touch his cap to an overseer he was transferred to a new station then being built at Impression Bay. Seen there in 1842 by a visiting writer, Frost was being treated no differently to the others on the chain gang, his only concession to be allowed to sleep alone at night.[16] But the experience and physical labour in the forests and quarries broke neither his spirit nor health, which he admitted later was in better shape when eventually he was moved to the garden gangs, reserved for the elderly and infirm.

Zephaniah Williams on the other hand had made an even worse start to his convict life. The Coal Mines were twenty-two miles from Port Arthur on the north-western coast of the Tasman Peninsular overlooking Norfolk Bay, a ten-mile wide expanse of water separating the convicts from the freedom of the bush. Like Port Arthur, it was also a punishment station and reserved for five hundred of the most hardened criminals. The discovery of coal there in 1834 caused great excitement in the colony, which until then imported its supplies from New South Wales at considerable expense. The coal was, however, of inferior quality, showering carpets and furniture with small hot fragments when lit. Joseph Lacey, a convict with practical mining experience, was sent from Port Arthur with a small party of convicts to start the mines. Others followed later to build the settlement from materials found locally, red sandstone and timber. Lacey was removed after a drunken brawl with the master of the *Swan River Packet*, by which time the mines had become *'sinkholes of vice and infamy.'*

Homosexuality was rife at Port Arthur but was concealed by the Commandant who insisted on recording *'unnatural acts'* as *'gross misconduct.'* During his year spent in the Commandant's office, Frost made copious notes of how Booth dispensed his so-called justice, particularly as regards those *'disgusting acts.'* One instance Frost noted illustrates the extraordinary lengths the Commandant went to hide the excesses of the penal regime. Two men were brought before the Commandant charged with crimes of the very worst kind. The witnesses told Booth that after hearing that abominable practices were carried out on the carrying gang, they had watched from the bush and saw the prisoners committing an unnatural crime. When the police clerk (quite possibly Frost himself) asked what name should be given to the offences, the Commandant said, *"Gross misconduct."* The constable was then sworn to give evidence but as he was about to explain what he had seen, Booth intervened, *"Stop! You witnessed a disgusting act.*" Entered in the record book as '*gross misconduct,*' the men were, consequently, flogged for no more serious an offence than possession of a pipe. Frost later claimed if Booth had "*committed these men under the real charge he would have displeased his masters, both in the colonies and at home.*" Men had been executed for buggery, at the very least sent to the Coal Mines or Norfolk Island. But there was a particularly bad case of this sort from which Booth could not escape by concealing is as '*gross misconduct.*' When a good-looking youth sent to the mines refused to participate in homosexual acts, six men seized him, and while four held him the other two violated his person. Despite attempts to conceal the attack, the victim refused to be intimidated, and the six were tried in the Supreme Court at Hobart. Two were hanged, the others sent to Norfolk Island.[17]

When Zephaniah Williams arrived at the Coal Mines, homosexuality was rampant, eventually becoming the main reason the mines were closed in 1848, the authorities no longer able to hide what was happening, although Booth tried had hard enough to do so with the connivance of the Governor Sir John Franklin, and his successors. Visitors were only allowed with the permission of the Colonial Secretary, and the crew of any vessel forced to seek shelter at Port Arthur or needing supplies was denied all contact with the convicts. For the same reason, Booth banned ships from fishing for oysters on the Tasman Peninsular, and entering its bays to collect rushes for whaling establishments. Rather than risk prying eyes, he had his convicts cut the rushes and forward them to Hobart Town.

Of the mines, Williams wrote, "*If ever there is a Hell that is one and the worst. I do not dread a greater. Consummate devils in human form in authority and though professed Christians, not the least ashamed to boast there was no conceivable crime as man could commit, they were guilty of. . . . My destruction was sought in every possible manner they could devise which rendered my situation most miserable.*"[18]

The coal was first worked from horizontal tunnels driven into the side of the cliff from near the water's edge. After the shaft was sunk, the miners were lowered to the pit bottom in pairs, astride a metal bar suspended from a rope. Below ground the seam was about four feet thick and worked by the pillar and stall system

Top: Norfolk Bay across which Zephaniah Williams made his escape from the Coal Mines at Slopen Main. *Bottom:* left, the shaft down which convict miners (right) were lowered in pairs, astride a metal bar suspended from a rope.

familiar to Zephaniah Williams from his experiences in Monmouthshire. The underground workings extended for about five miles, in many places the roof was so low it was only possible to crawl, the few lamps attached to the walls offering little to relieve the darkness, the faint light frequently snuffed out by the lack of oxygen. Half naked, and sweating profusely, most convicts were employed dragging coal on wicker baskets from the coalface to the bottom of the shaft, raising about 300 tons a week. An airshaft was eventually sunk, the ventilation system the same as that employed in early 19th century South Wales collieries, the shaft split by a wooden partition, then a fire lit to force warm air up the one side and fresh air down the other. The miners were given quotas, 25 tons to be raised in each eight-hour shift. For the worst offenders, five solitary confinement cells were carved out of the sandstone deep beneath the surface, the Commandant's *"pleasant little abodes."* Every class of criminal was crowded together in the most fraught and depraved conditions. With murderers, rapists, bigamists, highway robbers, burglars and deserters, slaving together below ground, it is not possible to imagine without feelings of horror, those naked figures, faintly perceptible in the gloom, involved in *'gross misconduct.'* In an effort to curb such acts, additional lighting was placed in the tunnels, augur holes cut in the doors and shutters of sleeping quarters and surprise visits made by constables. Over one hundred separate cells were built in an attempt to keep prisoners segregated at night but surveillance remained virtually impossible when the men were at work.

As an overseer, Zephaniah Williams had his own quarters at the Coal Mines. All that remains of these today are a few stones and a marker to this effect situated on the edge of the settlement, immediately beside the path running up to the mineshaft hidden in the bush a mile away. Through the trees, he would have seen the clear blue waters of Norfolk Bay, the mainland and freedom. Whether at the mines or Port Arthur, the chance of escape, no matter how slight, was the convicts' life-blood, the oxygen that kept him alive. There were few escape options. Either he could smuggle himself aboard one of the American sealers frequently anchored in Norfolk Bay, or build a primitive boat to cross the ten mile stretch of water, and once ashore disappear into the bush, there to join the army of bushrangers that more or less controlled the unfenced, uninhabited interior of Van Diemen's Land. If this failed, the final resort for the desperate was murder and suicide. Zephaniah Williams had witnessed this, admitting to his wife that but for his lingering hopes of being one day reunited with his family *"death would be preferable to being such a servile wretch."* Many he had known had murdered their fellow sufferers in order to expire on the gallows rather than continue to suffer.[19]

Williams' resolve to remain humble, obedient, and submissive was broken within three months of being assigned to the Coal Mines. He bolted into the bush with four other convicts, or, if his account is believed, was forced to escape with them as he was escorting the group to the mines for the start of the night shift. This explanation, which he also gave his wife Joan, as well as the magistrates, was not believed when it was discovered he had taken with him a compass belonging to the Commandant, a set of mathematical instruments, and clothing. Catching up with the absconders, Zephaniah's version of events was that they threatened to kill him, then forced him aboard a boat they had hidden to cross the bay. Reaching the opposite shore, the party split up, two remaining with the boat, the other pair heading off into the bush, taking Williams along as a hostage.[20]

Describing what happened in a letter to his wife, he said, *"For four successive days and nights I was driven along like a beast before them, and if at any time I attempted to remonstrate or appeal to their humanity I was instantly threatened with death. I might almost as well have incited them to do it for they nearly starved me notwithstanding they had more food than sufficed for the time. They would give me none but that they considered sufficient to sustain life."*

By the end of the fourth day, Williams was close to starvation. Since coming ashore they had travelled about 150 miles. His captors then placed him in a hollow tree, where he was told to remain for at least an hour while the fugitives made good their escape. Now completely lost in the bush, the Welshman wandered for about two hours before coming upon a hut occupied by six assigned servants and an overseer, whom he persuaded to join him in pursuit of the runaways. After a fruitless search, they arrived on the outskirts of the town of Richmond, at which point Zephaniah decided he had better explain his story to the local magistrate.[21]

"As a matter of course I was then lodged in jail till they ascertained the facts," he wrote to his wife. *"On the third day following I was taken before the police magistrate who, very patiently and apparently with sympathy, heard my woeful tale. He said he doubted not a word of what I had stated as he had seen one of the men that were left with the boat whose statement corroborated mine to the word. This man also said that if ever I should be found I would not be found alive."* Not long afterwards, Williams' captors murdered two shepherds for which they were subsequently hanged.[22]

Returned to Port Arthur, his story was dismissed by the Commandant who had witnesses alleging Williams was an accomplice in the escape attempt. Found guilty of absconding, and sentenced to two years hard labour in chains, he was paraded at Port Arthur before the Governor Sir John Franklin, a dozen guests, and 800 convicts, his head shaven, his legs chained to a log: *"I was fixed between two murderers, right in the centre of the settlement, in the most conspicuous place they could find, that I might not escape the notice of anyone that passed, and exhibited to every stranger as Williams the Chartist. Why treat me in such a manner more than the others unless the offence for which I was sent into the country was the cause. Twice I have been brought before such characters, and for the same purpose, and dare not speak a word in vindication."*[23]

The next sixteen weeks he spent in solitary confinement, his cell only six feet by four, his bed a wooden board, eighteen inches wide, suspended three feet from the ground, and his boots for a pillow. Zephaniah only kept warm by shuffling around his cell as much as his manacles would allow. For breakfast at 4.30 every morning there was a pint and a half of skilly (watered gruel) and half a pound of dark brown bread. For midday dinner the same measure of *'pig's wash'*, the water in which cabbage, potatoes, turnips and meat were boiled, a lump of bread, and two or three ounces of meat. Supper was the same as breakfast.[24]

To his wife he wrote, *"For sixteen weeks, and I believe three days, I was kept in this wretched situation, from which I was removed into the 'Huts', which were but very little better, except the privilege they afforded me of walking the yard a little between meals, and the opportunity of conversing with my fellow sufferers.*

*As for sleeping in the huts it was next to impossible, unless com-
pletely exhausted with labour and fatigue, for the place is infested
with bugs, fleas and lice. You will scarcely credit me when I
declare to you that I have at various times taken off my blanket
in the day time, 300 and 400 fleas at a time, and some blankets I
have seen almost alive with lice.*"

Williams suffered these conditions for almost three years, at
first employed in the logging gangs, the most exhausting work
at the penal settlement. After six months of this he was transferred, still in irons, to the garden gangs for the remainder of
his sentence. Then just eleven days before his sentence ended,
Zephaniah was suddenly ordered back to the cells, and his head
shaved. His appeals for an explanation ignored, he was returned
the next morning to the logging gangs, from which he bolted,
unable to endure the suffering any longer. This time he headed
not for the bush, but straight into the Commandant's office to
demand a reason for his treatment. Momentarily overcome with
indignation by this impertinence, Booth on recovering his
composure told Williams he had been returned to the logging
gang because he had spoken to a *"very suspicious character."*
This he understood to mean the man to whom he was actually
chained, for this was the only person with whom he could have
any kind of conversation! Williams escaped further punishment,
and was returned to the garden gangs due, he believed, to his
boldness in confronting the Commandant who was more accustomed to servility.[25]

His respite was to be short-lived. By the end of almost three
years at Port Arthur a convict expected, at the very least, a ticket-
of-leave, entitling him to work for wages anywhere within the
island colony. The Canadian political prisoners had received theirs
almost immediately, leaving Williams convinced that on account
of his crime against the state he was being treated as a special
category prisoner. During the 1840s, how and where a convict
served his sentence was at the discretion of the Commandant and
Governor, the former never hesitating to retain a man longer at
Port Arthur if it were useful for him to do so. For eighteen months
the Superintendent of Convicts at Port Arthur had been trying
without success to manufacture iron castings. A large quantity of
metal had been wasted in the process, and so in desperation he

turned to Zephaniah Williams. When the man from the Minerals District of South Wales took no time at all to produce a casting, Booth decided he was too useful an asset to lose – and kept him at Port Arthur another seven months superintending the manufacture of castings. Even then Booth still refused to give Williams a character reference. Finally transferred to the probation station at Impression Bay after four years of the most brutal prison regime in the world, the Welshman discovered his usefulness was still not exhausted. Now he was needed to prospect for a supply of fresh water. So desperate was the water situation at Impression Bay, that when Williams arrived seventy men were being treated for dysentery and the station looked as if it might be forced to close. Within two weeks he had found water, and piped it three miles through thick bush to the station. Instead of being rewarded, Zephaniah found himself back in the carrying gang, until a heavy log fell and broke his leg. By then Frost had also been moved to Impression Bay and was teaching at Cascades about three miles along the coast, still on the Tasman Peninsular.[26]

The third Chartist, William Jones, initially employed as an overseer the Point Puer juvenile prison, was removed from his position within a year for what the Commandant described as *"language calculated to have an evil effect on the minds of the boys."* This might have been another of Captain Booth's euphemisms concealing something more sinister. Zephaniah Williams hinted as much in a letter to his wife in which he described Jones as a character *"so repugnant and odious to my feelings, I forbade him ever to speak to me again."* Dismissed from Point Puer, Jones was admitted to hospital at Port Arthur for several months. After recovering from some mystery illness, which Booth assured the Colonial Secretary was not associated with his work, he was placed in Number One Garden Gang, and was seen in 1842 by the visiting writer David Burn saying grace before a meal in one of the convict messes. Burn wrote that while *"he wore the aspect of a sottish, dissipated mechanic and was disposed to talk rather freely"* he had *"learned his place."* A year later Jones was considered sufficiently reformed to be appointed a constable in Hobart Town, and according to Williams *"a more vigilant and efficient constable is not to be met with; he just suits the tyrants."* While at Port Arthur, the writer Burn also came across John Frost's stepson, William Geach, the solicitor who instructed defence counsel at the trail of the Chartist leaders. Soon afterwards Geach was himself convicted of defrauding an elderly client of £20,000 and transported to Australia, where he died in exile.[27]

By now Zephaniah was obsessed with the idea that he was being discriminated against for reasons known only to his captors. Still not fully recovered from his broken leg, his spirits were at rock bottom, writing to his wife from Impression Bay of his *"wretched, miserable, degrading and afflicting situation."* The scourge and whip, he told her, were not the only weapons of torture. *"Mental oppression is familiar and practised not in vain,"* he said. He had been cast among *"the most corrupt, desperate, and audacious of human beings to drag out a life of misery and woe, labour, toil, mess, sleep, pine, bleed and die midst the hecatombs of victims."*[28]

But Zephaniah Williams' letters provide more than a graphic account of his suffering. They are as remarkable for their sensitivity as love letters, Zephaniah pleading with his wife to forgive him for his 'insane' actions. *"My feelings are overcome, there I must conclude,"* he writes on one occasion. Then, *"Language is inadequate to express or portray my feelings . . . torn away from the nearest and dearest objects of my affection in the vale of years . . . has almost unmanned . . . nothing can exceed it, no calamity which hath befallen me could have struck so deeply into my heart, deprived me of those who was my only solace, death would have been far preferable and I would have courted, were it not for the hope I entertained that I might by some means or other extricate myself and get into some country where I might once more have the pleasure of rejoining your society . . . not a night have I laid myself down to rest, nor yet raised in the morning since I last saw you without being oppressed most unbearable with the thoughts and grief for your society."* His world, he told her, was a complete wilderness. *"I madly courted wretchedness for myself and filled the cup of bitterness to the brim for you. Many are the unhappy hours I have endured when reflecting upon that insane and infatuated course which led me to the awful separation."*[29]

Of his broken leg he said, *"What is the pain of a thousand broken limbs when compared with separating me from those from whom my affections were never estranged? A day, even an hour, of liberty in the society of a virtuous family, is worth a whole eternity of bondage destitute of all comforts. Nothing to cheer me, no friends to sooth my sorrows, no wife, no little ones to smooth the rugged path of life; I must number my days in misery and wretchedness, consume my thoughts or my reason in solitude, grief and bitterness."*[30]

In letter after letter Zephaniah expressed his undying love for his wife and family, alongside the graphic description of the atrocities committed against him and others trapped in the penal regime. But he did neglect to mention one matter: the punishment he received when he was caught with a female inmate in a locked room!

Three years into his exile and Zephaniah had become convinced his rule of conduct, *"implicit obedience, humility and the best merited assiduity under tyranny"* was not actually working. In fact on several occasions he had suffered as a consequence, it appearing to him that the most desperate and audacious were regarded more highly than the meek and innocent.[31] But there was some hope on the horizon in 1843, Sir J. E. E. Wilmot replacing Sir John Franklin as Governor, the latter having departed on his fatal voyage to discover the North West Passage. Williams planned to raise his grievances about the length of time he and Frost were detained in penal settlements when the new governor and his Controller General of Convicts, Captain Forster, visited Impression Bay. Even the Lancashire and London Chartists who were to follow the Welshmen into exile in 1848 were better treated. The Welsh pair had now started two years probation, having already spent three in the penal station at Port Arthur. Possibly it was on account of Zephaniah's personal appeal to Wilmot that both were shortly afterwards moved to Slopen Island, a transit station for convicts on route to Hobart Town. Recalling this later, Frost said they were held in the filthiest of huts, even by Van Diemen's Land standards. Afraid to complain, he asked the wife of the station superintendent for clean blankets, which she kindly supplied. The following day their overseer ordered the clean blankets removed and replaced with the filthy ones, at the same time issuing Frost with a stern warning of the consequences if he was again caught with his hand in his pocket! Before leaving for Hobart, Williams also narrowly escaped being sent back to Port Arthur after he was searched and found to be carrying letters given him by other convicts for posting in Hobart to avoid scrutiny by colonial authorities.[32]

The pair arrived in Hobart in November 1843, three and a half years after being sent to Tasman Peninsular. Neither of them mourned when the colony received news of Franklin's death in the Arctic. Frost was assigned as a clerk to a grocer, an individual he described as the cruellest man he had ever known. Without the few pounds sent by Chartist sympathisers, he believes he would never have survived. After three months in a quarry, Williams was made a convict constable but for only a month before being moved again, this time twenty miles inland to the town of New Norfolk, as a watch-house keeper supervising road gangs. Whether or not he had been singled-out for special treatment, his reputation certainly seemed to follow him. For once though he emerged the hero not the villain.[33]

At New Norfolk, Australia had built its first lunatic asylum for the most dangerous psychopaths. The gates were closed to all outsiders and the only inspections that ever took place were of the account books. What went on inside can only be imagined from the evidence in a case of malpractice brought before the Supreme Court, by an inmate blinded by the negligence of the medical superintendent. In April 1845, the lunatics broke loose, arming themselves with whatever weapons they found, bricks and stones. The keepers fled for their lives, leaving about seventy inmates on the rampage. It was a Sunday and police and officials were at church. When they eventually arrived none of them was willing to enter the ransacked building to reason with the lunatics. Instead they sent in Zephaniah Williams, hoping that as he was known to some of the inmates from Port Arthur, he might succeed in pacifying them. By then 700 large panes of glass were broken and the inmates threatened to break loose, killing everyone in their path before burning and plundering the town. Their leader boasted they could not be punished because they were certified as insane! On entering the ward, Williams found himself surrounded by inmates flourishing weapons, until their leader, recognising him from Port Arthur, instructed the rioters to lay their weapons at Zephaniah's feet, each shaking his hand as he did so. Then they gave him three great cheers, the roar convincing those waiting anxiously outside Williams had certainly been murdered. The reason for the riot was the asylum's chief medical officer, a Dr Brock who was universally hated by the inmates. After they promised Zephaniah they would remain quiet, he left the asylum to negotiate with the magistrate on their behalf. But the magistrate refused to consider the inmates' grievances until they returned to their cells, sending Zephaniah back into the lions' den with what seemed an impossible ultimatum. To his utter surprise, the rioters accepted his advice that it was in their best interests to surrender, even allowing him to lock them back into their cells.[34]

Changes were afterwards made at the asylum, the *Colonial Times* commenting, *"It appears that most of the men have at times passed under the charge of Williams who is well known to be a most humane and kind hearted man, especially so to those unfortunate creatures. Had Williams not had sufficient control the result might have been dreadful. . . . It is a pity Williams is not the head medical officer and Dr Brock the watch-house keeper."* Surely, Zephaniah thought, this display of bravery would earn him his ticket-of-leave. But while his courage was applauded throughout the colony, Zephaniah was still denied any respite by the penal authorities. *"Had any prisoner,"* he wrote his wife, *"done the one-fiftieth part as much as I have done, he would have received an absolute pardon."* Overwhelmed by despair, his latest letter must have left his wife fearing he was close to ending his life. Informing her, in unmistakeable terms, he preferred death to his continued slavery, Zephaniah went as far as alluding to the method he might choose, by citing instances of convicts who committed murder for the certainty of the gallows. Was it this state of mind that accounted for a rumour reaching Wales that he had been executed? Zephaniah himself suspected his former Chartist comrade-in-arms William Jones of maliciously spreading it.[35]

Zephaniah mentioned nothing to his wife that shortly after the asylum riot his impulsiveness had landed him in more trouble – this time, caught in a locked room with a female prisoner! Fined 10 shillings and removed from his post as watch-house keeper, Williams was dispatched to a logging camp in the bush for five months. From his declarations of unswerving devotion expressed in a subsequent letter, it seems Mrs Williams might have heard something of his romantic adventure. Although a half dozen of Zephaniah's letters have survived – copies translated from the original Welsh by his friend Israel Jacob and published first in the *Cardiff Times* – he was not a frequent correspondent, unless, as he suggested to his wife his letters were being intercepted by the authorities. At no time during the first two years of his imprisonment at Port Arthur did he ask for writing paper from the Commandant's office. What letters did enter the public domain, were filled with bitterness and despair, and angry denunciation of the penal system, especially its instruments of oppression, Commandant James O'Hara Booth, and the Governor, Sir John Franklin. The only reason his criticisms of the system got beyond the shores of Van Demain's Land was because he wrote in Welsh. On the other hand, Frost writing in English was very guarded in his observations after his remarks about Lord Russell, Secretary of State for the Colonies, cost him two years on the chain gang. As far as can be discovered, Frost wrote only once from Port Arthur soon after arriving, preferring to wait until his pardon to deliver his ringing condemnation of the penal system in a series of lectures and two open letters, one to the People of the United States which he visited in 1855 before returning to Britain a free man. As for Jones, he appears not to have written at all, even to his wife. The one occasion he asked for writing paper from the Commandant's Office, he never used it, according to Captain Booth in reply to a formal complaint from the Merthyr Chartist leader Morgan Williams that the trio were being held incommunicado.[36]

Returning from exile in the bush, Zephaniah was sent in August 1846 to Launceston on the island's northern coast, at that time about as far as settlement had extended. Jones and Frost had both received their tickets-of-leave, Jones twelve months previously. The only logical explanation Williams could find for his different treatment, was that because he was so useful, the penal authorities put every obstacle in his way in order to retain his services for as long as possible. As petition after petition was rejected, it became generally agreed the three Chartists would have to serve ten years, before the home government considered any respite. At least at Launceston, Zephaniah's life was easier. Assigned as a clerk to Edward Greenbank, owner of one of the largest hotels in the town, he was up at 3 a.m. every morning to prepare the three coaches leaving from the hotel for Hobart, then served in the bar until after midnight, as well as keeping the account books and collecting debts. It was as a direct consequence of this latter duty that Williams fell out with William Jones, over a debt he was sent by his master to collect from Jones who ran the *Cross Keys* in Launceston. Angry that Jones dared challenge his account of the debt, Williams told him just what he thought. Writing to his wife about the incident, he said, *"I then found it necessary to be plain, honest and candid, and did not fail to tell him of his pride, assumption and arrogance, at which my nature revolted, and knowing his origin and the course of life he pursued, I could not countenance nor associate with a character so repugnant and odious to my feelings and I forbade him ever to speak to me again."* Whatever was really behind the quarrel, the breakdown in their relationship was final and irretrievable although Zephaniah insinuated the reasons were far more serious than a disputed bill. Afterwards Jones went rapidly downhill, accumulating so much debt that by the time his wife eventually arrived to join him in exile, he could afford only two miserable rooms, one he used as a watch repair workshop, the other a kitchen-bedroom with scarcely a stick of furniture. By 1848 he was penniless, his business bankrupt, his only source of income the little he earned as a part time actor. Before this, however, he exposed to the authorities Zephaniah's plans for a second escape.[37]

Along with another convict, William Ellis, transported for his part in riots in the Potteries, Zephaniah arranged passages from Launceston to New Zealand aboard the cutter *Opossum*. From there they intended reaching the United States or France, in the case of the latter, their arrival, hopefully, coinciding with *"that glorious revolution which caused Louis Phillippe to quit the throne in so unceremonious a manner."*[38] For some reason he felt obliged to warn his employer Greenbank of the escape plan, although exhorting him not to mention a word to Jones, a regular at the hotel. The plan was for the pair to sail a small boat 43 miles to the mouth of River Tamar, where the *Opossum* was waiting to pick them up. But Greenbank let it slip, and hearing of the scheme Jones informed the local constable. The following day Jones immediately took the coach to Hobart, to provide himself with the alibi he was out of town at the time. As Williams and Ellis approached the river's mouth they spotted the police waiting, and realising their chances were hopeless quickly turned the boat about and headed back up river, in darkness almost making it back safely to their lodgings before being seized by police. Charged with attempting to escape the colony, they were detained in the watch house and visited a few days later by Jones, now back from Hobart. Offering his consolations and promising to do all he could to save them from further punishment, it was his statement that sentenced them to a further year's hard labour after Greenbank refused to give evidence. Loaded on to a cart and shackled together like murderers, in full public view, the pair were escorted across country to Port Arthur 200 miles away. Petitions for their release from 150 of Launceston's most respectable citizens and from three members of the island's Legislative Council all failed. The affair did, however, have the effect of propelling Zephaniah's grievances into the public domain, so that on his second visit to the penal settlement he suffered comparatively little, even though six months was spent at the Coal Mines.[39]

On his release into the Convict Barracks in Hobart Town, the dark shadows lifted somewhat and Zephaniah was sufficiently confident about the future to write to his wife with plans for her and the family join him in Tasmania. Now 53, he could no longer contemplate the voyage home even if the opportunity arose. *"Dearest Joan,"* he wrote, *"if it were a probability of my being allowed to return, with all my prospects in view, I would not ask you to undertake such a trip, not withstanding I believe I could scarcely survive the voyage home, for I find the more I advance in years, the more incapable I am of sea voyage."* Urging that they join him, he recommended the Tasmanian climate as one of the healthiest in the world, and with no scarlet fever or typhoid, no measles or smallpox it would add twenty years to their lives. Moreover, he was excited about his prospects, expecting soon to be earning £1,000 a year from a coal mine he was sinking for four local businessmen on 600 acres of minerals land he had advised them to purchase at Hobart. If all went well, he told Joan, his next letter would contain the detailed arrangements for the family's passage to Tasmania. *"Heaven bless you all,"* he concluded, *"and a pleasant voyage to this country, to the arms of him whose sole happiness depends on your society and welfare."* As it happened, it would be another six years before Zephaniah was re-united with his wife, daughter Rhoda, and his son Llewellyn. By the time the letter reached them he was already back on the Tasman Peninsular, not at the penal settlement at Port Arthur but the Salt Water River probation station where he was sent for another year.[40]

Zephaniah mentioned not a word of this to his wife, leaving her with the impression he was still actively engaged on his mining venture at Hobart which he boasted was worth £500,000, one-fifth of this his. No reason is given in his convict record for the further period of detention at Salt Water River probation station. One possible explanation is that he had been dismissed by his partners in Hobart, and returned to the Convict Barracks in Hobart after they accused him of duplicity. Without a ticket-of-leave, he was not free to enter into a legal contract with anyone, and his dissatisfied employers had only to return him to the Barracks from which he was then sent to the probation station for further rehabilitation.[41]

It was not until a year later, in December 1849, that Joan Williams heard from Zephaniah that he was no longer in the coal business, although his letter gives the impression this had just happened, Zephaniah making no mention of the intervening twelve months he had served at Salt Water River probation station. The story for his wife was that his partners had reneged on him. They were not as flush with funds as Zephaniah first thought and just as he was about to reach the coal, they accused him of duping them, and sent him back to the convict barracks in Hobart. This had occurred only six days before he received his ticket-of-leave, which meant he had no contract with his partners and, consequently, no recourse to law. While it all sounds plausible, the chain of events Zephaniah related to his wife occurred not six days before he received his ticket-of-leave in November 1849, but twelve months previously. The suspicion remains Zephaniah was covering up what his wife suspected was another *"indiscreet and foolish"* act. But he never really lied: Zephaniah simply 'lost' twelve months in recounting it!

Although free by November 1849 to work anywhere in the colony for wages, Zephaniah had not sufficient funds to pay his family's passage. Almost penniless, he nevertheless continued encouraging Joan and the two children to prepare themselves for the voyage, sending precise details of what they would need, including *"such luxuries as . . . spirits, wine, beer and porter, also fruit such as currants and raisins, cheese, bacon and some flour, for you will soon get tired of biscuit."*

"When you have the means yourself," he wrote, *"you can make yourself a cake or a loaf of bread, which by giving the cook a glass of spirits or bottle of beer he will bake it for you and supply you with the necessary yeast. By so doing you will keep him sweet and you will be able to enjoy many comforts you would not otherwise. A quantity of jam you had better get in order to make some tarts and puddings; and as you will find the berths for sleeping very uncomfortable, you had better furnish yourselves with a cot each, such that swing like a child's cradle. That will take off the rolling of the ship, which is very unpleasant. All such articles you may procure in London. You may require an additional quantity of bedding to what they will supply, for, recollect, it is very cold at sea the most part of the time."* [42]

Zephaniah also had words of encouragement for his son, Llewellyn, whose career as a harpist had suffered on account of his father's imprisonment. Llewellyn would be in great demand for performances in Tasmania, wrote Zephaniah, his harp the only one in the entire island. As a teacher he could expect to earn £600 a year! To what extent the son's career was blighted by his father's notoriety is clear from one incident, after Llewellyn (Pencerdd y De) was awarded first prize at an eisteddfod. Because of his father's disgrace, the committee decided to withhold half the prize money. For a moment the young man stared at the £1 he was given, before jumping to his feet and flinging it in their faces. Taking a small key from his pocket, he ran it across the harp, the crack of the strings breaking thundering around the hall, and sending the committee fleeing from the stage in fright. After the Chartist Uprising, in which Llewellyn played a part as one of the founders of the movement's youth section, he was ostracised by the Monmouthshire gentry, no longer welcome to give recitals at Lady Llanover's home. Gradually, he was reinstated as Monmouthshire's most renowned musician, and at the Great Exhibition in 1851 was presented with a triple harp by Queen Victoria. [43]

Little is known about Joan Williams, except that sometime after the family was evicted from the *Royal Oak* at Nantyglo she became landlord of the *Boar's Head* at Caerphilly, until they eventually left for Tasmania. But judging from the letters there existed a remarkably strong bond between the pair, even if Zephaniah might have strayed occasionally during their long separation. Not that he had much opportunity for female companionship, considering almost ten years were spent in detention, and that the ratio of males to females in the colony was three to one and most of those females children. Zephaniah was ambivalent, about whether Joan should risk the hardship of such a long voyage. The failure of his mining venture, for whatever reason, once again plunged him into the deepest despair. Neither were his immediate prospects good. The colony was in the grip of a severe economic recession, almost every able-bodied man leaving on the first ship for the Californian goldfields. But Zephaniah did not doubt he could support his wife and children if only he retained his health.[44]

After promising his wife never again to enter into a business partnership, Zephaniah promptly did, this time with one of the last remaining Canadian rebels, Robert Collins from New York City. Considering he had little time for the Canadians whom he believed had been treated leniently for offences no different to his, Williams needed a partner to complete a new mine shaft he was sinking at New Town on the outskirts of Hobart in 1852. Apart from 14 Canadian rebels who died either from the rigours of transportation or penal servitude, the Canadians had almost all returned to North America. The only capital Collins could offer was £30 but sufficient to allow Zephaniah to get into the coal. The discovery triggered a small coal rush with seven other speculators sinking shafts all around his site. Zephaniah christened his the Triumph Mine, delighted he had broken the coal monopoly operated by the businessman who two years earlier had unceremoniously dumped him, after exploiting his professional expertise. Very soon he was producing 30 to 40 tons a day, enabling him to undercut his competitors. The only thing that mattered now was to be re-united with his family, Zephaniah telling his wife, *"All I want now is the society of yourself and my dearest Rhoda and Llewellyn, the loss of which has been to me a world of trouble and misery. . . . I will see the Governor as soon as I pos-*

sibly can and inform you of the result, which I have no doubt will be favourable." [45]

By the middle of that year the reunion was postponed yet again, Zephaniah managing to dig himself into more trouble. Next to the Triumph Mine was the Queen's Orphans School, the superintendent of which, Mr A. B. Jones, had complained to the Governor that colliers were tunnelling beneath Crown property. Instructed to investigate, the Surveyor General found Zephaniah had removed 400 tons of coal to which he was not entitled, and on which royalties had not been paid. This would have sounded very familiar to those acquainted with Zephaniah's mining exploits in Wales prior to his transportation! On this occasion, the Governor Sir William Denison took the view the unpaid royalties were not worth recovering, although he fixed a scale to be paid by Messrs Williams and Collins on every future ton of coal they raised from beneath Crown property. Whether it was this, or because the coal seam was too severely faulted, which it was, Zephaniah sold his interest in the Triumph Mine for £800 shortly after the sudden death of his partner Collins. Still without his wife and family, he headed north to explore for coal in the remote north west of the island.

NOTES

1. Alexander Maconochie, *Parliamentary Papers 1837-8*, Vol. 22, pp5-21.
2. West, *History of Tasmania.*
3. Reports of the Commissioners of Inquiry into the State of Education in Wales, Part II, 1847.
4. West, *History of Tasmania.*
5. *ibid.*
6. *ibid;* Tasmanian State Archives, Hobart, Rev. Roger Thomas, review of report on transportation 1846.
7. NPL, Williams letter to wife, New Norfolk, 27 January 1846, *South Wales Daily News,* 12 May 1877, p4.
8. West, *History of Tasmania.*
9. NPL, Williams letter to wife, from New Norfolk, 3 January 1846, *South Wales Daily News,* 5 May 1877, p3.
10. J. Lempriere, *The Penal Settlements of Van Diemen's Land,* p94; NPL, Zephaniah Williams letter to his wife, 3 January 1846, *South Wales Daily News,* 5 May 1877, p3; NPL, Chartist Archives, Letter to the People of Great Britain and Ireland on Transportation, John Frost.

11. C. P. T. Laplace, *Campagne de Circumnavigation de la Fregate Liartemise, Pendant les Annees 1837, 38, 39 et 40, sous le commandant de M. Lapace* (Paris, 1841-54), six vols., V 134; David Burn, 'Port Arthur 100 years Ago', *Tasmanian Journal*, 1840.

12. *Colonial Times*, 24 September 1833, p3, cols 1-2.

13. NPL, Williams letter to wife, from New Norfolk, 3 January 1846, *South Wales Daily News*, 5 May 1877, p3.

14. *ibid*.

15. NSW, Mitchell Library, Doc. 67366, Frost letter to wife, 21 July 1840.

16. David Burn, 'Port Arthur 100 years Ago' (Hobart, 1840, Oldham, Beddome and Meredith PTY, Ltd.), extracted from the *Tasmanian Journal*.

17. NPL, Chartist Archives, Frost 'Letter to the People of Great Britain and Ireland on Transportation' (1855), and Oddfellows' Hall lecture.

18. NPL, Williams letter to wife from New Norfolk, 3 January 1846, *South Wales Daily News*, 5 May 1877, p3; close reading of Williams letters to wife from Van Diemen's Land, 20 September 1843, 21 April 1844, 3 January 1846, 18 November 1846, February (undated) 1847, 28 November 1848, 23 February 1849, 4 August 1851, published *South Wales Daily News*, 28 April, 5, 12, 19 May, 2 June 1877, NPL; Dora Heard, *The Journal of Charles O'Hara Booth* (Hobart, 1841,Tasmanian Historical Association).

19. *ibid*.

20. *ibid;* Tasmanian State Archives, Hobart, TSA/CS05/265/6910, letter, Commandant Booth to Colonial Secretary, 1 January, 1840.

21. Williams letters to wife, loc. cit.

22. *ibid*.

23. *ibid*.

24. *ibid*.

25. *ibid*.

26. *ibid*.

27. Burn, *Port Arthur 100 years Ago;* Tasmanian State Archives, Colonial Secretary's Office, 74/903/cc, 1842.

28. Williams letters to wife, loc. cit.

29. *ibid*.

30. *ibid*.

31. *ibid*.

32. *ibid;* NPL, Chartist Archives, Frost 'Letter to the People of Great Britain and Ireland on Transportation' (1855).

33. Tasmanian State Archives, Hobart, 56/768, Williams Convict Record.

34. NPL, Williams letter to wife from New Norfolk, 3 January 1846, *South Wales Daily News*, 5 May 1877, p3; *Colonial Times*, 29 April 1845; R. W. Gowland, 'Troubled Asylum', New Norfolk Library.

35. NPL, Williams letter to wife from New Norfolk, op. cit.

36. Tasmania State Archives, Hobart, Colonial Secretary's Office, 74/903/cc, 1842.

37. NPL, Williams letter to wife from Hobart, 28 November 1848, op. cit.

38. *ibid*.

39. *ibid*.

40. *ibid.*
41. NPL, op.cit, Williams letters to wife, Hobart, 23 February, 27 December 1849, printed *South Wales Daily News,* 26 May 1877, p4.
42. *ibid.*
43. NLW, Robert Griffith, *Llyfer Cerdd Dannau;* GRO, Evan Powell, *History of Tredegar,* page 111, lists Llewellyn Williams harp as one of the those items exhibited at the Tredegar Art Exhibition, 1884; NPL, Williams letter to his wife, Hobart, 4 August 1851, printed *South Wales Daily News,* 2 June 1877, p4.
44. *Merthyr Guardian,* 30 June 1854.
45. NPL, Williams letter to wife, Hobart, 4 August 1851, printed *South Wales Daily News,* 2 June 1877, p4.

CHAPTER 10

On the Rio Grande

Within a few months of Texas winning its independence at the Battle of San Jacinto, April 21, 1836, the new republic was in dire straits. Bankrupt, the value of its only asset – land – at rock bottom, it lived with the constant fear of attack by Indians or from across the Rio Grande by Mexico, which still refused to recognise the Republic of Texas. By rewarding its volunteer army with land for service, and issuing land scrip to raise overseas loans, it had sown the seeds of its own collapse. Most of the land scrip was sold in the United States where investors saw their prospects of recovering their investments disappearing by the day as the Republic squandered its public domain. From its birth, the only realistic answer to the republic's perilous financial, military and political instability was annexation by the United States, a move the overwhelming majority of settlers voted for in September 1836. But the abolitionists in the US Congress would have none of it, suspecting annexation would lead to the creation of more slave states swinging the balance in favour of the south. Annexation was not raised again until Sam Houston became the first directly elected President of Texas in 1841 but the US was not interested. Other influences were at work, however, which were about to change that.[1]

Britain had long had an interest in the wilderness territories of the Pacific west coast, where it was already in dispute with the US over the sovereignty of Oregon, which was claimed by both countries. In 1843 the US government became concerned the British had ulterior motives for opposing the annexation of Texas. This was true but not because Britain had territorial aspirations towards Texas, or Oregon for that matter.[2] Neither was thought to have much to offer, containing large areas considered uninhabitable and of little economic value. Both were sparsely populated,

Oregon by a few thousand trappers and fur traders, Texas run by slave owners and slave traders, a significant obstacle to British expansionism. Britain had set its own slaves free ten years earlier, following a sustained campaign of public abhorrence and was unlikely to want to fight that battle again. Its only interest in Texas was to maintain existing commercial links, cotton and tobacco in particular – and prevent the westward expansion of the US. But the Texas slave owners supported by the United States believed the British were seeking to tamper with the institution of slavery. So convinced were southern politicians of this, they alleged British agents were plotting to abolish slavery throughout North America, the allegation provoking such outrage, that the south demanded immediate annexation of Texas to protect the interests of plantation owners.[3]

Given the British Empire's expansionist record, Americans had good reason to conclude that the British were scheming to make Texas a satellite, at the very least, a client state. This, together with its perceived claim to sovereignty over Oregon in the Pacific north-west, was regarded by Americans as an Old World conspiracy to obstruct their 'Manifest Destiny' – the expansionist agenda for a trans-continental republic extending from the Atlantic to the Pacific. Convinced they had a mission to extend the boundaries of freedom to others, Americans were committed to exporting their idealism and democratic institutions to all those they believed capable of self-government, which, significantly, excluded Native Americans and blacks. The real driving force behind American expansionism was altogether less altruistic: population growth. It had been phenomenal, from five million in 1800 to 23 millions by the mid-19th century, in just thirty years four million of these moving west where frontier land was cheap, often free. For many settlers land ownership in the New World meant exactly the same as it did in the old: it was synonymous with wealth, self-sufficiency, self-government, and above all political power. And Mexico had plenty of it; vast northern territories acquired with its independence from Spain in 1821, much still uninhabited because of the 'hostiles,' Native Americans. Southern plantation owners, in particular, hungered after this great expanse of inhospitable territory to enlarge their slave empire, and for this reason were especially prominent in the expansionist movement.

If further proof were needed of British policy to restrict the westward expansion of the United States, the expansionists could point to Britain's close ties to Mexico. This more than anything finally persuaded the Democratic leaders in the US Congress to support the policy of *'Manifest Destiny,'* clearing the way in 1844 for the annexation of Texas as the 28th state of the Union. The only way, said Democratic President James Polk, to deal with *"John Bull is to look him straight in the eye."* By October the following year, annexation was ratified by popular vote in Texas and accepted by the United States Congress although the formal transfer of power did not take place until February 19, 1846 when the republic's last President Anson Jones declared, *"The final act in this great drama is now performed; the Republic of Texas is no more."* One hundred and sixty years later, there remain many in Texas who believe that was the blackest day in its history![5]

Britain had done everything, short of war, to prevent annexation, most significantly persuading Mexico to recognise the new Republic of Texas on condition that it remained an independent sovereign state. The year before the curtain came down on the Republic, the British envoy Mr Charles Elliott had written to President Anson Jones, who at that time was also opposed to annexation, advising him the French had joined Britain in exerting pressure on the Mexican government to concede formal recognition.

When the republic sent a deputation to Washington to discuss annexation, Elliott expressed the British government's hope the visit was only intended *"to avoid any cause of offence or irritation to the government of the United States, and to explain with frankness, that the government of Texas could not entertain the subject at all . . . after the former rejection of such an arrangement by the government of the United States."*[6]

Mexico suspended diplomatic relations with the United States as soon as it heard of the annexation talks. The support given by the US to the breakaway Republic of Texas had been bad enough, the latest move denounced by Luis Cuevas, the Mexican Foreign Minister, as an act unparalleled in the history of civilised nations. The Europeans responded to his appeal for help to fend off this American land grab by offering to guarantee Texas independence in return for Mexico's recognition of the struggling republic. But it was too late, and General Santa Anna, exiled to the island of

Cuba, was preparing to return to lead the Mexican army against the United States invaders.[7]

The suspicion was growing in the United States that Texans had encouraged Britain and France to make overtures to Mexico on their behalf, either to secure annexation on better terms than those offered by the US Congress, or sabotage the process, even orchestrate an auction between Britain, the United States and Mexico for the 'Lone Star' republic.

The Nyles Register commenting on the looming conflict in May 1845 declared, *"That England has many and powerful inducements to avoid a war with the United States, is obvious. That she would go to war about a remote section of the sterile northwest, may be questioned. . . . But apprehensions may be entertained by her in relation to nearer and more interesting territory and trade, which she may consider compromised by what she doubtless regards as a spirit of grasping and aggrandizement on our part, and may make the question of peace or war, one of much broader aspect than otherwise it would be. When such a state of affairs exists, a small matter may give the die a fatal cast. Mexico in all probability will have the sympathies of the European governments on her side. European governments may adventure a step too far in attempting to sustain Mexico in resisting annexation, and thereby make a general war inevitable."*

Besides Oregon and Texas, and fixing the international border with Canada at the 49th parallel, President Polk had his sights set on an even greater prize: California. Polk knew that was possible by engineering a war with Mexico, so he sent General Zachary Taylor with an army to the mouth of the Rio Grande where it built an earthen fort christened "Fort Texas."[8] Sooner or later Polk knew the Mexicans would be provoked into attacking, and Taylor was ordered to prepare for an invasion. Britain, meantime, now beset by internal disputes over Corn Law reform, stepped back from the brink, withdrawing all support from Mexico and abandoning its interest in Texas. Almost the very last act of the Republic, before finally accepting annexation, was to despatch an emissary to Britain. The annulment of the Texas Declaration of Independence and annexation by the United States was followed by the inevitable border incidents, good enough excuse for Polk to declare war. Among the very first skirmishes was the ambushing by the Mexicans between Point Isabel and "Fort Texas" of a company of Texas Rangers. One of these Rangers was a man named "John Reese."9

Fort Texas, garrisoned by Taylor's 2,300-strong army, was built on the east bank of the Rio Grande directly opposite the Mexican city of Matamoros. The fortified walls were of sand covered with brushwood, woven together like basketwork, and surrounded by a wide, deep ditch. Twelve heavy guns pointed towards Matamoros, a beautiful Spanish colonial city sited on the opposite bank in the neck of a horseshoe bend on the Rio Grande, and defended by 4,000 Mexican troops commanded by General Mariano Arista. Fort Texas was supplied from Point Isabel, located on a high bluff 29 miles down stream near the point Laguna Madre opens into the Gulf of Mexico. Because of the sand bar across its mouth, only vessels of shallow draught were able to enter the lagoon. Between it and the fort was a belt of desert stretching along the coast for two hundred miles. Not the best of bases from which to supply his army but the only one Taylor had, consequently there was regular traffic between it and Fort Texas up river.

Of the two opposing armies, the Americans were generally the better equipped with muzzle-loading rifles and muskets, mainly the latter which were quicker and easier to handle. The Texas Rangers among them were notorious for arming themselves to the teeth, stuffing pistols, knives and revolvers into boots, belts and shirts. Mexican soldiers mostly carried old flintlock muskets sold by the British as surplus. These they usually fired from the hip because to aim a flintlock from the shoulder delivered a painful kick from the *"flash in the pan"* caused by loading too much gunpowder. Even though outnumbering the Americans, their firing technique meant shots often sailed over the heads of their adversaries. As was the case during the Texas War of Independence there was no standard uniform, volunteers to the US army arriving at Fort Texas in a variety of buckskins, homemade trousers and shirts, and on their heads, everything from forage caps to straw hats. General Taylor set the tone, preferring to wear a straw hat and linen duster to cover his uniform for which he earned from his men the enduring epithet *"Old Rough and Ready."* The volunteers were paid $8 a month. There was a very good chance they would never get to collect even this, for although superior fighters, the Mexicans had a secret weapon – *"vomito,"* yellow fever. Disease was to kill more men than bullets.[10]

John Reese joined Captain Samuel Walker's Texas Mounted Rangers at either Point Isabel or Corpus Christi, in February or March 1846, enlisting for three months. Texas Rangers began life informally when Stephen Austin sent ten experienced frontiersmen on a punitive mission against a band of Indians in 1823. A makeshift force, they had no uniforms and furnished their own horses, weapons and ammunition. They became officially Texas Rangers during the Texas War of Independence and afterwards were sent by Houston to defend the frontier against Indian attacks, and repel the invasion of 1842 when the Mexicans again captured San Antonio and the Alamo. Samuel Walker, a celebrated Ranger with a string of battle honours, was given permission by General Taylor to raise his own company, although the general had at first resisted using them. Skilled horsemen, accustomed to outdoor living, experienced with weapons and driven by personal motives, the Rangers had a well-deserved reputation for ill-discipline, bordering at times on lawlessness. The one hundred riders recruited by Walker signed on with whatever they were wearing, and remained that way for the duration of their service.

When on April 25, 1846, Mexican troops crossed the Rio Grande and attacked a detachment of American troops, President Polk was able to declare, *"Mexico has passed the boundary of the United States, has invaded our country and shed American blood upon American soil. She has proclaimed that hostilities have commenced, and that the two nations are at war."* Americans saw the war as being fought to defend the right of free people, namely the citizens of the recently defunct Republic of Texas; Mexicans saw it, with certain justification, as an attack upon its sovereignty by the United States seizure of Mexico's northernmost territory, Texas, whose short-lived independence it had never recognised.

As Mexican activity on the Texan side of the Rio Grande increased, Captain Walker and a detachment of 24 Rangers including John Reese were camped alongside the supply road, between Point Isabel and Fort Texas. Before long, supply wagons were finding their way to Fort Texas was blocked by Mexican patrols. On April 28 Walker left with his Rangers to reconnoitre the area and re-open the supply line. After proceeding half way, the 24 Rangers suddenly found themselves confronted by 1,500 Mexican troops. In the ensuing battle, most of the Rangers scattered in panic, Walker claiming later this was because they were *"raw recruits."* He retreated to Point Isabel, followed later by six other survivors.

Charles D. Spurlin in his book *Texas Veterans in the Mexican War* describes a number of muster rolls one of which lists J. Reese in Samuel Walker's Company as *"being taken by Mexicans near Point Isabel on April 28, 1846, exchanged on May 11, 1846; discharged for . . . on May 30, 1846."* This is partially confirmed by an account published by the *Nyles Register* on May 30 of a dispatch from Fort Texas on May 14, stating, *"All the prisoners whom we had in Matamoros were exchanged the day before yesterday, besides which, we gave our enemy ninety-seven wounded men."* Spurlin obtained his information from a document in the National Archives in Washington but was unable to decipher the reason for Reese's discharge.[11] It could easily have been because of illness since nearly 10,000 men were discharged because of this during the Mexican War. Camp conditions were appalling, the same water often used for drinking, cooking and washing. Disease was rampant in the humid, sub-tropical heat along the Gulf coast, yellow fever, dysentery and measles taking thousands to an early death, buried in shallow graves on the chaparral, their blankets for a shroud. Despite the final victory it was the most disastrous war in American military history, 35 per cent of all those who served, mainly young, adventure-seeking volunteers, dying as a consequence, five times as many after the war from sickness and wounds than were killed by it. On the other hand, Reese may have deserted, 10,000 of his comrades did. The Mexicans offered inducements: for every private who deserted 320 acres of free land and Mexican citizenship. General Mariano Arista, commander of the Mexican troops at Matamoros, made his offer to the Americans facing his forces across Rio Grande, declaring, *"If in time of action you wish to espouse our cause, throw away your arms and run to us, and we will embrace you as true friends and Christians."*[12]

None of this proves that John Reese the Texas Ranger, captured at the skirmish near Point Isabel and briefly imprisoned by the

Mexicans in Matamoros, was John Rees, veteran of the Texas War of Independence, and fugitive leader of the Chartist Uprising in Wales. All that is positively known from his correspondence from Virginia five years earlier is that he was offered a commission to fight in Texas. That almost certainly would have meant along the disputed border with Mexico. Whether "John Reese" served as a private or officer in the Rangers is not known because the muster roll for Walker's company has not survived.

But the hunt for 'Jack the Fifer' was not exhausted. The last and most important clue of all to what became of him after arriving in Virginia would be his Donation Certificate for 640 acres awarded for his part in the Siege of San Antonio de Bexar. Unable to sell or mortgage the land during his lifetime, this worthless piece of paper travelled with Rees twice across the Atlantic, before resurfacing, not in Texas but just across the Rio Grande in Matamoros where "John Reese" had been imprisoned after his capture by the Mexicans at Point Isabel!

For whatever reason he was discharged, "John Reese," Texas Ranger, was discharged either at Matamoros, or not far away, on May 30, 1846. The war with Mexico would last another two years but the city had fallen to *"Old Rough and Ready"* on May 16 without a shot being fired after the Mexicans beat a strategic retreat. While most Mexican towns were usually not much more than a clutter of poor adobe buildings of mud, brushwood and bamboo, Matamoros was an exceptionally fine Spanish colonial city of about 7000 inhabitants, the streets lined with shade trees, opening on to cool piazzas, the buildings of brick, and protected on two sides by the waters of the Rio Grande. There was a cathedral, market and government buildings, all occupied by the Mexican army before its hasty retreat. Now in American hands, it was just the kind of place discharged soldiers with a few dollars to spend might decide to linger.

Besides the $24 earned from his three months in the army, the only thing of any potential value to Rees was the Donation Certificate. Although Texas had by then become the 28th state of the Union, the Welshman's entitlement to 640 acres of Texas remained valid, except that Rees could still not sell his land grant. Ignoring this he went to the office of a Mexican public notary, Joaquin Arguelles, and on November 18, 1846, transferred his land rights to George Blenis (or O'Blenis) from Louisiana on a 99-year lease in return for $50, the equivalent of seven cents an acre. The transaction was quite illegal, not only the disposal of the certificate by Rees, but the pretence that a Mexican notary had the authority to execute and certify the transfer of land, located according to Rees in "State of Texas, County of Nueces." The transaction was witnessed by Thomas B. Sealy and A. Wheeler. At the end of the transfer document Snr. Arguelles noted in Spanish, *"(I) the undersigned notary public, certify: That, before me, Mr John Rees has signed the preceding document of sale in favour of Mr Oblenis and that said signature is his usual and customary one. Matamoros, November 18, 1846. Joaquin (notary's sign) Arguelles. Notary Public."*[13]

It is stretching incredulity to breaking point to imagine the existence of another Rees impostor, in a remote Mexican town, eight years after the last fraudulent land transaction in which Rees or Reese was involved. No matter what the status of the land transfer, the Mexican lawyer Snr Arguelles testified that "John Rees" (this time spelt correctly) was personally present in his office in Matamoros in November 1846, no more than twenty miles away from where "John Reese" Texas Ranger was captured by the Mexicans six months earlier, then exchanged. If they were different men then this was a monumental coincidence.

Leasing land, which appeared otherwise worthless, was a clever way of getting around the prohibition on selling Donation certificates. The only problem was that, even if it had been allowed, no one was likely to lease un-located land for 99 years. Rees actually overcame that objection by designating a false location – the Texas County of Nuecas. For that to be valid, it would have been necessary for the land first to be surveyed before it could be patented, and none of that had happened by 1846. Whoever Blenis was, he had been swindled out of $50!

I picked up the Rees 'land trail' in March 2003 in the Mills County clerk's office at Mullin in central Texas. Deeds for the Hampton Creek property show that by 1853 John Rees's original Donation Certificate bearing rights to 640 acres had almost certainly been acquired by a man named J. D. Brown. It was Brown, not Rees as Ivor Wilks supposes in the *Welsh History Review*, who surveyed and patented the land on Hampton Creek in what was then Travis County (now Mills).[14] This was possible after March 2, 1848 when the restriction prohibiting grantees from selling or mortgaging their Donation land during their lifetime was lifted. Although the conveyance Rees signed in Mexico was never filed with the Texas General Land Office, it did find its way back to Travis County where Governor Peter Bell reckoned it proof of legal transfer, because the Matamoros assignment document is included with other papers in the Deed File for the Hampton Creek property even though the beneficiary it refers to is Blenis, not Brown.[15] Whether there was some relationship between Blenis and Brown we will never know. The fact remains, the document enabled Brown to satisfy the governor he was owner of the much-travelled Rees Donation Certificate and, consequently, title to the land was delivered to him. As explained in Chapter Five, the patent was executed in the name of John Rees only because he was the original grantee, and was immaterial to the current ownership of the Donation Certificate. With the execution of the donation complete, certificate No. 266 was returned to the Texas General Land Office for filing.

Surrounded by a well-watered area of rich soil, Hampton Creek and the bayou were famous among Comanches for an abundance of fish and mussels, ideal for settlers if ever the Texas Army had been able to provide security cover, which it had not. The few who dared settle the region faced frequent outbreaks of hostilities for encroaching on Comanche hunting grounds. Not even the establishment of reservations in 1854 stopped the raids. The situation became more confused by subsequent boundary changes, Hampton Creek first part of Brown County which was created from Travis and Comanche Counties, then later moving into Mills County when this was formed out of Brown and other counties in 1887. Although the administrative district for Hampton Creek changed several times, details of land transactions are not difficult to follow since the record always passed to the current administrative office.

The only proof the Rees Donation Certificate was patented to Brown is a light pencil notation on the jacket of the file, *"Delev d (delivered) to J. D. Brown 15th March 1853."* That this was noted the day after Governor Bell issued the patent indicates the land was transferred to Brown. Yet that was still not the end of the matter. No serious attempt was made to homestead the land by

Brown or anyone else until after the Comanches were forced on to reservations in 1874. Around this time the land on Hampton Creek was seized by the Texas Comptrollers Office in lieu of unpaid taxes and held by it until 1881 when James Winston and J. T. Rankin redeemed 280 acres after settling the outstanding tax bill.[16] Could that mean that somewhere along Hampton Creek there are several hundred acres of land to which the descendants of John Rees, the Welsh Chartist leader, could lay claim by proving the transfer of Donation certificate No. 266 in Matamoros, Mexico, was invalid?

By the time John Rees left Texas, he had traded in almost 6000 acres of prime real estate, with virtually nothing to show for it. He had also disappeared again – but where this time?

NOTES

1. Eugene C. Barker, 'The Annexation of Texas', *South Western Historical Quarterly*, 50, July 1946; GPO, Washington, George Pierce Garrison, *Diplomatic Correspondence of the Republic of Texas* (Washington, 1908-11), three parts.
2. Texas and Oregon Question, *The Times*, Jan 31, 1845; John Phillip Reed, *Contested Empire* (Oklahoma, 2002).
3. E. D. Adams, *British Diplomatic Correspondence Concerning the Republic of Texas, 1836-1846* (Austin, Texas State Historical Association, 1918).
4. Jesus Velasco-Marquez, 'A Mexican Viewpoint on the War With the United States', *Institudto Tecnologico Autonomo de Mexico*; Sam W. Haynes, 'Manfiest Destiny', University of Texas.
5. Polk Policy, *The Times*, 8 January 1845; Herbert Gambrell, *Anson Jones: The Last President of Texas* (New York, 1948, Doubleday); 'Anson Jones Papers', Barker Texas History Center, University of Texas, Austin.
6. Elliot, Richmond *Compiler*, 22 March 1845 (reprinted *Niles Register*).
7. Luis Cuevas, *National Intelligencer*, 22 April 1845, reports correspondent of New Orleans *Jeffersonian; Niles Register*, 3 May 1845; New York *Journal of Commerce*, 24 May 1845.
8. K. Jack Bauer, *The Mexican War, 1846-1848* (New York, 1974, Macmillan).
9. Captain Walker's Detachment, and the battle of Point Isabel, New Orleans, *Picayune*, 9 May 1846.
10. K. Jack Bauer, *Zachary Taylor: Soldier, Planter, Statesman of the Old Southwest* (Louisiana State University Press, 1985).
11. Charles D.Spurlin, *Texas Veterans in the Mexican War*, p213.

12. Hubert Howe Bancroft, *History of the North Mexican States and Texas*, (San Francisco, History Company, 1886, 1889); Diccionario Enciclopédico Hispano-Americano de Literatura, Ciencias y Artes, Barcelona: Montaner y Simón, 1887-98.

13. Texas General Land Office, Austin, Rees Donation Certificate 266; Mills County Clerk's office, Mullin, Texas, Deed File, patent 234, copy of the Mexican transfer document in the deed file for the Donation Land located on Hampton Creek.

14. Wilks, loc. cit. p88; also see Mills County Deed file, patent 234.

15. *ibid*, Mills County Deed File for Hampton Creek.

16. Mills County Clerk's office, Mullin, deed file for patent 234, Certificates of Redemption Nos. 5483, 5489, Winston and Rankin, Austin Texas, 7 September 1881.

CHAPTER 11

The Lost Welsh of Ballahoo Creek

At about the same time that John Rees's entitlement to 640 acres of Texas public land was being surveyed by *"J.D.Brown"* at Hampton Creek in Travis County (now Mills County), Zephaniah Williams was pioneering the coal mining industry at Ballahoo Creek in Devon County, Tasmania. But he was not the first to discover it. That distinction went to two wood splitters named Powell and Ayres working in the forests along the banks of the River Don. In 1851 when Zephaniah first visited this remote corner of northwest Tasmania, the only settlements in the dense forests were gangs of splitters cutting the giant trees into palings, fence posts, rails and shingles for export to Melbourne on the other side of the Bass Straits, where a building boom had followed the discovery of gold at Ballarat. The forest soil was a rich chocolate brown, but apart from a few potatoes and swedes grown in clearings between the trees, there was no room for farming, every hill and precipitous gorge covered by towering eucalyptus reaching to the edges of the shoreline. The aborigines had virtually been exterminated, replaced by roving gangs of bushrangers, for whom the dank, dreary woods with undergrowth of tangled vine and nettles provided perfect cover. There had been very little settlement, the forests generally considered too great an obstacle for even the hardiest colonists. If this wilderness was a test of human ingenuity and endurance, reaching it was almost as difficult. There were no roads or bridges across the numerous rivers and creeks, only boggy tracks cut by wild cattle grazing wherever wood splitters or bush fires left clearings open enough for grass to grow.

In April 1850 two of the early pioneers, William Dean and Benjamin Cocker, headed into this wilderness, carrying £1,000 in their pockets to purchase palings from a community of splitters.

By nightfall they were lost somewhere in the vicinity of the River Don. Conscious this was bushranger country, the pair headed cautiously for the smoke spiralling from the chimney of a hut they had seen in the distance. The primitive dwelling belonged to two wood splitters, Powell and Ayres. Splitters were Australia's original white bushmen, some just one step away from bushrangers, but the majority honest and hard-working, only emerging from the forests to stock up on provisions, carrying their few luxuries, beer, wine, spirits, tinned meats, pickles and other delicacies back to their shingle cabins. Accepting their offer of accommodation for the night, Dean and Cocker settled down with the two splitters in the hut's only room, a huge wood fire at one end. Unable to sleep, his mind filled with visions of severed windpipes and shattered skulls, Cocker noticed that around midnight Ayres stole gently from his bunk, picked up an axe and slipped out into the night. Digging his companion in the ribs, he whispered, *"Dean! Dean! It's all up for us; we are done men; one fellow has gone out with an axe."* But Dean was not unduly worried, reckoning a would-be murderer was more likely to enter with an axe rather leave with one. Sure enough Ayres returned a few minutes later with what appeared to be a large square log on his shoulder, which he threw on the fire. The log blazed like coal and after satisfying himself it really was, Dean persuaded the splitters to take them the following morning to outcrop on the bank of the River Don where a thin two-foot coal seam protruded from the surface. For five sovereigns Powell and Ayres promised to make no mention of their discovery, allowing Dean and Cocker sufficient time to return to Launceston 100 miles away with specimens of the coal to show potential investors.[1] The Mersey Coal Company was formed, and after acquiring 1700 acres in the vicinity of the discovery at 10 shillings an acre, it invited Zephaniah Williams up from Hobart to assess the potential value of the coalfield.[2] Favourably impressed with what he saw, Zephaniah was expecting to be asked to sink the first mineshaft, until some of the syndicate decided they wanted nothing to do with him on account of his convict past. Although disappointed by this, Zephaniah promptly sold his share in the Triumph Mine at Hobart for £800, having seen sufficient to excite what became a life long obsession with coal exploration in the wilderness region of the northwest.[3] At the very time fortunes were being made in the goldfields of Ballarat across the Bass Straits, Zephaniah began his search for an elusive four-feet seam of 'black gold,' which he never doubted lay beneath the original outcrop. For him this was the Tasmanian equivalent of the famous Black Vein of Mynyddislwyn, source of untold wealth in his native Wales.

Zephaniah disembarked from the coastal schooner *Titania* on to the bank of the Mersey in 1852 accompanied by George Atkinson, his 19-year-old son, George junior, and a group of miners. The elder Atkinson was a burglar from Roecliffe in Yorkshire, son of a public house licensee, and had been transported from Portsmouth aboard the convict ship *"Asia"* on April 6, 1841, reaching Hobart four months later on August 21. By 1850 he had received his ticket-of-leave, and sometime later joined forces with Zephaniah on the expedition to Ballahoo Creek. Just before this it seems he was given permission for his wife, daughter Elizabeth, and son George Junior to join him in Tasmania. A partnership was forged between the burglar from Yorkshire and the Welsh traitor that was sealed in perpetuity some years later, when George Atkinson Junior married Zephaniah's daughter Rhoda after she, her mother Joan and uncle Edmund Llewellyn joined Zephaniah in Tasmania.

The Mersey is a large tidal estuary, the 12-foot rise and fall exposing great expanses of mud at low water. The highest navigable point on the river for the *Titania* was Ballahoo Creek where it landed Zephaniah and his prospecting party. Soon they had built a crude settlement beside the creek, Zephaniah dividing his time between running its store and sinking his first shaft on nearby land, adjoining what was to become the small township of Tarleton. There could not have been a more propitious time to settle in Tasmania, the Lieutenant Governor Sir William Denison having introduced more generous arrangements to facilitate land purchase. Under the new regulations, a settler was permitted to select up to 500 acres of land for future purchase, conditional on his paying £1 per annum rent for every 100 acres for five years after which he could exercise his right to buy at £1 an acre. Thus, for 500 acres a man had only to pay £5 a year for five years, and could relinquish it at any time. Better still, not a penny was handed over until the land was officially allocated, and pegged out by the

Top: Ballahoo Creek on the Mersey River where Zephaniah Williams and his partner George Atkinson disembarked from the *Titania* in 1852 to begin prospecting for coal. *Bottom:* Coal Mines Road, an echo from the past at Tarleton.

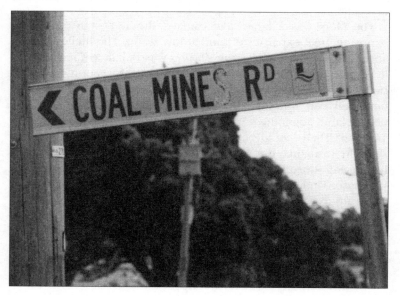

Government surveyor to the satisfaction of the prospective purchaser. If not, he could surrender his claim without any financial
loss whatsoever. Zephaniah acquired 500 acres immediately. A
syndicate of Hobart businessmen purchased a further 3,500 acres,
appointing the Welsh mining engineer the managing partner for
their coal interests in the area.[4]

There was still no coal of any quantity and finding it was proving
costly, Zephaniah's competitors at the Mersey Coal Company the
first to run into difficulties. After spending £20,000 sinking a shaft
and building a tram road five miles inland from Ballahoo Creek,
the company's mine flooded.[5] William Dean, its founder, concerned about the extravagant expenditure, resigned to open his
own mine nearer the spot on the River Don where the original
coal discovery was made. None of this, however, discouraged
others from joining the race to be the first to discover a commercially viable coalfield, to replace imports from Newcastle in New
South Wales, and in the case of the best anthracite from as far
away as Wales. Zephaniah was convinced huge rewards awaited
investors, his enthusiastic predictions largely responsible for a
frenzy of mining activity in the neighbourhood of Ballahoo Creek
and Tarleton. But the miners were not only competing with each
other in this wilderness: they had also to contend with the
bushrangers infesting the forests!

The settlement at Ballahoo Creek was not twelve months old
when it received a visit from James Dalton and Andrew Kelly,
survivors of a mass breakout from Port Arthur in 1852, which
claimed the lives of four of the absconders as they attempted to
swim past the dog chain at Eaglehawk Neck. Dalton and Kelly
went on a rampage, in the process of raiding remote farms killing
a police constable. Driven deeper into the bush, the fugitives
arrived at Ballahoo Creek in January 1853, bursting into a hut as
George Atkinson, his son George, and several others were having
supper. With a double-barrelled shotgun pointed at their heads,
the captives were marched down to Zephaniah's store. Zephaniah
had escaped into the bush but his store was ransacked, the bushrangers tearing up silk handkerchiefs to bind the wrists of their
prisoners before herding them aboard a boat moored in the
creek. By now, the resistance of the younger Atkinson, then only
19, was too much for Dalton and Kelly so he was released, while

his father was forced at gun point to navigate the small boat along the coast to the estuary of the Don. Failing to commandeer a whaleboat for crossing the Bass Straits to Port Phillip in Victoria, the fugitives together with their hostages pushed on further to the Forth estuary, where the schooner *Jane and Elizabeth* was riding at anchor in the river. Its owner Captain John Williams and the local constable Tom Clarkson were on board. As the crowded rowboat inched closer to the schooner, Captain Williams rejected Dalton's shouted demand for him to surrender, and the constable took a shot at the bushrangers, forcing them to beach the boat. Dalton and Kelly then seized the master's wife and lining her up with the other hostages in front of her house on the riverbank, threatened to burn it down. At this point Captain Williams agreed to surrender his whaleboat. Atkinson senior and several other captives were released, but Dalton and Kelly held on to Mrs Williams and the four strongest hostages to row them to the Australian mainland. Once clear of the river, Mrs Williams was dropped off on a beach, before the whaleboat pushed out into turbulent waters of Bass Straits and three days of hard rowing. Coming ashore near a cattle station, Dalton and Kelly set their remaining hostages free and headed for Melbourne where no sooner had they arrived than they were arrested, returned to Launceston, and hanged three months later.[6]

Dalton and Kelly were not the only bushrangers terrorising the area in the 1850s. A record number of convicts had taken to the bush assuming all manner of disguises, and aliases like Hellfire Jack, Dido, Wingy, and Long Mickey. Not all were hardened criminals. Some of the more educated would probably have become upstanding colonists, if they had not been brutalised by the prison regime from which they escaped into banditry. Nor were bushrangers always on the run. Some built semi-permanent homes deep in the forests; others struck deals with settlers to share their spoils in return for sanctuary. Highway robbery became so prevalent, however, that following the Dalton and Kelly raid, seven ticket-of-leave men were sworn in as constables to guard Ballahoo Creek and other fording places along the Mersey.[7] That so many bushrangers headed for Tasmania's northern coast was hardly surprising, given its proximity to Victoria and the goldfields at Ballarat. The traffic across the Bass Straits between the northern

Tasmanian ports and Port Phillip in Victoria was at its peak, ships ferrying men and supplies to the goldfields. Despite the protestations of the Victorian authorities unable to stem this flow of 'Vandemonians' into their state, free settlers and convicts all headed for the goldfields in a flood of emigration from Tasmania.

Gold fever did not for one moment distract Zephaniah Williams from his search for the black stuff, the presence of which was evident from outcrops of a thin seam about two feet thick, in the vicinity of the Don and Mersey rivers. Here the geology was not dissimilar from that which had excited early interest in the Monmouthshire coalfield. Zephaniah and his principal backer, Hobart businessman, Alfred Nicholas, a member Tasmania's Legislative Council, had every reason to feel confident they were on the verge of a major strike. But from the moment shaft sinking started in June 1852, work was hampered by a shortage of men and machinery, and all the problems associated with servicing a mine deep in the remote bush. Soon there were other difficulties. The rock through which Zephaniah was boring became increasingly harder, the shaft flooding the deeper he got. Notwithstanding this, special permission was obtained from the Lieutenant Governor Sir William Denison to employ convicts with whose help the shaft (now named the Denison Mine) was sunk to 200ft before striking quartz conglomerate as hard as adamant. At this point all his men quit, leaving Zephaniah to carry on single-handed for another 60ft when work was again halted by an in-rush of water. Reflecting on his predicament as he awaited the delivery of a steam pump from Hobart, Zephaniah evidently concluded the only way to prove his theory about the rich coal reserves beneath the Mersey Basin was to import professional colliers from Wales. It was late 1853, and despite the setbacks, public expectations remained high, stoked by regular progress reports in the Tasmanian media. After conducting a steam trial, the master and engineer of the *Titania* vouched for the quality of Mersey coal, pronouncing it equal to the best coals from Wales and Newcastle. Excitedly, the *Cornwall Chronicle* agreed: Mersey coal would prove a source of great prosperity for the island colony and the mine owners should get it to market as soon as possible.[8] And fortuitously for Zephaniah, the opportunity had arisen to recruit immigrant labour from Wales at very little cost!

By the mid-1850s the colony's excessive dependence upon convict labour had become a serious obstacle to its economic progress, exacerbated when most of the free settlers joined the gold rush to Ballarat, leaving behind a corrupted, slovenly labour force, generally regarded as the product of England's neglect and indifference. The legacy of transportation had become economic stagnation. Ticket-of-leave holders refused to work; convicts sentenced to the chain gangs spent most of their time lounging, ignoring the exhortations and threats of overseers. Female prisoners filled the police courts with their constant brawling.[9] In a belated attempt to remedy the situation, the Home Government offered assisted passages for free settlers and the London Agency Association, formed at Launceston with James Jackson its London agent, was commissioned to recruit suitable colonists. Writing to his son Llewellyn, then the landlord of the *Rolling Mill* public house in Nantyglo, Zephaniah asked him in November 1853 to recruit 40 workmen (33 colliers, 2 blacksmiths, 2 sawyers, 2 carpenters and one engineer). The free passages were to be arranged by the London Agency Association, the Home Government contributing £22 per migrant, the sponsoring employers in Tasmania purchasing Bounty Tickets at £3 per single person and £5 for a family.[10] The migrants, all to be of sober character, were required to pay their own expenses to the port of embarkation, which in the case of the Welsh colliers was London. Zephaniah's letter to his son was overly optimistic about the prospects awaiting the colonists. Besides detailing how much each collier would receive for every ton of coal raised, Zephaniah also offered them, and any farmers who might wish to accompany the party, the opportunity of leasing land from him on the most favourable terms, neglecting to mention most of it was covered by unbroken forest and scrub, and the Mersey coalfield had still to be discovered.[11]

That there was no shortage of Welsh interest in this expedition to the other side of the world was not entirely due to Zephaniah's enthusiasm. A devastating cholera epidemic then ravaging Britain, and the war looming in the Crimea provided very good reasons to leave the country. Zephaniah's competitors in the race for coal, the Mersey Coal Company, also took advantage of this opportunity to recruit Yorkshire miners, the London Agency Association chartering the 600-ton *Merrington* for its maiden voyage out of Newcastle. Among the Welsh contingent, men, women and children, that boarded in London were Zephaniah's wife Joan, then aged 54, daughter Rhoda (24), and Joan's younger brother, Edmund Llewellyn (52). For some reason Zephaniah's son Llewellyn chose not to emigrate, perhaps because he was married with two young daughters, although he changed his mind the following year, arriving aboard the *Donald McKay* after a remarkably eventful voyage but without his family. Aged 35, and describing himself as married and a plasterer by occupation, Llewellyn Williams, the celebrated Welsh harpist, was sponsored not by his father when he embarked on an assisted passage from Liverpool in the summer of 1855 aboard the *Fortune*, but by a 'William Williams.' The *Fortune*, with 290 passengers on board, had not long left Liverpool before she was driven aground by a storm in Dundrum Bay on the coast of Northern Ireland, two of its passengers drowning during the rescue operation. The remainder were eventually transferred to the *Donald McKay*, then one of the largest and fastest ships afloat, to continue the voyage to Tasmania, arriving in Hobart on September 6, 1855.[12] Llewellyn never settled in Tasmania, returning after a few years to pursue his musical career in Wales.

The only tragedy aboard the *Merrington* a year earlier was the death of one young Welsh collier, John Jones, aged 22, the remaining 201 men, women, and children, the youngest only five months, landing at George Town at the mouth of the Tamar River on October 20, 1854. Zephaniah had advised the new settlers to avoid the treacherous overland route to Ballahoo Creek, by transferring to the coastal barque *Titania* for the final leg of the journey.[13] Five years previously Zephaniah had braced his wife Joan for the arduous and treacherous voyage to Tasmania, in anticipation that his free pardon was not far away.[14]

Because the tide had turned when the *Titania* entered the Mersey, there was insufficient water to reach Ballahoo Creek five miles upstream. After wading ashore with their belongings on the muddy shoreline, a couple of miles below Zephaniah's mining camp, they completed the last leg of the journey by punt.[15] At the end of a voyage lasting 120 days the very first thing the men, women and children from Wales and Yorkshire did was to hold a

Extract from the passenger list of the *Merrington* on which Zephaniah Williams is named as sponsoring employer of the Welsh miners.

prayer service in a forest clearing, to give thanks for their safe passage. The historic moment was marked by enrolling 25 immigrant children in the first Baptist Sunday School established in this Tasmania wilderness.[16] Although the Mersey coalfield was not yet a reality, awaiting Zephaniah's wife was a fine two-storey house built on the banks of Ballahoo Creek just a few hundred yards from the water's edge, where he had also constructed the Williams Jetty, the timbers surviving to this day, at low water spread-eagled like a skeleton on the estuary bed. Much of what the Welsh colliers found at Tarleton must have seemed eerily familiar. Zephaniah had named his house *"The Manor"* and nearby was building a row of cottages for renting to the new arrivals. Before long, the Williams Mines would be linked to Williams Jetty by the Williams Tram Road, with Williams Cottages, and Williams Forge all in the shadow of *"The Manor."* [17] Some might have seen in this Zephaniah's obsession with his rehabilitation as a reputable minerals surveyor and coal owner; that he was seeking to replicate in this remote corner of the empire the life to which he had aspired in Monmouthshire, before becoming embroiled in the Chartist Uprising.

Top: Site of *The Manor,* the two-storey house Zephaniah Williams built for his wife. It was burned down in 1929. *Bottom:* The remains of the Williams jetty on the Mersey River at the bottom of the garden.

Only a few weeks after the Welsh immigrants had landed at Ballahoo Creek, the settlement at Tarleton received a visit from the Bishop of Tasmania, the Right Rev. F. R. Nixon aboard the Government schooner *Beacon*, and accompanied by the Surveyor-General. While the Bishop was on a tour of the remoter parts of his diocese, the Surveyor-General's staff had been sent to survey the Mersey River estuary, erecting buoys and beacons to mark a safe passage for shipping after a recent spate of accidents had discouraged vessels from using the muddy waterway.[18] Anchoring at the mouth opposite Torquay, then the only settlement of consequence on the banks of the river, the *Beacon* launched her long boat to transport the Bishop and his party five miles up stream on this, the first pastoral visit to the new Welsh community. The Anglican clergyman and his entourage landed at Zephaniah's new jetty, and then pushed a mile through the bush to a clearing where ten wooden huts were being erected for the colliers and their families. Tarleton may have been designated by the Colonial Government as a site for a future township, but when Bishop Nixon called in November 1854 it was a pitiful collection of wooden huts in various stages of completion, together with a shop, public house, and just beyond this Zephaniah's Denison Mine, complete with chimney, engine room and forge.[19] Certainly there was no evidence of the 40 brick-built cottages Zephaniah had reputedly erected to receive the new immigrant workers from Wales, and it is unlikely such substantial premises were ever constructed. A year after the Welsh arrived four of Zephaniah's cottages were blown down in a storm, suggesting they were most probably built of timber not brick. When the last was dismantled in Tarleton one hundred years later it was discovered the walls were made from flattened kerosene cans![20]

Abandoning his plans for an open-air service on account of the weather, Bishop Nixon gladly accepted the offer of a large room in Zephaniah's new house. While not openly hostile, the predominantly Welsh Baptist immigrants were distinctly unimpressed by his service, the Bishop attributing the poor attendance, and lack of devotion to the prevailing enmity between Wesleyans and Anglicans. Ironically, the Williams family, including Zephaniah who in Wales was vilified as a deist, were the only ones claiming membership of the Church of England, according to their entries

on the passenger list of the immigrant ship *Merrington* and
Zephaniah's convict record. In Zephaniah's case it had probably
been nothing more than an administrative convenience to volunteer some form of religious affiliation on entering the penal system.
Yet despite his legendary rationalism, Zephaniah was married in
St Tydfil's Parish Church, Merthyr Tydfil, on August 9, 1819, and
buried at St Paul's Anglican Cemetery, East Devonport.[21] The
likelihood is that he acquiesced in his wife's devotions. After all, it
was Joan who at the expense of more practical family possessions,
chose to carry the family Bible, a huge tome taking up valuable
space on the tiny immigrant ship, 14,000 miles to Tasmania. Considering the Bible's still pristine condition 150 years later, the pages
were rarely ever turned, apart from the front cover inside which
Joan scribbled the names, birth dates, and deaths of their children. As polite and hospitable as the Williams family certainly
were towards the Bishop, he was not impressed by his visit to the
Welsh colonists. Writing in his journal *"Cruise of the Beacon,"* he
recalled, *"Even here they have their 'local preachers,' who had
conducted their worship in the morning. It was not surprising
that this should have damped the willingness of their hearers to
listen to services of another character. The room, however, was
tolerably well filled; our congregation was manifestly unused to
the ritual of the Church of England, but few of them thinking it
necessary to kneel when offering up their petitions to Almighty
God. It was painful to see that there was but little heart in their
devotions, the touching prayers of our Church being apparently
to them nothing beyond the bare form or ceremony; listless as
they were here, they paid marked attention to the sermon."*

Despite Zephaniah's known convict background, the Bishop
declared himself impressed with his *"propriety and industry,"*
remarking that the colony was indebted to him for discovering
coal at New Town in Hobart and more lately his skill and enterprise in developing the Denison Mine. Having examined some
samples, Bishop Nixon considered the coal of excellent quality,
and if found in sufficient quantity predicted it would undoubtedly
reward all concerned. Zephaniah's wife, Joan, and daughter Rhoda
had settled down happily in the bush, *"the wild liberty compen-
sating for the isolation and privation."*[22]

No sooner had the Welsh arrived at Tarleton, than Zephaniah

was in trouble with the local constable, Thomas Clarkson, for selling illegal grog to miners. Whether or not this occurred as part of the arrival celebrations is not clear, but the incident complained of by Constable Clarkson allegedly happened on Sunday, October 22, 1854, the same day the immigrants were landed by the *Titania* in the Mersey. The case, however, was not proceeded with, after the magistrate's attention was drawn to an error in the information laid against Zephaniah by the constable, who had quoted the wrong section of the act. But the matter did not end there, controversy over the incident continuing for several weeks in the correspondence columns of the *Launceston Examiner*. Someone signing himself *"Miner"* sprung to Zephaniah's defence, accusing the newspaper's local correspondent of being mischievous and inaccurate in his reporting by alleging he was encouraging his colliers to squander their earnings on Sunday drinking. Then he criticised the reporting of the arrival of the Welsh immigrants on the Mersey, pointing out that they were not landed directly at Tarleton as the reporter had claimed, but a couple of miles below the township and then transported the remainder of the way by punt along with their baggage.

"He says (the newspaper's correspondent) *'most of them spoke positively as to the success of the coalfield.'* I (Miner) *cannot conceive how the most of them, or any of them, could speak so positively as to the success of the coalfield when they were all entire strangers to the country, and consequently not capable of forming anything like a correct idea about the subject. I am a practical miner myself and have been residing in the neighbourhood for a considerable time and am quite familiar with the different strata both in the locality of the Mersey Coal Company's Works and in that of Messrs Williams and Co yet I can by no means speak positively as to the success of the coalfield: that there is a seam of coal underneath in both localities I have not the slightest doubt; but the ultimate success of the coalfield depends entirely upon the means at the disposal of both companies."*

"Miner" concluded by describing Zephaniah as *"a man who has done more than any other man in this country to benefit the public, and is at the present moment struggling night and day to accomplish more both here and in Hobart Town – a man whose*

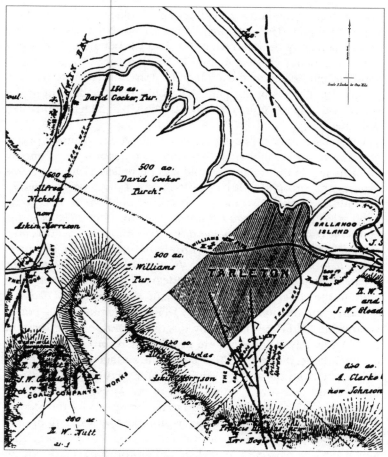

Map of the Mersey Coalfield showing the Williams Mines.

name ought to be wrote in letters of gold, instead of being held up to public ridicule by anyone."[23]

Whatever the truth of this spat between Zephaniah and the local constable, liquor was as big a problem on the Mersey, as it had been in the old country. So was another old enemy of the poor – credit! Before long Tasmanian employers introduced the loathsome practice of paying their men in credit notes cashed by publicans in return for a five per cent discount, and it was not uncommon for a relatively small group of colliers to spend £700 a week on liquor. The new arrivals must have been struck by the ghastly similarity between what they had left behind in Wales and what was being created in the Tasmanian bush. Worse still, it soon became clear to the immigrant miners there was no coal of any quantity, only the little that could be scratched from the surface outcrops. Within a few months they had all left Zephaniah Williams.[24]

Their suspicions, however, were not allowed to dampen public enthusiasm for a major coal discovery, to transform the economy of Tasmania, in the same way gold had propelled Victoria towards ever-greater prosperity. It had become not a question of whether the Mersey Coalfield would prove viable, only when. According to an editorial in *Cornwall Chronicle*, May 16, 1855, *"The quantity being inexhaustible, and the quality superior to any yet discovered in the southern hemisphere, it only remains to adopt means to bring it to market, to ensure for the vicinity of its depository the greatest prosperity."* Zephaniah's endeavours at the Denison Mine were in the vanguard of this excitement, the *Cornwall Chronicle* reporting, prematurely, on April 7, 1855 that thanks to "his perseverance and skill" he had finally discovered a three-foot seam of coal. A few days later the same newspaper received a sample of the coal recovered from 35 feet below the surface, and only half a mile away from the water's edge. Its informant claimed that one horse could deliver ten tons of coal to the Mersey for shipment every day.[25] There seemed no end to the prospects for the Mersey Coalfield, when Zephaniah Williams stumbled by accident upon a huge deposit of Yellow Coal, or Tasmanite, on his land, from which he was expected to realise a large fortune. His discovery was reported in a British publication *"The Builder"* which described how Zephaniah had been searching for coal below ground, when a lamp left on the surface accidentally set fire to a piece of yellow shale stone. Highly volatile, the shale on further examination was found to be similar to a deposit at Torbane Hill at Bathgate in Scotland from which 8,000 gallons of paraffin oil valued at £2,000 was distilled every week.[26]

There is little doubt Zephaniah did find Tasmanite, or Yellow Coal. But when a sample was sent to England for analysis, the results cast doubts over its value and attempts to exploit it commercially were largely unsuccessful. At the Denison Mine, the reality was also quite different to what was projected to the outside world. Whether or not they had been deliberately duped, or were simply the victims of one man's obsession, the Welsh colliers would have had serious doubts about the viability of the mine after the repeated flooding and the nature of the basalt through which the shaft was being sunk. Nevertheless, they set to work digging his shaft deeper and deeper, Zephaniah urging them on, the elusive coal seam just twenty feet away, he always insisted, until seeing that it was hopeless every Welsh collier left him by April 1855, within five months of landing at Ballahoo Creek. Undeterred, he pressed on, driven by the indomitable spirit for which he had become renowned, even shipping a few tons to Launceston although its source was unclear.

By now Zephaniah was not the only one prospecting for coal between the Mersey and the Don. Hundreds of thousands of pounds had been invested by four main companies, of which the Williams and Nicholas syndicate were one, as well as a number of smaller concerns. But very little coal was reaching the market, only reports of it being stockpiled on wharfs along the Mersey. Consequently, the Colonial Government sent its chief geologist, Alfred Selwyn, over from Victoria to assess the real potential. A prominent member of the Royal Society of Tasmania, Selwyn found a very different situation to what he had been led to expect. His main concern was the Denison Mine, the Government Geologist appearing to dash Zephaniah's already badly bruised optimism, when he reported the Welshman would not find coal if he sunk his shaft another 1,000 yards, because he was boring through strata older than the carboniferous levels.

"We have a shaft 270ft deep," Selwyn told the Governor and the prestigious Royal Society of Tasmania, *"sunk entirely thorough beds beneath the carboniferous series, and in which, of course, no coal was discovered – nor as I told Mr Williams would have the smallest chance of finding coal if he to sink another thousand yards. He, however, is firmly persuaded to the contrary and intends, if he can raise funds, and find men to undertake the work of sinking through quartz conglomerate nearly as hard as cast iron to carry the shaft deeper."* [27]

Until receiving his conditional pardon in 1854, Zephaniah had sensibly avoided public controversy, but could not contain his outrage at Selwyn's attack, as it jeopardised all his efforts to restore the public esteem and reputation his involvement in the Chartist Uprising had cost him sixteen years previously. The dispute was to rumble on for several months through the columns of the *Launceston Examiner*, Zephaniah accusing the government geologist of irresponsibility in basing his conclusions, not upon a personal investigation of the geology of the mine but on the accounts of competitors. At that time there were three main ones: the Mersey Coal Company, and those of Messrs Dean and Denny, all struggling to remain solvent. Clearly concerned at the effect the report would have upon prospective investors, Zephaniah wagered Selwyn £1,000 that he would reach coal within another 20ft. At the same time he wrote to the *Examiner* dismissing Selwyn's report as mischief making. If Selwyn had conducted a proper scientific investigation, he maintained, it would have been plain the coalfield at the Mersey had the potential to produce many hundreds of tons a day for centuries, its quality, the best ever discovered.[28] In fairness to Selwyn, his criticism focussed on the Denison Colliery only, not the entire area of potential coal reserves, noting in his report that Zephaniah was also working a two-feet thick seam outcropping alongside a small creek, and that this offered the prospect of him raising a considerable quantity of excellent coal at very little expense. For a time Zephaniah remained reluctant to abandon the Denison Mine but when even the new pump from Hobart could not handle another in-rush of water, it was closed after he and his partners had invested £10,000, and without producing a single ton of coal.[29]

Exactly why all the Welsh quit Zephaniah Williams within five months of their arrival is unclear. That they did, however, is confirmed in a series of letters published by the *Launceston Examiner* between April and June 1856. Richard Crompton, the manager of a mine on land close to where *"Frogmore"* presently stands, provides a graphic account of the all too-brief history of the Mersey Coalfield. In what he claims to be a *"plain unvarnished statement of facts,"* Crompton describes how Dean was the first to exploit the coal reserves, why Zephaniah's Denison Mine failed, and how the Welshman resorted to a spot of industrial espionage to locate another, more productive seam of coal.

According to Crompton, the Denison Mine was a quarter of a mile from the township of Tarleton, Williams and his Legislative Council partner Nicholas commencing operations in June 1852 by sinking what was then called the Williams Shaft. The difficulties were enormous: men and machinery were in short supply, the ground was rock hard, and the shaft flooded. Besides this, there was little or no communication between the mine, located in the middle of wild bush, and the outside world.

"These latter difficulties alone were sufficient to have cooled the ardour of any ordinary spirit but Mr Williams was not be deterred from prosecuting his favourite object, notwithstanding all of these obstructions," wrote Crompton. *"He obtained special permission from the government to hire passholders* (ticket-of-leave convicts) *into his service and with these and his own individual exertions he commenced and sunk his shaft to a depth of 300ft. The first 200ft was through ground best known to miners as 'marl' or 'blue bind,' which was pretty good sinking through. At this depth he encountered a quartz conglomerate as hard as adamant, which continued for 50ft. At this junction, too, nearly all his men left him when he was obliged to sink through it himself. The difficulty of sinking through ground of this kind can only be conceived by practical miners who have sunk through such ground themselves."*

At 260ft the shaft flooded and, at considerable expense, Zephaniah ordered a steam pump from Hobart. Meanwhile, he recruited some Scots with mining experience, at the same time sending to Wales for 40 colliers and tradesmen, these together with their families arriving aboard the *Merrington* in October 1854.

According to Crompton, *"These, after working a few months, for some reason or other, all left him and this circumstance together with a further increase in water which rendered the engine too small for its work caused him to abandon the shaft after having incurred an expense supposed to exceed £10,000 and this at a time when he was certainly not more than 20ft from the coal."* It was then that Zephaniah closed the Denison mine although never abandoning his conviction the shaft needed to be sunk only a few feet deeper to reach his fabled four-foot seam. Instead, he re-focussed his efforts *"with great vigour"* on recovering more accessible deposits nearer the surface, and completing the two-mile long Williams Tram Way to transport the coal to the Williams Jetty on Ballahoo Creek. The wooden tram way was a masterpiece of craftsmanship, all the rails secured to the sleepers by grooves and wedges without the use of a single nail. This would probably have been a matter of necessity, since supplies for the mines were brought by sea from Launceston, until Zephaniah started casting his own equipment at a forge powered by the steam pump from the abandoned Denison Mine.

While applauding the Welshman's *"indomitable spirit of perseverance and courage,"* Crompton insisted it was he, not Zephaniah, who discovered the seam from which coal was eventually mined for four years until 1859 for shipment to Launceston. On April 2, 1855 Zephaniah Williams wrote to his partner Nicholas in Hobart stating he had struck coal on their land. Crompton maintained, however, it was he who had found the seam the previous day, April 1, hidden in dense scrub, not a blade of which had been trampled or disturbed, proving no one could have discovered it before him. When Crompton and his employer returned the next day, April 2, to inspect the discovery they were followed by one of Zephaniah's men. The man later admitted reporting the location of the coal seam to Williams, who started working the deposit almost immediately. But Crompton levelled an even more serious allegation, suggesting Zephaniah had deliberately withheld news of the coal discovery from his partner until Nicholas had signed an agreement dissolving their partnership.[30] Whether or not this was a ruse, Nicholas never fell for it, coal production from the smaller seam and the partnership continuing until 1859 when after much acrimony, as the two men disputed ownership of the assets, their affairs were settled by arbitration and Zephaniah retired from mining to become a publican at Ballahoo Creek and Tarleton.[31]

Before then, however, Zephaniah Williams continued to be driven by his life long obsession. No matter how he had located the coal deposit Crompton claimed to have discovered, Zephaniah was quick to mine it, instead of sinking a shaft, driving a level into the side of the hill, loading his wagons underground, and then freewheeling down his tramway to the wharf.[32] Within a few months of Selwyn's damning report in 1855, Zephaniah had stockpiled 300 to 400 tones of coal on his jetty, awaiting shipment to Launceston.[33] While none came from his fabled four-foot seam, the period 1855-1898 was the only time the Mersey experienced anything that came close to a coal boom. At its height in 1858, three collieries – one of these Williams Mines – were being worked, exporting over 1000 tons of coal a month from six jetties on the Mersey. The value of the exports for the half-year ending July 1, 1858, was £18,000, Zephaniah Williams listed as being among the principal exporters.[34] Long before then, however, the Mersey Coal Company was facing bankruptcy having invested £20,000 in its mining operations five miles inland from the Williams pits. To save itself, it cut the wages of its colliers by half.[35] Zephaniah, who was, meanwhile, scouting around for new business ventures, built a sawmill at his jetty, finally quitting the coal business in 1859 to return to the licensing trade as landlord of the *Bush Hotel* in Tarleton. His friend and partner, George Atkinson Senior, ran another local tavern, the *Dalrymple Inn*, and later the *Beehive* at Tarleton before building *The Royal Charter* at Latrobe just across the river. At about the same time, Zephaniah's Chartist accomplice William Jones was landlord at the *Cross Keys* in Launceston.[36] Then came a diversion – the search for gold!

Ever since the gold strike at Ballarat had brought prosperity to Victoria, the legislators in Hobart had hoped something similar might occur in Tasmania, offering a £20,000 reward to the first person to discover a viable goldfield on the island. Hardly a week passed without some prospector reporting a Tasmanian El Dorado after spotting a few gold flecks swirling in the bottom of his prospector's pan. The most enthusiastic of these, James Smith, believed an extensive goldfield existed in the foothills of the central mountains at Gad's Hill. Arriving at Ballahoo Creek, he persuaded Zephaniah, the local constable Clarkson, and two other coal owners, William Johnson and another named Davies to join him prospecting an unexplored region of dense forest. The scrub was impenetrable, the country so rugged it took almost twelve days to reach the gold-bearing region, which they named Golden Point after washing a few flaky samples from a stream. Now running short of food, and without even sight of a kangaroo to shoot, they returned to Ballahoo Creek where for a time their discovery excited local interest, a certain James Jones claiming the reward. Gold fever soon subsided, 14 flecks the most anyone admitted having found at Gold Point.[37]

Ballahoo Creek and Tarleton prospered during the coal years, the population of the latter reaching 300 in its heyday with 34 houses, two inns, four stores, a police station and one school. Divine service was held twice on a Sunday, but Tarleton never shook off its reputation as a frontier town, the surge in population accompanied by an increase in drunkenness and violence, especially among the wood splitters, who were constantly quarrelling among themselves. Christmas at Tarleton was described in those days as a period of dark eyes, blood red cheeks, workers lounging about the bars recovering from bouts of dipsomania, occasionally carried off to the *'dead house'* at the back to sober up. Close on the heels of the dissolute came the teetotallers, the Mersey Total Abstinence Society conducting a 'pledge taking' service at Dean's Point every Boxing Day, the singing on those occasions led by *"Mrs Jones,"* schoolteacher.[38]

The Williams family had a major stake in the future of Tarleton, Zephaniah having either bought or taken an option on five hundred acres of Crown land extending along the boundary of the new township. When the boundaries of Tarleton were delineated by the Colonial Government in 1858, the *Gazette* reported on June 15 that the town limit was the *"south-eastern border of Lot 280 purchased from the Crown by Zephaniah Williams."* Even though Tarleton very quickly expired after it became clear there were no rich coal reserves waiting to be tapped, the coal search attracted new settlers and investment in logging, agriculture, and shipping. Zephaniah's daughter Rhoda had married George Atkinson Junior, who was to become one of Tasmania's most successful ship owners, eventually building *"Frogmore,"* an impressive brick house on the banks of the Mersey, complete with a tower from which he watched his ships sailing up river to load coal and timber at adjoining wharves.[39] When the coal bubble burst and Tarleton became a ghost town, George Atkinson Junior founded the present day town of Latrobe on the opposite bank. It was at *"Frogmore,"* the home he built for his new wife after Rhoda had died in 1876 aged only 46, that I discovered the Williams family Bible.

The failure to develop a viable coalfield on the Mersey caused huge disappointment, throughout a colony still heavily dependent on costly imports from New South Wales. Zephaniah's enthusiasm almost certainly exaggerated the coal prospects, but his persuasiveness and perseverance had attracted the interest of investors and won the unqualified support and confidence of his immediate neighbours on the Mersey. Even though his Welsh colliers had abandoned him, and his Denison Mine never produced a ton of coal, he remained on course to reclaim his reputation as a mining engineer. Throughout his imprisonment and exile, it was the sacrifice of his professional credibility and public status on the altar of Chartism that caused him the greatest mental anguish, complaining of this more than once in letters to his wife. Apart from some fleeting allusions to Chartism, never did he seek to justify his actions on November 4, 1839, when the men from the hills descended on Newport, nor did he ever refer to the merits of the Chartist cause. What tormented him most was his personal sacrifice, and how best he might redeem his prestige, reputation, and position.[40] Not surprisingly, the rest of his life was devoted as much to this personal crusade as to his search for coal, a mission that must have seemed close to realisation by 1855. Although recommended for a conditional pardon on November 6, 1852, official notification of this did not materialise until June 27, 1854. A free man at last, Zephaniah would still not have the right to return to Britain, unless granted an absolute pardon for which he would wait until February 24, 1857.[41]

But for the settlers along the Mersey, many of whom would also have had a convict past, Zephaniah was already a hero.[42] The Welshman was the one who put the Mersey on the map, even though coal production was more talk and expectations than actual tonnages. Now 60 years of age, Zephaniah must have felt his rehabilitation complete on October 23, 1855, when at a complimentary dinner given him by fellow settlers in the Mersey Hotel he was presented with a silver cup, in appreciation of his efforts in opening up the region to trade. Feted by some of the most influential people along the coast, among them a member of the Legislative Council, Zephaniah had at last recovered from his Chartist disgrace. The *Launceston Examiner* reported that, *"Several capital speeches were made and a very pleasant evening was spent."*[43] But Zephaniah's readmission into respectable society was barely noted compared to the public acclaim that greeted the release of William Smith O'Brien, leader of the "Free Irelanders" whose attempt at a rising was even more poorly planned and supported than the Chartist revolt in Monmouthshire. Smith O'Brien, son of the Irish aristocracy, and the three Monmouthshire Chartist leaders all received their conditional pardons from Lord Palmerston in May 1854, Smith O'Brien *"on account of his honourable conduct in not attempting to escape."* Also denied the right to return to Ireland immediately, O'Brien nevertheless embarked on the journey in anticipation his supporters would secure his absolute pardon within a short time. His first stop was the *Cornwall Hotel* in Launceston for a complimentary dinner and deputation *"composed of every grade of religious and political sentiment,"* according to the *Cornwall Chronicle*. *"They met to convey to a high principled gentlemen the universal esteem to which his magnanimity under his sufferings entitles him; whatever feelings may be entertained by persons influenced by opposite political views, all are satisfied of Mr O'Brien's purity of intention and of his ardent desire to serve his country."*[44] Zephaniah Williams had little sympathy for these Irish patriots whom he believed enjoyed privileged treatment on account of their aristocratic connections. No sooner had they arrived in the penal colony to serve life sentences for High Treason than most were issued with tickets-of-leave, entitling them to work anywhere on the island. While Smith O'Brien did spend a brief period at Port Arthur, it was in the relative luxury of his own cottage, attended by a servant, all courtesy of his influential brother, Sir Lucius O'Brien, 13th Baron Inchiquin, and heir to Drumoland. Even when he refused to give an undertaking not to attempt escape, Smith O'Brien was simply removed to another cottage on nearby Maria Island where after the briefest detention he received his ticket-of-leave without conditions attached. In fact, he and his fellow conspirators were on their way home to Ireland within five years of their life sentences, compared to the sixteen endured by Frost, Williams and Jones. Is it reasonable to conclude from this that for committing an identical offence, High Treason, the Chartists were considered by the British Government the greater rebels and threat to the nation?[45]

From Launceston, Smith O'Brien sailed to Melbourne for another testimonial dinner at which he was presented not with a silver cup but a gold one valued at £1,400, decorated with the family coat of arms, the shield inscribed, *"Presented to William Smith O'Brien by his friends in Victoria in testimony of their admiration for his patriotism, sympathy for his long suffering in the cause of his country, and congratulations for his release from captivity."* [46] Every stage of his return from exile was marked by cheering crowds until Gibraltar where the *Candia's* first class passenger dared venture no nearer Britain without an absolute pardon. O'Brien, like Zephaniah Williams' accomplice John Frost who on receipt of his conditional pardon in 1854 had set out to return via the United States, was prohibited from setting foot in Britain so he moved into a Paris hotel and later to Brussels to await the Crimean War amnesty for political prisoners. [47]

The men, women and children from Wales had travelled to Zephaniah Williams' promised land on the strength of largely empty promises. Stranded in the bush 14,000 miles from home, they probably felt like the Chartist demonstrator fleeing from the carnage outside the Westgate who exclaimed, *"The Devil shall have me before Zephaniah Williams has me with him again."* [48] Few, if any, would have had sufficient funds to return to the country from which they had severed all ties, for an expedition that in 19th century terms was tantamount to flying to the moon. As a condition of each £22 assisted passage, every immigrant aged over fourteen was required to sign a contract agreeing to remain in the colony for four years. Anyone returning to Britain sooner, was expected to refund the Immigration Agent in Hobart one quarter of the amount for each of the four years residency they failed to complete. [49] On top of which, returning immigrants would have to pay for their return passage. For single men it might have been possible, but for the larger families, like James Davies (aged 31), his wife Ann (31), son James (11), daughters Louise (9) and Margaret (7), and youngest son Samuel (1), the cost at today's values would have totalled several thousands of pounds. The largest family group aboard the *Merrington* were the Firth's from Yorkshire. Recruited by the Mersey Coal Company, William Firth (collier, 43), and his wife, had seven children, aged between eight and twenty-one. The 14 miners, two brick-makers, one quarryman, one navvy, two masons, two carpenters and two wheelwrights from Yorkshire where in difficulties from the moment they arrived, the Mersey Coal Company first halving their wages in its struggle to remain solvent, and two months later put up for sale.[50]

In all, 141 adults and 60 children had been destined for the mines on the Mersey. The Welsh immigrants consisted of 29 colliers, one engineer, two carpenters, two smiths, two sawyers, and their dependents, in all 77 souls, including one farmer, Edmund Llewellyn, Zephaniah's 52 year-old brother-in-law, Zephaniah's wife Joan (54), and daughter Rhoda (24). While the Home Government covered the cost of the free passages, the sponsoring employer, in this case Zephaniah, paid a £3 bounty for each single person aged over 14, and £5 for every family group he brought to Tasmania to work. In a letter transferring power of attorney to his son Llewellyn, then the licensee at the *Rolling Mill Inn*, Cwm Celyn Ironworks, Blaina, Zephaniah authorised him to complete the agreements with the migrant workers on his behalf. *"When executed,"* Zephaniah told his son, *"you will give the workmen one, and the other you will forward to me as their master. It is necessary for you to be very careful in the selection of good workmen, that they are not drunkards."* This was strictly a business arrangement, Zephaniah the employer recruiting the colliers in accordance with the Master and Servants Act. Under the provisions of the Act, an employee who refused to work, absented himself from his workplace, was drunk, or infringed numerous other constraints could be hauled before the court and punished. Usually the contract was for a specified period, in this case to work for Zephaniah for three years at 6 shillings a day. But he did offer them an alternative arrangement. Although contracted to work in his mines, instead of a wage, they could opt for piecework, and be paid for each ton of coal raised, thereby earning *"considerably greater wages than the stipulated price."* Those who chose to freelance in this way could earn between 10 shillings and 20 shillings a day, said Zephaniah.[51] Was it a combination of unfulfilled promises and shortage of readily accessible coal resources that persuaded the colliers from Wales to leave Zephaniah within a few months of arriving? There is no reason to doubt the assertion by Crompton, the mine manager, that either all or most did quit his employment not long after disembarking at Ballahoo Creek. But there is no evidence of Zephaniah Williams invoking the Master and Servants Act by bringing a single case of infringement before the courts, as was customary when workers proved unsatisfactory. Indeed, the master was at liberty to discharge the worker from the agreement if dissatisfied with his/her work. When the colony's labour force comprised mostly ticket-of-leave convicts entitled to work for wages anywhere on the island, a breach of the conditions usually meant they were returned to the Convict Barracks in Hobart Town to await relocation. Free settlers, however, objected to being shackled in this way on arriving in a colony portrayed to them by immigration agents and sponsoring employers as a land of liberty, flowing with milk and honey. Tension between employer and immigrant worker became especially strained once the latter saw their expectations did not match the reality of life in the Tasmanian bush. Almost every immigrant arriving in Tasmania felt aggrieved by the deceptions practised upon them, and the miners from Wales were probably no exception.[52]

At a time when the price of coal had slumped and his competitors on the Mersey were cutting wages, Zephaniah Williams offered carpenters, blacksmiths and engineers from Wales 5 shillings to 10 shillings a day, and promised sawyers up to 20 shillings a day. In fairness, he warned that the rates were *"subject to the rise and fall of wages."* The recruitment of the Welsh immigrants was delegated entirely to Llewellyn Williams. Not only was the son expected to supervise the choice of immigrant but also the completion of the agreements. These he then delivered to Mr Jackson, London representative for the London Agency Association, as proof for the Land Emigration Commissioners that Zephaniah Williams had purchased 40 Bounty tickets. The dependants of Bounty immigrants travelled free, but not Zephaniah's wife, daughter and brother-in-law who would have paid their own passages. All the immigrants were to be reminded, he told his son, to pay their own expenses from Wales to London, the port of embarkation aboard the *Merrington.*

By this time Zephaniah had an option to buy under the governor's land purchase scheme 2,600 acres, all of it thick, virgin bush needing to be cleared for cultivation. Zephaniah offered any small farmers in Wales prepared to pay their own way to Tasmania between thirty and one hundred acres rent-free for five or seven years on condition they cleared the land. No one took up this offer, the only farmer listed on the *Merrington*'s passenger list, his brother-in-law, Edmund Llewellyn. Zephaniah's letter to his son, post-marked Hobart Town, July 25, 1853, ended, *"I am now at liberty to go to any part of the world, except Great Britain,"* which was not exactly true, because while his conditional pardon was recommended on November 6, 1852, it was not finally authorised until June 27, 1854. Llewellyn Williams acted immediately, publishing the letter in the *Monmouthshire Merlin* on November 4 in the hope of recruiting the workers his father had requested.[53]

No addresses are listed for the passengers aboard the *Merrington*, the passenger list stating only their place of origin as being Wales and Yorkshire, except for two in the Welsh group from Somerset and Lincolnshire. Since Llewellyn Williams was responsible for recruitment, it is fair to assume most came from Monmouthshire, probably from the vicinity of his public house at Blaina. As might be expected, the names were mostly Jones, Davies, and Thomas:

William Lake (24), collier, and Margaret Lake (21); John Davies (24), collier; William Reece (24), collier; John Davies (33), collier, Margaret Davis (33), Mary (4), John (1), Mary (60); Lewis Davies (24), collier; Henry Davies (24), collier; David Thomas (31), collier; Philip Thomas (33), collier, Sarah Thomas (21), female child (under 1), David Thomas (60), collier, Thomas Thomas (8), Elizabeth Thomas (5); William Harrison (30), collier; John Jones (24), collier; Daniel David Jones (19), collier; William Reed (26), collier, Ann Reed (26), male child (12 months); Henry Hicks (22), collier, Priscilla Hicks (20); Charles Church (20), collier, Fanny Church (19): Robert Luke (26), collier, Sarah Luke (24); John James (22), died on passage; John Williams (22), collier; John Jones (31); David Thomas (35), collier, Mary Thomas (23), Catherine Thomas (13), Mary Jane Thomas (under 12 months); William Williams (28), collier, Sarah Williams (26), David Williams (6), Margaret Williams (1); Job Israel (28), collier, Ann Israel (22); Williams Saunders (44), collier, William Saunders (16); William Davies (40), collier, Jane Davies (40), Jane Davies (9); Thomas Williams (25), collier; David Selwyn (25), collier; William Marks (23), collier; Ebenizer Morris (23), collier; William Morgan (27), collier; Thomas Meredith (22), collier; Edmund Llewellyn (50),

farmer; James Davies (31), engineer, Ann Davies (31), James
Davies (11), Louise Davies (4), Margaret Davies (7), Samuel
Davies (1); David Phillips (23), carpenter; Isaac Harding (25),
carpenter; William Excel (23), smith, Eliza Excel (24), William
Excel (2), male infant (6 months); George Grant (21), smith; John
Jones (27), sawyer, Ann Jones (25), David Jones (13), Margaret
Jones (9); John Richards (22), sawyer, Martha Richards (27); Joan
Williams (55), Rhoda Williams (25); David Evans (48), collier.[54]

A vast amount of research would be necessary to identify from
where in Wales these emigrants came, and what became of them.
So far, I have traced only one family: William Excel, smith, wife
Eliza, son William, aged two, and an unnamed male infant evidently
born not long before the family left for Tasmania from their home
at No. 16 North Street, Tredegar. The 1851 census reveals that
William senior was born in Crickhowell, and his wife Eliza (maiden
name Dalley) in Radnorshire.

Despite perhaps a sense of betrayal, there was probably no
immediate exodus of the Welsh from Ballahoo Creek, because
where could they go? Some may have joined the thousands streaming across the Bass Straits to the goldfields in Victoria, while
others could have taken up small allotments of timbered land
being offered by the Colonial Government at West Devonport,
and on the Don River further west. What is certain is that the tree-
stump swamps along the banks of the River Mersey continued to
echo to the sound of Welsh and Yorkshire voices for several years
afterwards.[55] The arrival of these first assisted passage immigrants
had actually marked a watershed in colonial settlement, allowing
Van Diemen's Land, by now re-named as Tasmania, to begin the
process of shedding its convict past. Immigration was previously
synonymous with transportation, and workmen with convict
labour. The new immigrants were welcomed as a *"valuable acces-
sion,"* for once not the sweepings of the workhouse or refuse of
the parish. As men and women of character willing to work and
determined to be independent, there were hopes their arrival was
the beginning of a gradual change in the composition of Tasmanian society. Ironically, they also got the right to vote long before
adult suffrage was conceded in Britain, Zephaniah Williams one
of those on the list of registered voters in 1855.[56]

Zephaniah was indefatigable in his search for coal while most around him gave up. When William Dean, the early pioneer, decided to cut his losses, the Welshman took a lease on his Don Colliery, but even he could not make it pay.[57] All that the prospectors and miners had to show for their search was the one, severely faulted, thin seam of coal outcropping at various places between the rivers Don and Mersey. To mine it, they usually drove a level into the side of the hill, cutting away the underlying layer of rubble from the seam to allow the coal to collapse into the void that was left. Because it was scratched from the hillside in this fashion, the men who mined it were known as *"scratchers."*[58] Sometimes this generated great activity before leaving the men frustrated and poor when the disappearing vein pushed their employers towards the edge of bankruptcy. Soon the export of timber from Tasmania's seemingly endless forests became the more reliable and profitable activity along the banks of the Mersey.

Zephaniah's life-long passion for coal was not entirely unrewarded, despite Selwyn's damning indictment of his professional expertise. At least his rehabilitation as geologist and mining engineer was back on course when the Tasmanian Government's "Royal Commission on Tasmanian Coal" awarded him a £1,500 commission to investigate the viability of coal deposits at a number of sites on the island. One of these was Fingal on the east coast, where coal was still being mined a hundred years later. Zephaniah's instructions from the Government were to collect samples for scientific analysis against two tons of the best Welsh steam coal imported from Cardiff by the P and O Steamship Company. His results were encouraging, but Tasmania never developed much of a coal industry, although paraffin was distilled from the coal shale, Tasmanite, which Zephaniah was also credited with discovering.[59]

By the time Zephaniah had become landlord of the Bush Inn at Tarleton (1861), the population of the town had fallen to 61, its dream of becoming the commercial hub of the Mersey drowning in the accumulation of silt that soon made the river un-navigable to larger vessels at Ballahoo Creek. The search for coal would be consigned to history by the *Launceston Examiner* which wrote a stinging obituary in 1867, *"It is a deplorable fact that from mis-management and misfortune about one hundred thousand pounds of good money has been spent on futile attempts to procure a supply of coal from the district. For this there is nothing to show but abandoned pits, dilapidated and useless tramways, decaying machinery, and unoccupied land. The space between the Don and the Mersey contains a series of irregular faults. It seems as if the country had been crumpled up like a sheet of post paper pressed into all sorts of shapes by hand. There is no doubt that there was much ignorance, gross mismanagement, and perhaps something worse. Even the publicans who seemed to profit most largely, and at whose houses most of the workmen's 'piles' were knocked down, allowed their money to slip through their fingers."* These doubts about the viability of the Mersey Coalfield had existed ten tears previously among those who believed what had been found was not real coal at all. One of the *Examiner*'s regular correspondents *"Practical Miner"* was convinced from its charred, woody appearance, not dissimilar from pieces of burned wood, and the peculiar smell it emitted when burned, together with its failure to generate sufficient heat, that it was a form of lignite.[60]

Zephaniah meanwhile was dabbling in other business ventures besides the licensing trade, submitting a £13,675 tender to construct a twelve-mile section of the iron railroad planned to link Deloraine to Port Frederick (present day Devonport) at the mouth of the Mersey. While the Welshman failed to win the contract, he was appointed a trustee to assist in rescuing the project when the contractor went bankrupt in 1866. If Zephaniah had been a director of the company, rather than a trustee, he would have shared in tens of thousands of acres of land along the track promised by the government to the company building the railroad.[61]

His last project was, not unexpectedly, in the licensing trade: building the *Don Hotel* in 1869. Zephaniah's lifelong association with public houses in Wales and Tasmania would have automatically isolated him from the Temperance movements that had proliferated in both countries to combat the evils of the demon drink. A scattered community along the river, with a flourishing Temperance Society and Sunday School, the inhabitants of the

Don had successfully opposed public houses for fifteen years, and had no intention of surrendering to Zephaniah Williams. The *Launceston Examiner* reported that while not wanting to convey the impression *"that the Donites are a straight-laced, exclusive community of ascetics . . . the result of all this temperance, providence and industry, are to be seen in substantial and comfortable homes; in independent, self-reliant, and intelligent workmen; in their industrious happy looking and contented wives, and their robust healthy children."*[62] The first Zephaniah knew about the opposition was a letter signed by twenty-one people claiming to represent the community at large and giving him notice of their intention to use all legitimate means to prevent the *Don Hotel* from receiving a licence.[63] Incensed by this *"threatening letter,"* he sent a copy to the Editor of the *Cornwall Chronicle* for publication, asking his advice on what action to take. Not only did the Editor publish the letter, but included a supportive footnote advising Zephaniah to ignore the threat and *"go on raising coal or houses to meet the demand for them."*[64] The Welshman won the day, successfully applying for a licence despite opposition from the Don's Independent Chapel. Built on a hill on the eastern bank of the river on the old Tarleton Road, the hotel opened for business in 1870, becoming so popular that white-aproned housewives, reputedly, could be seen standing on the doorsteps of their cottages in the valley below watching for their husbands to leave the *Don Hotel* for their evening meal. Zephaniah only held the licence for a year, transferring it to George Lapthorne, one of those who signed the original protest letter! An examination of Lapthorne's account books reveals that despite the district's strong temperance tradition there were 230 customers on his 'slate'. The hotel burned down in 1905.[65]

By 1871 Tarleton was a ghost town and Zephaniah had moved to Latrobe, the new town his son-in-law George Atkinson Junior had founded across the creek. He had been alone since his wife Joan, aged 63, died on November 22, 1863, the first of the family to be buried in the family vault at St Paul's Anglican Cemetery, East Devonport. She had lived in the house overlooking Ballahoo Creek not for the twenty years Zephaniah had predicted, just nine. Afterwards Zephaniah settled on the coast at Torquay at the mouth of the Mersey, where he suffered a long and painful illness. Taken to hospital by his son-in-law for a serious operation, the Welsh Chartist leader never recovered and died at a temporary address in High Street, Launceston, on May 8, 1874, shortly before his 80th birthday. In a tribute published in July 1874, the *Illustrated Tasmanian News* concluded that Zephaniah Williams had taken *"no active part"* in the Chartist Uprising of 1839, a view it could only have formed from speaking to those closest to him.[66] What is certain is that throughout his 34 years of exile Zephaniah never made a single publicly recorded comment on those revolutionary events in Monmouthshire. Apart from coded references in his letters to his wife, which might be interpreted as regret for his stupidity, not once did he offer a word of explanation, only remorse that his involvement should have cost him and his family so dearly. The Tasmanian view of Zephaniah Williams as expressed in his obituary was uncomplicated. There was but one explanation for his involvement with Chartism: he was one of those celebrated Chartist leaders who dared claim their liberty by demanding the right to vote. *"While in Tasmania he was a valuable colonist always endeavouring to develop the mineral resources of the country, and investing all his means towards that end, as well as devoting to it his time, skill, and experience,"* commented the *News*. According to the newspaper, Zephaniah had been urged on many occasions to return to Wales and resume his old position as *"the largest shipper of coal from Newport where his name was idolised by the army of coal miners employed in the locality but he refused to leave Tasmania to which he had become attached and where his only daughter Mrs Atkinson is resident."* Evidently in considerable pain for some time before his death, this *"and the disappointments he had met with throughout a long life, had subdued his energy and iron will and he was prepared and resigned to the Divine will in case of the operation resulting fatally."*[67] Four months before this, William Jones, with whom Zephaniah had as little contact as possible after Jones had informed the police of his second escape attempt, also died in Launceston in St John Street on December 26, 1873 at the age of 68. He also suffered a long and painful illness and, in his case, in great poverty. Jones spent his final years repairing watches in a

The monument commemorating the contribution the Williams family, and Zeaphania's convict partner, George Atkinson, Senior, made to Tasmania's Mersey River region, was moved from Devonport Cemetery where they are buried to the banks of the river.

modest shop in Elizabeth Street, Launceston, but like most things he attempted in life was unsuccessful. When he died, he had not sufficient to pay the cost of his own funeral. The Loyal Cornwall Lodge of Odd Fellows, of which he was a member and official until his subscription lapsed, took pity and covered the cost of the internment.[68]

Zephaniah's daughter Rhoda Atkinson (aged 46) died two years after her father on March 20, 1876. Her husband George, six years her junior, and father of their two children, Joan and Llewellyn, was heartbroken, and left Tasmania for twelve months, first to visit his wife's native Monmouthshire, and then Europe. The very same year, Zephaniah's brother-in-law Edmund Llewellyn (aged 74) had also passed away on January 25, 1876.[69] All are interred in the family vault at St Paul's Anglican Cemetery, East Devonport, except for Llewellyn Williams, the family's celebrated harpist son who died in Wales two years before his father, after returning home to pursue his musical career.

A small, obscure plaque on the wall of a terraced house in Nantyglo, formerly part of the *Royal Oak*, is the only memorial in Wales to the remarkable part Zephaniah Williams played in the 19th century history of two countries. At least, Tasmania has not forgotten the pioneering efforts of Zephaniah. He, his wife Joan, daughter Rhoda, and brother-in-law, Edmund Llewellyn, are all remembered on a stone monument erected on the banks of the River Mersey at Latrobe, not far from the bush which swallowed up those early coal mines, their rusting equipment, and piles of waste. One hundred and fifty years later it is hard to imagine from the neat fields and the grazing livestock that coal ever passed this way.

But whatever happened to the Welsh of Ballahoo Creek? Did the men, women and children who were landed from the *Merrington* on a riverbank in the remote Tasmanian wilderness vanish into the bush, never to be heard of again? A close reading of the local newspapers for the ten years immediately following their arrival reveals only a few references to a Jones, Thomas, Davies. A John Williams became a well-respected horse breeder in the area; a John Thomas was reported prospecting for coal in the Dark Hollow in Launceston, and a Thomas Thomas died from an

ZEPHANIA WILLIAMS
1795 – 1874. A WELSH MINING
REFORMIST. HE WAS SENTENCED TO
VAN DIEMENS LAND. FROM CONVICT TO
OVERSEER TO OWNERSHIP ON THE
MERSEY COAL FIELDS AND A
DISTINGUISHED CITIZEN.

Zephaniah's commemorative plaque for services to a community where he regained his esteem after his *"infatuation"* with Chartism had destroyed his name and reputation

infection from a splinter in his arm. Then there was the bizarre case of the Welsh-speaking farmer, who had settled on the banks of the River Mersey. Called to give evidence against a neighbour accused of destroying a bridge on his land, it was discovered he could not speak a word of English. The appearance of farmer, Thomas Lloyd, in court caused considerable amusement, especially when his wife was asked to interpret.[70] Just how the couple came to settle in such a wild and remote area will probably never be discovered. There were no Lloyds among the passengers on the *Merrington*.

Some of the Welsh, and their descendants, who remained in the Tarleton area after it declined from potential boomtown to forgotten village, might have become coal *"scratchers."* Coal production along the Mersey did not end with the departure of Zephaniah Williams and the other major producers. The *"scratchers"* continued to mine small tonnages from shallow levels and out-crops until the very last closed, in 1961. Farming replaced the timber industry as the forests were felled, and in an area almost as sparsely populated as in its heyday, the agricultural calm is only occasionally disturbed when part of a field subsides, swallowing up an unsuspecting steer in a long forgotten shaft dug by those early miners. If the fate of the Welsh of Ballahoo Creek remains a mystery, so are their deaths because the cemetery in which most of the colliers may have been buried has also disappeared, either beneath the new road across the Mersey at Ballahoo Creek, or swallowed up by the bush. The last gravestone disappeared from public view in the 1940s; most would have been of wood and long since rotted away. Of the Williams cottages not a single stone remains, the only sign the Welsh ever existed in this remote corner of the world, the clumps of daffodils that flower on the spot each spring.[71]

In Wales, Zephaniah first achieved prosperity and status, then lost it, his aspirations bankrupting himself and his family, before engaging in what he himself regarded as an insane moment, the Chartist Uprising, ending with his transportation to a prison island and penal regime unparalleled for its brutality.[72] Incredibly, he survived to resume his life-long passion: the search for coal. But at Tarleton and Ballahoo Creek what he produced was largely smoke and mirrors, his enthusiasm an infection that gulled almost one hundred men, women and children to abandon everything to travel half-way round the world for the sake of his dream.

One of his great strengths was an indomitable spirit. Even this was stretched to breaking point when contemplating suicide in Monmouth Gaol, on the eve of what he thought was certain to be his execution, and again aboard the convict ship *Mandarin* when in desperation he might have joined an attempted mutiny. Exposed to the full rigour of the world's most brutal penal regime, his courage never deserted him. Afterwards, Zephaniah showed immense perseverance in his struggle to recover public esteem and along with it his reputation as a respected geologist and mining engineer. This he achieved in full measure, evidently to

Where the daffodils flower in spring, and the only evidence the Welsh Settlement on Ballahoo Creek existed.

the surprise of Frost who writing to a friend in London from New York after his conditional discharge observed: *"When I obtained my conditional pardon in July last, I determined to leave Van Diemen's Land. The prejudice which exists against prisoners there is so great that no conduct can remove it. Whatever a prisoner, or one who has been a prisoner, engages in is up-hill work; not a hand will be extended towards him, however meritorious may be the object of which he is in pursuit."*[73] Zephaniah Williams may have proved Frost wrong on this count, but the riches he sought eluded him to the very last. When Zephaniah died, his entire estate was worth less than £100. So much for the 'fortune' some writers claim that Williams made from coal.[74]

NOTES

1. Charles Ramsay, *With the Pioneers* (Devonport, 1957), p83.
2. *ibid*, p84.
3. NPL, John Frost, 'Letter to the People of Great Britain and Ireland on Transportation', Oddfellows Hall, lecture.
4. *Cornwall Chronicle,* 14 October 1854.
5. Richard Crompton, letter, *Launceston Examiner,* 26 April 1856.
6. Charles Ramsey, *With the Pioneers*, pp36-40.
7. LE, 12 December 1854.
8. CC, 20 December 1854; Richard Crompton, letter, LE, 26 April 1856.
9. *Melbourne Argus*, 13 April 1865.
10. CC, 26 July 1854; CC, 19 September 1855.
11. MM, 4 November 1853.
12. *The Times, a*ccount of grounding of the *Fortune,* 23 May 1855; Tasmanian State Archives, Hobart, Passenger List,, *Donald McKay,* arrived Hobart 6 September 1855.
13. MM, 4 November 1853.
14. CCL, Chartist Archives, Williams letter to wife from Hobart, 27 December 1849.
15. LE, 28 November 1854.
16. LE, 24 October 1854.
17. Dr John Malcolm, owner of *The Manor,* Latrobe: *"It was burned down in 1929, then rebuilt."*
18. CC, 20 December 1854.
19. Bishop Nixon, *Cruise of the Beacon* (Hobart, 1857).
20. LE, 17 November 1854; Gail and Terry Connelly, Henslow Road Farm, Ballahoo Hill.

21. GRO (Cardiff), Merthyr Tydfil Parish Records, St Tydfil's Church, p213, entry 637; East Devonport Anglican Cemetery ID: 62922, number DFH 07720.
22. Bishop Nixon, *Cruise of the Beacon*.
23. LE, 24 October 1854, 28 November 1854.
24. Crompton letter, LE, 26 April 1856.
25. CC, 11 April 1855.
26. Yellow Coal deposit, Crompton letter, LE, 18 April 1856; *Builder* account reported by CC, 16 May 1855.
27. Tasmanian State Archives, Hobart, Selwyn, Royal Society of Tasmania, Papers and Proceedings, LSC 506 1855-1859.
28. LE, 13 September 1855.
29. James Fenton, Bush Life in Tasmania, (London, 1970), p 85.
30. Crompton letter, LE, 26 April 1856; also LE, 2 May, 10 June, 17 June 1856.
31. 'The Coal Resources of Tasmania', Geological Survey, Bulletin 64, p142 (Booth, 1962).
32. Crompton, letter, LE, 26 April 1855.
33. LE, 29 September 1855.
34. Ramsey, *With the Pioneers,* pp124-136.
35. LE, 6 November 1855.
36. Ramsey, *With the Pioneers*, pp126, 178; LE, 30 January 1862; Faye Gardam, Port Sorell, Tasmania.
37. LE, 2, 9, July 1859.
38. LE, 30 June 1857, 31 December 1860.
39. Ramsey, *With the Pioneers*, p 128.
40. Williams letter to wife 27 December 1849, op. cit: "*My prospects have gone, my character as a miner or geologist likewise, unless I can by some effort yet redeem them.*"
41. Williams Convict Record, op.cit.
42. LE, 10 August 1856.
43. LE, 30 October 1855. Years later, the commemorative cup was donated to the Museum at Latrobe by Zephaniah's granddaughter, Mrs Joan Boadle.
44. CC, 8 July 1854.
45. Richard Davis, Revolutionary Imperialist: William Smith O'Brien, 1803-1864, (Dublin, 1998, Lilliput Press).
46. CC, 26 July 1854.
47. *Weekly News,* 4 November 1854.
48. NPL, Chartist Trials, 15, George Lloyd.
49. Bounty Emigrants Agreement, 24 January 1854, applicable to passengers aboard the *Merrington*. See *Merrington Passenger List,* Tasmania State Archives, Hobart.
50. LE, 6 November 1855, 24 January 1856.
51. MM, Zephaniah Williams letter to son Llewelyn, 4 November, 1853.
52. Editorial comment, CC, 5 January 1856.
53. MM, Zephaniah Williams letter to son Llewelyn, 4 November 1853; Richard Compton, LE, 26 April 1856; Williams Convict Record, op. cit.
54. Tasmanian State Archives, Hobart, *Merrington* passenger list.

55. K. R. von Stieglitz, *A Short History of Latrobe with notes on Port Sorrell and Sassafras* (reprinted Latrobe, 2000), p30.
56. LE, 15 September 1855.
57. Fenton, *Bush Life in Tasmania*, p84.
58. Gail and Terry Connelly, Henslow Road Farm, Ballahoo Hill.
59. Tasmanian State Archives, Hobart, Royal Commission on Tasmanian Coal, 30 June 1862.
60. LE, 2 December 1858.
61. Ramsey, *With the Pioneers*, p69; LE, 2 April 1865.
62. LE, 27 June 1871.
63. CC, 18 September 1869.
64. CC, 18 September 1869; Faye Gardam, *Sawdust, Sails and Sweat* (Devonport, 1996), p 248-249.
65. Gardam, *Sawdust, Sails and Sweat*, p250.
66. *Illustrated Tasmanian News,* July 1874.
67. *ibid.*
68. *ibid.*
69. Williams' granddaughter Joan Atkinson married Frederick Boadle, son of a Victorian pioneer family. The couple moved to *Frogmore* where for twenty years they raised dairy and beef cattle, Federick Boadle dying in 1937, Joan in 1965. By then she had moved to Devonport where her house in Oldaker Street was, reputedly, filled with family treasures, according to K. R. von Stieglitz (p29) in A *Short History of Latrobe*. It was she who presented Zephaniah's silver cup, commemorating his part in developing the region, to the Court House National Trust Museum at Latrobe. Her brother Llewellyn Atkinson, a prominent Latrobe solicitor, was for many years a member of the Australian House of Representatives. When he died on 1 November 1945 he bequeathed all his possessions and property to his sister Joan Boadle. Neither had children. (von Steiglitz, p29; will, Llewellyn Atkinson, Supreme Court of Tasmania, 28418, probate Dec 20, 1945.) Joan Boadle bequeathed her estate, worth £20,418 to relatives, friends and charities (will, Joan Boadle, Supreme Court of Tasmania, 47086, probate Jan 11, 1965). From this it would appear nothing has survived from *Frogmore* or the Zephaniah Williams estate apart from the family bible, two paintings, one of the house, the other believed to be a self-portrait of Joan Boadle, and a collection of old Hansards covering Llewellyn Atkinson's period in the Australian House of Representatives. All these items have remained at *Frogmore*.
70. LE, 9 July 1857.
71. Gail and Terry Connelly, Ballahoo Hill.
72. Auction Notice published in the *Monmouthshire Merlin* Oct 1833 announcing auction to be held 1 November 1833 at King's Head Hotel, Newport, "by order of the assignees of Messrs Webb, Pritchard and Williams, *bankrupts* (author's italics)." Webb and Pritchard were Zephaniah Williams's business partners in the failed mining venture at Bovil Colliery Machen, and earlier at Penrhiw Colliery, the subject of a restraining order issued against them in the Chancery Court. To be auctioned were

Zephaniah's two houses at Tredegar, and the one built by his father at Moggridge's Blackwood Garden Village in 1822.

73. Letter from Frost to friend, June 9, 1855, published *London Morning Advertiser,* reprinted *Cornwall Chronicle,* 21 November 1855.

74. Estate of Zephaniah Williams: Letters of Administration granted to George Atkinson, licensed victualler, son-in-law, by R. C. Gunn, Commissioner, Supreme Court of Tasmania 1874. "Goods, chattels did not exceed £100 at time of death." There is anecdotal evidence that before his death Zephaniah left the lease to the *Don Hotel* to his son-in-law; Prof. Gwyn A. Williams, *The Merthyr Rising* (1978), p83, quoting his source as Prof. David Williams, *John Frost: a study in Chartism* (1939).

CHAPTER 12

The Argonaut*

The announcement in the *Yreka Union* on November 23, 1893, said simply: *"Died. At Hornbrook, November 13th, 1893, Mr John Rees, a native of Wales, Great Britain, aged 78 years."*[1] Hornbrook is today a small town of 7,000 inhabitants in Siskiyou County in Northern California, just about as near as you can get to the Oregon state line, making its living from tourism and agriculture, with some recreational gold panning. Dominating this north-west corner of California are the rugged Klamath Mountains, a wilderness area of high craggy peaks, glacial lakes and fast-flowing rivers, but once an Eldorado, second only to the fabled Mother Lode in California in gold production. Much of the gold recovered from the Klamath Mountains was alluvial, panned from the rich blue gravel in the riverbeds, or mined from shallow shafts sunk into gold-bearing ground, the excavated dirt winched to the surface and washed. Between 1880 and 1959, Siskiyou County produced a massive 1.3 million troy ounces of gold, with probably as much again being mined but unrecorded in the previous thirty years.

The county town for Siskiyou is Yreka, founded in 1851 when Abraham Thompson, a member of a mule train travelling south from Oregon territory, discovered gold. First known as Shasta Butte City, that was changed by settlers because of confusion with a town of the same name in neighbouring Shasta County. So it became Yreka, deriving from the Indian word "Ieka," meaning white mountain, or cave. At the turn of the 19th century, Yreka had three newspapers, the *Union*, the *Journal*, and *Sisson Mascot*. The last published an identical announcement of the death of John Rees. But the Union went further with a brief account of an inquest that was held. According to this, when Rees's body was found by D. C. Earhart on open ground between the Hornbrook

Hotel and a local store, there was blood flowing from his mouth. On account of the circumstances and in the absence of witnesses, an inquest was held at which the coroner recorded a verdict of accidental death, after he concluded Rees, aged 78, who had for several years suffered from asthma, had died of a brain haemorrhage. While no official inquest report or death certificate survive, it is clear from other records that for thirty years before he died this John Rees had lived in a remote mining community called Cottonwood Creek, a few miles from Hornbrook.

In the second half of the 19th century just about everywhere in northern California was remote. But not as remote as it was before the discovery of gold in 1848 near Sutter's Mill, a saw mill owned by General John Sutter, a German settler who was hoping to establish a colony on a fork of the American River, where it joined the Sacramento. Desperate to find a new supply of timber for his mill, Sutter sent his contractor James Marshall to explore the mountains in the vicinity of Coloma. After he had been away a month, Marshall returned, indicating he wanted to speak to Sutter privately. When they were alone and the door locked, Marshall took a rag from his pocket and unwrapped about two ounces of yellow metal, which he thought was gold although others had said he was crazy. After testing the metal with aqua fortis, Sutter declared it was indeed gold of at least 23 carats. The following day on clearing out the gravel from the tail-race of the mill they found small pieces of gold on the bed; and every day it was the same, a piece of which Sutter made into a ring, inscribed, *"The first gold discovered in January 1848."*

The California Gold Rush had a greater impact on state-building than any single event in American history. Prior to the discovery of Sutter's Gold, the population was estimated at 15,000. By the end of the first year it had reached 100,000 and at the height of the gold rush in 1852 it was 240,000. California was acquired by the United States under the Treaty of Guadalupe Hidalgo, when the Mexican War ended in 1848, together with Arizona, New Mexico, and parts of Utah, Nevada and Colorado. For many Americans in the east, the acquisition of these new territories was an obstacle to growth, comprising, for the most part, a mass of arid wasteland. Worse still for the abolitionists, California and the new West might become part of the slave-holding south.

But the discovery of gold changed all this, and not just for California, which within two years was propelled by its new wealth into statehood. Recession had loomed at the end of the Mexican War as contracts were cancelled, and tens of thousands of discharged soldiers joined the ranks of the unemployed. Neither could continental Europe escape the recession that now overwhelmed the American economy. As for Britain, its trade had been stalled by rebellion in Ireland and an outbreak of cholera. But now the wilderness identity of California was shattered for ever by the cry, *"Gold, gold on the American River."*

The first gold was taken from an eighteen-inch thick layer of black sand on the banks of the American River, early prospectors scooping it out with spoons at the rate of $25 worth a day. In the boom that followed, that amount was barely sufficient to buy a spade or shovel. Washed down from the Sierra Nevada Mountains, gold deposits were discovered in river after river across the region. The news that even a child could pick three dollars worth a day from a stream, spread like a prairie fire, first to the east coast then beyond to Europe. The legendary city of Eldorado, it was claimed, was but a sand bank compared with the riches flowing down the rivers and streams of California. Londoners were soon as excited as Americans at the thought of picking up nuggets. The result was a shift of population the like of which has rarely been experienced. Three-quarters of the houses in San Francisco were deserted; every blacksmith, carpenter, lawyer had left; brick yards, saw-mills and ranches stood idle; the city's two newspapers ceased publication when their staff set out for the gold fields. Farmland was deserted, crops left to rot in the fields, stock unattended. Arriving at San Francisco, ships were abandoned by passengers and crew as they all rushed to catch the next steamer up the Sacramento River to the diggings where lawyers, judges and labourers jostled to stake their claims.

In the early days, nine tenths of the prospectors were foreigners, mostly arriving by the cheapest route – by ox-teams across the plains. Otherwise, California was a seven-month voyage by sailing clipper from New York around Cape Horn, or the shorter route across the Isthmus of Panama with a good chance of dying from cholera or yellow fever before ever reaching California. Many arrived too late, the most productive 'rivers of gold' already played out, leaving little alternative but to push further north towards the Oregon border in the hope of striking the fabled mother lode from which these glittering riches spilled down the rivers. That fountainhead was rumoured to be a distant volcano in the Klamath Mountains, and in 1850 an expedition set out to find it by penetrating a dense wilderness of redwood forests. Although failing to discover their Eldorado, the expedition did stumble upon rich gold deposits in Cottonwood Creek where it joined the Klamath River, twenty miles north-east of Yreka and to the west of Hornbrook. Very soon a thriving gold camp had sprung up, flourishing for five years with even a post office at one stage.[2] According to the 1870 census, Cottonwood Township had a population of approximately 200, one of those listed being "John Rees," described as a stock raiser and native of Wales.[3] The record shows his immediate neighbours were a family called Thomas and another by the name of Ellis, also from Wales, their occupation miners and farmers. It was not uncommon for men to divide their time between ranch work during the dry, hot summer months, and mining in winter, when water was more plentiful to work the sluices on the gold claims. The availability of water was critical for the gold mines. Without it, miners could not wash their pay dirt, and in summer they often chose to suspend operations rather than pay the exorbitant tariffs charged by those who controlled the water sources supplying the diggings.

Even when the peak of gold production had passed, California's population boom continued, reaching 650,000 by the 1870 census. By then it was evident that for the smooth administration of government, voter registration was essential and so California's *"Great Register of Voters"* was created.[4] The first of these in 1867 listed "John Reese, Cottonwood" but omitted all other detail. Nine years later, the *Great Register* of 1877 records "John Reese, Wales, miner, Cottonwood," but gives his age as 52 when actually it was 61. Two years later the listing reveals his true age as being 64 in 1879, describes him as a farmer, and discloses for the first time that Reese had become a US citizen. The naturalisation process took place at the 9th District Court, Siskiyou County on July 16, 1859, the official record stating that Reese was *"formerly of Schuylkill County, Pennsylvania"* and that he had taken the oath renouncing his previous citizenship. The legislation at that time required two witnesses to testify he was a right and proper person for American citizenship, but there is no record of such statements having been produced.[5] This is hardly surprising. Reese lived in a mining camp where not too many questions were asked about a man's past, and where the judges administering the oath of allegiance were often themselves miners, not too concerned about the letter of the law. Was Reese the Argonaut from Schuylkill County, Pennsylvania, the same John Rees the Chartist who escaped from Britain with a price on his head? Schuylkill County had one of the largest concentrations of Welsh miners in the whole of Pennsylvania and west Virginia. The sanctuary offered by towns like Ferndale, Jonestown, Llewellyn and Newtown would certainly have appealed to a Welshman on the run. Did Rees use the $50 he raised from the sale of his Donation Certificate in Matamoros to head for the Californian goldfields? For the vast army of unemployed after the Mexican War, the Rio Grande was the first leg of the southern route into California across the arid Sonora Desert, before striking north to San Francisco and the goldfields.

From the Rees (Reese) entries in the *"Great Registers"* of California, the impression is of a man who, while wanting to register to exercise his democratic right to vote, covered his tracks by lying about his age at almost every registration for thirty years. But in the year before he was found dead in neighbouring Hornbrook, he at last admitted to his true age! The *"Great Register"* of 1892 spells his name correctly as "John Rees," and gives his correct age, 77. Described as a miner, he is stated to be 5ft 7 inches tall, of light complexion, with blue eyes and, predictably, given his age, grey hair. This is unquestionably the Reese of previous Cottonwood Township registrations, because the naturalisation details, which are included from 1859, are identical. Besides the *"Great Register"* of 1892 there is further confirmatory evidence from the California Census of 1870 at which time Rees was a guest in a hotel at Etna. This records his age as 55, and born in 1815 in Wales, also stated to be the birthplace of his parents.[6] The significance of all this is that the birth date confirmed by the census return, and that listed in his last *Great Register* entry, tally with the age profile of John Rees, volunteer in the Texas War of Independence. When he enlisted for the second time in 1836, after his escape from the Goliad Massacre, and three years before returning to Wales and the Chartist Uprising, he gave his age as 21.

John Rees was still living on Cottonwood Creek in 1893, although by then it was a ghost town soon to disappear forever. The gold rush was over and the snow-covered Klamath Mountains no place for an aging miner. Winter arrives early in this part of northern California, persuading Rees perhaps to seek shelter and companionship in neighbouring Hornbrook. By now suffering from poor health, was Rees in the habit of moving to town to escape the harsh winters? His body was found only a short distance from the hotel where he was staying.

Unmarried, a 'loner' with a past, John Rees, the Texas War veteran, Chartist leader, California Argonaut in search of the Golden Fleece, must have shared at least one secret with someone: the date on which he was born and where. The Henley/Hornbrook cemetery is a small, well-kept plot with a large number of unmarked graves and indecipherable markers, the names worn away by time and weather. Most miners died penniless, a lump of anonymous rock set in some remote corner of some distant land, their only headstone. But not John Rees. His headstone is inscribed with the words, *"Rees, John, born March 4, 1815, died November 13, 1893. Native of Wales."*[7] Of the many Rees's from Wales who emigrated to the United States in the mid-19th century, there are only two born on or about March 4, 1815 whose births are recorded in the parish records. Both as it so happens were from Merthyr Tydfil. The first John Davis Reese was born on that very day, March 4, 1815. But he was not christened until 1869, by which time he was a Mormon, settled in Brigham City, Utah, with sixteen children and four wives, the first of these he married at St Mary's Church, Merthyr in 1842, two years *after* Rees the Chartist leader fled the country.[8] The second John Rees was christened on April 2, 1815, at Zoar Independent Chapel, Merthyr, the son of Thomas and Martha Rees.[9] This was a month after the birth date scrawled on that gold miner's gravestone in the Henley-Hornbrook Cemetery. Perhaps inconclusive and circumstantial, but the balance of evidence supports the contention that the last resting place of Jack the Fifer, Texas War veteran, and fugitive Chartist leader, is a cemetery in what was once a Californian gold mining town.

NOTES

1. *Yreka Union,* 23 November 1893, p3, col. 4; *Yreka Journal,* 22 November 1893, p3, col.4; *Sisson Mascot,* 13 November 1893.
2. Theodore H. Hittell, *History of California* (San Francisco, 1897, N. J. Stone and Co.), Vol. II.
3. John Rees, Census Microfilm Records, California 1870, series M593, Roll 89, Part 1, Page 590A.
4. Great Register, Siskiyou County, California, Genealogical Society of Siskiyou, *County Quarterly* (Yreka, CA), vol. 18:1 (Fall 1989), pp20-23: col. 18:2 (Winter 1989), pp12-15: vol. 18:3 (Spring 1990), pp16-19.**
5. John Rees, Naturalisation Certificate, Superior Court of California, Siskiyou County Office, Yreka.
6. John Rees, Census Microfilm Records: California 1870, series M593, Roll 89, Part 1, Page 590A; Great Register, Siskiyou County, California, Genealogical Society of Siskiyou, *County Quarterly* (Yreka, CA), vol. 18:1 (Fall 1989), pp 20-23: col. 18:2 (Winter 1989), pp12-15: vol. 18:3 (Spring 1990), pp16-19.
7. Hornbrook-Henley Cemetery, Hornbrook, Siskiyou County, California.
8. Church of Latter Day Saints, Family History Centre, Heol y Dero, Rhiwbina, Cardiff
9. GRO (Cardiff), Merthyr Parish records.

* Those who participated in the rush to the California Goldfields in 1849 were known either as the 49ers or Argonauts, the latter an allusion to Jason and the Argonauts, who in Greek mythology went in search of the Golden Fleece.

** **JOHN REESE (or Rees)** – Siskiyou County Great Register record:

1867: Reese, John, Cottonwood.

1876: Reese, John, 52 *(correct age 61),* Wales, miner, Cottonwood.

1877: Reese, John, 52 *(correct age 62),* Wales, miner, Cottonwood.

1879: Reese, John 64 *(correct age),* Wales, Farmer, Cottonwood, July 16, 1859, Siskiyou County, Cal., 9th District (naturalisation), Jan 31, 1879 (registration).

1886: Reese, John 64 *(correct age 71),* Wales, Farmer, Cottonwood, July 15, 1859 Siskiyou County, Cal., 9th District (naturalisation), Jan 3, 1879;

1888: Reese, John 64 *(correct age 73),* Wales, Farmer, Cottonwood, July 15, 1859 Siskiyou Co., 9th District (naturalisation), January 13, 1879 (registration).

1892: Rees, John 77 *(correct age),* 5ft 7, light complex, blue eyes, grey hair, Miner, Cottonwood, Hornbrook (postal district), July 15, 1859, Siskiyou Co., Cal District (naturalisation), September 2, 1892 (registration).

CHAPTER 13

Conclusion

Resolute, fearless, indefatigable, single-minded: Zephaniah Williams certainly had the distinguishing marks of a revolutionary, together with the esteem necessary to persuade others to follow where he led. But if he was an acknowledged leader of the working classes committed to toppling the established order, why then did he never at any time during the 34 years following that momentous event in Newport offer a word of explanation, or moral justification beyond the alleged confession aboard the *Mandarin* **after** his conviction and sentence, a confession Professor David Williams suggests was opportunistic?[1] The jury at his trial for High Treason saw only a broken man filled with remorse for what had occurred. Apart from deep contrition and his profound denials that it was ever the intention to wage war upon the monarch, Zephaniah had nothing further to add.[2]

The series of letters written to his wife from Van Diemen's Land do, however, provide some scraps of explanation but only because of one word, 'infatuation', the only word Zephaniah ever offers to describe his complicity in the Uprising. Writing about his disappointment at not being rewarded with some remission of sentence for his bravery in subduing the rioting lunatics at New Norfolk, Zephaniah blames this on the local magistrate *"one of the old faction and a bitter tyrant* (who) *never forgets the probable result of our infatuated design."*[3]

Judging from those few letters that have survived, the long separation from family and home weighed more heavily on Williams than on his two companions. An overwhelming sense of desperation and shame bleeds from almost every line of the correspondence, at times the writer sounding positively suicidal. *"Many are the unhappy hours I have endured when reflecting upon that insane and infatuated course which led me to the awful desperation,"* he wrote again from New Norfolk.[4] Zephaniah appeared to have difficulty convincing his wife of his determination to remain *"humble, obedient, submissive"* in the face of all provocation, almost as if she expected his impetuosity to lead to further trouble. He wrote, *"I hope (this) will set your mind at rest and exonerate me from all culpability ever since that infatuated affair which placed me in this unhappy and miserable situation."*[5]

No letters from Joan to her husband have apparently survived although there can be little doubt they were written from Zephaniah's response to his wife's concerns when he replies, *"The conduct of the Chartists towards you has been precisely what I had anticipated. It is as you justly observe, the man and not the principle they love, and even the very one, too, who has been the sole cause of our failures, misfortunes and sufferings."*[6]

This is the most intriguing of Zephaniah's few pronouncements on the Chartists and the Uprising, his reprimand implying betrayal by some unnamed person. Such a person could have been Fergus O'Connor, leader of the 'physical force' wing, whose bitter rivalry with William Lovett, the 'moral force' founder of the movement, ultimately caused its collapse. On the other hand, was Zephaniah referring to the 'darling' of the Monmouthshire Chartists, the young 'missionary' Henry Vincent who had charmed his way into the hearts and minds of the valleys' working classes, boosting their expectations, and urging them to prepare for revolutionary struggle, only to renounce physical force a month after the uprising failed outside the Westgate?[7] One of the most fluent and effective of the Chartist speakers, Vincent spoke with a rush, his torrent of words all sound and fury, sweeping everything and everyone before him. He achieved his greatest popularity among the Monmouthshire colliers, who suspected that after Vincent had endured two periods of imprisonment, the government had finally found a way to silence their favourite. Fergus O'Connor was his only rival as the movement's most popular speaker, the 'moral force' faction accusing the pair of making speeches inciting the Newport riot. After his release from prison, a restrained Vincent spoke only of a *"quiet revolution,"* believing Chartists should concentrate on *"mental and moral improvement"* by linking themselves to the temperance movement, not something calculated to appeal to members in Glamorgan and Monmouthshire. Vincent and O'Connor had been close allies, but they disagreed about temperance and, later, physical force, and the two drifted apart, O'Connor acquiring undisputed leadership of the Chartists in 1841.[8]

On balance, Zephaniah Williams more probably meant O'Connor, when he wrote to his wife of the person responsible for all their misfortunes, because it would seem that John Frost was also critical of the Irishman. Writing to O'Connor from aboard the convict ship *Mandarin,* Frost told him bluntly, *"Your prognostications were wrong; you have not proved yourself a true prophet, either as to the punishment or its extent."* Unable to unite the warring factions, O'Connor succeeded only in destroying Chartist credibility. Outside his personal circle of friends, he was regarded as a charlatan, an adventurer who traded on the passions of people for his own profit, at the very least a victim of his own delusions. At his best, however, O'Connor could touch a chord with the working classes that vibrated around the country, at the same time filling the pages of his *Northern Star* with the same fire and passion.[9] By 1850, the movement Karl Marx and Frederich Engels predicted would be the first political party of the proletariat in the socialist revolution, was as good as dead, its leader, O'Connor, himself dying from syphilis in an insane asylum five years later.

The few snatches of reflective recriminations contained in the Zephaniah Williams correspondence reveals a man who, while admitting to his own foolishness, insinuates others were responsible for involving him in the 'insane' affair. In some ways the letters are important for what they do not say about November 4, 1839, conveying, as this does, the impression Zephaniah, once a man of public stature and aspiring entrepreneur, considered the Uprising a shameful embarrassment that ruined his family and destroyed his reputation. This view is corroborated by his subsequent efforts to restore professional reputation and public status in Tasmania, a process of rehabilitation somewhat blighted by his extravagant claims for Tasmanian coal that persuaded nearly 100 souls from Wales to quit their homes for a life in the bush. Admittedly, Zephaniah could have provided his wife with the republican version of the affair in the letters he claimed he wrote during his first years of captivity at Port Arthur, but which Joan never received. Despite allegations by family and supporters in Britain he been held incommunicado, Zephaniah never once asked for pen and paper to write a letter during the three years he was detained at Port Arthur, according to the commandant, Captain James O'Hara Booth.[10] The commandant's office was the only source of writing materials for inmates, and the letterbox for all mail to and from the penal settlement.

The surviving correspondence confirms suspicions arising earlier from Zephaniah's mining ventures, that he was an altogether impetuous individual, quite different from the excessively cautious leader of the Chartist Uprising, which is how he is usually portrayed. Joan Williams is concerned not so much for her husband's health or well being in captivity, but for his conduct, to the extent of needing his re-assurance *"not to transgress."* She would have known more than anyone that the one thing her husband and John Rees had in common was that they were among life's adventurers, to the point even of recklessness. Not only had Zephaniah driven his family into bankruptcy, the same impulsiveness could so easily have landed him in gaol after the attempted hijacking of Cwrt-y-Bella Colliery, owned by two of the most powerful men in the county. To follow this, almost immediately, with what some believe was an ill-conceived, poorly executed plot to overthrow the government was irrational, or as he preferred to describe it, "insane."[11]

Zephaniah Williams's transportation to Van Diemen's Land as a political prisoner, was followed by the inevitable speculation his leadership of the Chartist Uprising must have been the inevitable consequence of a life devoted to political activism. If, as Ivor Wilks concludes, the roots of the uprising lay deep in the Welsh past, an explosion in class consciousness, then it follows the leaders might have been drawn from the ranks of the workers.[12] Some were, but certainly not Zephaniah Williams. Geologist, mining engineer, and ambitious coal owner, he would not have automatically related to the largely illiterate Chartists who descended from the hills, although this does not mean Zephaniah was unconcerned with their grievances. He had worked with them for thirty years, at times suffering the same hardships and sense of alienation, despite his essentially literate, middle-class background, and entrepreneurial aspirations. As R. R. W. Lingen, one of the Commissioners involved in the "Inquiry into the State of Education in Wales" in 1847, remarked, the workers inhabited an "*under-world,*" socially and intellectually isolated from all influences apart from those arising in their own "*order.*" In the works, the labourer had no hope of being promoted into the office either as a clerk or agent, his employer content to ignore his existence, accepting no responsibility beyond paying him a wage. The Government Inspector, Tremenheere, dispatched hurriedly to Wales at the end of December 1839, to investigate to what extent ignorance contributed to the troubles, had reached much the same conclusion that relations between employers and employed were of the "*worst description,*" the ignorance of the workers "*pitiable.*"[13]

It seems most unlikely that Zephaniah, the well-educated son of a relatively prosperous yeoman farmer, Minerals Agent for the Quaker Ironmasters, the Harfords, for ten years, could have risen from the "*stagnant pool*" described by Lingen, Tremenheere and others. The properties and possessions Zephaniah inherited from his father Thomas Williams at Blackwood and Tredegar, his marriage into the once wealthy family of Llewellyn Llewellyn, late of Machen and Penyderi, suggest the family enjoyed a quality of life, even gentility, unfamiliar to the tide of illiterate, largely immigrant, workers flooding into Monmouthshire from all parts of England and Wales. The influx had created a dreadful quagmire, physically brutal and socially crushing, from which there appeared to be no escape. That the workers, even the most uninformed among them, were genuinely aggrieved is undeniable: lacking in property rights, the labouring classes could not make their voices heard in the greatest capitalist revolution the world had ever seen. The vital role of labour was denied a partnership in this industrial and social revolution, leaving the workers resentful and with a deep distrust of their mainly English employers. In this regard, Ivor Wilks is correct when he says they saw their oppressors as alien oppressors.[14] The labouring classes of the Black Domain formed a proletariat sharing the same experiences and problems. But it was a proletariat that did not even own its own labour, so complete was the control exercised by the bourgeoisie, extending beyond its monopoly of the means of production to the food they ate, and all this legitimised and defended by a totally unrepresentative legislature. To stretch this as Ivor Wilks does, with the assistance of the Williams 'confession,' into a full-blown socialist revolution, an armed class struggle driven by a determination to seize control of the commanding heights of the economy, requires an act of political faith. This is not to say the workers of the Black Domain were not experiencing an emerging class-consciousness, but as was the case at the time of the Merthyr Rising of 1831 there was no sign of it having become politicised. That it also occurred *before* Marx began formulating his theories of working class consciousness and workers revolution is immaterial, apart from the confirmation afforded by hindsight. The *Communist Manifesto* (1848) and *Das Kapital* (1867) were not necessary for spontaneous combustion. But revolution and the creation of either an English or Silurian Republic was not on the agenda for the majority of Chartist marchers as they poured into Newport. Neither were their actions, as Wilks believes, in the tradition of Welsh self-determination, even though David Jones concedes that the idea of a people's army descending from the hills was not new in Welsh history. If an analysis of the depositions sworn by almost three hundred witnesses can be safely used as a yardstick, then a very large proportion of those participating in the march were English. Instead of being a manifestation of Welsh self-determination, the Chartist Uprising had repercussions that dealt a body blow to national aspirations. Sensibly dismissing the notion of a workers revolution, David Jones finds it hard to escape the conclusion that the Newport outbreak was a local occurrence, that may or may not have been conceived as part of a larger rising.[15]

The employers, ironmaster and coal owners, had no doubt the root cause of the troubles was ignorance and gullibility. The Varteg, Pontypool ironmaster R. Kenrick, probably closer to his workers than most, considered the large majority ignorant and impulsive, easily led. One wonders whether he had Frost, Williams and Jones in mind when he described the labouring class as *"predisposed to believe anything which these prophets may predict . . . the moving mass, which now on one side, now shifting to the other, like the Goodwin sands."* Not mentioned specifically by Kenrick in his lecture to Pontypool Mechanics Institute, few, however, would have doubted it was the Chartists he described as uninformed and credulous, prepared to believe anyone who told them they were *"oppressed, wretched, miserable."*[16]

Kenrick was not alone in branding the Chartist marchers as ignorant. Tremenheere found that a large proportion of the adult population in Bedwellty, Aberystruth, Mynyddislwyn, Trevethin, and Merthyr, the five parishes generally regarded as constituting the 'Disturbed District', could neither read nor write: very many had only acquired the art of knowing the letters and words.[17] Not insensitive or unsympathetic to the situation in Monmouthshire, Tremenheere was still blaming parental ignorance for the desperate social problems when he returned for a further inspection *thirteen* years later.[18]

The influence of O'Connor and Vincent through their speeches and radical newspapers, the *Northern Star* and *Western Vindicator,* on what was already a volatile society cannot be over-stated. The year both men spent in prison, 1841, coincided with the rapid decline in support for Chartism in Monmouthshire, following the massacre outside the Westgate. For a time, the movement continued to flourish in Glamorgan, especially in Merthyr where Morgan Williams remained active for a short time. Sent to London as a South Wales delegate to the Chartist Convention in May 1841, Williams told a meeting on Clerkenwell Green that Chartism had *"fallen off"* in South Wales, and that the families of the three transported leaders were in *"extreme want."*[19] Whether it was the depression that gripped the coalfield from 1840 onwards, forcing the workers to focus on survival rather than politics, Chartism very soon lost its appeal. Even Morgan Williams withdrew from active participation, eventually leaving Merthyr to return to Newtown, so that by 1842 the movement in Wales was effectively dead.

Unlike Frost, Zephaniah Williams had no proven track record as a spokesman for the Chartists until quite late in the campaign of 1839. That he then very quickly became prominent is undeniable. According to contemporary newspaper accounts, Zephaniah's Chartism did not surface publicly until the meeting at Nantyglo on March 31, 1839, addressed by the young firebrand Henry Vincent.[20] Although Chartism never captured the imagination of the rank and file until Christmas 1838, if Williams was a late recruit, as seems likely, there was good reason for him remaining in the background until Vincent's meeting outside the *Royal* Oak. Only the day before, March 30, the judge at Monmouthshire Quarter Sessions had, on account of a technicality, cleared him, his brother-in-law Edmund Llewellyn, and others of hijacking the Prothero/Phillips Cwrt-y-Bella Colliery at Penyderi; and this after criminal proceedings lasting almost a year. Even then the matter had not been resolved fully, the civil action arising from the affair was still awaiting judgement in the Chancery Court.[21] It was not until Zephaniah had walked free from court at the end of March that reports begun circulating, substantiated by witnesses at the trial, of the *Royal Oak* being used for Chartist meetings, recruitment, and in the last week before the uprising for the distribution of weapons, which Zephaniah always maintained were for defence only.[22]

Besides his frequent incursions into the licensing trade, Zephaniah's familiarity with colliers had just as much to do with the fact that as Minerals Agent for the Harford's he spent a large part of his working life employing them, to supply coal for the ironworks or in his own mines at various times. Public houses and beer shops were traditionally used by master miners to settle up with their colliers at the end of the 'long pay.'[23] Only the Saturday before the march, the Abergavenny Brewery Company had delivered £200 in silver to Zephaniah at the *Royal Oak* at Blaina, clearly unaware of what was about to happen. Zephaniah had returned to the licensing trade at the *Royal Oak* not many months before the march on Newport, not because, as Oliver Jones surmises, to plan the campaign, but more likely because he had lost his job as Minerals Agent for the Harfords following the Cwrt-y-Bella Colliery break-in.[24] The Chartist leader was concerned the affair would cost him his job when Summers Harford appeared as one of the examining justices.[25]

What little that has been uncovered about preparations for the march has led those wedded to the idea of a workers revolution to conclude the full extent of the rebel organisation will never be known; that they destroyed all records, and fled the area. This ignores the very real possibility the Chartists may not have kept records beyond a few account books for members' subscriptions.[26] Whatever preparations there were seemed confined entirely to the preceding week, and the meeting of delegates at the *Coach and Horses* in Blackwood on Friday, November 1. The question arises whether the delegates then agreed to a greatly modified plan. Zephaniah's 'confession' suggests so, while the account of the eccentric Pontypridd surgeon, Dr William Price, implies he pulled out at the eleventh hour because the proposed action had been reduced to the status of a united display of strength. That the doctor got no further than the door of the room in which the delegates were meeting, suggests perhaps an altercation with John Frost. It is clear from Price's memoirs forty years later he regarded the plan as very different from what had been agreed a few weeks earlier at the *King Crispin* (or *Twyn y Star*). Whatever that was – and it could have been the full-blooded rising described in the Williams' 'confession' – it had been replaced with something far less ambitious.[27]

If a national revolution was uppermost in the minds of Price and others like John Rees, the vast majority set off from Blaina, Blackwood and Pontypool for a demonstration in the centre of Newport in support of electoral reform, believing this was the only way to gain a more equitable share of the fabulously rich iron and coal wealth beneath the Black Domain. If there was a discernible 'call to arms' it did not spring from the tradition of Welsh self-determination or latent socialism as Wilks imagines, but something far more prosaic: pay and conditions. In an age when everyone has the vote but too few bother to do so, it is hard to understand the feelings of those who were denied it. Access to legislation through the ballot box would give the Chartists the opportunity to *"tackle the masters."*[28] The Uprising might have died in a maelstrom of competing interests, the *"mass of confusing evidence . . . several plans, last-minute decisions and divergence between intentions and execution,"* described by David Jones. But it was not born out of ignorance of how best to resolve the prevailing social and economic problems, nor was it a local rising conceived originally as part of a national insurrection.[29] Considering the inevitable financial turmoil that would have ensued, and the necessity for marchers to set aside resources as insurance for a period of enormous instability, how was it the level of withdrawals from local Savings Banks were no higher in the week preceding the march?

Furthermore, as the marchers gathered on the mountain above Blaina, the men were told they would be away two days only, hardly long enough to overthrow the British Empire![30] By November 1839, the Charter had mutated into a solution for all grievances, real and imagined, debated endlessly in public houses and beer shops across the Black Domain, arousing the labouring classes from their deprivation, and raising considerable expectations. Despite the disappointment of the rejected petition to the House of Commons, the failure of the 'Sacred Month' of protest, the collapse of the National Convention, and Frost's reluctance to lead them, Monmouthshire Chartism had become unstoppable. For some the march would be about *"making the poor as rich as the rich."* For John Rees ('Jack the Fifer'), his friend David Jones ('Dai the Tinker'), and the *"most aggressive leaders of the Welsh Chartist associations"* the intention would be to subvert the peaceful demonstration planned by Frost, Williams and Jones.[31]

Zephaniah Williams was drawn to Chartism because electoral reform was a just cause, and he realised more than the rank and file that without it, neither he, regardless of all his efforts to get a foothold in the mining industry, nor anyone else would break the monopoly of the employers. That on the day of the march he absented himself from the front line of the marchers, rounding up the stragglers at the rear, might indicate he feared for what would happen when they arrived in Newport, and certainly had no intention of providing the spark that ignited the confrontation outside the Westgate. When the shots were fired Zephaniah was 600 yards away at the top of Stow Hill, only able to watch as the smoke rose above the scene of the conflict. Although John Frost had reluctantly consented to lead the protest, the former mayor of Newport and magistrate had, despite his fiery speeches, no stomach for bloodshed, confiding in 1856, *"So far from leading the working men of South Wales, it was they who led me; they asked me to go with them, and I was not disposed to throw them aside."*[32] The Chartist rank and file wanted a figurehead, someone of repute and status whose presence gave their protest credibility. But by the time they wheeled around at the bottom of Stow Hill to face the Westgate and someone shouted, *"Mr Frost, appearance to the front"* the Newport draper had fled the scene apparently in tears in anticipation it was all about to go horribly wrong.

William Jones and his Pontypool contingent never got as far as Newport, the part-time actor a voice three miles off stage at Malpas when the soldiers threw open the shutters of the hotel windows. No matter what were the real intentions of the leadership, the majority of the marchers had no idea of any plan, beyond a demonstration of support for the Charter and the alleviation of the conditions suffered by Vincent and others in Monmouth Gaol. To this they now added the release of Chartist prisoners arrested the previous night and detained at the Westgate, which explains why on arriving outside the hotel the 'leader' of the marchers demanded of those inside, *"Surrender yourselves, our prisoners,"* *"Surrender yourselves as our prisoners,"* or *"Surrender our prisoners."* Considering the din, the exact words uttered and their meaning has always been disputed. What is certain is that by then neither Frost, Williams nor Jones were leading the marchers. Most of the demonstrators scattered when the soldiers unleashed their first murderous volley, the few who stood their ground inviting a further two volleys from the 45th. In ten minutes it was all over, twenty two men either dead or dying.

So who was this 'leader' who stepped forward from the crowd? The most likely candidate was John Rees. From the moment the Chartist column left Tredegar Park, Rees appears to have assumed the leadership, issuing instructions to the marchers at the Courtybella Weighing Machine to form ranks six or eight abreast, and positioning a gun carrier at the end of every other rank. At that point Rees was seen with a pistol in one hand, a pike in the other. When the column turned the corner into the front of the Westgate, he led the way, waving the marchers on with a sword. Rees was the only person identified as the likely leader of the attack on the Westgate.[33]

But did he fire the first shot? In the vanguard of the group that stormed up the steps of the hotel, pushing into the passageway was an unidentified person who pointed a pistol at the head of special constable Thomas Oliver stationed at the door, demanding of him to *"Surrender us our prisoners"* or words to that effect. Instinctively, as one of the constables standing behind him shouted *"No, never,"* Oliver slammed the door on his would-be assailant, the pistol discharging its shot three inches from the constable's head.[34] This could have been the shot Daniel Evans heard from the doorway of his house directly opposite the hotel. While it was generally thought a Chartist fired first, Evans was convinced the first shot came from within the passageway of the hotel immediately the demonstrators pushed their way in. But he also stated, contrary to the evidence given by the mayor and Lieutenant Gray, that the soldiers fired into the air *before* the shutters were removed from the windows, a suggestion contradicted by Lieutenant Gray, on the grounds that soldiers never fired other than at their targets. If they had fired at the men in the passageway, before their presence was revealed to the demonstrators by the removal of the shutters from the long room windows, this was not so much an act of High Treason by the Chartists as wilful murder by the 45th Regiment of Foot. The soldiers were an easy target when the shutters were removed, standing shoulder to shoulder in two ranks, muskets loaded and ready. Pressed by Lord Chief Justice Tindal to state how many were wounded by incoming fire after they were exposed to the Chartists gathered outside, Lieutenant Gray insisted, *"Only one, Sergeant Daily."* Consequently, the defence made much of this in the hope of convincing the jury that immediately the crowd saw soldiers at the window it desisted, and as it did not knowingly fire on them, Frost, Williams and Jones were not guilty of High Treason. Sergeant Daily never gave his evidence of the incident after he was withdrawn as a witness on account of a technicality, the Chief Justice ruling his address had been incorrectly stated. In his deposition before the magistrates, however, Daily said they returned fire into the passage and street after the Chartists entered the hotel and tried to force their way into the long room. Daily spent thirteen days recovering from his wounds at the home of the mayor, a kindness for which he expressed himself infinitely grateful.[35]

Gray was mistaken or lying when he told the court that Daily was the 45th's only casualty. No mention was made at either the trial or in contemporary accounts of Sergeant John Armstrong, a second member of the regiment wounded at the Westgate. It beggars belief that the existence of this second casualty, who was treated in the Workhouse sick bay for several days afterwards, completely escaped the attention of the army, and the wounded soldier's commanding officer, Lieutenant Gray. Why was Armstrong never called to give evidence, nor even asked to provide a statement to the examining magistrates? Was it because his evidence might have contradicted the lieutenant's account of the affair as far as it referred to who fired first? Such suspicions are perfectly legitimate, and material to the part played by the detachment from the 45th, because on November 13, 1839, only nine days after the massacre outside the Westgate, Armstrong was rewarded for his part in the affair by the Duke of Wellington with an immediate promotion to the Tower of London as a yeoman warder. To this day, the Tower has only 36 yeoman warders, these positions reserved for deserving, gallant and meritorious army sergeants of long-standing and exemplary character. The appointments, within the gift of the Duke of Wellington as Constable at the Tower, came with a range of benefits, such as free accommodation and extra pay. Besides their duties at the Tower, yeoman warders attend coronations, lying-in-state, and other state functions. Within nine days of the massacre, the *Iron Duke'* had removed a material witness from the scene of a crime that would end in the last great show trial in British legal history.[36]

Was there some ulterior motive for Sergeant Armstrong's hurried re-assignment? Wellington was certainly no friend of electoral reform. His opposition to the 1832 Reform Act is most remembered for his description of the then existing constitution as so perfect that he could not imagine anything better. Not only did this lead directly to his Government's defeat, it also earned him the epithet of *Iron Duke'* after railings were erected to protect his London home from stone-throwing crowds. If 160 years later a former Prime Minister and former Commander-in-Chief of the British Army removed a material witness in the manner Wellington had acted at Newport, it is not difficult to imagine the public outcry and the allegations of cover up and conspiracy. As for Armstrong, his sinecure did not last long; he died three years later from natural causes and is buried in the Tower. What part his injuries contributed to his early demise is not known.[37]

If the removal of Sgt Armstrong was an isolated incident it might have been explained as a coincidence, not an attempt to cover up potentially damaging evidence about the battle at the Westgate. But Sergeant Daily was also rewarded in a similar fashion, Wellington appointing him to an equally august military corps: a Yeoman of the Queen's Guard, the oldest of the royal bodyguards and the oldest military corps in Britain. Lieutenant Basil Gray was promoted major and given his own company. Soon afterwards, however, he was struck down by a paralysis and forced to retire on half pay to Ceylon where he died in 1889.[38]

The majority of the Chartists fled the moment the soldiers opened fire and they saw their first comrades fall. The whole incident would have been over within less than the ten minutes it was reported to have lasted, had it not been for the extended action in the passageway. From a close scrutiny of the available evidence, the conflict could just as easily have been started by the soldiers firing on the Chartist intruders in the passageway, or by the discharge of a pistol knocked aside by a door closing against it. On the other hand, that first shot could also have been fired deliberately by the person forcing his way through the door with the intention of escalating into bloody confrontation what many marchers thought was merely a display of unity. What is certain is that John Rees, the revolutionary from the Texas War of Independence, was the only Chartist leader placed at the centre of the action at this critical moment. Minutes later he was seen hurrying away from the scene of the carnage, down Commercial Street, boasting as he passed Samuel Smith the engine driver, *"Thank God; we have had one cut at them and knocked down three or four and they have not lost one of us,"* an admission that someone had *planned* to fire on the Queen's soldiers. If nothing else, this new evidence of the injuries suffered by Sergeant Armstrong, proves the Chartists were right in claiming a conspiracy by the Army to conceal the true scale of the casualties suffered by the 45th at the Westgate. The marchers believed there were even more.[39]

Whether the insurrection was real or something the prevailing mood led them to imagine, the mayor, Thomas Phillips, and Lieutenant Gray, were in no doubt an attack was imminent, positioning the troops in a room with immediate access to the main hotel passageway.[40] Monmouthshire's gentry had been expecting trouble for months, long before Chartism ever appeared on the political horizon, as the resentment of an alienated labour force incubated in the deteriorating conditions of the disturbed valley communities. Fear for their property and lives had become endemic among the gentry, the tyrannical ironmaster Crawshay Bailey, for one, sufficiently concerned to build a pair of fortified towers to defend his home at Nantyglo House, in addition to which he was reputed to have a secret escape tunnel from his works across the valley.

Insecurity and instability in the Black Domain had deteriorated to such an extent that three months before the attack on Newport, the Home Office sent the company from the 45th Regiment of Foot into the town, the presence of troops on the streets and in the public houses only adding to the tension.[41] While the role of the 45th at the Westgate has never been properly scrutinised, the revelation that it quite deliberately withheld information about its casualties, and spirited away a material witness within days of the massacre, adds credibility to this book's contention the regiment was not an entirely innocent party to the affair: that its niche in history as brave defenders of the town against a bloodthirsty mob needs to be challenged. The regiment had not long returned from India and the Burmese War, and as its nickname, the *"Old Stubborns"* implied, had an impressive list of battle honours, the most extraordinary of which, also involving Lieutenant Gray, occurred the previous year when the 45th brutally suppressed another set of rioters.

Bossenden Wood at Dunkirk in Kent on May 31, 1838 – and not the Chartist Uprising the following year – is generally considered to be the scene of the last armed rising on British soil. Though close to Canterbury, people of the neighbouring parishes were desperately poor, families close to starvation following the widespread unemployment caused by the introduction of farm mechanisation. This, and the new Poor Law meant many spent much of their lives in and out of workhouses. Into this scene of rural deprivation came a colourful character calling himself Sir William Courtenay, real name John Thom. Just 38, he was tall, dark and handsome, with immense charm, plausible and mad enough to have spent four years in an asylum. In earlier life he had attended meetings of the Spencean Society, a proto-socialist organisation, and he identified strongly with society's underdogs. He stood for Parliament in East Kent, but not surprisingly, since only the rich had the vote, he failed to get elected. Figuring that constitutional means would never solve the country's ills, or rid it of its conservative Establishment, he decided that rebellion was the only answer, aided by what he considered were his divine powers.

So raising a ragged army of jobless farm labourers, Courtenay announced, *"I'm now going to strike the bloody blow! The streets that have heretofore flowed with water shall flow with blood for the rights of the poor."* When a constable was sent to arrest some of the runaway labourers for deserting their master, Courtenay shot him dead. Accompanied by forty followers, he fled into the woods at Bossenden pursued by Lieutenant Gray and a detachment from the 45th Regiment of Foot. Although cornered, he refused to surrender, rushing upon one of the regiment's young officers and shooting him dead. A moment later Courtenay was knocked to the ground by a police constable and as he regained his feet he and seven others were shot dead by the soldiers. Twenty-seven of Courtenay's 'army' were arrested, not for High Treason, nor conspiracy, nor riot but for murder. Three were sentenced to death, commuted to transportation, the prosecutions against the others dropped. Eight rioters had been killed on the spot; others who were wounded died later and were buried by their friends.[42]

Eighteen months later the action taken by the 45th to suppress the Chartist Uprising in Newport was remarkably similar. So was what occurred at Free Derry Corner in the Bogside in 1972, when the first Parachute Regiment shot dead 13 Catholics during a civil rights march in Northern Ireland. According to the British Army version of events, the 1st Parachute Regiment was fired upon by IRA snipers, when it went to Derry's nationalist Bogside to arrest rioters. The return of fire by British troops culminated in what is now known as *'Bloody Sunday.'* Some eye witnesses have claimed only a single shot was fired at the soldiers before they opened up with their high velocity rifles, firing indiscriminately into the crowd in a calculated act to teach the nationalists of Derry a lesson. In all, the paratroopers fired 100 shots at the nationalist marchers, much the same as the three volleys discharged into the crowd outside the Westgate by the thirty soldiers from the 45th regiment. The main exchanges in the battle of the Bogside also lasted ten minutes, leaving seventeen injured in addition to the thirteen dead. As at Newport, there was also a suspected agent provocateur accused of firing the shot that triggered the Derry massacre.[43] Was the confrontation outside the Westgate a 19th century *'Bloody Monday'* and was it John Rees's finger on the trigger? Whether by design or accident, the 45th certainly taught the 'ignorant' Welsh a lesson, encouraged and supported by a bourgeoisie determined to defend its paramountcy against the radical demands of the men from the hills.

John Rees and others of a like mind failed in their attempted revolution at Newport, because the rank and file had not signed up to it. The factors competing for their support were as varied as they were contradictory, republicanism only one of these. While nothing is more germane in unravelling the contradictions that still swirl around the Uprising than a clearer understanding of the role of Rees, it would be an exaggeration to suggest he was the only republican among the leadership. Whether the Zephaniah Williams 'confession' is genuine or not, the Black Domain was awash with republican sentiment. Underpinning the demand for universal suffrage was the burning desire among Monmouthshire Chartists for freedom, which, as they saw it, was a prerequisite for purging public life of corruption and injustice, so that the common good could prevail above the interests of only one class. This was classical republicanism, *Res publica,* which means seeking to do what is best for the whole community. While its origins lay deep in the period of the Roman republic, the concepts were adopted by the leaders of the American Revolution who placed equality at the heart of a republican society in which distinctions were based only on merit. Emerging Welsh republicanism could not fail to have been influenced by the Declaration of Independence, the *"glorious 4th of July"* as Frost once observed. But there was a significant difference. Monmouthshire Chartists, on the whole, appear to have had no quarrel with the Monarch: it was the idle aristocracy, sponging upon the royal prerogative, and misappropriating tax revenue that they held responsible for all their grievances. Welsh republicanism was born out of a sense of political injustice and social deprivation, which might explain why Zephaniah Williams' admission to a republican plot, if indeed true, was not incompatible with his profound and abject denial in court that he had any intention to wage war on the Queen. Neither anti-monarchists nor revolutionaries, in the sense of seeking violent confrontation, they believed that given the opportunity through the ballot box they could run the country better and fairer than the Tory/Whig establishment. In this regard, the majority wanted to make republicans not revolutionaries: illogical perhaps by today's definition of political republicanism, and our ideas of violent revolution, but not ideological.

Ivor Wilks mistakenly applies the more common interpretation of republicanism, in reaching his conclusion that the men who marched on Newport *"aspired to a condition of self-determination that entailed separation from the bourgeois state."*[44] Even the most enthusiastic nationalist would find it hard to draw out from the mass of confusing evidence a shred of support for the notion of Welsh self-determination. If anything, the rising and the social clampdown that followed, set such ideas back a hundred years, maybe forever, by marginalizing Welsh nationalist radicalism. Any future progress down that road would, for the most part, be confined within the constitutional process. If the marchers never thought in terms of a nationalist revolt, neither did they reveal ambitions to seize the commanding heights of the economy. A greater share of the spoils from the Black Domain was one thing; seizing control of the ironworks and collieries was never on the agenda, and in that respect the Newport Uprising cannot be seen as a workers revolution. Beyond the claims made for it in Zephaniah's 'confession' and the recollections of Dr Price, the case for the Uprising being part of a general insurrection throughout Britain is poor. There was some suggestion that Newcastle Chartists had manufactured 60,000 pikes, and were stockpiling muskets, bayonets, shells and hand grenades for a rising to coincide with events at Newport. Northern Chartists had also been formed into companies of twelve each with a captain, all sworn to obey orders, maintain secrecy and execute traitors. When the night arrived and only 70 Chartists reported for action in Newcastle, it was decided that rather than rise they would burn the town to the ground. Then the news came about the defeat at Newport and the Newcastle Chartists resolved to await developments.[45] Professor David Williams had good reason to conclude, from the evidence of what transpired elsewhere in the country, that what happened at Newport was not part of a co-ordinated plan.[46]

In the aftermath of the attack on the Westgate there was plenty of verbal fury among Chartists across Britain; there was little by way of practical help for those in Monmouthshire, apart from launching a series of nation-wide campaigns and petitions for the release of Frost, Williams and Jones. None succeeded, and the Monmouthshire Chartists were left feeling alienated, abandoned by some of their national leaders for reacting prematurely, even unnecessarily. Frost, Williams and Jones had become local folk heroes, not so much for what they had done but for the unjust punishment they had suffered. Ironically, a most unexpected source of sympathy for the Chartist rank and file was the Government Solicitor General. In his closing speech to the jury at Monmouth, he absolved the vast majority of Chartist marchers from incrimination in High Treason on the grounds they were *"unfortunate and ignorant persons, with regard to some of whom the very object of the excursion was obliged to be translated into Welsh – persons who did not even understand our language, brought in immense masses to the spot, without knowing the object to which their attention was to be directed – told to bring arms in their hands, without knowing how or against whom they were to use them."* [47]

But for the ruling class of South Wales the battle at the Westgate was an alarm call, and its root causes, ignorance and Welshness, were synonymous. Whatever had produced this explosion of violence would not be permitted to occur again. That meant an immediate crack down on the lodges and beer houses the gentry regarded as the *"nucleii of sedition and hotbeds of treason,"* the suppression of pernicious unstamped newspapers, attacks on the evil of Chartism from the pulpits, and the reinforcement of the police throughout the county. Troublemakers were dismissed from the iron works and collieries. In the longer term, ignorance and Welshness would be throttled at birth by accelerating the process of Anglicisation and assimilation through education. [48]

By 1839 English had already made huge advances in the South Wales valleys. Although Welsh was still predominantly the language of the labouring classes, the influx of immigrants from England into Monmouthshire in particular had diluted its influence by 40 per cent in some districts like Trevethin. Conscious of the effect of immigration, the indigenous Welsh had, nevertheless, already reached a compact with immigrant English speakers, their resentment directed instead at the employers, and also the Irish, who were accused by Welsh and English alike of under-cutting wages. [49] In spite of its occasional flirtation with Welsh, the English language was regarded by the Monmouthshire gentry as the key to suppressing dissent, social and religious. The sentiments of Dr Edward Phillips, of Pontypool, contained in his statement to the "Commission of Inquiry into the State of Education" (authors of the Blue Books) in 1847 were not uncommon when he observed that English *"would tend to destroy the jealousy which more or less exists between the Welsh and the English by cementing them more closely together; it would extend the influence and power of the Established Church . . . there would be a general improvement of the people in due deference to their superiors and respect for the law of the land."* Another Commission witness, Rev. James Hughes, rector of Llanhilleth, considered Welsh to be *"a nuisance and an obstacle both to the administration of the law and to the cause of religion, imposing on pastors a double degree of work (or duty) by them having the Welsh and English portions of the community to attend to."*[50] In some day schools, by 1847 English was already the only language taught.[51] Soon it would become the principal instrument for the suppression of everything Welsh.

The Newport protest failed on almost all counts. If it is judged, as I believe it should be, as a peaceful demonstration in favour of increased political power through the ballot box, then it took another eighty years after the men from the hills had paid with their lives, before this was finally realised in Britain. Working class consciousness still had many miles to travel before it could be said to have asserted itself. If the plan was as stated in the Zephaniah Williams' confession *"to overthrow the Government of England and establish a Republic,"* then it has to be the most hopeless, ill-conceived coup ever attempted. The most satisfactory answer seems to be that what would otherwise have been a peaceful demonstration for electoral reform in the centre of Newport was subverted by the revolutionary John Rees and his supporters; that after the first shot was fired in the hotel passageway, the 45th Regiment of Foot responded with excessive vigour believing it was confronting a local rising not unlike the one it had crushed a year earlier in Bossenden Wood.

If the outcome had been different and Newport had fallen, Frost, Williams, Jones, and Rees would be remembered as the architects of the only Welsh insurrection since Owain Glyndŵr, and the last on mainland Britain. That is what the Crown and opponents of the labouring classes believed, at a time of constitutional instability throughout Europe. Given all the circumstances, the prosecution for High Treason, the most serious felony in the land, was inevitable. Still, the greatest of all the contradictions surrounding the affair is that the ringleaders are thought of in their native Wales as martyrs in a class struggle, from which socialism was eventually to spring. This investigation into the lives of two of the Chartist leaders, Zephaniah Williams and John Rees, should go part of the way towards adjusting that picture. If the Uprising is judged at all, it should be as a conjunction of circumstances and competing interests arising from a unique and isolated industrial society, culminating in a needless massacre, a Welsh *"Bloody Monday."*

NOTES

1. David Williams, *John Frost: a study in Chartism*, pp287-288.
2. MM, trial report, 18 January 1840.
3. NPL, Williams letter to wife from New Norfolk, 3 January 1846, *South Wales Daily News*, 5 May 1877, p3.
4. NPL, Williams letter to wife from New Norfolk, 21 April 1844, *South Wales Daily News*, 5 May 1877, p3.
5. NPL, Williams letter to wife from New Norfolk, 3 January 1846, op. cit.
6. NPL, Williams letter to wife from Enfield Hotel, Launceston, 25 February 1847, *South Wales Daily News*, 28 April 1877, p4.
7. *Western Vindicator*, 26 October, 16 November, 7 December 1839.
8. W. E. Adams, *Memoirs of a Social Atom* (1903), p499; R. G. Gammage, *History of the Chartist Movement* (1855).
9. NLW, Tredegar house Papers, 40/1, Frost letter to O'Connor from the convict ship *Mandarin*, 4 May 1840; Adams, *Memoirs of a Social Atom*, p209.
10. Tasmanian State Archives, Hobart, Colonial Secretary's Office, Tasmania, 74/903/cc, 1842.
11. Close reading of Williams letters to wife.
12. Wilks, *South Wales and the Rising of 1839* (1984), p1.
13. Lingen, *Merthyr Guardian*, December 1847; Tremenheere autobiography, *I was There*, pp37-39, Cardiff Law Library; close scrutiny of witness depositions at Newport Public Library reveals almost half were unable to write their name.
14. Wilks, loc. cit. pp246-251.
15. Jones, loc cit. p208.
16. NPL, Chartist Archives, Kenrick lecture, Pontypool Mechanics Institute, 1840, p 2.

17. Seymour Tremeneere on the State of Elementary Education in the Mining District of South Wales, app.11, p180, Cardiff Law Library.
18. MM, 'The better promotion of education in the mining districts', report, Tremenheere, 4 November 1853.
19. PRO, HO 45/102, informer's account of Chartist meeting on Clerkenwell Green, 15 May 1841.
20. Williams with Vincent at Nantyglo meeting, *Western Vindicator*, 6 April 1839.
21. *Merthyr Guardian* account, 13 April 1839, of judge's statement at Monmouthshire Quarter Sessions, 30 March 1839, concerning case brought against Williams and others for damaging Cwrt-y-Bella Colliery; GRO, 124.0078, sworn deposition of Thomas James in the case of 'Thomas Prothero and Thomas Phillips, appellants, and Henry Goude, Jane Llewellin and Henry Llewellin, defendants, Chancery Court'.
22. NPL, close reading of Chartist witness depositions, Vols. 1-24.
23. Tremenheere, p185.
24. The silver was never distributed and returned by Joan Williams the following Monday, *Hereford Times,* 9 November 1839; GRO, Miscellaneous series, D124.0800, letter Thomas Llewellyn, Bedwas, Williams brother-in-law, to J. Maughan, solicitor, confirms Penyderi Farm secured by Goude for £5,000 mortgage.
25. *ibid*; GRO, Conv. 0053, Mid Summer Sessions, 21 June 1838, for case against John Thomas and Rowland Richards, employed by Williams for the break-in at Cwrt y Bella Colliery.
26. Wilks, p2.
27. NPL, Chartist Trials, 5, Richard Pugh.
28. Wilks, p251.
29. Jones, pp206, 209.
30. Kenrick lecture, p16.
31. Jones, p210.
32. *ibid*, p210; NPL, also Chartist Trial depositions.
33. Daniel Evans, Gurney pp226-230.
34. Thomas Oliver, Gurney, pp215-216.
35. Basil Gray evidence, Gurney p254; James Daily deposition, Chartist Trials, 4.
36. For Armstrong and Daily, see Tower of London Archives, and their military service cards at The Sherwood Foresters Museum, Nottingham Castle; GRO, D3135/1.162,163, Duke of Wellington letters to Lord Fitzroy Somerset, 13 November, 10 December 1839.
37. *ibid*.
38. *Ceylon Observer*, account of 'The Death of Mr French Gray', 11 May 1874.
39. NPL, Chartist Trials, 14, Samuel Smith; *Northern Star,* 7 December 1839, *Champion*, 17 November 1839, *Northern Liberator*, 9 November, 7 December 1839; Gurney, John Harford evidence.
40. Basil Gray evidence, Gurney, pp247-254.
41. MPL, Chartist Trials, 4, James Daily.
42. Thomite Riots: Canterburiensis, 'The Life and Extraordinary Adventures

of Sir William Courtenay', Canterbury 1838; P. G. Rogers, *Battle in Bossenden Wood* (OUP, 1961, and Readers' Union Book Club 1962); Barry Reay, *The Last Rising of the Agricultural Labourers* (Clarendon Press, 1990).

43. *Guardian Unlimited,* Bloody Sunday Inquiry, 2003.
44. Wilks, p251.
45. Thomas Ainge Devyr, *The Odd Book of the 19th Century* (New York, 1881).
46. Williams, *John Frost: a study in Chartism.*
47. John and Thomas Gurney, *The Trial of John Frost for High Treason.*
48. Jones, p223; PRO, HO 40/45; NLW, Tredegar Park Papers, 57/148; MM, 4 January 1840; CCL, Bute Papers XXII 20, Napier Report, 6 September 1842.
49. See Kenrick lecture, p6, p13.
50. 'Commission of Inquiry into the State of education in Wales', p295, Witness Statement No. 2.
51. *ibid,* pp301-302, Witness Statement No. 10.

Bibliography

W. E. Adams, *Memoirs of a Social Atom* (London, 1903).

E. D. Adams, *British Diplomatic Correspondence Concerning the Republic of Texas* (Austin, 1918).

Austin Book Exchange, *Biographical Directory of the Texan Conventions and Congresses, 1832-1845* (Austin, 1941).

Dewitt Clinton Baker, *A Texas Scrapbook* (Austin, Texas, 1991).

Hubert Howe Bancroft, *History of the North Mexican States and Texas* (San Francisco, 1886, 1889).

K. Jack Bauer, *The Mexican War, 1846-1848* (New York, 1974).

K. Jack Bauer, *Zachay Taylor: Soldier, Planter, Statesman of the Old Southwest* (Louisiana, 1985).

Miles S. Bennet, *The Battle of Gonzales: The Lexington of the Texas Revolution* (1899).

William Blackstone, *Commentaries on the Laws of England* (Oxford, 1735).

Gary Brown, *New Orleans Greys* (Texas, 1999).

Daughters of the Republic of Texas, *Founders and Patriots of the Republic of Texas* (Austin, 1963).

E. T. Davies, *Monmouthshire Schools and Education to 1870* (1957).

Richard Davis, *Revolutionary Imperialists: William Smith O'Brien, 1803-1846* (Dublin, 1998).

Thomas Ainge Devyr, *The Odd Book of the 19th Century* (New York, 1881).

Ness Edwards, *John Frost and the Chartist Movement in Wales* (Abertillery, 1924).

Herman Ehrenberg, *Texas und seine Revolution* (1844).

James Fenton, *Bush Life in Tasmania* (London, 1970).

Herbert Gambrell, *Anson Jones: The Last President of Texas* (New York, 1848).

R. G. Gammage, *History of the Chartist Movement* (1855).

Hans Peter Nielson Gammel, *Laws of Texas, 1822-1897* (Austin, 1898).

Arthur Gray-Jones, *Histoy of Ebbw Vale* (Ebbw Vale, 1970).

Allan Greer, *Patriots and the People: The Rebellion of 1837 in Rural Lower Canada* (University of Toronto Press, 1993).

Joseph and Thomas Gurney, *The Trial of John Frost for High Treason* (London, 1840).

Mrs Hardcastle, *Life of Lord Campbell* (London, 1881).

Theodore H. Hittell, *Histoy of California* (San Francisco, 1897).

John H. Jenkins, *The Papers of the Texas Revolution* (Austin, 1973).

David J. V. Jones, *The Last Rising: the Newport Chartist Insurrection of 1839* (Cardiff, 1985).

David J. V. Jones, *Before Rebecca* (London, 1973).

Gareth Elwyn Jones and Dai Smith, *The People of Wales* (Llandysul, 1999).

Ieuan Gwynedd Jones, *Mid-Victorian Wales: The Observers and the Observed* (Cardiff, 1992).

Oliver Jones, *The Early Days of Sirhowy and Tredegar* (Tredegar, 1969).

Paul C. Lack, *Texas Revolutionary Experience* (Austin, 1992).

W. R. Lambert, *Drink and Sobriety in Victorian Wales* (Cardiff, 1983).

C. P. T. Laplace, *Campagne de Circumnavigation de la Fregate Liartemise, Pendant les Annees, 1837, 38, 39 et 40 sous le commandant de M. Lapace* (6 vols., Paris, 1841-54).

J. Lempriere, *The Penal Settlements of Van Diemen's Land.*

John Macdonell, *Reports of State Trials* (London, 1891).

Thomas Lloyd Miller, *Bounty and Donation Land Grants of Texas 1835-1888* (Austin, Texas, 1967).

Thomas Lloyd Miller, *The Public Lands of Texas 1519-1970* (University of Oklahoma Press, 1972).

David Morgans, *Music and Musicians of Merthyr and District* (Merthyr, 1922).

Joseph Milton Nance, *After San Jacinto: The Texas-Mexican Frontier, 1836-1841* (Austin, 1963).

Bishop Nixon, *Cruise of the Beacon* (Hobart, 1857).

A. C. Owell and J. Littleton, *History of Freemasonry in Bristol* (Bristol, 1910).

Evan Powell, *History of Tredegar: subject of competition at Tredegar chair eisteddfod,* 1884 (Newport, 1902).

Charles Ramsey, *With the Pioneers* (Devonport, Tasmania, 1957).

Barry Reay, *The Last Rising of Agricultural Labourers* (London, 1990).

John Phillip Reed, *Contested Empire* (Oklahoma, 2002).

P. G. Rogers, *Battle in Bossenden Wood* (London, 1961).

George Rude, *Protest and Punishment* (Oxford, 1978).

Samuel Snow, *The Exiles Return* (Cleveland, 1846).

M. N. Sprod, *The Convict Probation System: Van Diemen's Land 1839-1854* (Hobart, 1990).

Charles D. Spurlin, *Texas Veterans in the Mexican War* (Victoria, Texas, 1984).

K. R. von Stieglitz, *A Short History of Latrobe with Notes on Port Sorrell and Sassafras* (Latrobe, 2000).

W. W. Tasker, *The Sirhowy Tramroad and Railway in Monmouthshire* (Shrewsbury, 1960).

E. P. Thompson, *The Making of the English Working Class* (London, 1980).

John West, *History of Tasmania* (Hobart, 1852).

Charles Wilkins, *The History of the Iron, Steel, Tinplate and Other Trades of Wales* (1903).

Charles Wilkins, *The South Wales Coal Trade and its Allied Industries* (1888).

Ivor Wilks, *South Wales and the Rising of 1839* (University of Illinois Press, 1984).

David Williams, *John Frost: a study in Chartism* (Cardiff, 1939).

David Williams, *The Rebecca Riots* (Cardiff, 1955).

Gwyn A. Williams, *The Merthyr Rising* (Croom Helm, 1978).

Glanmor Williams, *Wales and the Reformation* (Cardiff, 1999).

Sian Rhiannon Williams, *Oes y Byd I'r Iaith Gymraeg* (Cardiff, 1992).

A. Wright, *The History of Lewis School, Pengam* (Newtown, 1929).

NEWSPAPERS

The following newspapers provided valuable source material:

In Britain: *Northern Star; Western Vindicator; The Times; Monmouthshire Merlin; Monmouthshire Beacon; Cambrian; Seren Gomer; The Workman/Y Gweithiwr.*

In Australia: *Cornwall Chronicle; Launceston Examiner.*

In United States: *Nyles Register.*

Index

OTHER BOOKS FROM GLYNDŴR PUBLISHING

The Book of Welsh Saints ISBN 1903529018 Terry Breverton* 606pp hardback 2000 – *'an enormous work of research'; 'full of fascinating information . . . a must for anyone interested in the history of the Church in Wales, indeed for anyone interested in learning the glorious heritage bequeathed to them from the time when Wales was the only Christian country in the world'; 'this book is a really extraordinary achievement: a compilation of tradition, topography and literary detective work that can have few rivals. I have enjoyed browsing it immensely, and have picked up all sorts of new lines to follow up' –* Rowan Williams, Archbishop of Canterbury.

The Secret Vale of Glamorgan ISBN 190352900X Terry Breverton 230pp **2000 Millennium Award** – *'shows a local man's pride in the history and culture of his native patch, combined with a historian's delight in tracing the past and relating it to the present'; 'for anyone born or living in the Vale, this should be essential reading.'*

A Rhondda Boy – The Memoirs of Ivor Howells ISBN 1903529050 – Ivor Howells (ed. Owen Vernon Jones) 144pp 2001 – *'A charming evocation of the childhood of a 93-year-old Welshman. Son of a miner, Rhondda born and bred, Rhondda educated apart from his degree years at Aberystwyth, Ivor Howells spent all his professional life as teacher and headmaster in Rhondda schools.'*

100 Great Welshmen ISBN 1903529034 Terry Breverton 376pp 2001 **Welsh Books Council 'Book of the Month'** – *'From heroes of Waterloo and computer engineers to lethal pirates and gold medallist champions, Breverton has attempted to include them all, and that's no mean feat given our colourful heritage. Hats off to him for the painstaking research involved in every one, a trademark which is typical of his previous work'; 'a revealing volume illustrating the great and good with Welsh connections'; 'a veritable goldmine of a book'; 'the amount of research that went into this book is astounding.'*

100 Great Welsh Women ISBN 1903529042 Terry Breverton 304pp 2001 – *'this book is an absolute must for all those who value their Welsh heritage, and for all those who wish to see women accorded their rightful place in history'; 'His latest book has finally arrived to fulfil the enormous gap in our knowledge of the enormously important, but sadly unheralded achievement of women, not only to Welsh society, but to Western civilization itself . . . a most invaluable addition to every bookshelf and library.'* (Of 100 Great Welshmen and 100 Great Welsh Women – *'Both are really extraordinary achievements by a single author whose energy seems to know no bounds –* Terry Breverton is to be congratulated.'*

The Dragon Entertains – 100 Welsh Stars ISBN 1903529026 Alan Roderick 230pp 2001 – *'a celebration of Welsh talent in all its vibrant variety'; 'this is the book to reach for, the next time someone tells you that Wales has not nurtured any great talent in the world of entertainment or show-biz.'*

The Welsh Almanac ISBN 1903529107 Terry Breverton 320pp hardback 2002 Welsh Books Council **'Book of the Month'** – *'a tremendous undertaking, and a very worthwhile and absolutely fascinating addition to the library of Welsh history'; 'It will take its place on the bookshelf with other works of reference'; 'it's a must for anyone with a drop of Welsh blood in them'; 'a wonderful book.'*

Glyn Dŵr's War – The Campaigns of the Last Prince of Wales ISBN 1903529069 Gideon Brough (ed. T. Breverton) 240pp 2002 – *'A massive undertaking . . . tackled with immense confidence and success'; 'The Great Liberation War is THE defining moment in our nation's history. Had it not been for Owain Glyn Dŵr and the men and women who stood at his side against overwhelming odds, there would be no Welsh nation today. You will find all the details here.'*

The Path to Inexperience ISBN 1903529077 Terry Breverton (poetry) 160pp 2002 – *'a tortured energy runs through this book'; 'the poem Chalice will surely help Aberfan to always stay in our memories'; 'magnificent, compassionate and moving.'*

(continued overleaf)

From Wales to Pennsylvania – The David Thomas Story ISBN 1903529085 – Dr Peter N. Williams (ed. T. Breverton) 112pp 2002 – *'The story of the man who emigrated from Ystradgynlais, to transform the American iron industry and make America a superpower . . . though Dr Thomas's correspondence with Wales, Dr Williams shows the Welshman's immense contribution to the industrialisation and economic growth of America.'*

Glamorgan Seascape Pathways – 52 Walks in the Southern Vale of Glamorgan ISBN 1903529115 Terry Breverton 144pp **2003 ARWAIN Award** *'fascinating . . . useful to anybody interested in the topography, geography and history of the southern Vale of Glamorgan'; '12 linked coastal paths and 40 inland walks with a wealth of information on the history, flora and fauna of the Vale, its coasts and rivers, plus notes upon all the Vale's notable saints, who gave names to our landscape . . . well-researched and well-written . . . presented in a totally accessible and user-friendly manner.'*

The Book of Welsh Pirates and Buccaneers ISBN 1903529093 Terry Breverton 388pp 2003 **Welsh Books Council 'Book of the Month'** – *'absolutely fascinating'; 'an immense work of great scholarship . . . effectively, a study of the whole genre of piracy . . . exemplary, yet the writing is light and accessible . . . wonderful, fascinating detail and essential reading.'*

Black Bart Roberts – The Greatest Pirate of Them All ISBN 1903529123 Terry Breverton 208pp 2004 – *'meticulously researched and well written . . . the writing is fluent and easily accessible'; 'the definitive account of the most successful pirate in history, who took over 400 ships in three years.'* (Available in the USA from Pelican Publishing, Louisiana).

The Pirate Handbook – A Dictionary of Pirate Terms and Places ISBN 1903529131 Terry Breverton 288pp 2004 Welsh Books Council **'Book of the Month'** *'This wonderful source book is an absolute "must" for anyone who is interested in nautical matters . . . if you ever wondered where phrases like "bit the deck" and "let the cat out of the bag" come from, then this is undoubtedly the place to look . . . the amount of detail and depth is phenomenal'; 'this book is a vitally important addition to the canon of literature about naval history.'* (Available as The Pirate Dictionary in the USA from Pelican Publishing, Louisiana).

* Terry Breverton is also the author of ***'An A-Z of Wales and the Welsh'*** ISBN 0715407341 – published by Christopher Davies 2000 304pp – *'impeccable research – an important addition to the Welsh bookshelf'; 'Hwyl and hiraeth, heritage and history, people and places, myths and imagination all come together in Terry Breverton's comprehensive anthology and compendium of Welshness'; 'a massive treasure chest of facts and figures'; 'great fun'; 'the first Welsh encyclopaedia!'*

All these books are available from www.gwales.com

FORTHCOMING PUBLICATIONS:

Henry Morgan – The Greatest Buccaneer of Them All ISBN 1903529158 Terry Breverton. (Available in the USA from Pelican Publishing, Louisiana).

William Williams and the First American Novel ISBN 1903529166 Terry Breverton – the unknown Welsh privateer, poet, painter and polymath who wrote America's first novel, and the modernised transcript of the first story of buried treasure.

Heroes of Science and the Royal Institution of South Wales ISBN 1903529190 Ronald Rees – at one stage in then Industrial Revolution, Swansea was a world centre of scientific developments.

Ramblings of a Patagonian ISBN 1903529239 Rene Griffiths – the biography of a troubadour and his travels between his twin homes of Patagonia and Wales.